About this book

The need for a "Yellow Pages" telephone book for Saint Petersburg, Russia is clear to all who visit, work and live there. In June 1991 we began work on a proposal for a full size Yellow Pages in Russian for the Leningrad phone company. This project evolved into the concept of a compact, practical *"Traveller's Yellow Pages and Handbook for Saint Petersburg"* in English, designed especially for travelers and foreign businesses coming to Saint Petersburg. In October 1991, InfoServices International, Inc. was founded to publish a series of *Traveller's Yellow Pages* for St. Petersburg, Moscow and other major cities in Russia, CIS and Eastern Europe. In March, 1992, we established Telinfo A/O in Saint Petersburg, Russia to collect information and to be the first to bring the concept of advertising in the Yellow Pages to the business community of Saint Petersburg.

The result is this practical telephone book and handbook for Saint Petersburg with more than 4000 telephone numbers and addresses of shops, restaurants, hotels, services, institutions and everything else useful for visitors and residents of Saint Petersburg. Hundreds of small informational ads were written by the editor together with the advertisers. All this information is classified under 432 categories of goods and services, like the well-known "Yellow Pages" used throughout the world. Our book, written in English, is designed for the world traveller and has indexes in English, Russian, German, French and Swedish.

The Traveller's Yellow Page for Saint Petersburg is not intended to be a complete Yellow Pages Telephone Book for the entire city, but rather a convenient reference book and guide for travelers and residents. Our goal was to include all or some of the best or at least two and three good verified listings for each category.

The information is up to date as of 1 July 1992, but Saint Petersburg is changing rapidly. As the book goes to press, we are discovering new shops, little cafes, more good doctors, and special craftsmen. Old shops and institutions are closing for "remont" and repair. Some are simply disappearing forever.

So we need your help to make the next edition even better. Tell us about your special findings: a good clothing shop, a great restaurant, a fascinating tour guide, a little cafe, a new stationery shop, or a talented artist. Tell us what new information you want. And above all, tell us about incorrect numbers, bad experiences with any Institutions listed in our book and any wrong information. Write us, fax us or even call us. We want to hear from you.

Acknowledgments

The book was researched and produced by American and Russian staffs in New York and Saint Petersburg, Russia. Their long hours, dedication to the concept and enthusiasm were essential to the success of this project.

The American staff was led by Natalie Kotlyar and included Sylvia Lajko, Andrew David, Roman Bover, Arina Fridman, Marina Peunova, Elena Rakovskaya, Rebecca Tsiu, Nelson Kirshner, Julie Rogers and Douglas R. Dohan. Natalie Kotlyar and Bob Hagen of Garvan, Inc. of Hicksville, New York designed the original model of the *Yellow Pages for Leningrad*. Acknowledgment must also be given for the support provided by the Social Science Laboratory for Research and Teaching at Queens College of the City University of New York. Hans Opsahl assisted in the final copy editing.

The staff in Saint Petersburg, Russia included Aleksandr G. Zakirov, Dmitriy A. Gudramovich, Ramilya A. Zhafyarova, Oksana A. Rossinskaya, Flera A. Khusyainova, Tatyana V. Nikitina, Marina V. Bevza, Olga A. Kholodova, Svetlana N. Petrachenkova, Olga E. Gazina, Michael B. Dohan, and Svetlana Kashina. A special acknowledgment must be give to Nataliya P. Makarova, the vice-president of Telinfo, who excelled at problem-solving and selling the concept of advertising in the *Traveller's Yellow Pages* to the Russian business community in St. Petersburg. The translators included Svetlana V. Tkachenko, Catharina Jameson, Heike Doll, Sergei and Marina Orloff, Nina Paulsen, Jean Delfoe, Rudolf and Gisela Hunermund and Tarcisio Costa. We should also acknowledge the editorial help and support of Andrey A. Belykh, Ph.D., Alla V. Belykh, Ph.D., and Marina A. Golli, MD.

A special thanks is given to our 165 advertisers which include the leading Russian and Western firms in St. Petersburg. Their support and confidence are making a major contribution to the economic prosperity of their city.

The text, ads and informational commentary were written by the editor with the help of the Russian staff. Rita Stasiak and the technical staff of Accurate Web, a major printer of directories in New York, provided technical advice, enthusiastic encouragement, fast press times and infinite patience.

Finally, and most importantly, the support and encouragement of Blanche B. Dohan, my wife, was central to the success of the entire project.

Michael R. Dohan, Ph.D.
Editor and Publisher
Cold Spring Harbor, New York, USA
Saint Petersburg, Russia

About the editor:

The editor, Michael R. Dohan, received his Ph.D. in Economics from the Massachusetts Institute of Technology. He is a specialist in Soviet (now Russian) economics and is currently an Associate Professor of Economics at Queens College of the City University of New York and Director of the Social Science Laboratory for Research and Teaching.

About the typography and printing

The book was written using Word for Windows 2 on Dell 386 20 MHz laptops and 486 50 MHz desktop systems. The text is set in 7 pt Univers (WN) Adobe. The Russian Glasnost fonts were designed by Cassidy and Greene of California. The graphics were drawn in CorelDraw by our designer Aleksandr G. Zakirov. The manuscript was prepared for printing on a Hewlett Packard Laserjet IIID. The cover was printed by Levon Graphics Corp. NY. USA on 10 pt coated 2 sides, and the book was printed by Accurate Web Press, Long Island, NY, USA on 40 lb. offset paper especially selected to keep the book compact.

THE TRAVELLER'S
YELLOW PAGES

and *HANDBOOK for*

SAINT PETERSBURG

Suburbs of Lomonosov, Pavlovsk, Petrodvorets, Pushkin
Cities of Novgorod, Pskov, Vologda and Vyborg

FALL 1992 -SPRING 1993

Gelbe Seiten
für Reisende mit
deutschem Suchwortregister

Pages Jaunes
pour le voyageur
avec index en français

Gula Sidorna
för resande
med anvisning på svenska

Жёлтые Страницы
с алфавитным указателем
для иностранных гостей
Санкт-Петербурга

Michael R. Dohan, Ph.D.
Editor

When calling from outside
of St. Petersburg

The City Code For
Saint Petersburg
812
The County Code For
Russia
7

INFOSERVICES INTERNATIONAL, INC., New York, USA

The *Traveller's* Yellow Pages and Handbook
for Saint Petersburg, 1992-1993 Edition
(Effective July 1, 1992)

Michael R. Dohan, Ph.D., Editor

Published by InfoServices International, Inc., NY, USA
Distributed in Russia by Telinfo, Saint Petersburg, Russia

For information, contact InfoServices International, Inc., 1 Saint Marks
Place, Cold Spring Harbor, NY 11724, USA (516) 549-0064.
In Russia, contact Telinfo, Saint Petersburg, Russia, 190000, Nab. reki
Moyki, 64, Tel: (812) 315-64-12, 315-98-55, Fax: (812) 312-73-41, 315-74-20.

Large volume purchases with your imprint for promotional purposes or
premiums are available at a special discount.

The name "The *Traveller's* Yellow Pages" is a registered trademark.

ISBN 1-881832-00-7
First Printing: July 1, 1992

Although the editors, staff and publishers have made every effort to in-
sure the accuracy and completeness of the information contained in this
book, we assume no responsibility for errors, inaccuracies, omissions or
any inconsistency herein or for any harm or any inconvenience from
using this book or from being included in or omitted from this book.
Readers should be aware of the rapid changes in telephone numbers
and business conditions in Saint Petersburg, Russia and should take
appropriate measures to verify the information. We are grateful for
corrections and suggestions for improvement.

PRINTED IN THE UNITED STATES OF AMERICA

TABLE OF CONTENTS
Содержание, Inhaltsverzeichnis
Sommaire, Innehållsförteckning

◆СОДЕРЖАНИЕ◆

◆SOMMAIRE◆

◆INHALTSVERZEICHNIS◆

◆INNEHÅLLSFÖRTECKNING◆

Introduction

The Traveller's *Yellow Pages and Handbook for Saint Petersburg, Fall 1992 - Spring 1993,* the first Yellow Pages for Saint Petersburg, contains over 4000 up-to-date telephone numbers and addresses most frequently needed by travelers to (and residents of) Saint Petersburg and near-by cities. You will find everything from airlines and art galleries to veterinarians and video rentals, all organized into 432 categories of goods and services like the well-known "Yellow Pages" telephone books. All the category headings are written in English, Russian, German, French and Swedish. The book has much useful information on telephone services, postal rates, sizes and measures, medical care, Cyrillic alphabet, climate, customs regulations, visas, etc., seating charts for major theaters and concert halls, a check list of what-to-bring, and more. It also has a walking map of Nevskiy Prospect, a metro map (subway or underground) and a large fold-out street map of Saint Petersburg with transport routes.

How to live and shop: The *Traveller's Yellow Pages* is especially designed to help you enjoy this beautiful historic city by showing you how to live, work, dine and shop in Saint Petersburg, to make international phone calls, buy good theater tickets, hail a taxi, find flowers, listen to jazz, mail a package home, picnic in the park, get a replacement contact lens, and do your laundry as well as visit museums, dine at great restaurants, browse in old book stores and take an architectural tour with an art historian. It is the perfect complement to a good guidebook such as Baedeker's *Guide to Leningrad (Saint Petersburg),* or Fodor's *Guide to Russia and the Baltics.* See "TRAVEL BOOKS" under "T".

On business: When coming here on business, you will find everything you need for working, living and running a business in St. Petersburg: banks, auditing firms and business consultants, shipping, trucking, and customs clearance, computers and cellular phones, office space, furniture and apartments, fax and E-mail, car rentals and repairs, presentation banquets in a palace, temporary help and translators, advertising agencies, business service centers, accountants and lawyers.

Learn the Cyrillic Alphabet: Visitors, who do not know Russian, will find many aids to help them get about the city. The Cyrillic alphabet is on page 11 and the back cover, and a pronunciation guide is on the inside back cover. It is well worth the few hours needed to learn the 33 letter Russian Cyrillic alphabet and you will soon be able to recognize street signs, shops, and Metro stops. In the book, the names of many signs and shops are not only translated, but are also given in Cyrillic and transliterated into Latin letters. The foreign languages spoken in shops, restaurants and other establishments are indicated in many display ads. Interpreters are found under TRANSLATORS.

Suburbs and nearby cities: Our section with telephone numbers and addresses for the suburbs of Lomonosov, Pavlovsk, Petrodvorets and Pushkin and for the nearby cities of Novgorod, Pskov, Vologda and Vyborg, is one of the few sources of this information in Russia as well as abroad.

New Names: Names are changing rapidly in St. Petersburg as many "old" Soviet names being dropped in favor of the "new" Tsarist names. Which names to use in our book? Old or new? Our policy in this edition is to use "old" Soviet street names because most people still use them, and most street signs, stationery, business cards, etc., still have the "old" Soviet names. For names of organizations, buildings, concert halls and shops, however, we used the newest name available because these are already in use by the firms and people themselves. Consult our short article on "New Names" and a list of the "new" Tsarist street names on page 241.

Transliteration: The reader should be aware that there is no agreed upon system for writing (transliterating) Russian words in regular "Latin" letters. We chose the simplest system possible as discussed on page 11 "The Russian Alphabet". Our map, the best available map, however, uses a slightly different Russian (and also the German) system of transliteration. Spend a few minutes studying the differences on page 11.

Who is included: We selected those shops, restaurants, institutions and agencies of the greatest interest to the traveler and include them free of charge. These are usually better known, better quality and located in the central part of Saint Petersburg. More than 165 of these better establishments have chosen to describe their specialties, services, products, qualifications, hours, currencies, credit cards, location and languages spoken in informative ads. Please patronize our advertisers.

A complex economy: In Saint Petersburg the visitor will find a very complex economy using two currencies with widely different price levels. The information provided in this book will help both visitors and residents to quickly find a wide variety of goods and services at reasonable prices.

Keeping up-to-date: Saint Petersburg is changing rapidly with new shops, restaurants and businesses opening every day, many firms closing for repairs, and some closing forever.

All numbers were verified in June 1992, and all advertisers were interviewed. We know, however, that numbers change rapidly, business conditions change, and errors can be made. So we ask your help in keeping our Traveller's Yellow Pages up-to-date. We are planning the all-Russian edition for the residents of St. Petersburg and the Spring-Summer 1993 English edition with many improvements and more addresses and numbers.

So, if you have any corrections, suggestions or if we have not included your favorite restaurant or shop, please give us a call while you are in Saint Petersburg at 812-315-98-55, fax us a note at 812-315-74-20, or send a note to Telinfo, 64 Moyka Embankment, Saint Petersburg, Russia 190000. Outside of Russia, contact us at: InfoServices International Inc., 1 Saint Marks Place, Cold Spring Harbor, New York 11724, USA. Fax 516-549-2032 and Tel. 516-549-0064.

We look forward to hearing from you.

Michael R. Dohan
Editor and Publisher

HOW TO USE THE TRAVELLER'S YELLOW PAGES

Categories of goods and services are arranged in English alphabetical order: The stores, restaurants, services, institutions and information are classified into more than 400 different categories of goods, services and topics, which are *organized in the* Yellow Pages *in alphabetical order according to their English headings.* These headings are also given in Russian, German, French and Swedish.

Within each category, the listing are arranged alphabetically, usually by the English name, unless the "transliterated" Russian name is better known. Both are often given.

Where and what to expect: Most firms listed here are located in the center of the city. Unless otherwise stated, they accept rubles, do not speak much English and are open normal working hours. (See HOURS.)

What we have not included: We have not included factories, wholesale suppliers, detailed listings for government agencies, local schools, etc. Similarly, the many hundreds of small food stores, cafeterias and clinics, especially if located in the outlying regions of Saint Petersburg, have been omitted.

Similarly, this is not a guide book and information about the history, culture and arts are not included either.

What is in each listing: Each listing includes the name, address and telephone. Additional information is often listed (especially in the ads), including fax, telex, hours of operation, currencies and credit cards accepted, languages spoken, and nearest metro station.   Here are some conventions used in our listings.

Hours of operation are given on the 24 hour clock, so that 8:00 is 8 a.m.and 20:00 is 8 p.m. in the evening.

The abbreviation *VO* in front of a street name refers to its location on Vasilevskiy Ostrov (Island) on the northwest side of the Neva River and *PS* refers to Petrogradskaya Storona (side) on the north side of the Neva across from the Hermitage.

English or "Eng" means that some English is spoken by some personnel. Similarly with German (Ger), French (Fren), Swedish (Swed) and Finnish (Finn).

The symbol $* means that the establishment accepts "hard currency". This always includes US dollars and depending on the establishment may also include German and Finnish marks, French and Swiss francs, Scandinavian currencies and English pounds. Other currencies may be harder to use. *The symbol "$ and rubles" means that both are accepted *or* that part of the cost is in hard currency and part is in rubles.

Use the indexes: Look directly in the Yellow Pages for the categories most closely related to the product, service or information you are seeking. Or use the indexes in English, Russian, German, French and Swedish. For example, to extend your visa, look under "VISA"; to buy a cake, look under "BAKERIES"; to reschedule your flight, look under "AIRLINES"; to find out the average temperature in November, look under "CLIMATE"; for official holidays and vacations, look under "HOLIDAYS".

If you don't find the category for a specific good, service or information, look under *related* categories. For "paper", look under "STATIONERY" and for a winter coat, look under "CLOTHING".

Use the many cross references to related categories. Cross references are given in CAPITAL LETTERS. For example, under the category of RESTAURANTS, you are given the following "cross reference" to other related categories.

> *See also* CAFES, PIZZA, FAST FOOD, FOOD DELIVERY,
> DELICATESSENS and ICE CREAM.

Translation and transliteration of Russian words: In the text, we often give the English *translation* so you can understand it, the English *transliteration* of the Russian word so that you can pronounce it, and the Russian word in *Cyrillic* so that you can recognize it in Russian. For example, "bakeries" (bulochnaya, Булочная).

We use a simple English system of transliteration, described in *The Russian Cyrillic Alphabet* on page 11 and printed also on the back cover. Our system is compared with other systems on page 11 and differs from most in that we substitute "y" for the Russian й regardless of where it occurs in the word. Thus, "Nevsky" becomes "Nevskiy" and "Bolshoi" becomes "Bolshoy".

Street names: The names of all streets, prospects, lanes, boulevards, avenues, etc. are listed with the ***principal name first*** followed by *ul.* (street), *pl.* (square), etc. regardless of their actual order in Russian. Thus we write "Sadovaya ul." rather than "Ul. Sadovaya". This simplifies finding streets on maps, etc. The exception is the Russian word for embankment "Naberezhnaya." For examples, in "Nab. reki Moyki, 64", Nab. comes first.

Abbreviations of Russian words for street, etc.: The Russian words for street (*ulitsa*), square (*ploshchad*), etc. rather than their English translations of street, square, etc. are used because you will find that it helps you (and Russians) find the right street or square more quickly. The full list of abbreviations and their Russian equivalents is given on page 32.

The more important ones are listed here.

ul.	=	ulitsa	Улица	= street
pr.	=	prospekt	Проспект	= prospect or avenue
kan.	=	kanal	Канал	= canal
pl.	=	ploshchad	Площадь	= square
per.	=	pereulok	Переулок	= lane
Nab.	=	naberezhnaya	Набережная	= embankment
V.O.	=	Vasilevskiy Ostrov	Васильевский Остров	= Vasilevskiy Island
P.S.	=	Petrogradskaya Storona	Петроградская Сторона	= Petrogradsky Side

The Russian Cyrillic Alphabet and Russian Names and Transliterations used in the Traveller's Yellow Pages and the City Map of Saint Petersburg

TRANSLITERATION of Cyrillic letters into our Latin letters is difficult because there is no agreement among experts on one system of converting from Cyrillic.

Indeed, each language has one or more methods of converting Russian into English or German or French, based on their own pronunciation of letters. In addition there is an official Russian of transliteration from Cyrillic. In the text of the Traveller's Yellow Pages, (TYP) we usually use a simplified system of transliteration based on the English system of transliteration.

The transliteration system used in this "old" map of St. Petersburg, the best available map with the old commonly used street names, differs slightly from the street names given in the book. The principal differences between the transliteration used in the text of the Traveller's Yellow Pages and the official Russian transliteration and the German transliteration in the map are for the letters Й, Я, Ч, Ш, and Щ.

TRANSLITERATION SYSTEMS FROM CYRILLIC

| RUSSIAN | | TRANSLITERATION SYSTEMS | | |
Cyrillic Alphabet		Traveller's Yellow Pages	Russian Official Method	German Used on Map	English Systems in Use
А	а	a	a	a	a
Б	б	b	b	b	b
В	в	v	v	w	v
Г	г	g	g	g	g
Д	д	d	d	d	d
Е	е	e	e, je	je	e, ye
Ё	ё	e	o, jo	jo	yo
Ж	ж	zh	ž	sh	zh
З	з	z	z	s, z	z
И	и	i	ji, i	i	i
Й	й	y	j	j	i, y
К	к	k	k	k	k
Л	л	l	l	l	l
М	м	m	m	m	m
Н	н	n	n	n	n
О	о	o	o	o	o
П	п	p	p	p	p
Р	р	r	r	r	r
С	с	s	s	s	s
Т	т	t	t	t	t
У	у	u	u	u	u
Ф	ф	f	f	v, f	f
Х	х	kh	ch	ch	kh
Ц	ц	ts	c	z	ts
Ч	ч	ch	č	tsch	ch
Ш	ш	sh	š	sch	sh
Щ	щ	shch	sc	stsch	shch
Ъ	ъ	*hard sign*			
Ы	ы	y	y	y	y
Ь	ь	*soft sign*	'	(j)	
Э	э	e	e	e	e
Ю	ю	yu	u, ju	ju	yu, iu
Я	я	ya	ja	ja	ya, ia

The Country Code for **Russia**

7

The CITY CODE for
SAINT PETERSBURG
812

RUSSIAN ABBREVIATIONS AND WORDS USED IN ADDRESS

Bulv	Boulevard	Бульв .... Бульвар
Der	Village	Дер .... Деревня
D.	House/ Apt.	Д .... Дом
G. .	City / Town	Г .... Город
Gos.	State (adj)	Гос .... Государственный
Im.	Named after	Им .... Имени
In-t	Institute	Ин-т .... Институт
K	Room	К .... Комната
Kan.	Canal	Кан .... Канал
Kv.	Apartment	Кв .... Квартира
Kladb.	Cemetery	Кладб .... Кладбище
Km.	Kilometer	Км .... Километр
Komb	Factory complex	Комб .... Комбинат
Kop	Kopeck	Коп .... Копеек
Korp.	Building Number	Корп .... Корпус
Mag	Shop/ Store	Маг .... Магазин
Min	Ministry	Мин .... Министерство
Nab	Embankment	Наб .... Набережная
Obshch	Society	Общ .... Общество
Ob'edin.	Enterprise	Объедин .... Объединение
O.	Island	О .... Остров
Per.	Lane	Пер .... Переулок
P.S.	Petrogradsky Side	П.С... Петроградская Сторона
Pl.	Square	Пл .... Площадь
Pod	Entrance	Под .... Подъезд
Pos	Planned Settlement	Пос .... Поселок
Prodolzh	Continuation	Продолж .... Продолжение
Pr.	Prospect	Пр .... Проспект
R	River	Р .... Река
Rem	Repair	Рем .... Ремонт
R-n	District	Р-он .... Район
Sm.	Look (for...)	См .... Смотрите
St.	Station	Ст .... Станция
Str.	Page	Стр .... Страница
Stroit	Construction	Строит .... Строительство
Tel.	Phone	Тел .... Телефон
Ul	Street	Ул .... Улица
V.O	Vasilevskiy Ostrov	В.О......Васильевский Остров
Zal	Bay	Зал .... Залив
Z-d	Plant	З-д .... Завод

ENGLISH ABBREVIATIONS and TERMS USED IN ADS AND LISTINGS

Mon	Monday	понедельник
Tue	Tuesday	вторник
Wed	Wednesday	среда
Thu	Thursday	четверг
Fri	Friday	пятница
Sat	Saturday	суббота
Sun	Sunday	воскресенье
Rm	room	комната
Bldg	building	корпус
Apt	apartment	квартира
Clsd	Closed	закрыто
Hrs	Time on the 24 hour clock.	время работы
Rbl	Accepts rubles	рубли
CC	Accepts Credit Cards	кредитные карточки
$	Accepts or requires hard currency	валюта
Eng	English spoken to some extent	английский
Ger	German spoken to some extent	немецкий
Fren	French spoken to some extent	французкий
N.A.	Named after	имени

☎ ACCOUNTING AND AUDITING FIRMS
АУДИТОРСКИЕ ФИРМЫ
BUCHFÜHRUNGSFIRMEN
COMPTABILITE, SOCIETES DE REVISORER, OCH
HANDELSKONSULTER

ARTHUR ANDERSEN

Saint Petersburg Office, Russia

Audit and Business Advisory
Tax and Legal Services
Systems Consulting

V.O., Bolshoy pr., 10 350-49-84
.... 350-48-13
Fax................................ 213-78-74

Association of Accounting Firms
Rossi ul., 3/1 311-12-66
Income Tax & Accounting Services
Audit Firm
Dzerzhinskogo ul., 30...... 310-48-05
Auditor
Dumskaya ul., 1/3, flr. 3
.... 110-59-99
Bosy
1-ya Krasnoarmeyskaya ul., 11
.... 292-56-58
Infraudit
Malaya Posadskaya ul., 22
.... 246-50-90

Coopers & Lybrand | Solutions for Business

Moscow & St. Petersburg

Accountants, Management Consultants
Tax Advisers

In Saint Petersburg
At the Astoria Hotel, Room 528
Gertsena ul., 39 210-55-28
Fax.. 311-42-12

In Moscow
Shchepkina ul., 6 ....(095) 971-69-61
Fax.............................(095) 284-52-73

Deloitte & Touche

DRT - Inaudit
St. Petersburg Office

Accounting and Auditing
Management Consulting
and Tax Services

Petropavlovskaya krepost, 11
.... 247-82-11

ERNST AND YOUNG
SAINT PETERSBURG OFFICE
AUDITING & CONSULTING
Tax, accounting, market & feasibility studies
business plans, legal & personnel issues
partner selection
V.O., 13 Liniya, 20 (local)... 116-01-57
Outside of St. Pb.................. 906-01-57
Fax 218-79-40

ICPA Corp., A full-service accounting firm
*Auditing, tax management, financial mgmt
Financial evaluation of Russian enterprises
Staff of 30, Affiliate of Marcum & Kliegman, NY*
Profsoyuzov bul., 4, apt. 14
TEL....................... (812) 311-61-30
.... 312-23-39
FAX .... (812) 311-78-22
English, Deutsch, Francais

Leningradintekh
Auditing, Bookkeeping & Accounting
Saint Petersburg 197022, Russia
Chkalovskiy pr., 52 235-58-74
Fax...................................... 230-13-07

LENAUDIT
Nevskiy pr., 7/9.............. 312-37-00
.... 315-89-85
*Accounting services available,
Preparation of taxes & financial records.*

MCD Marketing, Consulting and Design
Voynova ul., 52, rm.13
.... 275-56-23
.... 275-54-55
Region-Expert, audit and consulting
Sofi Perovskoy ul., 14 315-96-30
Fax 315-96-30
Express-Pravo-Information
Sofi Perovskoy ul., 7 312-15-69

☎ ACCUPUNCTURE
АКУПУНКТУРА
AKUPUNKTUR
ACCUPUNCTURE
AKUPUNKTUR

Arkrus
Krasnaya ul., 69, apt. 224
.... 210-99-39
Karlson
Oleko Dundicha ul., 26
Children's Clinic No. 64 ... 177-74-36
At home & hotel visits
Zdorove
Gagarina pr., 28, bldg. 2
.... 264-25-94

☎ ADDRESS BUREAU
АДРЕСНЫЕ БЮРО
ADRESSENBÜROS
ADRESSES, BUREAU D'
ADRESSBYRÅER

Call the "Address Bureau" for help in finding new telephone numbers and addresses. This Bureau was traditionally run by the Ministry of Internal Affairs (MVD). Unfortunately, many of the new numbers and firms are not listed. You must visit the address bureau on your own; there is no phone.

Address Bureau (In Person)
Liteynyy pr., 6.................*(see text)*

Address Bureau (by Phone)
Gertsena ul., 24
Dial .... 009 + your phone number.

Please phone 009 + your own phone number. They will tell you the address of a person in St. Pb. in 1 hr, if you inform them of his (her) date of birth, place of birth and full name. If he (she) lives outside of St. Pb., you will receive the information in 2-2.5 hrs. The cost of this "paid information" was about 10 rubles for 1 address. Information is available only in Russian.

These two organizations are located at different places, but are closely connected.

☎ ADVERTISING AGENCIES
РЕКЛАМНЫЕ АГЕНТСТВА
WERBEAGENTUREN
PUBLICITE, AGENCES DE
REKLAMBYRÅER

Alcor Technologies Inc., USA
Stepana Razina ul., 8/50
.... 310-44-01
Fax.............................. 310-44-70

Advertising Agency
Yuriya Gagarina pr., 28, bldg.1
.... 264-03-54
Fax.............................. 299-39-82
Telex...................... 121017 YCM
Stands, audio-advertisements
Art Designer
Pushkin, Tolstogo bul., 38, apt. 3
.... 465-85-48
Development of Trademarks and Logos
Association "All Petersburg".
Sadovaya ul., 2, rm. 46
(Mikhaylovskiy zamok)..... 210-48-79
.... *272-36-89*
Newspaper and video advertising
AVIR
Mokhovaya ul., 31 275-62-57

BMP REKLAMA. A/O
ADVERTISING
Design and Implementation of Advertising Programs for the Saint Petersburg Market
Commercial Artists • Image Design
Fine-quality printing of brochures, cards, stationery. • Silk Screen Printing
Mezhevoy kan., 5 114-95-41
Fax.............................. 186-83-44
Telex........................... 121501 SU

Eskart-Saint-Petersburg
Gertsena ul., 28, rm. 524
.... 315-47-81
Electronic Display Newspaper
Nevskiy pr., 52............... 310-17-68
Nevskiy pr., 102 279-43-53
IGREK
Profsoyuzov bul., 19 311-95-95

IMA-Press
Zodchego Rossi ul., 1/3 ... 110-46-51
.... 110-49-96
.... 110-49-94
Fax.............................. 314-48-23
Newspaper and Radio Advertising

IMPEX
Gertsena ul., 35.............. 310-94-41
.... 110-65-02
Fax:.............................. 319-97-09
Telex .... 121302 LIMEX SU

**Inform Progress-St. Petersberg,
USA**
194295, St. Petersberg, P.O., Box 11

IRA
Babushkina ul., 25, apt. 2
.... 567-30-07
Newspaper

Florman Information Russia
Public Relations in Russia
Publisher of
Saint Petersburg News
*Advertising to Air Travelers on Aeroflot
and Residents of St. Petersburg*

Media Relations, Press and TV,
Printed Matter and Brochures,
Company Events and Presentations
Legislation Monitoring
Editorial Products, Newsletters, Videos
Market Research on Market Potential

Kamennoostrovskiy (Kirovskiy) pr., 14b
.... 233-76-82
Fax: 232-80-17
Telex: 121609

Kira Magazine
Please call 239-73-25
Kommet *Advertising on St. Pb. Metro*
Moskovskiy pr., 28, rm. 450
.... 259-74-15

Len_{expo}   Advertising
*20 years experience in publicizing
exhibitions and conferences in St. Pb
Press releases & posters to direct mail
Television, radio, newspapers, magazines*
Bolshoy pr., 103 355-19-89
fax 355-19-85

Lenizdat
Nab. reki Fontanki, 59, apt. 118
.... 210-84-11
*Advertising in Nevskiy Vestnik , Televidenie-Radio,
Kinonedelya Sankt Peterburga*
Len-Sof
Aptekarskiy pr., 16 234-28-88
Advertising shorts for St. Petersburg TV
Leningrad
Proletarskoy Diktatury, 6, rm. 424
.... 278-14-08
Fax: 271-16-82
Lentelefilm
Chapygina ul., 6 234-77-75

L I C
Information & Publishing Agency, Ltd.
Gertsena ul., 20 314-59-82
Fax 315-35-92
*Aurora, Khudozhestvennaya
Literatura i Sudostroenie*

Neva News
Pravdy ul., 10 .... (812) 164-47-65

Potential
Kolpino, Pavlovskaya ul., 42
.... 481-95-24
Fax 463-90-00
Advertising spots on TV-1 in Russia
Pulkovo-2 International Airport
Aviagorodok.................. 291-87-84
.... 122-98-51
Advertising stands at the airport
Reklama
Apraksin per., 11, apt. 56
.... 113-49-30
Audio-advertisements in major cinemas
RUMB
Zaytseva, 41 183-46-39
Fax: 185-08-69

Rossy Agency
*We offer you a NEW kind of advertising
on computerized screens at the entrance
of the Metro station "Gostinyy Dvor."*
Nab. reki Fontanki, 51/53, apt. 17
.... 310-10-68

Rostorgreklama
Sedova ul., 13................ 567-47-68
TV, films and radio advertisements

Russian Trade Express Media
*Advertising to the business
community in English.*
Manezhnyy per., 19 275-84-66
Fax 275-84-66

SAMSON (NEWSPAPER AD)
Nab. Morskaya, 15.......... 356-99-20
.... 356-73-38

SANTA LTD Advertising Agency
Publisher of
St. Petersburg
Today & Tonight
For visitors to Saint Petersburg
Quarterly in English and German
Nab. Makarova, 30 279-73-29

Sankt Petersburg
Productive Creative Firm
Gertsena ul., 56.............. 311-07-94
*Creative TV and print advertising of your
product on the territory of former USSR*

The City Code for Saint Petersburg
Dial 812 + Number

St. Pb Association of Ballroom Dance
Nab. reki Moyki, 94, rm. 96
.... 314-89-95
.... 166-38-23
Display Advertising at Int'l Dance Competitions

Smart
Admiralteyskiy pr., 8/1 110-66-55
.... 110-66-34
Fax:................................ 110-65-70
Telex: .... 121432 Smart SU

Sonex
Professora Popova ul., 7/8, apt. 6
.... 234-58-00
Newspapers, radio, TV

Sovmarket
1-ya Sovetskaya ul., 10... 277-53-71
Newspaper , TV-1 in Russia

Soyuz Dizaynerov
Nab. reki Moyki, 8 311-72-63
Fax:................................ 312-43-74

Stiba
Malaya Posadskaya ul., 8
.... 233-32-74

Sport and Concert Complex
Yuriya Gagarina pr., 8...... 264-89-58
Advertising stands in the complex

Startplus
Ulyany Gromovoy ul., 8 ... 277-53-18
.... 277-02-13

Svega
Nevskiy pr., 52/14 310-17-68
.... 314-72-88
"Running line"

TELINFO, publisher
The Traveller's Yellow Pages
For Saint Petersburg
and
The City Map of Saint Petersburg
In Russia, copies can be obtained at
✉190000, St. Petersburg, Russia:
Nab. Reki Moyki, 64
.... 315-64-12
.... 315-98-55
Fax................................ 315-74-20
Fax................................ 312-73-41
For the rest of the world
InfoServices International, Inc.
1 Saint Marks Place
Cold Spring Harbor, NY 11724, USA
Tel..................USA (516) 549-0064
Fax........................ (516) 549-2032
Telex ....221213 TTC UR
Telinfo is a wholly-owned subsidiary of
InfoServices International, Inc. NY, USA

***TVID** Advertising*
A full service ad agency in St. Petersburg
Public relations for foreign firms
Kamennoostrovskiy pr., 42
.... 230-80-22

Taiwan
Nab. reki Fontanki, 11 110-68-32
.... 311-07-19

Transport
Energetikov pr., 50.......... 225-63-98
On the side of vehicles

Veles
Olgina ul., 2b (Krestovskiy ostrov)
.... 235-30-80

Vika Design Group
Nab. Obvodnogo kan., 215, apt. 12
.... 251-43-33
All types of commercial design

☎ **AIR CARGO**
АВИАПЕРЕВОЗКИ
LUFTFRACHT
AIR CARGAISON
FLYGTRANSPORT

See also EXPRESS MAIL PARCELS,
FREIGHT FORWARDING AGENTS,
SHIPPING, TRUCKING

Aerobalt Service
Pilotov ul., 38................ 104-18-75
Dept. Manager................ 104-18-12
Fax 104-18-36
Telex.................... 121317 ACA SU

Aeroflot

Aviagorodok, Warehouse
Domestic cargo 104-34-11
.... 104-34-48
International cargo 104-34-95

EuroDonat *FREIGHT FORWARDERS AND TRANPORT*
TRUCK, SHIP, AIR, RAIL
Specializing in transport to/from
Russia, the Baltic States, & CIS
from/to USA, Canada & Europe
All Customs operations
Modern truck fleet
Warehouse in St.-Pb.
Moldagulovoy ul., 7/6...... 224-11-44
Fax.............................. 224-06-20
Telex.................... 121118 DFS SU
Hrs: 9-18, $ & rubles, English

FEDOROV TRANS EXPRESS

Air Cargo Agency

Official KLM cargo agent

Worldwide, Russia & CIS

Pilotov ul., 8 104-34-49

Fax............................... 481-69-98

TNT Express Worldwide

St. Petersburg
Liteynyy pr., 50

**Express Freight To One Ton
To 30 cities in CIS & Baltics
Over 200 Countries Worldwide
Customs Clearance in St. Pb.**

Immediate free pick-up

.... 273-60-07

.... 272-58-86

Fax 272-90-51

Telex................. 121663 ABS SU

Moscow Office:(095) 156-56-89

Lenvneshtrans

Mezhevoy kan., 5 251-41-97

Fax............................... 186-28-83

Telex .... 121511 SVT SU

☎ AIR CHARTER, RENTALS
АВИАЦИЯ, АРЕНДА
АВИАСРЕДСТВ
FLUGZEUGVERMIETUNG
AVIONS, BAIL
FLYGPLAN, ATT HYRA

KUSTANAY AIR

*Sightseeing flights to the Tsars palaces
Helicopter flights to all of the North-West*
Pushkin, Leningradskoe shosse

.... 465-88-10

Aeroflot
АЭРОФЛОТ
Soviet airlines

Aviagorodok, Warehouse

.... 122-97-90

☎ AIRLINES
АВИАЛИНИИ
FLUGGESELLSCHAFTEN
AVION (LIGNES AERIENNES)
FLYGBOLAG

Austrian Airlines

Gogolya ul., 19............... 312-43-48

Pulkovo-2, Airport........... 104-34-31

Aeroflot
АЭРОФЛОТ
Soviet airlines

Main offices: corner of Nevskiy pr. and
Gogolya ul., 7/9

Domestic arrivals/departures

.... 293-90-21

Information 293-90-31

Inter'l arrival/departure..... 314-69-43

Tickets.......................... 311-80-72

.... 311-80-93

Ticket sales office

Aprelskaya ul., 5 225-99-15

Freight transport 314-69-59

International department
Dzerzhinskogo ul., 47. 310-45-81

*From St. Petersburg
More flights to more places
than any other airline*

Air-France (c/o KLM)

Pulkovo-2, Airport offices

.... 104-34-40

.... 104-34-41

Service To Paris

BALKAN AIRLINES

Gertsena ul., 36

Information 315-50-30

.... 315-50-19

Pulkovo-2, Airport........... 104-34-36

Airline to Central Europe

BRITISH AIRWAYS

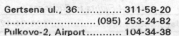

(c.o. Delta)

Gertsena ul., 36.............. 311-58-20

.... (095) 253-24-82

Pulkovo-2, Airport........... 104-34-38

*Direct flights to London
3 times a week*

CSA (Czechoslovakia Airlines)
Gertsena ul., 36 315-52-64
.... 315-52-59
Pulkovo-2, Airport 104-34-30
Direct flights to Prague

Gertsena ul., 36 311-58-20
Pulkovo-2, Airport 104-34-38
*Convenient connections to the USA
2 times a week*

Gogolya ul., 19 315-97-36
Pulkovo-2, Airport 104-34-39
Fax 131-89-87
Telex .... 121533 SU

*Daily Flights To Helsinki,
Europe and North America*

KLM
Pulkovo-2, Airport 104-34-40
.... 104-34-41
Amsterdam - Gateway to Europe

LOT (Polish Airlines)
Pulkovo-2, Airport 104-34-37
Direct Flights to Warsaw

✈ Lufthansa

FROM ST. PETERSBURG
VIA FRANKFURT
TO 182 DESTINATIONS
IN 73 COUNTRIES
Mayorova pr., 7 314-49-79
.... 314-59-17
Fax 312-31-29
Pulkovo-2, Airport 104-34-32

Malev, Hungarian Airlines
Mayorova pr., 7 314-63-80
.... 315-54-55
Pulkovo-2, Airport 104-34-35
Direct Flights to Budapest

Jat 104-34-42

**Look in
Traveller's Yellow Pages
before calling!**

☎ AIRPORTS
**АЭРОПОРТЫ
FLUGHÄFEN
AEROPORTS
FLYGPLATSER**

There are two major airports in Saint
Petersburg, Pulkovo I for domestic flights
and Pulkovo II for international flights and
international airlines. They are about five
kilometers apart. The small Rzhevka
Airport north of St. Pb. provides air
services to Northwest Russia.

Pulkovo-1 Domestic Airport
For Domestic Flights
Pilotov ul., 18, bldg. 4 293-90-21
.... 293-90-31
*Bus 39 from Metro Moskovskaya
Fixed- route taxi from Metro Moskovskaya
Express Bus from Gertsena ul., 13*

Pulkovo-2 International Airport
for international flights and
international airlines

Information 104-34-44
Intourist Service 104-33-29
International Flights 293-99-11
Cargo Arrival 104-34-95
Cargo shipped 122-99-13

Rzhevka
of Kovalevo in Leningradskaya Oblast
Information 227-85-62
Levashevo
Please call
Information 594-95-19
.... 594-88-89

☎ AIRPORT
TRANSPORTATION
**АЭРОПОРТЫ, ТРАНСПОРТ К НИМ
TRANSPORT ZU FLUGHÄFEN
AEROPORTS, TRANSPORT
FLYGTAXI**

The Pulkovo airports are about 30
minutes by taxi from center of St. Pb.
Taxi prices vary. From hotels it costs
about $15, otherwise about $3-5 in rubles.
There is also good, frequent
comfortable Airport Express Bus service to
Pulkovo 1, the Domestic Airport. Catch the
bus at the corner of Gertsena ul. 13 and
buy tickets at the Ticket Office there; the
price in June 1992 was 25 rubles. It
takes about 45 minutes to get to Pulkovo-1.

Buses leave about every 20 minutes during the day, 30-40 minutes in the morning and the evening and every hour and one-half at night.

Getting public buses to Pulkovo-2 International Airport is more difficult. Bus No. 13 from Hotel Pulkovskaya is infrequent and not recommended. Call instead the AIRPORT TRANSPORTATION SERVICES or TAXI or LIMOUSINE listed below.

TAXI

At Pribaltiyskaya Hotel

Taxi and Limousine Service
24 Hours/Day,
Featuring Fords
Korablestroiteley ul., 14

Dispatcher	356-93-29
Director	356-10-74
Fax	356-00-94
Fax	356-38-45

$, English, German, Finnish

MATRALEN
AIRPORT LIMOUSINE SERVICE

Call to be met at or driven to the airport
Featuring FORD automobiles & mini-vans

Lyubotinskiy proezd, 5	298-36-48
	298-12-94
Fax	298-00-73
Telex	121028 MATRA SU

24 Hours Daily, $, English, German

☎ **ALARM SYSTEMS**
СИГНАЛИЗАЦИЯ
ALARMANLAGEN
SYSTEME D'ALARME
ALARM, UTRUSTNING

See also SECURITY
Alarm systems are used in many offices and homes.

Kontak
Moskovskiy pr., 182 298-86-35
.... 298-69-43
Bikar
Mayorova pr., 16 274-42-91
.... 315-84-91
Valeri
Pochtamtskaya ul., 5, apt. 1
.... 312-86-54
Fax: 312-41-28

Concern SOPPOL
Alarms

Alarm systems for
offices, banks, stores & apartments
sound, motion & fire detectors
TV surveillance systems.

2-ya Krasnoarmeyskaya ul., 7

Tel............................. 110-14-32
24 hours/day, $ & rubles, English

Zashchita
Dobrolyubova pr., 13 233-82-62

☎ **ALCOHOL/OFF-
LICENSE/LIQUOR**
СПИРТНЫЕ НАПИТКИ, ПРОДАЖА
SPIRITUOSEN
ALCOOL, VENTE
SYSTEMBOLAG

The easiest place to buy imported liquor and beer at fairly reasonable prices is in the INTERNATIONAL SHOPS.

Russian and imported vodka, wine, beer and soft drinks are also sold for rubles by kiosks and street merchants around markets, metro stations and in many kiosks at lower prices. Cognacs, champagne, wines and beer are also sold in restaurants and cafeterias for rubles at a reasonable price (in Western terms).

Many Russian shops sell domestic wines, beer, cognac and vodka. For late hour purchases, try GERA.

Cognac and Wine Tasting
Gogolya ul., 4 315-89-78

Empire Brands Inc.

Authorized distributors
Pierre Smirnoff Company
in Russia

Zhelyabova ul., 27	315-87-38
	314-76-62
Fax:	315-87-38

GERA

Gifts for Your Friends

Spirits, wine, beer.

Zhelyabova ul., 1 315-74-90
Open 24 hrs/day (except 9-10, 15-16)
Metro Nevskiy Pr.

Dagestan "*Cognac & Wine*"
Nevskiy pr., 172 277-43-12
Metro: Alexandra Nevskogo pl.
Konyak, Shampanskoe
Nevskiy pr., 130 277-18-26
Metro: Alexandra Nevskogo pl.
Hrs: 11-19

AGANIMOV
VODKA

Old Family Recipe 1860.
Three Distinguished Vodkas
Distillers & Distributors
Livag Ltd., St. Petersburg

Sinopskaya nab., 56-58... 271-86-31
.... 274-59-82
Fax: .... (812) 274-61-63
Fax (Helsinki) .... (90) 803-85-66

Nektar
Malodetskoselskiy pr., 25
.... 292-52-44
Tasting Hall & Store.
Night Alcohol Retail
Nevskiy pr., 156 277-10-63
Hrs: 21-7
Wine, Vodka
Moskovskiy pr., 38 292-33-83
Moskovskiy pr., 74 292-34-83
Nab. kan. Griboedova, 152
.... 114-08-36
Dzerzhinskogo ul., 34 310-82-70
Nevskiy pr., 88 273-40-41
Tolmacheva ul., 2 210-47-37

☎ AMBULANCE
СКОРАЯ ПОМОЩЬ
AMBULANZEN/KRANKENWAGEN
AMBULANCE
AMBULANSTJÄNST

FOR MEDICAL EMERGENCIES
See EMERGENCY
MEDICAL CARE.
AMBULANCE **03**

☎ AMERICAN EXPRESS OFFICE
АМЕРИКАН ЭКСПРЕСС
AMERICAN-EXPRESS-BÜROS
AMERICAN EXPRESS BUREAU
AMERICAN EXPRESS

See also TRAVELER'S CHECKS

American Express Office
In Saint Petersburg
Travel Services Around the World
At the Grand Hotel Europe
Brodskogo ul., 1/7 (& Nevskiy)
Tel. 315-74-87
Moscow: .... (095) 254-45-05
.... (095) 254-43-05
.... (095) 245-44-95

☎ ANTIQUES
АНТИКВАРИАТ
ANTIQUARIATE
ANTIQUITES
ANTIKVARIAT

See also ART GALLERIES
and ART APPRAISERS.

Antiques are found in strange places in Saint Petersburg. Often they show up in "COMMISSION SHOPS" or in street markets.

Komissionnyy Magazin
Nevskiy pr., 52 311-16-51

Antik Enterprise
M. Govorova pr., 43 252-74-74
Restoring furniture, paintings, ceramics.

'HERITAGE'
Representative work from the finest weavers, painters, silversmiths, woodcarvers, & potters

Paintings, tapestry, embroidery, jewelry , Palekh boxes, samovars china, silver, ceramics

Nevskiy pr, 116 279-50-67
Hrs: 10-19, Rbl, Eng & Ger

Salon "Sankt-Peterburg"
Petra Lavrova ul., 42 273-03-41
Hrs: 11 - 19:30, Rbl.

☎ ANTIQUARIAN SHOPS
(Old Books)
АНТИКВАРНЫЕ МАГАЗИНЫ
ANTIQUITÄTEN (GESCHÄFTE)
ANTIQUAIRES LIBRAIRIES
ANTIKVITETS AFFÄRER

Bukinist on Liteynyy
Books from the Tsarist Times.
Liteynyy pr., 59 273-25-04
Hrs: 11-20

Bukinist on Nevskiy
Nevskiy pr., 122 277-26-86
Hrs: 10.00-18.30 Close: Sunday

Kniga
Used Soviet and Western Books.
Nevskiy pr., 18 312-66-76

Rus
Petra Lavrova ul., 42 273-03-41
Hrs: 11-18, Metro: Chernyshevskaya
Staraya Kniga (Old Book)
Marata ul., 43 164-94-15
Hrs: 10-19
Staraya Kniga (Old Book)
P.S., Bolshoy pr., 19 232-17-65
Staraya Kniga (Old Book)
V.O., Bolshoy pr., 29 218-42-86
Hrs: 10-19
Staraya Kniga (Old Book) No. 75
Nevskiy pr., 122 277-26-86
Hrs:10 19 Closed Sun, Metro: Pl. Vosstaniya
St. Petersburg Shop Salon
Nevskiy pr., 54 311-40-20
Hrs: 11-19

☎ APARTMENT CLEANING
КВАРТИРЫ, УБОРКА
GEBÄUDEREINIGUNG,
WOHNRÄUME
APPARTEMENTS NETTOYAGE
STÄDNING

Apartment Cleaning Svcs "Gefest"
Marshala Govorova ul., 31
.... 252-25-26
Apartment Cleaning Svcs. No. 7
Rizhskaya ul.,12 221-25-49
Apartment Cleaning Svcs. No. 8
Gaza pr., 52.................... 252-04-63
Apartment Cleaning Svcs "Losk"
Voynova ul., 30 272-91-41
Aparment Cleaning Svcs.
Kalyaeva ul., 14.............. 273-38-51

☎ APARTMENT RENTALS
КВАРТИРЫ, АРЕНДА
WOHNUNGEN, VERMIETUNG
APPARTEMENTS LOCATION
LÄGENHETER, ATT HYRA

Apartments can be rented in St. Pb. for longer stays. Prices range from very cheap to outrageous, depending on connections, currency, locations, and negotiating ability. Staying in a private apartment legally is still tricky from the viewpoint of old regulations and should be clarified. For example, prolongation of a visa often required that your passport be registered with the "registration office" and this in turn requires permission to stay in other than an official hotel or as an invited guest in somebody's home. See VISA.

There are a growing number of BED and BREAKFASTS that offer you a room and meals. See HOTELS, MOTELS, BED & BREAKFASTS, DACHA RENTALS.

Chayka
Hotel for foreign specialists
.... 301-75-85
Rentals of apartments of various sizes for foreign firms and companies.

Astoria-Service
Borovaya ul., 11/13, apt. 65
.... 112-15-83
Baltika
Marata ul., 28 164-21-35
.... 164-96-22

DOM PLUS
A G E N C Y

We buy, sell and rent commercial, industrial and residential properties.
Full service agency providing assistance with negotiations and documents.
Kanal Griboedova, 3 312-11-32
Fax 312-83-51

Chic
Blokhina ul., 33 233-16-16

 Ecopolis
OFFICES & APARTMENTS
Zanevskiy pr., 32, Bldg. 2
No. 3...528-26-66

INPREDSERVICE
APARTMENT RENTALS
Nab. Kutuzova, 34 272-15-00
Fax................................ 279-50-24
*INPREDSERVICE is the Municipal Office for Service to
Foreign Representatives & their Staff*

K-Keskus
Ordinarnaya ul., 7 232-07-23
Kovcheg
Klyuchevaya ul., 15, apt. 33
.... 544-98-82
MP "Burgo"
Myasnikova ul., 4, apt. 11
.... 113-41-11

Nationale
Moskovskiy pr., 104........ 297-13-31
Rooms in hotels for foreigners

Nevskie Zori
Nevskiy pr., 95............... 277-42-52
Secretary....................... 274-00-90
Pomoshnik
Nab. reki Moyki, 72......... 310-24-57
.... 310-00-52

☎ APARTMENT REPAIRS
КВАРТИРЫ, РЕМОНТ
WOHNUNGEN RENOVIERUNG
APPARTEMENTS, PETITE
REPARATION
LÄGENHETER, REPARATION

See also CARPENTERS, ELECTRICAL
INSTALLATION, AND LOCKSMITHS

Apartment repairs are carried out by four groups.

Most major apartment repairs, such as painting, are still supposed to be done by local "municipal repair offices" listed below under "District Apartment Repair".

Repairs and small installations of electrical outlets and wiring, locksmith, sewers, heating, plumbing system, and water, in theory, can be solved with help of ""PREO"(ПРЭО) or "REU" (РЭУ) offices. These operate on a very specific regional basis, almost street by street, so that you have to get the right one to solve your problem. Best get somebody to look in the "Short Leningrad Telephone Book 1991" and call for you. The emergency numbers for PREO and REU as well as other emergency response services are listed under our category EMERGENCY ASSISTANCE.

The third major provider of repair services are the Nevskie Zori and Peterburgskie Zori who provide all sorts of services from locksmiths to electricians, carpentry on an individual craftsmen basis, pay-as-you-go.

Fourth, many people look for good individual craftsmen to get work done more quickly. Ask your friends and look under CONSTRUCTION *and* CARPENTERS.

DISTRICT APARTMENT REPAIR OFFICES

Dzerzhinskiy District
Chaykovskogo ul., 15
.... 273-23-52
Frunzenskiy District
Budapeshtskaya ul., 37-120
.... 260-74-88
Kalininskiy District
Vernosti ul., 10, bldg. 3
.... 535-27-71
Kirovskiy District
Veteranov pr., 21............ 156-07-24
Krasnogvardeyskiy
Bolsheokhtinskiy pr., 25
.... 227-16-96
Leninskiy District
Moskovskiy pr., 61 292-21-02
Moskovskiy District
Kosmonavtov pr., 42....... 299-80-07
Nevskie Zori
Nevskiy pr., 93............... 274-00-90
Nevskiy District
Babushkina ul., 42, bldg. 1
.... 560-55-96
Oktyabrskiy District
Dzerzhinskogo ul., 49 310-85-56
Petrogradskiy District
Kirovskiy pr., 27.............. 232-12-24
Primorskiy District
Koroleva pr., 15/30 393-65-62
Pushkinskiy District
Oktyabrskiy bul., 10........ 476-01-95
Smolninskiy District
Nevskiy pr., 175 274-24-07
Vasileostrovskiy
11-ya Liniya, 40.............. 213-13-78
Peterburgskie Zori
Nevskiy pr., 93............... 277-17-17
.... 277-45-47
Vika
Mytninskaya ul., 19......... 274-48-04

**Pleased with a restaurant!
Call Telinfo / InfoServices
See page 237 for info.**

☎ ARCHITECTS
АРХИТЕКТОРЫ
ARCHITEKTEN
ARCHITECTES
ARKITEKTER

 Ecopolis
ARCHITECTS

Staff of 60 Architects Engineers & Designers
European Architectual Standards
International Fashion Center, Moscow, 1992
Commissioned by Steilman & Kronen, Germany
Buildings in St. Pb, Black Sea, & Vyborg
From a single apartment to an entire building
Zanevskiy pr., 32, Bldg. 2, No. 3
☎ 528-26-66

**St.-Petersburg Organization of the Russian
Union of Architects**
Gertsena ul., 52 311-45-57

☎ ARCHIVES
АРХИВЫ
ARCHIVE
ARCHIVES
ARKIV

**Central State Archives of Film & Photo &
Phono Documentary**
Muchnoy per., 2 310-52-48
**Central State Archives of Literature & Art
of St. Petersburg**
Shpalernaya ul., 34 272-53-97
Central State Historical Archives
Nab. Krasnogo Flota, 4 311-09-26
**Department of Archives
of St. Petersburg**
Nab. Krasnogo Flota, 4 311-14-89
**Central Historical Archives of
St.Petersburg**
Pskovskaya ul., 18,........ 219-79-61
State Archive of St. Petersburg
Varfolomeevskaya ul., 15
.... 560-40-01
**St. Petersburg Affiliation of the Archive
of the Russian Science Academy**
Nab. Universitetskaya, 1
director 218-05-12
.... 218-03-12
Military Medicine Archives
Lazaretnyy per., 2........... 315-73-28
Petra Lavrova ul., 52 272-26-41
ZAGS Archives
Petra Lavrova ul., 52 272-26-41

☎ ART APPRAISERS
ХУДОЖЕСТВЕННАЯ ЭКСПЕРТИЗА
GUTACHTEN,
KUNSTGEGENSTÄNDE
ART, EXPERTISE D'
KONST, VÄRDERINGSEXPERT

PALITRA
ART APPRAISERS & RESTORERS
Appraisal, authentication & analysis
of Russian icons and Russian and
European paintings.
Consultants from the Hermitage,
Russian Museum, & Academy of Art
Restoration of Old Masters of Russian
and European Schools, icons and
antique furniture by certified restorers
from Hermitage & ICAR.

Nevskiy pr., 134, apt. 7.................274-21-73
Fax...274-09-11
Telex.............................. 121498 PAL SU
Daily 11-17, English

☎ ART GALLERIES
ХУДОЖЕСТВЕННЫЕ ГАЛЕРЕИ
KUNSTGALERIEN
ART, GALLERIES D'/
GALLERIES D'ART
KONSTGALLERIER

*The art galleries listed here specialize in
paintings & graphics and often have
permanent exhibitions of contemporary
Russian painters. For sculpture, tapestry,
embroidery, and Russian handicrafts, see
ARTS & HANDICRAFTS.*

Alivekt
Nevskiy pr., 22/24............. 315-59-78
Hrs: 10 - 19

ANNA
Nevskiy pr., 16 312-85-35
Hrs: 11-20; Closed: Sun.
Plekhanova ul., 39 311-87-55
OFFICE

*Autograph Avtograf
Studio & Gallery*
Limited Editions Etching & Lithographs
Book Illustration & In House Graphics
Lomonosova ul., 5 310-26-02
Hrs: 9-18, English, French, German, Japanese

Association of St. Petersburg
                Humanitarian Organization
Serpukhovskaya ul., 38..... 292-24-88
Fax   292-29-29

ARIADNA
Best of the modern artists in St. Pb.
Profsoyuzov bul., 11, apt. 17
Tel................................ 311-69-97

Atus, art salon, Russian-Austrian JV
Ispolkomovskaya ul., 7...... 277-02-63

BLOCK LIBRARY Art Gallery
Nevskiy pr., 20............... 311-77-77

BLUE DRAWING ROOM
Golubaya Gostinaya
Art Gallery-Salon
Featuring well known artists of the
Realism movement
Gertsena ul., 38.................. 315-74-14

THE BOREY ART GALLERY
Liteynyy pr., 58 273-36-93

Babush
Lenina pl., 5 542-09-31
Coop Gallery
Pushkinskaya ul., 10/10
Iskusstvo
Nevskiy pr. 16................ 312-85-35

GRIFFON
Paintings & Folkart with Export Documents
Gertsena ul., 33

Exhibition Center for the Association
of Artists of St. Petersburg
*Exhibition and sale of paintings, graphics,
sculpture, drawings, watercolors
Portraits & reproductions from Hermitage*
Gertsena ul., 38 314-64-32
Hours13-19, Closed Mondays, English

 In Saint Petersburg,
and need extra copies of
The Traveller's Yellow Pages
of Saint Petersburg
1992 July - December
Call (812) 315-98-55, 315-64-12
Fax: (812) 312-73-41, 315-74-20

'HERITAGE'
*Representative work from the finest
weavers, painters, silversmiths,
woodcarvers, & potters*

*Paintings, tapestry, embroidery,
jewelry , Palykh boxes, samovars
china, silver, ceramics*
Nevskiy pr., 116........ 279-50-67
Hrs: 10-19, Rbl, Eng & Ger

Klenovaya Alleya
A large outdoor market of
Russian art and handicrafts
Manezhnaya pl. 219-21-29
Modern Art

Kolomna
Rimskogo-Korsakova pr., 24
.... 114-31-50
Lavka Khudozhnikov (Artist's Shop)
Nevskiy pr., 8................. 312-61-93
Gallery of the Russian Artists' Union
Lenart (Russian-Finnish JV)
Nevskiy pr., 40............... 312-48-37
Lenkommisiontorg Shop
Plekhanova ul., 39 312-72-53
Lecturer's Association of St. Petersburg
                        State University
Universitetskaya nab., 7/9
.... 218-96-27
.... 218-97-19

MILENA - ART - GALLERY
Private collection & exhibition of
St. Petersburg's best painters
Please call to visit gallery
Khalturina ul., 11 235-39-01
After 19:00 (ask Diana)
.... 311-05-13
Fax 312-78-84
*We cooperate with foreign galleries to
present our painting abroad*

 Modern Art Gallery
*Classic, realist & avant-gard
graphics and paintings from
recognized & new
artists in Saint Petersburg.*
Nab. reki Moyki, 83 314-47-34
Hrs 13-18, closed Sun & Mon, English

☎ **ART MUSEUMS**
ХУДОЖЕСТВЕННЫЕ МУЗЕИ
KUNSTMUSEEN
ART, MUSEE D'
KONSTMUSEER

See MUSEUMS

☎ **ART SUPPLIES**
ХУДОЖЕСТВЕННЫЕ
ПРИНАДЛЕЖНОСТИ
KÜNSTLERBEDARF
ARTISTES, MAGASINS POUR
KONSTMATERIAL

Lavka khudozhnikov
Nevskiy pr., 8................ 312-61-93
*Hrs. 10:00-19:00, Closed: Sun., Mon.
Paints, brushes, canvases.*

U Fontanki (Near Fontanka)
Pestelya ul., 8 273-54-04
*Hrs. 10:00-19:00, Closed: Sat., Sun.
Everything for artists.*

☎ **ARTISTS**
ХУДОЖНИКИ
KÜNSTLER
ARTISTES
KONSTNÄRER

To find artists, try also the ART
GALLERIES *and* ARTIST ASSOCIATIONS

☎ **ARTISTS ASSOCIATIONS**
ХУДОЖНИКИ, АССОЦИАЦИИ
KÜNSTLERVERBÄNDE
ARTISTES, ASSOCIATIONS DES
ARTISTFÖRMEDLING

Association of Amateur Artists
Exhibition Hall
Nevskiy pr., 20, the Blok Library
Repair............................... 311-01-06
Hrs: 11-21. (-18, Sat &, Sun), closed Fri

☞ Fish for salmon, ripus, ugor
Look up "Hunting & Fishing" on page 132

House of Artists   Dom Khudozhnikov
and
Exhibition Center for the Association
of Artists of St. Petersburg
Gertsena ul., 38 314-64-32
Hours13-19, Closed Mondays, English

☎ ARTS & HANDICRAFTS
(National Crafts)
ХУДОЖЕСТВЕННЫЕ ПРОМЫСЛЫ
VOLKSHANDWERK
KUNSTHANDWERK
ARTS et ART MANUEL
BOUTIQUES D'
KONST OCH
HANTVERKSAFFÄRER

The shops and galleries listed here carry
a wide variety of handicrafts from the
traditional Palekh painted boxes, Pavlo-
posadskiy and Orenburgskiy scarves,
Khokhloma painted wooden ware, and
Matreshkas to beautiful silver, glassware,
tapestry, jewelry and sculptures from
contemporary Russian artisans and artists.

ROSDESIGN
Custom works in colored glass by reknown artists
at Baron Shtiglits Art Institute. Interior decorating
& custom pieces in metal, ceramics, & textiles
Solyanoy per., 13............. 279-41-96

The Russian Arts
Master craftsmen of glass and decorative arts
Saltykova-Shchedrina ul., 53
Closed Monday

Borey
    Liteynyy pr., 58............. 273-36-93
Index
    Nekrasova ul., 6 273-28-59
    273-26-03
Nasledie (Heritage)
    Nevskiy pr., 116............. 279-50-67
Plakat
    Lermontovskiy pr., 38...... 251-94-28
Polyarnaya zvezda
    Nevskiy pr., 158............. 277-09-80
Rosvuzdizain
    Voinova ul., 11............... 273-08-39
    Ordered items on individual samples

The Decorative Arts At

Petrograd

Kirovskiy pr., 54 234-43-77

Art Shop Varyag
Outstanding collection of Russian crafts
Palekh, Fedoskino, Kholui lacquer, Zhostov
painted trays, Pavlovo-Posad scarfs, Baltic
amber, and many Matreshkas.
At the Hotel Gavan: Worth the trip.
V.O., Sredniy pr., 88
☎ 356-61-39
Hrs: 7 am- 2 am, $, Eng, Fran, Finn, Deutsch

☎ ASSOCIATIONS, CLUBS & SOCIETIES
АССОЦИАЦИИ,КЛУБЫ И
ОБЩЕСТВА
VEREINE UND VERBÄNDE,
GESELLSCHAFTEN
ASSOCIATIONS, CLUBS et
SOCIETES INTERNATIONALES
FÖRENINGAR, KLUBBAR

See also CLUBS and BUSINESS
ASSOCIATIONS
There are many clubs, charities asso-
ciations and societies in St. Petersburg
from the Amateur Handweaving Ass-
ciation to War Veterans. Get a copy of
the LBG LENINGRAD BUSINESS GUIDE
1991/92. (See BUSINESS DIRECTORIES).
For a list of local clubs, see CLUBS. Here
we list a few societies of international
interest.

The All-World Club of St. Petersburg
Uniting St. Petersburgers from around the
world in the cultural, intellectual & spiritual
revival of the city of Saint Petersburg.
Meetings in Kseshinskaya Palace.
St. Petersburgers from around the world are
invited to join our projects and activities.

✉ 197046 Russia, St. Petersburg
Kuybysheva ul., 4
☎ 355-04-48

Association For the Development of Dentistry in Saint Petersburg.

An Associaton of Western and Russian Businesses Providing Financial Support To the Private Dentists and Dental Clinics in Saint Petersburg

International Exchange of Dentists
Training In Latest Western Techniques
Provision of Modern Equipment & Materials
Financial Support

Your support is invited.

✉ 193124, Saint Petersburg, Russia, Tverskaya ul., 12/15

Tel	110-02-06
Fax	552-20-06

Union of Russian Friendship Societies & Cultural Links with Foreign Countries
Nab. reki Fontanki, 21 314-06-70
International Centre of Russian Culture
P.S., Bolshoy pr., 75 232-91-40

 Red Cross Society of Russia (Krasnyy Krest)
Rakova ul., 25 311-36-96

ROTARY (Club of Friends of Rotary)
Nab. reki Fontanki, 14 113-58-96

Association of the Victims of Stalin's Repressions
Sankt Petersburgskaya Assotsiatsiya Zhertv Stalinskikh Repressiy
Nab. reki Moyki, 59, rm. 14
Information 535-34-59

☎ AUCTIONS
АУКЦИОНЫ
AUKTIONEN
VENTE AUX ENCHERES
AUKTIONER

See also FURS, REAL ESTATE AGENTS and CURRENCY EXCHANGE

☎ AUDIO EQUIPMENT
АУДИО-ВИДЕО СЕРВИС
HIFI-/VIDEOGERÄTE ANLAGEN
AUDIO-VISUEL, SERVICES D' AUDIO/VIDEO UTRUSTNING

Imported audio equipment, from a simple Walkman to a surround-sound system and CD players, can be purchased in a wide variety of shops in St. Petersburg. Look at COMMERCIAL STORES and COMMISSION STORES, ELECTRONIC GOODS, INTERNATIONAL SHOPS and TELEVISION SALES.

☎ AUTO PARKS
АВТОПАРКИ
PARKPLÄTZE (LKW, BUSSE)
AUTOPARCS
PARKERINGSPLATSER

See PARKING LOTS

☎ AUTOMOBILE ACCIDENTS
ДОРОЖНО-ТРАНСПОРТНЫЕ ПРОИСШЕСТВИЯ
VERKEHRSUNFÄLLE
AUTOMOBILES, ACCIDENTS D' BILOLYCKOR VAD GÖRA INSTR.

In case of an automobile accident, call the traffic police, called "GAI", (ГАИ) (State Auto Inspectorate) at 234-26-46. Don't touch or move the car or at least fix the car's position by chalk. GAI also recommends that you use Sovinteravtoservice (292-12-57) to tow or transport your car. Be prepared to present all your papers to the GAI. If there is any question about fault, get the names of witnesses and a lawyer experienced in such matters. See LAW FIRMS. Drinking while driving is a serious matter. Get a lawyer at once.

☎ AUTOMOBILE EMERGENCY ASSISTANCE
АВТОМОБИЛИ, СРОЧНЫЙ РЕМОНТ
RETTUNGSDIENST
AUTOMOBILE, ASSISTANCE D'URGENCE
BIL, BÄRGNING

Getting emergency assistance in case of breakdown is difficult. Try calling the G.A.I. (State Automobile Inspectorate) and Sovinteravtoservice listed below. . See also MILITIA (Police). Try some of the shops listed under AUTOMOBILE SERVICE.

GAI *(State Automobile Inspectorate)*
Professora Popova ul., 42
.... 234-26-46
.... 234-26-52
Sovinteravtoservice (towing)
.... 292-12-57
Towing service
Udelnyy pr., 28 554-08-64

☎ AUTOMOBILE PARTS
АВТОМОБИЛИ, ЗАПЧАСТИ
AUTOERSATZTEILE
AUTOMOBILE, PIECES DE RECHANGE D'
BILDELAR

See also AUTOMOBILE SALES, AUTOMOBILE SERVICE & REPAIRS.

Parts and most tires for foreign and Russian cars are increasingly available in stores. This is especially true for Volvos. For a price, most other parts can be ordered for quick delivery from Helsinki or Rotterdam.

On Saturday and Sunday mornings, hundreds of car owners gather at the corner of Prazhskaya and Fuchika ul in the Kupchino District to buy and sell auto parts, mostly for Russian models.

Autotechnicalservice
Automobile Parts & Tires
Lubricants & Accessories
All Domestic & Foreign Models

Purchase & Sale of New and Used Cars and Car Parts on Commission

Sadovaya ul., Apraksin Dvor, Bldg. 1
Tel.	311-79-42
Tel	314-89-77
Fax	110-60-99
Fax	395-36-96

Hrs: 10-19, Closed Sun, $ & rbl, English

Car Service International
Jan Ligtharstraat, 9A 3083 AL, Rotterdam, Netherland
	010-484-55-08
Fax	010-484-16-04

Sovinteravto service

Everything for the
AUTO PARTS

Parts, accessories & supplies
for foreign cars, truck, buses
Specializing in Volvo, Mercedes, VW, Opel
Our Shop on Gogolya ul. 19, near Astoria Hotel
Gogolya ul., 19	315-97-58
Telex	121412 LTOS SU
Fax	292-00-28

M-F, 10 a.m. -6 p.m., Eng, $

☎ AUTOMOBILE RENTAL
АВТОМОБИЛИ, ПРОКАТ
AUTOVERMIETUNG
AUTOMOBILE, LOCATION
BILUTHYRNING

Automobiles, mini-vans and buses can readily be rented in St. Pb. with driver. Car rentals without drivers are also available. Often renting a car with driver, however, can be less expensive and more comfortable than without a driver. The roads in St. Pb. tend to be in poor condition, especially crossing over trolley tracks.

Alias A/O
Muchnoy per., 2 310-61-25

Bank Konvers
Please call 239-60-34
Automobiles Available for Rent.
Drivers Available at your option.

AYS" - Car Rentals
Please call 226-95-39

InNis
Automobile Rental
at the Hotel Astoria
Featuring NISSAN cars
Immediate availability & reasonable rates
From the economical MICRA to the
Minibus & luxurious MAXIMA
With or without drivers
Gertsena ul., 39	210-58-58
Fax	210-58-59

Hrs: 9-23, $ & rubles, English

INTERAVTO - Hertz Int. Lic.
Large selection of cars & minibuses with or without drivers. Reservations at the Grand Europe & Moscow Hotels
Ispolkomskaya ul., 9/11
	277-40-32
Fax	(812)274-26-62
	277-46-77
Telex	121347 KRUIS SU

Complete 24 hrs service $, English

☎ AUTOMOBILE SALES
АВТОМОБИЛИ, ПРОДАЖА
AUTOVERKAUF
AUTOMOBILES, VENTE
BILFÖRSÄLJNING

Commercial Store
Savushkina ul., 15 166-42-74
.... 239-98-19
Buy and sell used and new cars.

Kommercheskiy Magazin-Salon
Ligovskiy pr., 142 166-42-74
Savushkina ul., 15 239-98-19

Logo Vaz
Krasnoy Konnitsy ul., 12.. 274-09-33

Orimi- Broker
Kostyushko ul., 3, bldg. 2
.... 290-78-55
.... 290-75-83

Soltransavto

SOVAVTO ST. PETERSBURG
with Klein Trucks, Netherlands

Imported Automobiles

Wide selection of used foreign cars
Volvo, Opel, Ford Scorpio or by order
Excellent prices

Vitebskiy pr., 3 298-46-50
Fax 298-77-60
Telex......................................121535 AVTO
Hrs. 8:30-17:30, English, German

Tiztus (Citroen)
Please call 292-39-76

 TDV–AUTO ТДВ–АВТО

NEW CAR SALES & WARRANTY SERVICE
Authorized Dealer of Ford Europe
in St. Petersburg & NW Russia

FORD-EUROPE CARS & MICROBUSES
Adapted To Russian Road Conditions

Showroom, Service & Parts
Kommuny ul., 16.................... 521-46-14
....521-77-19
Fax...521-85-47
Telex ....121263 TDV SU
Hrs: 9-18, Closed Sunday, $ & rubles, CC, English
Transco N.V. & DTI Holdings (Belgium)
& LRC Avto-Vaz.

Triada
Zhukovskogo ul., 22
Direction........................ 275-79-22
.... 275-79-21

BKR-Service
Authorized Volvo Dealer

VOLVO

Sales, Parts, Service
Bolshaya Podyacheskaya ul., 24,
.... 312-79-44

Volvo. Service by Inavtoservis
Vitebskiy pr., 17/2 298-39-10
Volvo cars sales, service.

Zapad-vostok avto
Moskovskiy pr., 7, apt. 36
.... 314-63-24

☎ AUTOMOBILE SERVICE AND REPAIRS
АВТОСЕРВИС
AUTOWERKSTÄTTEN
AUTOMOBILE, REPARATION (GARAGE)
BIL SERVICE, BILVERKSTÄDER

Automobilist
Lodeynopolskaya ul., 7 235-70-78

AvtoVAZ
St.-Petersburg Regional Autocentre
Krasnoe Selo,
Kingiseppskoe shosse, 50
....132-44-50

Interavto
Alexandra Nevskogo ul., 12
.... 277-40-32
Fax 274-26-62
Telex.................. 121347KRUIS SU

ON ST. PETERSBURG- VYBORG ROAD
InNis AutoService at Olgino
Nissan & Foreign Cars
Autoservice, Repair & Washing
Located At "Olgino Motel" & Camping
Primorskoe shosse, km 18
Tel 238-37-09 $ & rubles

Kontrakt
Maksima Gorkogo pr., 63
.... 233-57-09

LogoVaz
Krasnoy Konnitsy ul., 12
.... 274-09-33

Predpriyatiye po Obsluzhivaniyu Transportnykh Sredstv
Nakhimova ul., 5, bldg. 1
.... 356-77-01

A/O Piter-Lada
Kingiseppskoe shosse, 50 132-52-55

Service Station No. 1 (VAZ)
Salova ul., 70................. 166-47-06
Hrs: 9-17
Service Station No. 3 (GAZ & VAZ)
Staroderevenskaya ul., 5
.... 239-22-31
Hrs: 9-18
Service Station No. 4 (ZAZ)
Kosmonavtov pr., 69....... 126-02-20
Service Station No. 7 (MOSKVICH)
Luzhskaya ul., 3 530-47-82
Sitroen
Moskovskoe shosse, 13a
.... 293-23-04
Hrs: 9-17
Volvo service by Inavtoservis
Vitebskiy pr., 17/2 298-39-10
Volvo cars sales, service.
Sovinteravtoservice
Malodetskoselskiy pr., 24
Secretary...................... 292-24-58
Repairs........................ 292-75-63
Trade Dept.................... 292-17-45

SERVICE

Service, parts, gas, oil & repairs
Specializing in Volvo, Mercedes, VW, Opel
& other foreign cars.
Service centers throughout Russia
Service Center in Saint Petersburg
Predportovyy proezd, 5.... 290-15-10
(Next to Hotel Pulkovskaya)
Daily, 9 a.m. - 8 p.m., Eng, $ & Rbl.
For other services, call
Malodetskoselskiy pr., 24 .. 292-77-18
Telex...................... 121412 LTOS SU
Fax 292-00-28

 TDV-AUTO ТДВ–АВТО

WARRANTY SERVICE & REPAIRS
PARTS, TIRES & ACCESSORIES
Authorized Dealer of Ford Europe
In St. Petersburg & NW Russia

Kommuny ul., 16.................... 521-46-12
Fax.. 521-85-47
Telex............................. 121263 TDV SU
Hrs: 9-18, Closed Sunday, $ & rubles, CC, English
Transco N.V. & DTI Holdings (Belgium)
& LRC Avto-Vaz

"Zenit" Avtoservisnyy Kooperativ
Yuriya Gagarina pr., 32 .....No Phone

VAZ Warranty Services
"Rzhevka"
Kommuny ul., 16........ 521-37-00
.... 521-37-12
"Parnas"
Parnas, 4-yy proezd 598-56-94
"Shuvalovo"
Prokofeva ul., 10........ 515-14-08
GAZ Warranty Service
Pushkin,
Kolpinskoe shosse, 2-oy entrance, 12
.... 470-19-40
Closed Sat.,Sun.
ZAZ Warranty Service
Simonova ul., 13 515-38-06
MOSKVICH Warranty Service
M. Balkanskaya ul., 59 101-54-01

☎ **AUTOMOBILE WASH**
АВТОМОБИЛИ, МОЙКА
AUTOWASCHANLAGEN
AUTOMOBILE, LAVAGE
BILTVÄTT

See CAR WASHES

☎ **BABY FOOD**
ДЕТСКОЕ ПИТАНИЕ
BABYNAHRUNG
BEBES, NOURRITURE POUR
BARNMAT

*Special shops sell prepared baby food
and are called Children's food (Detskoe
Pitanie, Детское питание); some foods
require a note from the doctor.*
COMMERCIAL SHOPS *also sell baby food.*

Dieta No. 12
Moskovskiy pr., 23 292-31-57
Dieta No. 18
Sadovaya ul., 38............. 315-94-53
Malysh (Food for Infants)
Nevskiy pr., 30 312-16-33
Zdorove
Moskovskiy pr., 172 296-17-20

☎ **BAKERIES**
БУЛОЧНЫЕ, КОНДИТЕРСКИЕ
BÄCKEREIEN, KONDITEREI
BOULANGERIES , CONFISERIES
BAGERIER, KONFEKTAFFÄRER

*There are two types of bakeries in
Russia; the more than 320 "bakeries",
almost one on every block (bulochnaya,
булочная) with bread, rolls, and
occasional cakes and pastries and the
more than 30 "konditerei" (konditerskaya,
кондитерская) which has pastries, cakes,
cookies, candy and often coffee*

and cognac, and even a section selling ice cream. They are both listed. Some of the shops listed here have something special and are often joint ventures.

Belochka *Confectionery*
　　V.O., Sredniy pr., 28 213-17-63
Bulochnaya No. 609
　　Nevskiy pr., 66 314-85-59
Bulochnaya No. 74
　　Nevskiy pr., 74 273-50-23
Bulochnaya No. 458
　　P.S., Bolshoy pr., 4 232-02-91
Bulochnaya No. 350
　　Bolshoy pr., 61 232-87-84
Bulochnaya No. 222
　　Nevskiy pr., 142 274-01-50
　　　　Metro: Pl. Vosstaniya, Hrs: 8-20
Bulochnaya-Konditerskiy Magazin
　　Nevskiy pr., 93 277-08-81
　　　　Metro: Pl. Vosstaniya
Bulochnaya-Konditerskiy Magazin
　　Nevskiy pr., 139 277-15-97
　　　　Metro: Pl. Vosstaniya
Bulochnaya-Konditerskiy Magazin
　　Nevskiy pr., 134 277-19-12
　　　　Metro: Pl. Vosstaniya
BUSHE
　　Ryleeva ul., 23 272-01-68
　　...................................... 273-74-98
　　　　From 11 to 17
　　　　Good pastries, rubles
Dr. Oetker Bakery-Konditerei
　　Nevskiy pr., 27 312-10-80
　　　　Hrs: 8-20 daily, rubles
Mechta (Dream)
　　Nevskiy pr., 72 272-98-56

Dr. Oetker Nevskiy 40
BAKERY-KONDITEREI-CAFE
Fine pastery, sweets and great bread
Enjoy coffee, fresh-baked cakes and pasteries
　　Nevskiy pr., 40 312-24-57
　　　　Hrs: 12-24 daily, $

Sever (Cakes)
　　Nevskiy pr., 44 311-25-89
　　　　French Croissants & Pasteries
Torty, Pirozhnye
　　Nevskiy pr., 154 277-29-16
　　　　Hrs: 11-21
Torty
　　Nevskiy pr., 10 312-60-86
Vostochnye Sladosti
　　Moskovskiy pr., 27 292-75-56
Yubileynyy
　　V.O., 7-ya Liniya, 40 213-11-62
Yubileynyy
　　Chernyshevskogo pl., 3
　　...................................... 298-15-47

Zolotoy Uley
　　Nevskiy pr., 22 312-23-94

☎ BALLET
БАЛЕТ
BALLETT
BALLET
BALETT

See THEATER/BALLET

☎ BANKS
БАНКИ
BANKEN
BANQUES
BANKER

See also CURRENCY EXCHANGE &
TRAVELER'S CHECKS &
INVESTMENT BANKS.

　　Saint Petersburg is rapidly becoming a banking center of Russia with more than 28 commercial banks, some new, some from the old state banking structure. These banks perform most of the usual banking operations including deposits, transfers and lending, and often currency exchange. Payments to other firms are done through the less convenient way of "transfer requests" directly through the payer's bank rather than sending a check to the payee for deposit. The commercial banking industry is growing rapidly in a very uncertain economic climate and changing regulations. The stability of banks should be investigated carefully before making significant deposits. We list some of the larger and better known banks.

　　Foreign firms should look for banks with good foreign departments and the right to buy and sell foreign currency.

　　Some firms are similar to Western "investment bankers". See INVESTMENT BANKS.

　　For changing money or traveler's checks, see CURRENCY EXCHANGE *and* TRAVELER'S CHECKS". *Note that you can receive* CASH ADVANCES *from your VISA card at the St. Petersburg Savings Bank.*

　　As of June 15, 1992, one Western bank, the Dresdner Bank, has representatives in St. Petersburg , but it is still not operating as a bank. Many Western banks have offices in Moscow. Several are listed separately at the end of this section.

Aeroflotbank
  Gertsena ul., 28 315-51-57
  311-45-42
Astrobank
  Nevskiy pr., 58............... 311-36-00
  Fax.................................. 311-08-25
Baltiyskiy, commercial bank
  Sadovaya ul., 34 310-05-80
  168-87-66
  Fax 310-92-74

BANK «SAINT PETERSBURG»

The leading bank in St. Petersburg
◇
Ruble & currency accounts
All foreign exchange operations
Direct currency transfer, member of SWIFT
Moscow Interbank Currency Exchange
Market research & evaluation of firms
◇
Correspondent with: Barclays Bank, Deutsche Bank,
Credit Lyonnais, Nordwest, Kansallis-Osaka-Pankki &
leading Western banks
◇
Nab. reki Fontanki, 70/72
....219-80-71
Fax................................315-83-27
Telex .... 121226 LBANK SU
Office 8:30-17:00,
Banking Operations: 9:30-13:00
Bureau D' Exchange: 9:30 -12:00
English spoken

Central Bank of Russia
Saint Petersburg Operations
Nab. reki Fontanki, 70/72
.... 219-85-19
.... 312-39-40
Leningrad Regional Operations
Nab. kan. Griboedova, 13
.... 311-19-45

CREDOBANK
Saint Petersburg

24 Branches throughout Russia
28 Correspondent banks in Europe, UK
and United States
❧
Ruble and Currency Accounts
Interest bearing accounts
Lending to industry and commerce
Currency exchange and transfer
❧
Member of SWIFT & VISA International
Credo card Credit Card
❧
Mokhovaya ul., 26 275-03-33
.... 275-06-06
Fax 275-03-31
Telex....................... 121105 SPFCB
Hrs: 9:30-13, 14-18, English, German, French

Industry & Construction Bank
Saint Petersburg, A/O
Est. Volzhsko-Kamskiy Bank 1863

Full Service Bank for Business & Industry
in Saint Petersburg and Northwest Russia
Ruble & currency accounts for foreign companies
Currency exchange & transfer operations, shares
& loans, certificates of deposit. Corresp. banks:
Deutche Bank & Unibank, Copenhagen
Nevskiy pr., 38................ 110-47-03
Fax 310-61-73
Telex...................... 121612 ICB SU
Office: 8:30 - 17:30, Teller Hrs 9:30 - 12:30
Closed Saturday and Sunday
Bureau of Exchange: 9.30-19 Daily

Energomashbank, joint-stock bank
  Tolmacheva ul., 1 311-95-02
  Fax 315-99-27
Investorbank
  Nab. reki Fontanki, 70/72
  219-80-48
Konversbank
  Nab. Chernoy rechki, 24
  239-75-01
  239-52-22

LADABANK
Ruble and foreign exchange accounts
Banking operations
Currency Exchange
Zanevskiy pr., 6.............. 528-59-01
Fax................................ 528-03-03
Hrs: 9:30-12:30

Lenagroprombank, commercial bank
Nab. kan. Griboedova, 13
.... 315-44-92
Telex .... 121205 LKAPB
Leningrad Innovation Bank
Chaykovskogo ul., 24-8... 279-00-04
Lesopromyshlennyy bank, *see* Petersburg
Lesopromyshlennyy Bank

Petersburg Lesopromyshlennyy Bank
Moving, Please call 541-82-17

Petrovskiy Commercial Bank
Kalyaeva ul., 14.............. 275-76-36
Fax................................ 275-76-35
Telex .... 121624 COUNT SU
Rossiya, commercial bank
Smolnyy, entry 4 278-10-48
.... 278-19-43

 Russian Commercial Industrial Bank
Full-Service Bank
Hard currency & ruble accounts
Safe Deposit, Certificates of Deposit,
International transfers

Gertsena ul., 15 315-78-33
Fax 311-21-35
Hrs for Int'l Payments: 9:00-12:30, Eng.

Russian State Bank
See CENTRAL BANK OF RUSSIA

SAINT-PETERSBURG BANK

St. Petersburg Savings Bank
LARGEST BANK IN SAINT PETERSBURG
Five million accounts • 23 Full Service
Branches •• 254 Savings Bank Offices
9 Currency Exchange Offices
A LEADER IN BANKING INNOVATION
Sberbank Cash Card & Visa Cash Advance

A FULL SERVICE BANK
Foreign Currency & Ruble Accounts
All Lending & Credit Operations
International Currency Transfer

VISA $ CASH ADVANCE
At Hotel Pulkovskaya
Pobedy pl., 2....................... 264-51-47
At Branch No. 1991, Nevskiy pr., 38
Tel.. 110-49-45
Fax 110-47-91

CURRENCY EXCHANGE
9 Currency Exchange Offices in St. Pb
See Ad in Currency Exchange

Head Office: Mayorova pr., 16
Tel..............................314-32-60
Fax...........................315-56-18
Telex............................ 121353 LSB SU
Hrs: 9-18, Closed Sat & Sun, English

Severnyy Torgovyy Bank
Nekrasova ul., 14............ 275-76-00
.... 275-87-98
Stankinbank
(branch of Moscow Stankinbank)
Nab. reki Fontanki, 145/14
.... 275-55-40
Fax 273-16-71
Phone in Moscow .... (095)209-28-57
Tekhnokhimbank
Nab. Krasnogo Flota, 10
.... 311-68-36
Fax................................ 311-69-94
Tokobank
Zagorodnyy pr., 5 112-43-80
Vitabank, commercial bank
Gertsena ul., 59.............. 311-51-93
.... 311-49-48
Fax................................ 311-83-61
Vikingbank, commercial bank
Nab. reki Moyki, 72......... 314-61-31
Fax 272-90-43

*The following bank plans operations but still
had no banking operations in St. Pb.*

*These are a few of the many foreign
banks in Moscow:*

Bank of America Moscow
Krasnopresnenskaya nab., 12
.............................(095) 253-70-54
Chase Manhattan Moscow
Krasnopresnenskaya nab., 12
office 1709 .... (095) 253-28-65
Midland Bank Moscow
Krasnopresnenskaya nab., 12
office 1305 .... (095) 253-21-44
Svenska Handelsbanken Moscow
Pokrovskiy bulvar, 41/17, rm. 35
.............................(095) 207-60-18

☎ BARBER SHOPS
ПАРИКМАХЕРСКИЕ
FRISEUR
COIFFURES, SALONS DE
FRISÖRER

See HAIRCUTTING

☎ BARS
БАРЫ
BARS
BARS
BARER

*There are many types of "bars" in St.
Pb. from the 50 simple bars (bary, бары)
and 20 beer joints (pivnoy, пивной) to
sophisticated "Night Bars", Beer Bars, Grill
Bars and restaurant bars. Westerners
tend to gather at "hard currency only"
Western-style bars located in hotels and
restaurants. There are many good bars
and restaurants with a more limited
selection accepting rubles which serve
wine, champagne, cognac, and, with
perseverance, even vodka. Sometimes,
imported liquor is sold for hard currency
and the meals for rubles.*

HOTEL BARS
See HOTELS *for addresses*

THE NIGHT BAR ASTORIA
*At the Hotel Astoria, Bldg. B
Music and Dancing
to the Wee Hours of the Morning*
Gertsena ul., 39 210-59-06
Hrs: 11 to 5, $, CC, English

Night Club in Hotel Pribaltiyskaya
.... 356-44-09
Hrs: 20 pm-3 am
Kareliya Hotel Bars
2-d floor......................... 226-57-31
Hrs: 12 noon-2 am
8-th floor....................... 226-30-78
Hrs: 12 noon-6 am
11-th floor..................... 226-30-79
Hrs: 8 am-4 am
Oktavian Hotel Bar
8-th floor....................... 356-11-62
Hrs: 4 pm-6 am
Sovetskaya Hotel Bar
5-th floor....................... 259-34-03
Hrs: 2 pm-5 am
St.-Peterburg Hotel Bar
5-th floor....................... 542-90-55
Hrs: 8 am-2 am
Pribaltiyskaya Hotel Bars
Express-bar.................... 356-38-97
Hrs: 8 am-4 am
15-th floor bar............... 356-18-74
Hrs: 8 am-4 am
Beer Bar "Stella" ....No Phone
2-d floor Business Bar ......No Phone
Moskva Hotel Bar
Night Bar....................... 274-00-26
Hrs: 9 am 4 am

BAR ANGLETERRE
THE ENGLISH BAR
At the Hotel Astoria, Bldg. B
**WHERE EVERYBODY MEETS
IN SAINT PETERSBURG**
Gertsena ul., 39 210-59-06
Hrs: 12- 1, $, CC, English

RUBLE BARS

Here are some centrally located bars:

Gogolya ul., 4
Zhelyabova ul., 5
Zhelyabova ul., 6
Sadovaya ul., 13
Nevskiy pr., 44
Nevskiy pr., 113

Bar #1
Mokhovaya ul., 41 273-53-79

Bar #2
Solidarnosti pr., 11 583-09-73

Beer Bar
Dzerzhinskogo ul., 27..... 314-07-18
Hrs: 10 - 17

Belaya Loshad
Chkalovskiy pr., 16 235-11-13
Hrs: 11 - 22

Belye Nochi Bar
Mayorova pr., 43 319-96-60

Fortetsiya
Kuybysheva ul., 7 233-94-68
Hrs: 12 - 17, 19 - 23

Grot
Park Lenina 238-46-90

Kolos
Nab. kan. Griboedova, 20
.... 310-28-83
Hrs: 11 - 22

Victoriya
Skorokhodova ul., 10 232-42-34

Visla Beer Restaurant
Dzerzhinskogo ul., 17 210-68-07

Zhiguli Beer Bar
Vladimirskiy pr., 8 113-16-68
Metro: Vladimirskaya & Dostoevskaya

HARD CURRENCY BARS

Chayka $
Nab. kan. Griboedova, 14
.... 312-21-20

☎ BATHS, RUSSIAN
БАНИ
BÄDER
BAINS
BAD

*There are more than 30 "Russian
baths" in St. Pb. Baths of the Highest
Class often have a sauna room, showers
and a small swimming pool. Often men
and women attend on different days. In
such cases, bathing suits are not customary
in the steam baths and even the pools.
(See also SAUNAS)*

Banya (Highest Class)
O. Forsh ul., 6................ 592-76-22

Banya
Gavanskaya ul., 5 356-63-00

Banya
Karbysheva ul., 29a 550-09-85
Metro: Muzhestva Pl.

Banya No. 43
Nab. reki Moyki, 82......... 312-31-51

Banya
V. O., 5-ya Liniya, 42 213-42-75

Banya
Chaykovskogo ul., 1........ 272-09-11

Banya
Tallinskaya ul., ... 221-34-53

Banya
Malaya Posadskaya ul ., 28
.... 233-50-92

Pravoberezhnye
Novoselov pr., 51 266-13-46

☎ BEACHES
ПЛЯЖИ
STRÄNDE
PLAGES
STRÄNDER

For swimming, the nearest good sand beaches are on the Gulf of Finland in nearby Sestroretsk, Repino and Solnechnoe, about 40 minutes by train from Finlyandskiy Vokzal (Finland Station). Take a picnic or buy some snacks. For sun-bathing only, try any park. See PARKS. Many people sunbathe on the small beach in front of the Peter & Paul Fortress, but don't swim there.

☎ BEAUTY SALONS
САЛОНЫ КРАСОТЫ
SCHÖNHEITSSALONS
SALONS DE BEAUTE
SKÖNHETSSALONG

For women's hairdressers and beauty salons, see HAIRCUTTING. The so-called "cosmetic salons" have nothing to do with cosmetics, but rather include plastic surgery and dermatology. See MEDICAL CONSULTATIONS.

☎ BED & BREAKFAST
ПАНСИОН С ЗАВТРАКОМ
ÜBERNACHTUNG MIT FRÜHSTÜCK
CHAMBRE AVEC PETIT DEJEUNER
PENSIONAT/RUM MED FRUKOST

See also DACHA RENTALS, HOTELS and MOTELS.

Many families are now opening up their homes to foreign visitors as "bed and breakfasts". They will usually arrange for the necessary VISA invitation, provide you with a private room in their apartment, or sometimes an entire fully furnished apartment, and provide as many meals as you want. Often they will guide you around the city, arrange for tickets, get translators, and arrange meetings with people in the professions, business and government. Be clear about what is included in the cost of an overnight's stay. There are organizations in many foreign countries who can arrange such home stays. Here is one you can call directly in Saint Petersburg. The prices can be very reasonable.

Kontakt
Student Center at St. Petersburg Electotechnical University
Prof. Popova ul., 5............... 234-69-59
Accommodations for Foreign Students

HOST FAMILIES
ASSOCIATION
BED & BREAKFAST IN RUSSIA
Saint Petersburg, Moscow, Kiev, Vilnyus, Tallinn, Bishkek, Alma-Ata, Tashkent, Irkutsk, Khabarovsk

"THE BEST WAY TO SEE RUSSIA"
"WE'LL KEEP IN TOUCH FOREVER".
"SAW THINGS WE COULD NEVER SEE."
Stay with faculty & research staff of universities & technical institutes.
Apartments Arranged. Visa Invitations
Full program of cultural, educational, sightseeing, business & professional contacts.
Car tours, stay in a dacha, overnight in a village
Tel.............................. 275-19-92
Tel.............................. 535-78-24
Fax ... 312-41-28   Attention HOFAK
Tavricheskaya ul., 5, kv. 25
Saint Petersburg 193015 Russia

☎ BEEPERS
БИПЕРЫ
BEEPER
BEEPER
PERSONSÖKARE

Pocket pagers or beepers have, to our knowledge, still not arrived in St. Pb.

☎ BEER
ПИВО
BIER
BIERE
ÖL

Western beer is sold in the hard currency shops at big hotels and in many kiosks. Russian beer is sold everywhere, at open markets, and on the street as well as in many shops. The best Russian beers are: Nevskoe, Martovskoe, Petrovskoe, Admiralteyskoe, Zhigulevskoe and Rizhskoe.

See BARS, ALCOHOL, BEVERAGES

☞ Try one of our more than 38 hotels from very reasonable to very elegant, from center city to seaside resorts.
See page 127

☎ BERIOZKA SHOPS
ВАЛЮТНЫЕ МАГАЗИНЫ БЕРЕЗКА
BERIOZKA- GESCHÄFTE
(DEVISEN)
BERIOZKA, BOUTIQUE
AFFÄRER HARDVALUTA

See INTERNATIONAL SHOPS

Beriozka shops are a chain of hard currency shops run by the former state trade organization to sell Russian art, handicraft, jewelry, vodka, cigarettes and a selection of other imported goods for hard currency. For complete listing, see INTERNATIONAL SHOPS.

☎ BEVERAGES-SOFT/DRINKS
НАПИТКИ
GETRÄNKE
BOISSONS
DRYCKER

Beer, Mineral Water, Juice, Pepsi

EAST-REST, beverage distributor
Distributor of **Lapin Kulta Beer**
Soft Drinks, Spring Water
Podolskaya ul., 23
.............................292-63-22
Fax 292-38-58

PEPSI
St. Petersburg favorite soft drink distributor.
Plant Mineral water "Polyustrovo"
Tukhachevskogo ul., 4 226-56-96
.... 226-57-44

Coca Cola
Representation
Nab. kan. Obvodnogo, 93a
..................................315-76-32
..................................113-31-60
..................................210-17-27

Narzan
Nevskiy pr., 34 ....No Phone
Mineralnye vody No 2
Kirovskiy pr., 20 232-60-13

```
To Direct  Dial The USA
DIAL  8,  wait for Dial Tone
DIAL  101 + Area Code + #
```

☎ BICYCLING (Rentals, Clubs)
ВЕЛОСИПЕДЫ, ПРОКАТ, КЛУБЫ
FAHRRADVERLEIH, CLUB
CYCLISME
CYKELAFFÄRER

You can rent bicycles from these three organizations for a modest sum. The 1-st and 3d are sport schools for children, the 2d is the Sports Club "Burevestnik". See also RENTALS

Admiralteyets Velosipednyy Klub at Sport-School for Children
Truda pl., 6..................... 311-25-90
Bicycling Club "Burevestnik"
Engelsa pr., 81 554-17-41
Organizes bike trips and tours.
Bicycling at Sport-School for Children
Vyborgskoe shosse, 34
.... 553-32-03

☎ BOAT EXCURSIONS
ЭКСКУРСИИ ВОДНЫЕ
BOOTSAUSFLÜGE
EXCURSIONS EN BATEAU
BÅTTURER

St. Pb. is the Venice of the North and now many firms offer boat trips on the canals & rivers as well as hydroils out on the Gulf of Finland to Petrodvorets. Many canal boat trips in small motor boats leave from corner of Nevskiy & Fontanka at the Anichkov Bridge. The larger sightseeing tours leave from the piers opposite the Hermitage & the Square of the Decembrists (Dekabrist's Ploshchad).

To Petrodvorets
The boats to Petrodvorets leave from the Neva Embankment opposite the Hermitage Museum. There are hydrofoil boats every 30 minutes from 9:00 in the morning. The trip takes about 30-40 minutes and costs about 40 rubles (June 1992). You cannot buy tickets in advance.

Boating Excursions on Neva.
Boat excursions on the Neva leave either from the Dvortsovaya Embankment opposite the Hermitage Museum or a bit further west near the Admiralty. The schedule in summer is about every two hours and costs about 25 rubles on weekdays, more on weekends. Advance purchases of tickets are difficult, but possible.

A Trip at Night on the Neva

During the summer and especially during the White Nights, there are boats tours at night on the Neva and the canals. One boat trip leaves from the Dvortsovaya Embankment (near the Hermitage) at 10:00 am and lasts about 1 hour. Another leaves from Anichkov Bridge at 12 midnight and returns at 5 am.

Anichkov Bridge Boats (various)
From the pier by the Anichkov Bridge (near Nevskiy pr.) ....No Phone
(Also "White Night" cruises
from June 10 to July 10)

AKVA EXCURS, boat tours
Explore the rivers & canals of St. Pb.
from early morning to late at night.
White night & under-the-bridges tours
Vozrozhdeniya pr., 34...... 237-14-36
.... 110-11-92
.... 237-14-36
Reservations: 9 to 11& 18 to 23, Tours in English

Evening Boat Trips 312-24-47
Concerts On Board Boat By St. Pb.
Performers - Departures From the
Decembrists' Square Landing-Piers.

Hermitage
Information 311-87-71
22:00 - 1:00

Regata
Nab. Maloy Nevki
at Kamennoostrovskiy Bridge
.... 234-49-89

Uliss
Lesnoy pr., 61, bldg. 1, entr. 8
.... 245-09-80

☎ BOAT RENTALS
ЛОДКИ, ПРОКАТ
BOOTSVERLEIH
BATEAUX, LOCATION
BÅTUTHYRNING

See also YACHT CLUBS

AKVA EXCURS, boat rentals
Explore the rivers & canals of St. Pb.
from early morning to late at night.
Custom tours with your own captain.
Vozrozhdeniya pr., 34...... 237-14-36
.... 110-11-92
.... 237-14-36
Reservations: 9 to11& 18 to 23

Breakwater Ltd.
Nab. Martynova, 94 235-27-22
MALAKHIT (Yacht's rental)
Please call...................... 264-65-10

☎ BOOK BINDERS
КНИГИ, ПЕРЕПЛЕТ
BUCHBINDEREIEN
RELIURE, ATELIER DE
BOKBINDARE

Book Binder
Belinskogo ul., 11 272-35-92
Book Binder
Sedova ul., 37................ 560-33-03
Mon., Wed., Fri.
Pereplet
Nekrasova ul., 41............ 279-54-53

☎ BOOKS
КНИГИ
BUCHHANDLUNGEN
LIVRES
BÖCKER

Academic Books   **Akademkniga**
Liteynyy pr., 57 272-36-56
Scientific and technical literature
Hrs: 10-20. Clsd: Sun., Mon.
Aktsioner *books & newspaper*
Petra Lavrova ul., 42 272-66-33
Old Books
     Antikvarno-Bukinisticheskaya Kniga
Nevskiy pr., 18 312-66-76
Second hand books
Bukinist
Liteynyy pr., 59 273-25-04
Second hand books
Burevestnik
Nevskiy pr., 141 277-15-22
Children's Book World
Ligovskiy pr., 105 164-23-94
Hrs: 10-19
Construction Books
     Dom Stroitelnoy Knigi
Bolsheokhtinskiy pr., 20... 224-08-73
Specializing in construction books.

Dom Knigi (House of the Book)
Largest Selection of Books in St.
Petersburg

Nevskiy pr., 28............... 219-94-43
Hrs: 10-20 Clsd: Sun. & first Fri. of the month.

Military Books   **Dom Voennoy Knigi**
Nevskiy pr., 20............... 311-07-51
Specializing in Military Books.

"Hippokrat" Medical Books   **Gippokrat**
Lenina ul., 20.................. 232-54-69
Books on medicine

Iskusstvo (art)

*Albums and prints from Eastern
Europe, China, Mongolia and
Yugoslavia*
Nevskiy pr., 16........... 312-85-35
Hrs: 10-19, Closed Sunday

Lover of Books   **Knigolyub**
Novoizmaylovskiy pr., 40, bldg. 1
.... 295-90-28

Writer's Book Corner
       Knizhnaya Lavka Pisateley
Nevskiy pr., 66....... 314-54-58
New books, old books, old prints

Leningrad
Nevskiy pr., 52.............. 311-16-51

The Mask   **Maska**
Nevskiy pr., 13.............. 311-03-12
Theater books & actors accessories

MIR

Nevskiy pr., 13.............. 311-51-46
Books from Eastern Europe & China

Nauka   **Science**
Liteynyy pr., 64............. 273-50-12

Otkrytki   **Postcards**
Liteynyy pr., 63............. 273-48-97

Planeta

Liteynyy pr., 30............. 273-88-15
A Large Variety of Imported Books.

Rapsodlya

Sheet Music and Music Books.
Zhelyabova ul., 13...... 314-48-01
Nekrasova ul., 38....... 273-45-26

Shipbuilder   **Sudostroitel**
Sadovaya ul., 40 315-31-17
Specializing in Shipbuilders Books

Tekhnicheskaya Kniga

Technical and Scientific Books.
Pushkinskaya ul., 2 164-65-65

TYP

Visit our more than
25 Art Galleries
See page 43

TELINFO
publisher

*The Traveller's Yellow Pages
For Saint Petersburg
and
The City Map of Saint Petersburg*

In Russia, copies can be obtained at
✉ 190000, St. Petersburg, Russia:
Nab. reki Moyki, 64

.... 315-64-12
.... 315-98-55
Fax.............................. 315-74-20
Fax.............................. 312-73-41

For the rest of the world
InfoServices International, Inc.
1 Saint Marks Place
Cold Spring Harbor, NY 11724, USA
Tel.................USA (516) 549-0064
Fax........................ (516) 549-2032
Telex..................... 221213 TTC UR

*Telinfo is a wholly-owned subsidiary of
InfoServices International, Inc. NY, USA*

Transportation Books
       Transportnaya Kniga
Pushkinskaya ul., 20 164-98-07

☎ **BOOKS, OLD**
   КНИГИ АНТИКВАРНЫЕ
   ANTIQUARIATE
   LIVRES, ANCIENS
   ANTIKVARIAT

See ANTIQUARIAN SHOPS

☎ **BOWLING**
   КЕГЕЛЬБАН
   KEGEL- UND BOWLINGBAHNEN
   BOWLING
   BOWLING

Hotel Pribaltiyskaya

Korablestroiteley ul., 14 ... 356-16-63
Hrs: 12-21 Daily

Kirov Stadium
Krestovskiy Ostrov, Morskoy pr.,
.... 230-07-09

☎ BRIDGES
МОСТЫ
BRÜCKEN
PONTS
BROAR

The main bridges over the Neva and Nevka Rivers in the city open at the following hours of the night between April and November (depending on ice and weather) to allow ships to pass. This can cause major problems trying to get home across the rivers late at night. On the public holidays of 1st and 2d May, 7th and 8th of November, the bridges are not raised. The Russian word for bridge is Most (Мост).

Alexandra Nevskogo Most
.... 2:35-4:50
Birzhevoy (Exchange) Most
.... 2:25-3:20 & 3:40-4:40
Bolsheokhtinskiy Most
.... 2:45-4:45
Bolshoy Krestovskiy Most
.... 2:05-2:35 & 4:45-5:20
Bolshoy Petrovskiy Most
.... 1:25-2:00 & 5:00-5:45
Dvortsovyy (Palace) Most
.... 1:55-3:05 & 3:15-4:45
Grenaderskiy Most
.... 2:45-3:45 & 4:20-4:50
Kamennoostrovskiy Most
.... 2:15-3:00 & 4:05-4:50
Kantemirovskiy Most
Kirovskiy Most
.... 2:10-4:40
Leytenanta Shmidta Most
.... 1:55-2:55 & 3:15-4:50
Liteynyy (Foundry) Most
.... 2:10-4:40
Svobody (Freedom) Most
.... 2:10-2:25 & 3:20-4:25
Tuchkov Most
.... 2:00-3:10 & 3:40-4:40
Ushakovskiy Most
.... 2:15-2:55 & 3:55-4:30
Volodarskiy Most
.... 2:05-3:45 & 4:30-5:45

☎ BROKERS
БРОКЕРСКИЕ КОНТОРЫ
MAKLER
AGENTS DE CHANGE
MÄKLARE

Ameros
Stepana Razina ul., 8/50
.... 251-03-88
BOSY
1-ya Krasnoarmeyskaya ul., 11
.... 292-56-58
Brok Master
Babushkina ul., 53, 2d fl.
.... 274-21-39
.... 560-51-56
Fax 274-21-38
Metro: Lomonosovskaya
DISLA
5-ya Krasnoarmeyskaya ul., 20, apt. 6
.... 292-14-52
Fax 292-78-38
Mb: Moscow International Stock Exchange
Interles-Birzha Brokers
Mikhaylova ul., 17 542-99-05
Broker on International Lumber Exchange
Invert Brokerage Firm
Manezhnyy per., 19, apt. 27 ....
.... 275-53-20
.... 275-59-10
Major Stock & Commodity Exchanges
ITEC Brokerage Firm
Manezhnyy per., 19 ....
.... 275-57-71
.... 279-46-10
Fax: 275-57-73
Kiin Inc.
Chernyakhovskogo ul., 73 164-49-65
.... 164-12-96
.... 164-13-96
Kronverk Enterprises
Gertsena ul., 56.............. 110-66-56
.... 110-67-27
.... 275-45-78
Major Stock Exchanges
Montazhsnab
please call...................... 310-78-00
.... 310-34-31

Nadezhda Brokerage Firm
Nab. kan. Griboedova, 15
.... 311-73-47

ORGTEKHNIKA
Antonenko per., 6........... 315-93-82
Fax............................... 315-74-20
St.-Petersburg Stock & Commodity Exchanges

Oksen
V.O., 17 Liniya, 62 355-72-58
Orion
Stepana Razina ul., 8/50.. 251-03-88
Roster
Nab. kan. Griboedova, 15
.... 314-52-96
Fax............................... 314-43-34

Broker-Signal, Ltd.

Commodity Brokers

Lumber, oil products, grain, & metals
Mbr: Interlesbirzha & Agroprombirzha
Shpalernaya ul., 52, apt. 23
Tel.......................................273-21-24
Fax......................................275-31-12

RUMOR 2
Kalyaeva ul., 25.............. 275-61-61
Fax: .... (812) 275-61-47

Trilogika
Khalturina ul., 27 184-06-88
Twin
Krasnykh Tekstilshchikov ul., 2
.... 271-40-89
Fax............................... 274-01-80

SCORPION

A FINANCIAL INVESTMENT COMPANY

Dealers in Investments ❖ Loans
Moscow & St. Pb Currency Exchanges
St. Petersburg Stock & Commodity Exchange

Founded by Bank Saint Petersburg
Sberbank and Unicombank
Nab. reki Fontanki, 70/72...............219-80-37
....277-47-37
Fax.......................................277-49-21

Spektr
.... 528-84-54
Fax............................... 291-09-19
*Brokerage services for St. Petersburg &
Kaliningrad Stock Exchanges*
Universal Brok Gratis
P.S., Bolshoy pr., 56/1 233-06-11

Vostok
Tavricheskaya ul., 39, rm. 347/348
.... 271-41-04
Krylova per., 2................ 310-20-64
VTS
Glinki ul., 13, apt. 8 114-77-11

☎ **BUILDING SUPPLIES**
СТРОИТЕЛЬНЫЕ МАТЕРИАЛЫ
BAUSTOFFE
CONSTRUCTION, MATERIAUX DE
BYGGNADSMATERIAL

See also HARDWARE STORES *and*
PAINT STORES
*Building supplies and lumber are
bought in shops, called "building material
shops (Stroymaterialy, Стройматериалы)
and the "Young do-it-yourself store"
(Yunyy tekhnik, Юный техник) as well as
an increasing number of private shops.*

Building Supplies — **Stroymaterialy**
Baskov per., 36 279-18-56
Building Supplies — **Stroymaterialy**
Babushkina ul., 71 262-16-22
Building Supplies — **Stroymaterialy**
Grecheskiy pr., 27 271-21-74
Building Supplies — **Stroymaterialy**
Ligovskiy pr., 161 166-13-34
Building Supplies — **Stroymaterialy**
Moskovskiy pr., 134........ 298-21-15
Building Supplies — **Stroymaterialy**
Zamshina ul., 31 543-31-77
Dizayn-Gruppa
Kompozitorov ul., 1, bldg. 2
.... 592-25-36
Hardware Store
— **Khozyaystvennye tovary**
Yakornaya ul., 1 224-38-03
Yakornaya ul., 2 224-34-86

MESAV, Ltd.

Wood Products for Construction
Doors, flooring, windows
*Current production committed to
Finnish Contractors in Saint Petersburg*
Shpalernaya ul., 52, Apt. 23
Tel................................ 275-31-12
Fax 275-31-12
Telex............... 121745 GARDA SU

Prazdnik
Gagarina pr., 14 294-05-30
.... 298-61-81
Stroitel
Chkalovskiy pr., 54-56..... 234-23-84
Store Salon
Krasnykh Zor bul., 8........ 267-39-56
Hrs: 10-19, closed Sun, Lomonosov

Stroitelnye Tovary
    Moskovskiy pr., 4 310-17-33
Supplies for Apartment Renovation
    Nab. Chernoy rechki, 6
    239-84-90
Vesta
    Smirnova pr., 16............. 242-09-51

☎ **BUSES (City & Municipal)**
   АВТОБУСЫ, ГОРОДСКИЕ
   BUSVERBINDUNGEN, STADT
   BUS (MUNICIPAL)
   BUSSAR LOKALTRAFIK

*People rely on public transportation in
Saint Peterburg, so that the city and
suburbs are covered with bus, tram and
trolley bus routes. For example, you can
go to Pushkin, Pavlovsk, Gatchina by bus
or by the smaller "fixed route taxi" from
H. Pobedy at Metro Moskovskaya". Note
that in some suburbs, you pay the city
bus driver directly.*

*To use the bus, you need one coupon
(talon), which cost 50 kopecks in June,
1992, or use a monthly transportation
card. See TRAMS and METRO for further
information on how to use public
transportation.*

TRANSPORT SIGNS

BUS,   TRAM,   TROLLEYBUS

☎ **BUS & MINIVAN CHARTER**
   АВТОБУСЫ, ПРОКАТ
   BUSVERLEIH, KLEINBUSVERLEIN
   BUS ET MICROBUS, BAIL
   BUSS OCH VANS ATT HYRA

See also AUTOMOBILE RENTAL

☎ **BUSES INTERCITY
& INTERNATIONAL**
   АВТОБУСЫ, МЕЖДУГОРОДНЫЕ И
   МЕЖДУНАРОДНЫЕ
   BUSVERBINDUNGEN, ÜBER LAND
   BUS LONGUE DISTANCE
   BUSSAR, INRIKES

*Buses serve many of the nearby cities,
such as Novgorod, Vologda, Narva and
the Baltic's. They leave from the two
terminals listed below. There is now daily
express bus service to Finland.*

BUS TERMINALS - INTER-CITY

Bus Terminal No 1
*Buses to Vyborg, Priozersk on Lake
Ladoga, Volosovo, Kingissep, Osmino and
other cities in Leningrad Oblast (region)*
    Nab. kan. Obvodnogo, 118
    292-16-83

METRO Baltiyskaya;. BUSES: 10, 49 60
67,109; TROLLEY BUSES: 3, 24;
TRAMS: 1, 2, 19, 29, 34, 36, 43

Bus Terminal No 2

Buses to the Northern Region,
Vologda, Petrozavodsk, Estonia,
Novgorod, Pskov, Pushkinskie Gory.

Nab. kan. Obvodnogo , 36

.... 166-57-77

METRO Ligovskaya; .BUSES: 3, 14, 26,
44, 57, 74, TROLLEY BUSES 42;
TRAMS: 10, 19, 26, 44, 49

☞ Before you come to
Saint Petersburg
Look at our "WHAT-TO-BRING"
Checklist to be sure you have the most
essential items for your trip.

 **BUSINESS ASSOCIATIONS
AND CLUBS**
БИЗНЕС-АССОЦИАЦИИ
WIRTSCHAFTSVERBÄNDE
BUSINESS ASSOCIATIONS DE
AFFÄRSKLUBBAR

There are many Business Associations
in St. Petersburg. See the "Business
Directories" listed under and BUSINESS
PUBLICATIONS, *and* BUSINESS
CONSULTANTS and ASSOCIATIONS,
CLUBS & SOCIETIES. *A few of the larger*
and more active clubs are listed below.

Arendator (Lease Holder)
Liteynyy pr., 42.............. 279-51-74
Business club attached to the board of
the Znanie (Knowledge) Society.

**Association of Small and Medium Sized
Firms in Leningrad for Foreign Economic
Activity**
Zagorodnyy pr., 68 292-14-55
Fax................................ 315-17-01

**Association of Soviet Maritime Trade
Ports**
Gapsalskaya ul., 4 114-92-14
Fax................................ 251-14-92

**AVEKS, the Association for Cooperation
in Foreign Economics of Leningrad
Enterprises**
3-ya Krasnoarmeyskaya ul., 12
.... 292-48-37
.... 110-13-13
Fax................................ 292-14-53

**Baltika, Foreign Economic Association
for Leningrad Region**
.... 164-60-08

Business Forum
Plekhanova ul., 42 315-47-01

**Business People's Club of the Leningrad
Association of Scientific, Scientific &
Technical, Scientific & Production
Cooperatives and Small Enterprises**
Gertsena ul., 67.............. 312-87-67

Leningrad Association of Joint Ventures
Plekhanova ul., 36, rm. 602-605
.... 312-79-54
Fax............................... 315-94-70
Telex...... 121132 GVLEN SU

**Lenstroyinter, Leningrad Foreign
Economic Association**
Nevskiy pr., 1 (up to August)
.... 312-60-42
Fax................................ 315-81-73

Progress, Leningrad Management and Marketing Centre
Institutskiy pr., 22 552-13-38
.... 552-69-62
.... 552-58-11

Sovamtrade, Association for Business Cooperation with the USA
Prosveshcheniya pr., 87-1
.... no phone

Technoimpex, Leningrad Foreign Economic Association
V.O., 6-ya Liniya, 27 213-06-05
Fax 218-42-75

Voyage, Foreign Economic Association
Chekistov ul., 28 135-18-55

WORLD TRADE CENTER
TRADE INFORMATION & BUSINESS SERVICES
Proletarskoy Dictatury ul., 6... 274-1970
Fax.....278-1808   TLX.....121003 WTASA SU

☎ **BUSINESS CARDS**
ВИЗИТНЫЕ КАРТОЧКИ
VISITENKARTEN
CARTES DE VISITE
VISITKORT

Enterprise AYU
Voronezhskaya ul., 33 166-03-20

EXPRESS PRINT
Pushkinskaya ul., 20 113-18-08
Express Printing of Business Cards
Hours: Mon.-Fri. 10 - 19

Institute of Printing
Krasnaya ul., 3 315-24-36

DESIGN & PRINTING

Printers to the banks, businesses & government of Saint Petersburg.
Stationery and Business Cards
Logos & Trademarks
📠 Gromova ul., 12, apt. 5, 195196 St. Pb.
Tel: .... 232-18-90 & 221-96-03
Fax 232-18-90
Hrs: 9-21, Closed Sundays

Leningrad Art Factory
Nab. reki Fontanki, 71, flr. 4., rm. 46
.... 310-40-01

Offset
Dzhambula per., 13 164-96-24
Manufacturing of business cards and stationery.

PetroSpek
Grazhdanskiy pr., 111 531-14-11

Rikki-Tikki-Tavi MP
Dekabristov ul., 62 219-76-92
.... 114-19-20

SKIF, business cards
Russian & English while-you-wait
Letterheads & Logo Design
Vosstaniya ul., 32 275-53-45
.... 275-47-53
Fax 275-58-71

Taiwan
Nab. reki Fontanki, 11 110-68-32

Trionika
Nevskiy pr., 41 311-03-33
Hrs: 14 - 17

Product complex TRUD
Saltykova-Shchedrina ul., 30
.... 275-77-07

Vika
Nab. kan. Obvodnogo, 215, apt. 12
.... 251-43-33
Stationery & logos, etc.

☎ **BUSINESS CENTERS**
БИЗНЕС-ЦЕНТРЫ
BUSINESS CENTERS
BUSINESS CENTERS
BUSINESS CENTER

See BUSNESS SERVICES CENTERS

☎ **BUSINESS CONSULTANTS**
БИЗНЕС-КОНСУЛЬТАЦИИ
WIRTSCHAFTSBERATER
BUSINESS, CONSULTATIONS
AFFÄRSKONSULTER

ABC
Sadovaya ul., 55/57, rm. 505
.... 310-84-36
.... 315-77-14
Consultation for opening a company.

A. J. EST S.U
Representative for
French & Spanish Firms in Russia
Profsoyuzov bul., 4, Entr. 6
.... 110-64-96
Telex.................. 121732 CGTT SU

ALLIANCE *Business consultants*
At the Hotel Sovetskaya
We find and evaluate Russian firms.
Investment advice & full registration of JV
Assistance in finding office space
Lermontovskiy pr., 43 259-34-42
Fax 251-88-90

AsLANTIS

A Consortium of Interpreters
to Business

For Your Business Negotiations & Trips
Let us capture the subtle nuances in your
Publicity, Advertising & Legal Documents
Fax & Phone Translation and Transmission

We are well acquainted with the business &
political community in Saint Petersburg

Tel... 213-76-81
Fax/Tel.................................... 298-90-07
We can answer your call in English

Concord Agency
Rubinshteyna ul., 3 315-18-32
Bazis
Please call 310-39-59
Broteck
Please call 248-25-56
BOSY
1-aya Krasnoarmeyskaya ul., 11
.... 292-56-58

Business Center T.A.M.
Consultancy services, selection and
checking of partners for business.
Processing of documents required to
commence business in the Russia
Nevskiy pr., 16, Floor 2 ... 312-77-37
Fax................................. 311-57-01
Hrs: 10-17.; Clsd: Sat. & Sun.

Business Management International
Nab. reki Moyki,18.......... 307-79-04
.... 314-10-91
*Business accounts in US banks
Offices in California*

City
Tambasova ul.,27/2
Please call after 15:00..... 130-14-79
Please call after 21:00..... 145-07-76

Consofin J.V. Fin (Technical)
Ogorodnikova pr., 58....... 259-91-06
Fax................................ 251-76-11
Timber, paper & cellulose industry.

Coopers &Lybrand | Solutions for Business

Moscow & St. Petersburg
Accountants, Management Consultants
Tax Advisers

In Saint Petersburg
At the Astoria Hotel, Room 528
Gertsena ul., 39...................... 210-55-28
Fax..................................311-42-12

In Moscow
Shchepkina ul., 6 ....(095) 971-69-61
Fax................................(095) 284-52-73

G.V. Bear Bros. "ALKOR"
Apraksin Dvor, bldg. 33, 2nd Fl.
.... 255-76-56
Fax................................ 310-44-70

ERNST AND YOUNG
SAINT PETERSBURG OFFICE
AUDITING & CONSULTING
Tax, accounting, market & feasibility studies
business plans, legal & personnel issues
partner selection

V.O., 13 Liniya, 20 (local)
.... 116-01-57
Outside of St. Pb.................. 906-01-57
Fax 218-79-40

Hill-Baltiyskaya Konsultatsionnaya firma
Hill-Baltic Consultation Firm
Executive Search Firm
Berezovaya Alleya, 5-a..... 275-72-82
Fax 275-76-98
Let us help you find the staff you need

Inex, Japan
Business services, organization of exhibitions,
assistance in export-import operations.
Egorova ul., 18............... 292-50-13

Informatika
Nab. Krasnogo Flota, 8 312-28-73
Innovative Consulting Centre
Nab. Universitetskaya, 7/9
.... 218-96-27
.... 218-97-19

Intourist-Nauka-Service

CONSULTANTS ON THE RUSSIAN
TRAVEL INDUSTRY, HOTELS & SERVICES

MARKET RESEARCH ON TOURISM

TRAVEL MANAGEMENT TRAINING

Isaakievskaya pl., 11..... 210-0907
Fax............................ 312-28-18
Telex ....121559 INTUR SU
Hrs: 10-18, $ & rubles, Eng., Ger, Finn.

Lenaudit AKG
Rakova ul., 33................ 311-19-49
.... 312-06-33
.... 310-53-11
Fax.................................. 310-53-33
Leningrad-Goteborg Company
Leninskiy pr., 101 153-57-65

M.A.G. Logistic GmbH
Mezhevoy kan., 5, rm. 806
.... 186-83-44
Fax.............................. 251-86-62
Telex ....121691 MCT SU
Business consultations, legal & financial, services, contacts in Europe & Asia.

Novyy Sankt-Peterburg
Nab. reki Fontanki, 76 315-80-58
Registration of all types of ownership

NATARI
BUSINESS LAW CONSULTANTS
Antonenko per., 6b 315-93-82

Permafrost Consultants
Soil Mechanics
& Engineering Cryology
Put Your Enterprise on Solid Ground

Frost Heaving & Soil Mechanics, Experts on Soil Conditions in Russia Specifications for Road Surfaces, & Paving, Construction, Dams, Large Structures & Refrigerated Storage.

Contact: O.R. Golli. Laboratory of Engineering Geology, Geocryology and Soil Mechanics, Research Institute of Hydraulic Engineering
Gzhatskaya ul., 21
195220, St. Peterburg, Russia
(812) 535-88-68

Pari
Nekrasova ul., 40 273-67-46
Fax.............................. 273-67-46
Pinta, Stock Co.
Professora Popova ul., 47
.... 234-51-78

INFADOC
Krasnaya ul., 69, apt. 215
.... 210-96-41
Experts on business & technical projects
RUSTEX (USA)
Belgradskaya ul., 6, bldg. 4, apt. 46
.... 109-69-14
.... 273-44-40

Russkaya Torgovaya Kompaniya
Russian Trading Company
At the Hotel Pribaltiyskaya
Korablestroiteley ul., 14 ... 356-21-29
Going to change address

SEVOS
High Municipal Business School
Dvinskaya ul., 5/7 251-63-92
.... 221-76-95
Selena
Liteynyy pr., 20 278-86-94

SMENA, business consultants
Understanding the Russian business world

Learn negotiation and organizational methods to help you establish and manage your business in Russia. Inter-cultural and social values

We assist in negotiations and analyze & evaluate investment projects

Labutina ul., 20 114-37-70
.... 114-70-16
Fax 311-01-44
Hrs: 9 -18, $ & rubles, English, Norwegian

Concern SOPPOL
BUSINESS LAW CONSULTANTS
Experienced lawyers & law professors
Contract law, tax advice & customs
Full registration with all documents
2-ya Krasnoarmeyskaya ul., 7
Tel 110-12-09
24 hours/day, $ & rubles, English

SOU
Nevskiy pr., 177, rm. 6
.... 277-44-94
.... 277-49-00
St. Petersburg
The Centre of International Commerce
Proletarskoy Diktatury ul., 6,
rm. 417-419................... 274-19-70
Fax 278-18-08
All Trading Consultations

Sigma Apeks
Primorskiy pr., 6 239-97-60
Fax................................. 239-53-74

St. Petersburg Information Centre (SPIC)
Manezhnyy per.,19, apt. 27
.... 275-63-15
Fax................................. 275-18-59

Trilogika
Millionnaya ul., 27 184-06-88

ITS
.... 292-50-13
Egorova ul., 18............... 292-77-29

The Traveller's Yellow Pages
For the *World Traveller* is published by
InfoServices International, Inc., USA
and by its wholly-own subsidiary
Telinfo, St. Petesburg, Russia

InfoServices International, Inc.
1 Saint Marks Place Cold Spring
Harbor, NY 11724 USA
Tel.: (516) 549-0064
Fax: (516) 549-2032

Telinfo
64 Moyka Embankment
Saint Petersburg, Russia, 190000
Tel: (812) 316-98-55, 316-64-12
Fax: (812) 312-73-41, 316-74-20

Vostochnyy predprinimatelskiy Ekspress
Gogolya ul., 14............... 312-80-97
Fax............................... 315-09-54

☎ BUSINESS INSTITUTES
БИЗНЕС-ИНСТИТУТЫ
WIRTSCHAFTSSCHULEN
BUSINESS, INSTITUTS DE
AFFÄRSINSTITUT

**International Business School of the
Leningrad Organization of the Znanie
(Knowlege) Society**
Karla Marksa pr., 88.........No Phone

**Leningrad Institute of Finance &
Economics**
Nab. kan. Griboedova, 34
.... 310-52-31

**St. Petersburg International Management
Institute (LIMI)**
Rastrelli pl., Smolnyy, entrance 9
P.O.B. 450.................... 273-41-48
Fax............................... 271-07-17

Magistr
Dvinskaya, 5/7 (LIVT), rm. 487
.... 259-06-05
.... 114-98-72

**International Institute of Developement
and Teaching the Banking and Business**
Mezhdunarodnyy Institut Razvitiya I
Obucheniya Bankovskoy I Birzhevoy
Deyatelnosti
Nevskiy pr., 58, rm. 103

Khalarovi (business-school)
Fax 249-84-67
Fax/Ph (Stockholm) 08 929090
soon will change their address

Polyus
Nab. kan. Griboedova, 176,
room 43 114-50-61
.... 114-79-55
.... 114-79-49

Shkola Menedzherov
Sadovaya ul., 21, rm. 263a
.... 110-55-81

Konta
Please call 127-93-45
.... 273-63-22
*Five to six week courses in business
development.*
Hrs: 17-21 Mon.-Fri.

VNESHVUS-CENTRE

Business in Russia Seminars
Taxes, Laws, Banking, Privatization
Seminars in English
Other Languages by Translation
Write to: Post Office Box 14
199226 Saint Petersburg Russia
V.O., Nab. Morskaya, 9 356-99-05
Fax 355-69-87

☎ BUSINESS PUBLICATIONS
ДЕЛОВЫЕ ИЗДАНИЯ
WIRTSCHAFTSPUBLIKATIONEN
PUBLICATIONS D'AFFAIRE
AFFÄRSFÖRLAG

See also NEWSPAPERS & MAGAZINES

Aktsioner [Auctioner]
A newspaper on economics of Russia.
Shpalernaya ul., 52, apt. 19
Tel 272-96-76
Fax 275-76-11

**Moscow Business Survival Guide 2d
Edition, 1991** Russian Information
Service. $32.00

Business Navigator (Russian)
*An excellent guide to business
in St. Petersburg & Moscow. 1991, 126 rbl.*
IMA Press,
Laboratornyy proezd, 23 .. 544-62-85

St. Petersburg Business Guide
1992/93
Published September 1992
*Most complete and up-to-date guide to
businesses and organizations in St. Pb.
Business regulations • Who is Who
Financial and Commercial Services
Tax and customs regulations
Business Services • Charities*

Published by and available from
LIC Information & Publishing Agency, Ltd.
191065 Saint Petersburg, Russia
Gertsena ul., 20
☎ 314-59-82
Fax 315-35-92
InfoServices International, Inc., USA
(See "TELINFO" ad below)

Business-Shans (Russian)
Advertisement newspaper printed in color
Nab. reki Fontanki, 59 210-84-57

Commersant ℔ (Russian & English)
On sale in Kiosks

Delovye Lyudi (Business People)
The well-known Business in USSR *now
with a new name* Delovye Lyudi *meaning
"Business people". Excellent,
English and Russian Editions.*
Moscow, Profsoyuznaya ul.,73
.... (095) 333-33-40
Fax .... (095) 330-15-68

TELINFO, publisher
*The Traveller's Yellow Pages
For Saint Petersburg
and*
The City Map of Saint Petersburg
In Russia, copies can be obtained at
✉ 190000, St. Petersburg, Russia:
Nab. reki Moyki, 64
.... 315-64-12
.... 315-98-55
Fax 315-74-20
Fax 312-73-41

For the rest of the world
InfoServices International, Inc.
1 Saint Marks Place
Cold Spring Harbor, NY 11724, USA
Tel ....USA (516) 549-0064
Fax .... (516) 549-2032
Telex .... 221213 TTC UR
*Telinfo is a wholly-owned subsidiary of
InfoServices International, Inc. NY, USA*

Reklama-Shans
  Weekly newpaper for private
  advertisement and information
  Nab. reki Fontanki, 59 210-84-41

Russian Trade Express
  Morskoy Slavy pl., 1, rm. 7044
  355-16-44
  Will soon change their address

Saint Petersburg Business Directory
  1991, 305 p.
  Leninform 234-03-18

☎ **BUSINESS SERVICES CENTRES (Fax, Telex, Photocopying, Computer, Interpreters)**
  БИЗНЕС-ЦЕНТРЫ (ФАКС, ФОТОКОПИЯ, ТЕЛЕКС И Т.Д.)
  BÜROSERVICE (FAX, KOPIEREN, TELELEPHONE U.S.W.)
  BUSINESS SERVICES DE (FAX, PHOTOCOPIEUSE, ORDINATEUR ,TELEX)
  AFFÄRSSERVICE (KOPIERING O.S.V.)

  See also EXPRESS MAIL/PARCEL SERVICE, FAX SERVICES, COMPUTERS, PHOTOCOPYING, TELEPHONES, TELEX, TELEGRAM, BUSINESS CARDS, BUSINESS CONSULTANTS, OFFICES, OFFICE EQUIPMENT.

ALLIANCE BUSINESS CENTER
  At the Hotel Sovetskaya
  International Communications, Fax
  Photocopies, Computers & HP Laser
  Lermontovskiy pr., 43...... 259-34-42
  Fax 251-88-90
  Hrs: 9:30-18, $ & rbls, English

AsLANTIS

  A Consortium of Interpreters to Business

  For Your Business Negotiations & Trips
  Let us capture the subtle nuances in your
  Publicity, Advertising & Legal Documents
  Fax & Phone Translation and Transmission
  Tel.. 213-76-81
  Fax/Tel................................. 298-90-07
  We can answer your call in English

In the Traveller's Yellow Pages
  for Saint Petersburg
  The SPORTSMAN can find
  Tennis, Swimming, Rowing
  Shooting, Horseback Riding
  and Skating

AVEX Business Centres
  Full Service for the Business Traveler
  PC', Fax, Copier, Paper, Telex, Phone
  Two Locations
  Hotel MORSKAYA
    Tel & Fax 365-14-01n
    Telex ....121367 BUSHM SU
  Hotel SOVETSKAYA
    Business-Club 'AIRLINES',
    Tel 251-88-90
    Fax.......................... 259-34-42
    Telex .... 121367 HSSU SU

Business Center Varyag
  At the Hotel Gavan, 4th Floor
  Full-Service Business Center with tele-
  communications, secretaries, copying.
  Sredniy pr., 55 355-67-18
  Fax 356-85-52
  Telex............... 121101 VARAG SU
  Daily, 8 am.-8 pm, $ & rbl, Eng, Fran, & Deutsch

A/O "Innovatsii of Leningrad Institutes"
  Professora Popova ul., 47
  (Dvoretz Molodyozhi), fl. 11, rm. 1-7
  234-55-11
Hialaimpex (J.V.Rus-Bulgarian)
  Gagarina pr., 1 297-81-22
DHL
  Profsoyuzov bul., 4, apt. 22
  311-23-46
  311-96-82
Alliance
  Hotel Sovetskaya
  Lermontovskiy pr., 43/1 ... 259-34-42

BUSINESS CENTER **GRAND HOTEL EUROPE**

  ★★★★★

  ST. PETERSBURG RUSSIA
  Fax, telex, telephones, computers, photocopiers
  Audio-visual support and projectors
  Secretarial and interpreters
  Six meeting rooms

  Mikhaylovskaya Street 1/7
  Saint Petersburg, 191011
  Info/Switchboard .... 312-00-72, Ext. 6230
  Fax: 311-88-61

Hotel Helen
  Lermontovskiy pr.,43/1 259-20-48
International Phone Station
  Gertsena ul., 3/5............. 314-01-40
M.A.G. Logistic GmbH
  Mezhevoy kan., 5, rm. 802
  186-83-44
  251-86-62

MCT (Management Consulting Training)
.... 251-86-62
Fax 186-83-44
Telex 121691

Perekrestok (Crossroads)

Information & Consultancy services.
*Communications, photocopying,
computer, audio & video technology.
Premises for business meetings.
Interpreting & translating.
Chauffeur-driven cars.*
Poltavskaya ul., 10 277-41-97
Fax 273-43-04
Telex .... 121060 LBUSC SU
Hrs: 10 -18 daily.

Petr Velikiy
Nab. kan. Obvodnogo, 117
.... 392-17-79
Retur
Gertsena ul., 39, Hotel Astoria, Floor 2
.... 311-73-62
Hrs: 9-21 daily
Smart
Admiralteyskiy pr., 8 110-66-34
.... 110-66-55
Fax: 110-65-70
Telex: .... 121432 Smart SU
"St. Petersburg"
    Centre of International Commerce
Proletarskoy Dictatury ul., 6,
rm. 417-419 274-19-70
Fax 278-18-08
Telex .... 121003 WTASA SU

☎ **CABLE TELEVISION**
  КАБЕЛЬНОЕ ТЕЛЕВИДЕНИЕ
  KABELFERNSEHEN
  TELEVISION DE CABLE
  TV, KABEL

See TELEVISION, CABLE

☎ **CAFES**
  КАФЕ
  CAFÉS
  CAFES
  CAFÉ'R

See also RESTAURANTS

*Cafes in St. Petersburg are usually smaller
than restaurants with a lighter menu and a
variety of drinks (but not always coffee).
The better ones are listed under*
RESTAURANTS, *as well. For fast service,
look for "Cafe Express" or "Bistro".*

Dr. Oetker Nevskiy 40
BAKERY-KONDITEREI-CAFE
Fine pastry, sweets and great bread
Enjoy coffee, fresh-baked cakes and pastries
Nevskiy pr., 40 312-24-57
Hrs: 12-24 daily

Bistro
Dzerzhinskogo ul., 13 314-66-14

"Around the corner and down the steps"
The CAFE "Bristol"
For a quick cup of good coffee and snack
Black & red caviar, pizza, & khachapuri
Nevskiy pr., 22 311-74-90
Hrs: 10-20, Ruble, English

Cafe at the Saint Petersburg
Nab. kan. Griboedova, 5 .. 210-76-73
Desertnoe
Sadovaya ul., 59............. 312-35-16
Donuts
Nevskiy pr., 119 ....No Phone
Retro
Shchorsa pr., 23............. 230-83-91
Syurpiz
Nevskiy pr., 113 277-00-97
Zakarpate
Gertsena ul., 14.............. 110-69-97
Hrs: 11-20

CHILDREN'S CAFE

Ice Cream Parlour
Nevskiy pr., 24 311-00-71
Konek- Gorbunok
Industrialnyy pr., 10 520-20-33
Shokoladnitsa
Pestelya ul., 19 272-98-46

RUSSIAN CUISINE

Avtomat Kafe
Nevskiy pr., 45 311-15-06
Elf
Stremyannaya ul., 11 311-22-17

The Traveller's Yellow Pages
For the *World Traveller* is published by
InfoServices International, Inc., USA
and by its wholly-own subsidiary
Telinfo, St. Petersburg, Russia

InfoServices International, Inc.
1 Saint Marks Place, Cold Spring
Harbor, NY 11724 USA
Tel.: (516) 549-0064
Fax: (516) 549-2032
Telinfo
04 Moyka Embankment
Saint Petersburg, Russia, 190000
Tel: (812) 315-98-55, 315-64-12
Fax: (812) 312-73-41, 315-74-20

Fregat
  V.O., Bolshoy pr., 39 213-49-23
Petrogradskoe
  P.S., Bolshoy pr., 88 232-34-55
Kvas bar & ice-cafe
  Belinskogo ul., 6 273-64-98
U Samovara
  Piskarevskiy pr., 52 538-30-95

CAUCASIAN CUISINE

Iveriya
  Marata ul., 35 164-74-78
Rioni *Georgian shashlyk*
  Nevskiy pr., 136 277-58-93
  Metro: Vosstaniya pl., Hrs. 11-20

☎ **CALLING HOME**
   ТЕЛЕФОН МЕЖДУНАРОДНЫЙ
   TELEFONVERBINDUNGEN
   TRANSMISSION
      TELEPHONIQUE,INTERIEURE
      ET EXTERIEURE
   TELEFON, INTERNATIONELL

See TELEPHONE INTERNATIONAL CALLS

☎ **CAMERAS**
   ФОТОАППАРАТУРА
   FOTOAPPARATE
   APPAREILS DE PHOTOS
   KAMEROR

See PHOTOGRAPHY FILM & DEVELOPING,
PHOTOGRAPHY-CAMERAS AND SUPPLIES

☎ **CAMPING**
   КЕМПИНГ
   CAMPING
   CAMPING
   CAMPING

Olgino Motel
CAMPING
Primorskoe shosse, 18 km
.... 238-35-50
Fax 238-39-54

☎ **CAMPING SUPPLIES**
   ТУРИЗМ, ТОВАРЫ В ДОРОГУ
   CAMPINGZUBEHÖR
   CAMPING, FOURNITURES
   CAMPINGUTRUSTNING

*Camping supplies can be bought in
special travel stores called "Tourist"
(Turist, Турист), in special departments at
the department stores and in sporting
goods stores.*

See also DEPARTMENT STORES &
            SPORTS EQUIPMENT

TOURIST, goods for travelers
  Nevskiy pr., 122 277-02-79
TOURIST, goods for travelers
  Kondratevskiy pr., 33 540-13-94
GOSTINYY DVOR, department store
  Nevskiy pr., 35 110-51-45
  312-41-74
APRAKHSIN DVOR, department store
  Sadovaya ul., bldg. 85-95
  310-18-93

☎ **CANDY STORES**
   КОНФЕТЫ
   SÜBWAREN
   BONBONS
   KONFEKTYR

*Candy, especially Russian chocolates,
is sold in many places and especially in
"confectionery" shops (Konditerskaya,
кондитерская) which are listed under
BAKERIES. INTERNATIONAL SHOPS
usually have a good selection of candy,
especially imported chocolates. Some
DEPARTMENT STORES have whole
departments selling candies.*

MARS, candy, cakes, a cup of coffee

Nevskiy pr., 40 311-90-66
.... 312-24-57
Fax 272-22-73
Open: 8-20

Vostochnye Sladosti
Oriental Sweets
Russian & Imported Sweets & Chocolates
Middle Eastern halvah, nougat, pastries
Nevskiy pr., 104 273-74-36
Moskovskiy pr., 27 292-75-56

MECHTA confectionery shop
Nevskiy pr., 72 272-98-56

☎ CAR ACCIDENTS
ДОРОЖНО-ТРАНСПОРТНЫЕ
ПРОИСШЕСТВИЯ
AUTOUNFÄLLE
VOITURE, ACCIDENTS DE
BILOLYCKOR

See AUTOMOBILE ACCIDENTS.

☎ CAR PHONE
РАДИОТЕЛЕФОН
AUTOTELEFON
AUTOTELEPHONE
BILTELEFONER

See CELLULAR PHONES.

☎ CAR RENTAL
АВТОМОБИЛИ, ПРОКАТ
AUTOVERMIETUNG
VOITURES, LOCATION
BILUTHYRNING

See AUTOMOBILE RENTAL.

☎ CAR REPAIR
АВТОМОБИЛИ, РЕМОНТ
AUTOREPARATUR
VOITURES, REPARATION
BILREPARATIONER

See AUTOMOBILE SERVICE & REPAIR.

☞ In Saint Petersburg,
and need extra copies of

The Traveller's Yellow Pages
of Saint Petersburg
1992
July - December

Call (812) 315-98-55, 315-64-12
Fax: (812) 312-73-41, 315-74-20

☎ CAR SALES
АВТОМОБИЛИ, ПРОДАЖА
AUTOVERKAUF
VOITURES, VENTE
BILFÖRSÄLJNING

See AUTOMOBILE SALES.

☎ CAR WASHES
АВТОМОБИЛИ, МОЙКА
AUTOWASCHANLAGEN
VOITURES, LAVAGE
BILTVÄTT

Car Wash
Salova ul., 70 166-47-06
Open: 10 a.m. - 6 p.m.

Car Wash
Nakhimova ul., 5/1 356-77-01
Open: 8 a.m. - 7:30 p.m.

Car Wash
Energetikov pr., 65 226-56-88
Open: 1 p.m. - 2 p.m.

Car Wash
Staroderevenskaya ul., 5
.... 239-22-31
Open: 8 a.m. - 8 p.m.

Car Wash
Luzhskaya ul., 3 530-47-82

Car Wash
Kosmonavtov pr., 69 126-02-20
Open: 8 a.m. - 9 p.m.

☎ CARPENTERS
ПЛОТНИКИ
SCHREINEREIEN TISCHLEREIEN
CHARPENTIERS
SNICKARE OCH HANTVERKARE

See also CONSTRUCTION
& RENOVATION, APARTMENT REPAIRS

Carpenter
Tsiolkovskogo ul., 10 251-26-16

Kontrakt
Gorkogo pr., 63 233-56-32
.... 235-12-98

MESAV, Ltd.
Custom Carpentry &
Cabinetmakers
Shpalernaya ul., 52, Apt. 23
Tel. 275-31-12
Fax 275-31-12
Telex .... 121745 GARDA SU

Nevskie Zori
Nevskiy pr., 95 277-42-52
Secretary 274-00-90

Peterburgskie Zori
Nevskiy pr., 95 277-17-17

Sentex
Zanevskiy pr., 6.............. 221-47-89
Sosna
Yuzhnoe shosse, 61........ 269-30-94
Uspekh
Kirovskiy pr., 16b 230-91-25

☎ CARPETS
КОВРЫ И ДОРОЖКИ
TEPPICHE
TAPIS
MATTOR

See RUGS & CARPETS.

☎ CASINOS
КАЗИНО
CASINO
CASINOS
CASINO

777 Kazino
Nevskiy pr., 22-24 311-31-41
Hrs: 13-24

Nevskie Melodii
(at restaurant)
MOST EXCITING CASINO IN ST. PB.
Nab. Sverdlovskaya, 62
.... 227-26-76
Hrs: 22-03

Nordvest
Kima pr., 4...................... 350-12-91
Slot machines

Spielbank Casino
In the Hotel Pribaltiyskaya
Korablestroiteley ul., 14 ... 356-41-53
Hrs: 20.- 03

☎ CATERED BUSINESS
FUNCTIONS
ПРЕЗЕНТАЦИИ
PRÄSENTATION
PRESENTATIONS

Many RESTAURANTS *and* CONFERENCE
HALLS *will also "cater" for your party.*

PAVLOVSK PALACE
Introduce your company to St. Pb.
Catered company receptions in the
beautiful palace and park of Paul 1st
Revolyutsii ul., 20 470-29-61
.... 470-21-55

☎ CELLULAR PHONES
РАДИОТЕЛЕФОНЫ
MOBILTELEFONE
CABINES TELEPHONIQUES
MOBILTELEFONER

Petrovich
Knippovich ul., 10........... 567-23-16
Fax............................... 567-23-49
Sitek
Rentgena ul., 3, 4 fl. 233-20-91

☎ CEMETERIES
КЛАДБИЩА
FRIEDHÖFE
CIMETIERES
KYRKOGÅRDAR

Cemetery Care

Cemeteries

Armenian Smolenskoe Cemetery
V.O., Nab. reki Smolenki, 29
(at church)...................... 350-53-01
Visit historic Armenian Cemetery in St. Pb.

Bogoslovskoe Cemetery
Laboratornaya ul., 4a 544-75-24
Bolsheokhtinskoe Cemetery
Metallistov pr., 5 224-27-29
Evreyskoe (Jewish) Cemetery
Aleksandrovskoy Fermy pr., 66-a
.... 262-03-97
Kazanskoe Cemetery
Pushkin, Lermontovskiy pr., 1
.... 465-28-53
Kazanskoe Cemetery
Rybatskoe, Yunnatov pr., 34
.... 107-55-44
Levashovskoe Memorial Cemetery
Pos. Levashovo, Gorskoe shosse, 135
.... 594-95-14
Nikolskoe Cemetery
Nab. reki Monastyrki, 1.... 274-25-39
Novo-Volkovskoe Cemetery
Salova ul., 80................ 298-09-29
Piskaryovskoe Cemetery
      (Memorial to the Siege)
Nepokorennykh pr., 74 247-57-16
      (excursions)
Serafimovskoe Cemetery
Serebryakov per., 1......... 239-31-51
Severnoe Cemetery
Pargolovo-3.................... 594-86-26
Smolenskoe Cemetery
V.O., Kamskaya ul., 24.... 355-99-93
Shuvalovskoe Cemetery
Vyborgskoe shosse, 106-a
.... 554-16-59
Volkovskoe (Lutheran) Cemetery
Nab. reki Volkovki, 1....... 166-33-34
Volkovskoe (Orthodox) Cemetery
      (Literatorskie Mostki)
Rasstannyy proezd, 30
.... 166-28-83
Volkovskoe Pravoslavnoe Cemetery
Rasstannyy proezd, 7a
.... 166-04-00
Yuzhnoe Cemetery
Vostochnoe shosse, 1..... 183-15-34
Zelenogorskoe Cemetery
Zelenogorsk, Lenina pr..... 231-32-19

☎ CERAMICS
КЕРАМИКА
KERAMIK
CERAMIQUE
KERAMIK

See **CRYSTAL & PORCELAIN**

☎ CHAMBERS OF COMMERCE
ТОРГОВЫЕ ПАЛАТЫ
HANDELSKAMMERN
CHAMBRES DE COMMERCE
HANDELSKAMMARE

See BUSINESS ASSOCIATIONS
VNESHPOSYLTORG
191084, Moskovskiy pr., 98
.... 298-67-25

Finnish-Russian
4-aya Krasnoarmeyskaya ul., 4a
.... 292-16-41
Fax............................... 112-72-52

Leningrad Chamber of Trade and Industry
191194, Chaykovskogo ul., 46/48
.... 273-48-96

☎ CHESS CLUBS
ШАХМАТНЫЕ КЛУБЫ
SCHACHVEREINE
ECHECS CLUBS
SCHACK-KLUBBAR

City Chess Club
         Gorodskoy Shakhmatnyy Klub
Zhelyabova ul., 45 314-75-61
.... 314-72-61
Rook (in renovation)   **Ladya**
Vladimirskiy pr., 3........... 113-36-97
Chess Club of St. Petersburg University
Nab. Morskaya, 15.......... 351-71-78
Chess Club of Frunze District
         Shakhmatnyy Klub
         Frunzenskogo rayona
Dunayskiy pr., 48/1......... 172-16-16
City's chess club
         Gorodskoy Shakhmatnyy Club
Zhelyabova ul., 25 314-75-61
.... 317-72-61

☎ CHILD CARE
НЯНИ
KINDERMÄDCHEN
BONNES D'ENFANTS
DAGHEM, BARNPASSNING

Most baby-sitting is done by grandmothers or by well-known highly recommended older women. The American system of baby-sitting is still developing. Children are usually sent to nursery schools and kindergartens.

Kompleks
Mayorova pr., 16............ 298-85-76
.... 127-90-90

☎ **CHILDREN'S CAFE**
ДЕТСКИЕ КАФЕ
KINDER KAFES
CAFES POUR LES ENFANTS
BARNKONDITORIER

See CAFES

☎ **CHILDREN'S CLOTHES**
ОДЕЖДА ДЕТСКАЯ
KINDERBEKLEIDUNG
VETEMENTS POUR ENFANTS
BARNKLÄDER

See CLOTHING, CHILDREN

☎ **CHINA & CRYSTAL
STORES**
ФАРФОР, ХРУСТАЛЬ
PORZELLAN,KRISTALL
PORCELAINE ET CRISTAL
PORSLIN OCH GLASAFFÄRER

See CRYSTAL & PORCELAIN

☎ **CHURCHES, OTHER**
Including
Temples and Mosques
ЦЕРКВИ РАЗЛИЧНЫЕ
KIRCHEN, VERSCHIEDENE
EGLISES: AUTRES
KYRKOR: ALLMÄN

ARMENIAN APOSTOLIC CHURCH

Armenian Church of St. Catherina (1771)
Nevskiy pr., 40/42
Closed for renovation.

BAPTIST CHURCH
Baptist Church
              Evangeliskikh Khristian-Baptistov
Bolshaya Ozernaya ul., 29a
.... 553-45-78

EVANGELICAL CHRISTIANS CHURCH
Christian Evangelists
              Evangeliskikh Khristian
3-ye Pargolovo pos.,
Polevaya ul., 21,.......... 594-81-43
Evangelical Christians (Pentecostal)
Slavyanskaya ul., 13 100-40-92
Dom evangelistov
Borovaya ul., 52 166-28-31

LUTHERAN CHURCH
Lutheran, town of Pushkin
Proletkulta ul., 4 470-99-63
Lutheran (Deutsch) Church (Inactive)
Nevskiy pr., 20................. no phone
*This church, built in the 1830's, is now
used as a swimming-pool. It is to be
returned to the church.*
Seventh Day Adventists
Volodarskiy pos.,
Internatsionalnaya ul., 7
.... 138-98-11

ROMAN CATHOLIC
Church of Our Lady of Lourdes
Kovenskiy per., 7............ 272-50-02
Roman Catholic Church (Inactive)
Nevskiy pr., 34.................No Phone
Inactive, but will be reopened soon.

HOUSES OF WORSHIP NON-CHRISTIAN

BUDDHIST
Buddhist Temple
Primorskiy pr., 91............ 239-03-41

JEWISH
              See SYNAGOGUES
Jewish Religious Center
              Evreyskaya Obshchina
Lermontovskiy pr., 2 114-11-53

MUSLIM
Mosque of the Congregation of Moslems
Maksima Gorkogo pr., 7
.... 233-98-19

☎ CHURCHES
RUSSIAN ORTHODOX
ЦЕРКВИ ПРАВОСЛАВНЫЕ
KIRCHEN,ORTHODOXE
EGLISES: ORTHODOXES
KYRKOR: ORTODOX

There are hundreds of churches in the St. Petersburg area. Many of the closed one are slowly be reopened. We have included here many open and some closed churches of historical significance.

Finding churches can be confusing because one church can have several names. Also the same name has been given to different churches in different areas of the city. To help identify the church, the traditional English name first, then the Russian name and then the area.

Alexander Nevskiy Monastery,
       Cathedral of the Holy Trinity
Nab. reki Monastyrki, 1
.... 274-04-09

Alexander Nevskiy Church
       [Shuvalovskiy District]
Vyborgskoe sh., 106-a, ... 595-06-66

Cathedral of the Transfiguration
       Spaso-Preobrazhenskiy Sobor
Radishcheva pl., 1.. 272-36-62
.... 279-51-20

Cathedral of Prince Vladimir
       Vladimirskiy Sobor
Blokhina ul., 16 232--76-25

Church of the Resurrection
       Voskresenskaya Tserkov
Nab. Obvodnogo kanala, 116
.... 292-00-93

Church of Nativity of John the Baptist
Kamennoostrovskiy pr., 7

Church of Valaam Monestary (Podvore)
       Church of Lady of Kasan
Valaam Island................ 252-20-66

Church of the Savior on the Blood
       Tserkov Spasa na Krovi
Nab. kan. Griboedova, 2a
.... 314-40-53

Church of the Serafim
       Serafimovskaya Tserkov
Serebryakov per., 1......... 239-15-50

Church of the Icon of the
       Lady of Smolensk
Kamskaya ul., 24............. 213-54-24

Church of the Icon of the
       Lady of Vladimir
Vladimirskaya pl., 20....... 113-16-14

St. Iov's Church
Kamchatskaya ul., 6........ 166-27-49
.... 166-25-44

St. Peter's Church
Lakhtinskiy pr., 94 ....No Phone

St. Nicholas Church
       Bolsheokhtinskoe Cemetery
Metallistov pr., 5 224-27-08

St. Nicholas Cathedral
Kommunarov pl., 1/3....... 114-08-62
.... 114-08-13

Spasskaya Tserkov
Konyushennaya pl., 1 ....No Phone

Staroobryadcheskaya Obshchina
       Bespopovtsev Pomovskogo soglasiya
Poselok Rybatskoe,
Yunnatov ul., 32...............No Phone

> **St. Andrei's Cathedral**
> V.O., 6-ya Liniya, 11 213-17-32
> 213-62-39
> *Needs Restoration, visitors welcome*
> *Services Sun 12:00*

St. Isaac's Cathedral
Isaakievskaya pl. 315-97-32

Church of Holy Trinity
       Svyato-Troitskaya Tserkov
       "Kulich" i "Paskha"
Obukhovskoy Oborony pr.,235
.... 262-13-87

St. Dmitriy Church
Kolomyagi, 1-ya Nikitinskaya ul., 1-a
.... 395-34-10

Alexander Nevskiy Church
Krasnoe Selo,
Shuppa ul., 10................ 136-46-16

Archangel Michel Cathedral
       Sobor Arkhangela Mikhaila
Lomonosov, Yunogo Lenintsa pr., 63
.... 422-39-62

Cathedral of Sofiya
Pushkin,
Sofiyskaya ul., 1............465-47-47n

Spasskaya Tserkov
Poselok Pargolovo, Vyborgskoe
shosse, 106-a 554-16-58

St.Peter & Paul Cathedral
       Sobor Svyatogo Petra i Pavla
St. Peterburgskaya ul., 32
.... 427-92-68

Church of the Icon of the Lady of Kazan
Zelenogorsk,
Primorskoe sh., 547 231-80-06

St. Ilya Church in Porokhovye
Revolyutsii sh., 75 227-88-15

Cathedral of the Transfiguration
       Spaso-Preobrazhenskiy Sobor
Vyborg,
Teatralnaya pl., 1.....(8-278) 2-58-37

☎ CINEMAS, MOVIES
КИНОТЕАТРЫ
FILMTHEATER
CINEMAS
BIOGRAFER

Avrora
Nevskiy pr., 60.............. 315-52-54
Barrikada
Nevskiy pr., 15.............. 315-40-28
Dom Kino (House of Films)
Tolmacheva ul., 12 314-81-18
Gigant
Kondratevskiy pr., 44 540-90-00
Khudozhestvennyy
Nevskiy pr., 67.............. 314-00-53
Kolizey
Nevskiy pr., 100 272-87-75
Ladoga
Shosse Revolyutsii, 31 227-24-18
Leningrad
Potemkinskaya ul., 4 273-31-16
Meridian
Novo-Izmaylovskiy pr., 48
.... 295-76-70
Molniya
Bolshoy pr., 35.............. 233-11-36
Molodyozhniy
Sadovaya ul., 16 311-00-45
Moskva
Gaza pr., 6 251-29-18
Neva
Nevskiy pr., 108 273-75-52
Films from Lenfilm Studio
Parisiana
Nevskiy pr., 80.............. 273-48-13
Primorskiy
Kirovskiy pr., 42 230-80-14
Prometey
Prosveshcheniya pr., 80... 531-77-82
Rekord
Sadovaya ul., 75 114-22-94
Rodina
Tolmacheva ul., 12 470-61-94
Rubezh
Veteranov pr., 121 135-17-44
Slava
Bukharestskaya ul., 47 260-87-26
Smena
Sadovaya ul., 42 310-13-01
Spartak
Saltykova- Shchedrina ul., 8
.... 272-78-97
Old movies, special subject movies
Stereokino
Nevskiy pr., 88.............. 272-27-29
Stereoscopic Films

Titan
Nevskiy pr., 47.............. 319-97-26
Zenit
Gastello ul., 7................ 293-13-20
Znanie
Nevskiy pr., 72.............. 273-51-83

☎ CIRCUS
ЦИРКИ
ZIRKUS
CIRQUES
CIRKUS

On the Scene (Na Stsenye)
Sergeya Tyulenina per., 4
.... 312-01-10
.... 311-02-60

The State Circus
April - June
"Lions, Tigers and Horses"
a program by animal trainers Lyudmila
and Vladimir Shevchenko

Nab. reki Fontanki, 3
.... 210-43-90
Administrator...................... 314-84-78
.... 210-41-98

Palitra
Nevskiy pr., 134, rm. 7.... 274-21-73
Shapito (Big Top) Summer Circus
Avtovskaya ul., 1a.......... 183-15-01
May 15 - September 30   Metro Avtovo
Performances by artists
of the Moscow circus

☎ CITY GOVERNMENT
ГОРОДСКОЙ СОВЕТ
STADTVERWALTUNG
CONSEIL MUNICIPAL
STAOSFULLMÄKTIGE

See ST. PETERSBURG CITY GOVERNMENT
- CITY COUNCIL
- MAYOR'S OFFICE

☎ CLEANING SERVICES
УБОРКА, СЛУЖБЫ
REINIGUNGSFIRMEN
NETTOYAGE, SERVICE DE
STÄDHJÄLP

See APARTMENT CLEANING

 DIAL 01 for FIRE

☎ CLIMATE
КЛИМАТ
KLIMA
CLIMAT
KLIMAT

The climate in Saint Petersburg usually comes off the Baltic sea and the Gulf of Finland. It is highly changeable with crystal clear sunshine followed by heavy showers and again by sunshine, especially in summer. A collapsible umbrella is useful. A good raincoat (with a liner) will be used from March to October. Even in summer, it can get chilly, so a sweater & windbreak may be useful, especially in the evening.

Something warmer may be needed from November to February. A good top coat, fur coat, or ski parka with scarf, gloves, and fur hat will be welcome. Note that the interiors of most buildings are usually well heated.

	Average Daily Temperature Fahr		Days with some	
	Celsius			
	Lo/High	Low/High	Rain	MM
Jan.	8/19	-13/-7	21	35
Feb.	11/22	-12/-5	17	30
March	18/32	-8/0	14	31
April.	33/46	0/8	12	36
May.	42/59	6/15	13	45
June.	51/68	11/20	12	50
July.	55/70	13/21	13	72
Aug.	55/69	13/20	14	78
Sep.	47/60	9/15	17	64
Oct.	39/48	4/9	14	76
Nov.	28/35	-2/2	18	46
Dec.	18/26	-8/-3	22	40

☎ CLINICS
КЛИНИКИ
KLINIKEN
CLINIQUES
KLINIKER

See MEDICAL CARE AND CONSULTATIONS

☎ CLOCKS/WATCHES
ЧАСЫ
UHREN
HORLOGES/MONTRES
KLOCKOR OCH ARMBANDSUR

See WATCHES

☎ CLOTHING
ОДЕЖДА
BE KLEIDUNG
VETEMENTS
KLÄDER

See CLOTHING-CHILDREN'S, CLOTHING-MEN'S, CLOTHING-WOMEN'S, FASHION SALONS, DEPARTMENT STORES, COMMERCIAL SHOPS, INTERNATIONAL SHOPS and COMMISSION SHOPS, FURS and SHOES, HATS and HABERDASHERY

The favorite places to buy clothing in general are the DEPARTMENT STORES, Gostinyy Dvor, Apraksin Dvor, and the Univermags. Imported clothing can be bought in the COMMERCIAL SHOPS such as Babylon, COMMISSION SHOPS, and INTERNATIONAL SHOPS as well as in Passazh. Raincoats and coats can be bought at the large DEPARTMENT STORES. Sports clothing and swimming suits are bought at SPORTS SHOPS.

Bolshevichka
Ligovskiy pr., 107 164-93-10

Center for Trade
        Tsentr Firmennoy torgovli
Clothing, shoes and apparel from the best domestic and imported manufacturers
Nab. Novosmolenskaya, 1
.... 352-11-34

"DLT" Leningrad Trading House
     Dom Leningradkoy Torgovli
Men's, Women's, and Children's Clothes
Zhelyabova ul., 21-23...... 312-26-27

Enterprise im. Volodarskogo
Stachek pr., 21 186-43-66

DOM MOD Fashion House
            Dom Mod
Fashionable Women's Clothing
P.S., Kirovskiy pr., 37...... 234-90-40
.... 234-69-23
.... 234-90-55
Marshala Tukhachevskogo ul., 22
.... 543-65-78
.... 225-19-19

Lencomissiontorg Shops

Sadovaya ul., Apraksin dvor,
section 35-36................ 310-30-58
Sadovaya ul., Apraksin dvor,
section 40-48................ 310-29-67
Moskovskiy pr., 50
.... 292-54-52
Gallery-102
Nevskiy pr., 102............. 273-68-42
P.S., Bolshoy pr., 44 232-01-29

Jeans and Jackets

Petrograd

Kirovskiy pr., 54 234-43-77

Yubiley
*Dress clothes, suits, clothes for special
occasions, such as weddings.*
Nab. Sverdlovskaya, 60 ... 224-25-98

☎ CLOTHING, CHILDREN'S
ОДЕЖДА ДЕТСКАЯ
KINDERBEKLEIDUNG
VETEMENTS POUR, ENFANTS
KLÄDER, BARN

*Children's clothing can be bought in
many of the shops mentioned above as
well as special children's shops called
"Children's World"* (Detskiy Mir, Детский
Мир). *DEPARTMENT STORES have a
special department for children.*

Aist   *Clothing for infants*
Sredniy pr., 16 213-26-37
Alenka   *for girls*
Stachek pr., 80 183-01-60
Andreika   *for young boys*
Stachek pr., 55 183-04-88
Bele   *for infants*
Nevskiy pr., 63............... 311-45-33

Detskiy Mir (Children's World)
                              Детский Мир
Moskovskiy pr., 191........ 293-50-75
Prosveshcheniya pr., 46-1
.... 597-33-16
Sedova ul., 69................ 560-61-92
Shkolnaya ul., 6 230-87-01
*The Complete Store for Children
Clothing, Shoes, and Toys*

Leningrad Trading House
           Dom Leningradskoy Torgovli
Zhelyabova ul., 21-23...... 312-26-27
Clothing for Children
                         Odezhda dlya detey
Bolshoy pr., 25 233-56-36

☎ CLOTHING, MEN'S
ОДЕЖДА МУЖСКАЯ
HERRENBEKLEIDUNG
VETEMENTS POUR, HOMMES
KLÄDER, HERR

*See DEPARTMENT STORES,
COMMERCIAL STORES, INTERNATIONAL
SHOPS, COMMISSION STORES,
SHOES and HABERDASHERY.*

*The favorite places to buy men's
clothing are the DEPARTMENT STORES,
Gostinyy Dvor, Apraksin Dvor, and the
Univermags. Raincoats and coats can be
bought at the large DEPARTMENT
STORES. Belts and neckties can be
bought at HABERDASHERY shops. You
can also buy neckties at Necktie shops,
called "Neckties" (Galstuki, Галстуки).*

Bogatyr (Big sizes for men)
Nalichnaya ul., 33........... 352-65-60
Elegant Store - Men's Department
P.S., Bolshoy pr., 55 232-86-19
Rassvet (for shirts)
Ligovskiy pr., 38............. 314-42-20
Ruslan
Smirnova pr., 27............. 246-15-15
Sokol
Metallistov pr., 77........... 540-21-01
.................................540-20-26

☎ CLOTHING, WOMEN'S
ОДЕЖДА ЖЕНСКАЯ
DAMENBEKLEIDUNG
VETEMENTS POUR, FEMMES
KLÄDER, DAM

*See FASHION SALONS, DEPARTMENT
STORES, COMMERCIAL STORES, INTER-
NATIONAL SHOPS, COMMISSION
STORES, FURS, SHOES and
HABERDASHERY*

*The favorite places to buy women's
clothes are the stylish Dom Mod, Passazh,
Gostinyy Dvor, Apraksin Dvor, and the
Univermags. Imported clothing can be
bought in the COMMERCIAL SHOPS,
INTERNATIONAL SHOPS as well as in
Passazh. Used clothing can be bought in
COMMISSION SHOPS.*

Avrora
    Prosveshcheniya pr., 5 599-69-51
Bogatyr (Big sizes)
    Nalichnaya ul., 33........... 352-65-60

Bolshevichka

Ligovskiy pr., 107........... 164-93-10
*("Bolshevichka" collection designed by
the Leningrad House of Fashion, known
for elegance and style)*

DOM MOD Fashion House
                     Dom Mod
    Fashionable Women's Clothing
    P.S., Kirovskiy pr., 37...... 234-90-40
    234-69-23
    234-90-55
    Marshala Tukhachevskogo ul., 22
    543-65-78
    225-19-19

Dress Salon
       Salon zhenskikh legkikh platev
    Nevskiy pr., 11............... 314-70-21
Elegant Store - Women's Department
    P.S., Bolshoy pr., 55 232-86-19
Lyudmila
    Torzhkovskaya ul., 7 246-48-09

ᏒᏌᏁᎧ **clothing for women**

Hand-tailored blouses, dresses, skirts
P.S., Bolshoy pr., 22/24 .. 233-67-18
Metro: Petrogradskaya. Hrs. 10-19. $ & Rbls. Fng

Salon Prestige

Nab. reki Moyki, 3 ....110-66-85n
Fax.............................110-68-82n
Telex .... 121394 PCG SU
Hrs: 9 -18 Clsd: Sat. & Sun.

Vesna
    Zamshina ul., 44............. 540-78-14
Yaroslavna
    Narodnaya ul., 5 263-81-90
Yubiley
    *Dress clothes, suits, clothes for special
    occasions, such as weddings.*
    Nab. Sverdlovskaya, 60
    224-25-98

☎ CLUBS & SOCIETIES
КЛУБЫ И ОБЩЕСТВА
VEREINE UND VERBÄNDE
CLUBS ET SOCIETES
KLUBBAR OCH FÖRENINGAR

The All-World Club
of St. Petersburg

Uniting the St. Petersburgers from around the
world in the cultural, intellectual & spiritual
revival of the city of Saint Petersburg.
Meetings in Kseshinskaya Palace.

St. Petersburgers from around the world are
invited to join our projects and activities.

    ✉ 197046 Russia, St. Petersburg
             Kuybysheva ul., 4

    ☎..355-04-48

Atlantis   **School of photomodels.**
               Amateur Photographers
    Nab. kan. Obvodnogo, 114
    168-24-91
Airplane Model Club   **Aviamodel's**
    Novo-Izmaylovskiy pr., 101
    295-15-50
Alliance Francaise
    Nab. reki Moyki, 20.......... 311-09-95
Amateur Hand-Weaving Association
    Mayak Club
    Sadovaya ul., 125........... 311-43-11
Automotive Society
                  Avtolyubiteley
    Zhukovskogo ul., 55........ 272-11-21
Aviation & Parachute Club
                     Aviaclub
    Kosmonavtov pr., 28, bldg.3
    299-08-26
Bridge Club
    Tambovskaya ul., 63, rm. 13
    166-46-96
    President of the Club 112-09-95
    Wed: 18:15-22:00, Sun: 16:45-22:00
Cinematographists Union
    Tolmacheva ul., 12 314-71-47
German Cultural Center of St. Petersburg
    Grivtsova per., 10........... 315-83-35
    221-75-05
    315-85-35
Geographic Society
                 Geograficheskoe
    Grivtsova per., 10........... 273-36-12
House of Nature   **Dom prirody**
    Zhelyabova ul., 8............. 314-08-48
    311-47-31

Hunting and Fishing
                    Okhotnikov I Rybolovov
Nab. reki Pryazhki, 32...... 219-70-74
International Charitable Foundation
                    for the Renaissance
.... 278-18-02
Kis Cat Lovers Club
Zhelyabova ul., 8............ 230-26-27
Musical Society
                    Muzykalnoye Obshchestvo
Nab. reki Moyki, 20......... 314-10-37
Metsenat
Nab. reki Fontanki, 34, apt. 19
.... 272-21-23
Philatelists Union   Filatelistov
Nab. kan. Griboedova, 27
.... 314-72-78
Pushkin Club
Nab. reki Moyki, 12......... 312-08-29
.... 271-77-42
Rock Club, Young People Musical Center
Rubinshteyna ul., 13 314-96-29
Vegetarian Club (of Shatalina method)
Please call 106-59-76
.... 176-22-94
Society of Collectors
                    Kollektsionerov
Rimskogo- Korsakova pr., 53
.... 114-33-41
Women's Club
Rubinshteyna ul., 28 312-63-80
Youth for Renaissance of St.Petersburg
Nevskiy pr., 39............... 314-57-52

☎ COMMERCIAL STORES
КОММЕРЧЕСКИЕ МАГАЗИНЫ
KOMMERZIELLE LÄDEN
MAGASIN COMMERCIAL
AFFÄRER, PRIVATÄGDA,
KOMMERSIELLA

A large number of COMMERCIAL
SHOPS have opened up in recent months
in St. Petersburg, which basically sell
products at market prices and where you
can buy a wide variety of products at free
market prices, which are substantially
higher than '"state prices'" and are
resented by many Russians. Some tend to
be badly organized and rely on buying
"new" goods on (15-20%) commission
from Russian citizens returning from
abroad. Thus, the selection and
guarantees are highly variable.
Increasingly, however, commercial shops
and the so-called "commercial
departments" of the largest department
stores in St. Pb, such as Gostinyy Dvor,

Passazh and most Univermags are
establishing permanent relations with
foreign and good domestic firms and are
stocking their shelves with a good
selection of goods purchased regularly
from a growing number of wholesalers of
foreign goods.

AKKA Hrs: 11-19
Zhelyabova pr., 3............ 311-92-75
Amela
Vladimirskiy pr., 3........... 113-22-84
Atribut
Nevskiy pr., 87.............. 279-43-75
Azeri
Sadovaya ul., 49............. 312-12-20
Biona
Nevskiy pr., 111 ....No Phone

"BOSKO International Shop"
Imported clothing, electronics & food
Two locations in St. Petersburg
Nevskiy pr., 8................. 219-18-56
Zhukovskogo ul., 20........ 273-70-92
Rubles & $

Charter
Vladimirskiy pr., 16 311-26-08

GERA
Gifts for Your Friends
Open 24 hours a day for last minute gifts
Exquisite Porcelain Gifts Imported Liquors
Flowers, Chocolates & Cigarettes
Zhelyabova ul., 1 315-74-90
Open 24 hrs/day (except 9-10, 15-16)
Metro Nevskiy Pr.
On V.O., visit our other shop
V.O., Zheleznovodskaya ul., 9
☎ 350-74-98
Hrs: 11-19, Closed Sat & Sun
Metro Primorskaya

Gloriya Hrs: 11-19
Nevskiy pr., 166 277-41-09
Goods Hrs: 11-19
Nevskiy pr., 20............... 311-57-90
Gorbi
Sadovaya ul., 51............. 315-98-34
Donon CS
Gertsena ul., 17.............. 315-89-68
Elf Food
Gertsena ul., 25/11 314-64-43
.... 311-97-33
Europe-shop
Dzerzhinskogo ul., 25 315-50-08
Iris Hrs: 11-20
Liteynyy pr., 23.............. 273-21-53

Luma *Hrs: 11-19*
  Nevskiy pr., 164 277-45-62
  277-07-23
Magazin-Salon
  Sadovaya ul., 89 114-43-52
Magazin-Salon
  Moskovskiy pr., 63 292-48-93
Magazin-Salon *Hrs: 10-19*
  Nevskiy pr., 147 277-18-93
Natasha *Hrs: 11-20*
  Zhelyabova ul., 13 315-54-41
Novinka *Hrs: 11-19*
  Vladimirskiy pr., 17 112-52-22
Poisk *Hrs: 11-19*
  Nevskiy pr., 170 277-15-53
Podsolnukh *Hrs: 10-19*
  Liteynyy pr., 32 273-74-62
Prezent
  Vladimirskiy pr., 14 106-75-94
Reys
  Nevskiy pr., 120 277-41-11
Russia *Hrs: 10-19*
  Zhelyabova ul., 5 315-79-52
Skif *Hrs: 10-21*
  Nevskiy pr., 175 271-01-01
  274-24-07
Shop
  Nevskiy pr., 105 277-06-29
Shop
  Sadovaya ul., 13/15 311-76-42
Shop-61
  Sadovaya ul., 61 114-45-21
Stella
  Liteynyy pr., 36 273-34-88
TATA
  Blagodatnaya ul., 41 .... No Phone
Tatyana *Hrs: 11-19*
  Vladimirskiy pr., 7 113-13-92
Terra *Clothing, Radio-Electronics*
  Sadovaya ul., 49 314-82-47
Tornado
  Office: Nevskiy pr., 132, apt. 77
  272-72-80
  Shop: Nevskiy pr., 22, *Hrs: 10-20*
Vika *Hrs: 10-19*
  Zhelyabova pr., 4, apt. 6-8
  312-96-72
U Lavry *Hrs: 11-20*
  Nevskiy pr., 188 .... No Phone

**Walk down
Nevskiy Prospect
with our
*DETAILLED WALKING MAP
OF NEVSKIY*
Pages 252 - 255**

☎ COMMISSION STORES
**КОМИССИОННЫЕ МАГАЗИНЫ
KOMMISIONSLÄDEN, SECOND-
HAND-LÄDEN
MAGASINS D'OCCASION
PROVISIONS AFFÄRER**

  There are a lot of Commission (Second hand) shops specializing in buying and selling on commission clothes, footwear, furniture, refrigerates, carpets, electronics, automobiles, etc. In contrast to commercial shops, things are not necessarily new. They charge the seller up to 25%. Now there are commercial departments in some second-hand shops.
  Commercial stores, in contrast, sell brand new imported Western goods: clothes, foot-wear, canned food, cigarettes, coffee, tea, drinks, cosmetics, electronics, souvenirs. In addition, there are a lot of commercial stalls (kiosks - commercial shops) throughout in the city.

Lenkomissiontorg Shop
  Apraksin dvor, Sadovaya ul.,
  section 70-71 310-03-36
Commission Shop
                  Komissionyy Magazin No.4
  Kirovskiy pr., 2 233-51-53
                  Furs and Leather
Commission Shops Goods
                  Komissionyy Magazin No.5
                  (receiving of goods)
  Sadovaya ul., 84 114-45-12
Commission Shop
                  Komissionyy Magazin No.6
  Liteynyy pr., 34 273-65-26
                  Furs
Commission Shop
                  Komissionyy Magazin No.10
  Apraksin dvor, Sadovaya ul.,
  section 35-36 310-30-58
Commission Shop
                  Komissionyy Magazin No. 11
  Lermontovskiy pr., 31 114-20-02
Commission Shop
                  Komissionyy Magazin No. 35
  Nevskiy pr., 124 277-23-01
                  Clothing ,Furs and Textiles
Commission Shop
                  Komissionyy Magazin No.16
  Apraksin dvor, Sadovaya ul.,
  section 32-34 110-45-59
                  Children's Clothing

Commission Shop
      Komissionyy Magazin No.17
Apraksin dvor, Sadovaya ul.,
section 64-65
.... 273-68-42
      Textile, Rugs
Gallery No. 102
Nevskiy pr., 102 273-68-42
      Clothing, Textiles
Commission Shop
      Komissionyy Magazin No.29
Apraksin dvor, Sadovaya ul.,
section 40-48
.... 310-29-67
Commission Shop
      Komissionyy Magazin No.32
Kirovskiy pr., 2 233-49-53
      Clothing and Textiles
Commission Shop
      Komissionyy Magazin No.40/41
Ligovskiy pr., 96............. 164-98-65
      Shoes and Clothing
Commission Shop
      Komissionyy Magazin No.42
Marata ul., 53 164-75-33
.... 164-72-92
.... 164-73-00
Commission Shop
      Komissionyy Magazin No.43
Nevskiy pr., 54............... 311-40-20
      China and Crystal, antiquariat
Commission Shop
      Komissionyy Magazin No.46
Stachek pr., 82 183-42-74
      Home Electric Supplies
Commission Shop
      Komissionyy Magazin No.64
Apraksin dvor, Sadováya ul.,
section 25-27................. 310-36-29
Commission Shop
      Komissionyy Magazin No.69
Kirovskiy pr., 4 232-85-80
      China and Crystal

☻ **Komissionyy Magazin No.75** ●
Apraksin dvor, Sadovaya ul.,
section 13-15................. 310-20-03
      Sporting Goods, Hunting Goods

Commission Shop
      Komissionyy Magazin No.76
Plekhanova ul., 39 312-72-53
      Arts and Crafts

TYP   *NEED A SYMPHONY*
          ORCHESTRA
Look under ORCHESTRA
page 159

☎ **COMMODITY EXCHANGE**
БИРЖИ
WARENBÖRSEN
BOURSE DE MARCHANDISES
VARUBÖRS

See STOCK & COMMODITY EXCHANGE

☎ **COMMUNICATIONS**
СВЯЗЬ, УСЛУГИ
NACHRICHTENWESEN/ POST-
UND FERNMELDEWESEN
COMMUNICATION
TELEKOMMUNIKATION

See also TELEPHONE-INTERNATIONAL,
TELEPHONE, TELEGRAM, EXPRESS
MAIL/PARCEL SERVICE, ELECTRONIC
MAIL, TELEX, FAX, CELLULAR PHONE.

BUSINESS SERVICES CENTERS *often
specialize in communication.*

Alcatel
Gertsena ul., 16.............. 315-89-38
SPRINTSET (USA-RUSSIA J.V.)
Nab. Sinopskaya, 14 265-27-50
.... 265-05-71
International phone station
Gertsena ul., 3/5............. 314-01-40
      send fax: 9 a.m.-5 p.m.
Bikar
Mayorova pr., 16 274-42-91
.... 315-84-91
Dauer
Ispolkomovskaya ul., 4/6
.... 277-54-85
Kaiya
Myasnikova ul., 6
.... 113-76-09
LDM
Professora Popova ul., 47
.... 234-06-96

LENCELTEL
International Communications
by Satellite
"Call Home Today"
International calls, fax, and E-Mail
directly from your office or home
Mobile international calling for your events.
Vereyskaya ul., 34/36, St. Pb.
Telephone & fax 274-46-41
In USA .... (609) 354-60-66
Hrs: 9:00 - 17:00

LENFINKOM

Gertsena ul., 3/5 314-00-60
Deputy Director 110-69-17
Accountant.................... 314-50-84

Sileks
Volodi Ermaka ul., 9 219-75-87
Teleset-Service
Sovetskaya ul., 80, P.O. Box 55

☎ COMPACT DISKS
КОМПАКТ ДИСКИ
COMPACT DISCS
COMPACTES-DISQUES
SKIVOR, CD

See also RECORDS, MUSIC SHOPS

DLT
Zhelyabova ul., 21/23...... 312-26-27
Elektronika
Gagarina pr., 12 299-38-49
Gostinyy Dvor, Perinnaya Liniya
Nevskiy pr., 35............... 110-53-66

☎ COMPUTER COURSES
КОМПЬЮТЕРНЫЕ КУРСЫ
COMPUTERKURSE
ORDINATEUR, COURS
DATAKURSER

Many institutes teach computers.
Obuchenie
Leninskiy pr., 149 293-13-35
Zagorodnyy pr., 58 292-40-05
St. Pb. Uchebnyy Tzentr
Aerodromnaya ul., 4........ 394-54-06
.....................................394-50-04
Scientific-Training Centre
Energetikov pr., 60, bldg. 2
.... 225-60-92
.... 226-11-27
**Center for Computing Technology at
St.Petersburg State Technical University**
Politekhnicheskaya ul., 29
.... 552-76-62

☎ COMPUTER PROGRAMMING
КОМПЬЮТЕРЫ,
ПРОГРАММИРОВАНИЕ
COMPUTER, PROGRAMMIERUNG
ORDINATEUR, PROGRAMME
INFORMATIQUE
DATAPROGRAMMERING

Askod
Nab. reki Fontanki, 6....... 112-25-23
.... 275-58-15
Dialog-Invest
Dostoevskogo ul., 19/21
.... 164-88-74
.... 164-27-07
.... 164-89-56

MasterCode ltd

Software Programmers
32 Russian Fonts for Desktop Publishing
Computer Security Programs
Protect Your System and Data Against
Malicious and Accidental Tampering
Shpalernaya ul., 52, Apt. 3
Tel............................... 273-21-24
Fax 275-31-12

Association of Artificial Intelligence
Leningrad Institute of Management and
Computer Technologies Training
Gastello ul., 12............... 293-32-68
.... 293-44-06
*Software in developing of expert systems,
computer education and tutoring.*

Intercompex(USA-Russia J.V.)
Kalinina ul., 13 221-75-64
.... 221-76-31
Fax .... (812) 186-33-90
Elinor
Khalturina ul., 27 311-78-46
Etlas JV
V.O., 14-ya Liniya, 39 218-08-87
DBASE for beginners & experienced
Intellekt Bank
197046 p/b 401 272-30-38
**St.Petersburg International
                    Management Institute**
.... 278-56-50
.... 271-34-33
Fax 271-07-17
We offer courses in Lotus 1-2-3.
LIPK
Metallistov pr., 115......... 540-93-69
Mif
Lermontovskiy Pr., 7/12... 114-28-54
Fax 219-55-08
Obuchenie
Leninskiy pr., 149 293-13-35
Zagorodnyy pr., 58 292-40-05
Service-Informatika
Nevskiy pr., 81 277-04-80
**Center for Computing Technology
at St. Petersburg State Technical University**
Politekhnicheskaya ul., 29
.... 552-76-62

☎ COMPUTER REPAIR
КОМПЬЮТЕРЫ, РЕМОНТ
COMPUTER, REPARATUR
ORDINATEURS, REPARATION
DATAREPARATIONER

Arnika Association
Aptekarskiy pr., 9/8 234-32-70
Repair & computer parts

Askon Enterprise
Nab. Obvodnogo kan., 132
.... 259-18-49
.... 259-18-48
Repairs Guaranteed

Dialog-Invest
Dostoevskogo ul., 19/21.. 164-88-74
.... 164-27-07
.... 164-89-56

Elinor
Khalturina ul., 27 311-78-46

Mister PC
Shvernika pr., 49 534-64-00

Repairs
.... 272-74-06
Repairs of Color TV's & PC's

Nienshantz
Kalyaeva ul., 25/12 275-35-06
.... 275-49-79
.... 275-50-55
We install various computer systems:
IBM Compatible, VAX, UNIX.

Sfinks, J.V. (Fin-Rus)
Gertsena ul., 55 312-75-40

Stalker
V.O., 25-ya Liniya, 8 217-08-58
.... 217-76-42
.... 217-90-01
We repair all makes of computers.

St. Petersburg Business Center
Marata ul., 78 164-40-37
Cartridges for Xerox Sharp Z-50 filled

SVEGA
Please call 310-17-68
.... 314-72-88

☎ COMPUTER SOFTWARE
КОМПЬЮТЕРНО-ПРОГРАММНЫЕ
ПРОДУКТЫ
COMPUTER, SOFTWARE
ORDINATEUR, COMPUTER
SOFTWARE
DATATILLBEHÖR, MJUKVARA

MasterCode ltd

Software Programmers
32 Russian Fonts for Desktop Publishing
Computer Security Programs
Protect Your System and Data Against
Malicious and Accidental Tampering
Shpalernaya ul., 52, Apt. 3
Tel. 273-21-24
Fax 275-31-12

Etlas (the official dealers of Borland)
14-ya Liniya, 39 218-08-87

◈◈ soft-tronik

Authorized distributors in Russia
Novell Netware & SCO Unix
Networks and Multi-User Systems
Nab. reki Fontanki, 88 315-92-76
Fax 311-01-08
Telex .... 121-184 SOFT SU
Hrs: 9-18, $ & rbl

Intellegence Bank
197046, P.B. 401 272-30-38

Microprotsessornye Tekhnologii
St. Pb., 198052 P.B. 260
.... 210-70-94

Computer Center of Simulation
Technology Institute of Russian
Academy of Sciences
Liteynyy pr., 57 292-64-70
Fax 292-00-64

☎ COMPUTER STORES
КОМПЬЮТЕРЫ, ПРОДАЖА
COMPUTER, FACHGESCHÄFTE
ORDINATEURS, MAGASINS D'
DATAAFFÄRER

See also COMPUTER REPAIR

AJAX LTD.
Krasnaya ul., 55 314-39-45
Fax 312-24-79

Bive
Profsoyusov bul., 4, entr. 4, rm. 20
.... 312-78-35
Fax 315-39-51

ComputerLand ®

Saint Petersburg
SALES, SERVICE, TRAINING
SUPPORT

Personal computer systems
Office electronics
Complete solutions

Authorized Dealer
IBM, Compaq, Apple
and other leading firms

Authorized Distributor
Microsoft, Lotus, Borland, Aldus, Novell
Nab. Sverdlovskaya, 64 224-09-32
Fax 224-04-55

Balteks
Altayskaya ul., 1 293-29-67
*Assembling, installation and sale of
computer systems*

Dialog-Invest
Dostoevskogo ul., 19/21
.... 164-88-74
.... 164-27-07
.... 164-89-56

Elinor
Khalturina ul., 27 311-78-46

EVM-Fredriksson
Tushina ul., 3 166-82-75

Irik, *Computers, Copiers, Fax*
Nab. reki Monastyrki, 3.... 274-38-88

Intertal Election
Apraksin per., 1 310-63-39
.... 310-57-86

Kompan JV,
Marshala Govorova pr., 52
.... 252-17-73
.... 252-15-64
Fax............................... 252-41-84
Telex .... 121412 COMP SU

Konkurent
Nab. Obvodnogo kan., 132
.... 259-18-48
.... 259-18-00
Fax............................... 259-18-40

Nienschanz
Zakharevskaya ul., 25/12
.... 275-49-19
.... 275-49-79

Novoindeks
Mozhayskaya ul., 6 292-27-85
.... 292-39-19

Peterburzhets
Zagorodnyy, 40 113-55-94

Meridian
Varshavskaya ul., 58 293-33-44

soft-tronik

Branch office St. Petersburg
soft-tronik GmbH, *Germany*

Specializing in
Networks and Multi-User Systems
Authorized distributors in Russia
Novell Netware & SCO Unix,
3Com, U.S. Robotics, APC ups, Everex, Wyse
Complete systems, sales and service
from small shops and offices
to large banks and factories

Nab. reki Fontanki, 88.......... 315-92-76
Fax 311-01-08
Telex .... 121-184 SOFT SU
Hrs: 9-18, $ & rbl

Sinus
Morskoy Pekhoty ul., 8, bldg. 1, apt. 4
.....................................157-57-94

TRIONIKS, computers

Apple/Macintosh
Authorized Seller and Warranty Exchange
Povarskoy per., 8............. 112-38-44
Fax................................. 112-53-59
Telex .... 121222 SPRES SU

UNiREM
computers

Authorized dealer Hewlett Packard
Sales, Services, and Repairs
Laser printers, scanner, plotters, &
computer systems
Authorized dealer of Farbax
refill-services, and laser printer
photocopiers

Office automation and LAN Network
Installation, warranty service & repairs
Large stock of parts available.

We carry a large selection of computer
systems, peripherals and accessories.

If we don't have it, we can get it quickly"

Near the Peter & Paul Fortress

Dobrolubova pr., 6/2 235-22-98
.... 235-23-98
Fax 232-21-11
Hrs: 10-20, Ruble, English & German.

Vesta
Vyborgskaya nab., 27...... 542-88-09
Tolmacheva ul., 12 272-94-25

☎ COMPUTER SUPPLIES
КОМПЬЮТЕРНОЕ ОБОРУДОВАНИЕ
COMPUTER, ZUBEHÖR
ORDINATEURS, FORNITURES
DATAMATERIAL

Alternativa Sinitsy
.... 164-47-87
.... 184-75-33

Ascod
Nab. reki Fontanki, 6....... 164-52-50
.... 275-58-10
Fax 112-00-01
Fax 275-57-55

Bive Enterprise
Profsoyuzov bul., 4, entr. 4
.... 312-78-35
We re-ink ribbons for printers.

Eltek
Nab. Obvodnogo kan., 143
.... 110-18-06
.... 113-03-46
Specializing in printer ribbons.

Informpap (paper for computers)
Babushkina ul., 3 567-21-80

Inftel
Moldagulovoy ul., 7/6, 5 flr., 51-52
.... 224-39-61

Lek
Mytninskaya ul., 19/48-20 274-38-85
.... 271-06-57
.... 271-13-36

Sinus
Morskoy Pekhoty ul., 8, bldg. 1, apt. 4
.... 233-20-91

Sitek
Rentgena ul., 3.............. 233-20-91

**To Contact The Editor of
The Traveller's Yellow Pages**
In Russia
TELINFO
✉190000, St. Petersburg, Russia:
Nab. Reki Moyki, 64
Tel.................315-64-12, 315-98-55
Fax 315-74-20, 312-73-41
For the rest of the world

InfoServices International, Inc.
✉ 1 Saint Marks Place
Cold Spring Harbor, NY 11724, USA
Tel...............USA (516) 549-0064
Fax ....(516) 549-2032
Telex...................... 221213 TTC UR
*Telinfo is a wholly-owned subsidiary of
InfoServices International, Inc. NY, USA*

Vesta
  Nab. Vyborgskaya, 27 542-88-09
  Tolmacheva ul., 12 272-94-25
Polradis
  Gagarina ul., 1 297-89-36
RIK
  Nab. reki Monastyrki, 3
  274-38-88
  Fax................................ 274-33-25
Sever
  Olminskogo ul., 13.......... 567-00-86
  567-19-93

☎ CONCERT HALLS
КОНЦЕРТНЫЕ ЗАЛЫ
KONZERTSÄALE
CONCERT, SALLES DE
KONSERTHUS

See also THEATER/BALLET

All concert halls are listed under THEATER/BALLET. We have SEATING PLANS on pages 245-251 for 6 theaters and concert halls.

Lenkontsert. State Concert Association
  Nab. reki Fontanki, 41 110-40-00
Direktsiya Teatralno-Kontsertnykh i
          Sportivno-Zrelishchnykh Kass
  Nevskiy pr., 190............. 277-59-24
  Metro: pl. Alexandra Nevskogo
Dom Kompozitorov (Composers House)
  Gertsena ul., 45 311-02-62
Glinka Small Hall
  Nevskiy pr., 30.............. 312-45-85
  Box Office 311-83-33
St. Pb. Inkultsentr
  Nab. Pirogovskaya, 5/2
  542-90-56
Leningradskiy
  Lenina pl., 1................... 542-94-22
Smolnyy Sobor (Smolnyy Church)
  Rastrelli ul., 3/1 311-36-90
  Box Office 542-09-42
  271-91-82

☎ CONFECTIONARY SHOPS
КОНДИТЕРСКИЕ МАГАЗИНЫ
KONDITOREIEN
CONFISERIES
KONFEKTAFFÄRER

See BAKERIES *and* CANDY STORES

☎ CONFERENCE ROOMS
КОНФЕРЕНЦЗАЛЫ
KONFERENZRÄUME
CONFERENCES, SALLES DE
KONFERENSLOKALER

See also BUSINESS SERVICES CENTERS

Sankt-Peterburg Hotel
  Nab. Vyborgskaya, 5/2 542-80-34
Pulkovskaya Hotel
  Pobedy pl., 1.................. 264-51-79
  264-51-90

Pansionat Zarya
  Repino pos., Primorskoe shosse, 423
  231-65-39

Tavricheskiy Palace
Voynova ul., 47.............. 278-95-04
Dom Ofitserov
Liteynyy pr., 20.............. 278-86-40
Dom Uchenykh
Nab. Dvortsovaya, 26...... 312-82-58

☎ CONSTRUCTION
& RENOVATION
СТРОИТЕЛЬСТВО И
РЕКОНСТРУКЦИЯ
BAU UND RENOVIERUNG
CONSTRUCTION ET RENOVATION
BYGGNATION

Adzhi Corporation
Severnyy pr., 8 /3, rm. 84
.... 592-67-30
*We develop and provide all types
of construction work.*
Apraksin Dvor
Apraksin Dvor, bldg. 33... 310-48-47

Gamma Service
Voytika ul., 11 114-64-57
Gera
Please call 538-70-08
Ibar (Russian-Yugoslavian J.V.)
Please call 227-40-82
.... 227-47-14
Fax............................... 227-47-98
Kachestvo (Quality)
Rimskogo-Korsakogo ul., 5
.... 311-84-95
Komfort
Bol. Porokhovskaya ul., 24
.... 224-27-52

Lenstroyinter
Ryleeva ul., 1 312-60-42
Magazin-Salon *Flat renovation*
Moskovskiy pr., 61 292-21-02
Malakhit
Bolshevikov pr., 33/1....... 586-63-88
*Decoration of Walls and Windows
Renovation of Apartments*
Montazh
Vereyskogo ul., 31 292-25-32
Nastilka parketa (parket floors)
Please call 186-35-16
Call from 20 to 22. High quality work
Neval
Salova ul., 33................ 166-52-16
Nord-Vest
Grazhdanskiy pr., 105, rm. 1
.... 114-29-54
Oreol
Liflyandskaya ul., 3 186-48-93
Renovation of industrial & civil buildings.
Okhta
Utkin proezd, 17 392-11-16
Panorama Enterprise
Bol. Pushkarskaya ul., 41
.... 235-47-75
*Construction and renovation works
Project developments.*

Sodruzhestvo
Nab. Sverdlovskaya, 14/2
.... 524-89-26
.... 225-10-84
Fax .... (812) 524-57-12
**St.-Petersburg Construction and
Renovation Enterprise**
Nab. kan. Griboedova, 174a
.... 114-27-80
Construction of country houses and villas

Vneshstroyservice. Soviet-Norwegian j/v
Nab. reki Fontanki, 46 311-37-56

☎ CONSULATES
КОНСУЛЬСТВА
KONSULATE
CONSULATS
KONSULAT

See also EMBASSIES

Bulgaria
Ryleeva ul., 27 273-73-47
China
V.O., 3-ya Liniya, 12 218-17-21
Cuba
Ryleeva ul., 37 272-53-03
Czechoslovakia
Tverskaya ul., 5 271-04-59
Finland
Chaykovskogo ul., 71 272-42-56
.... 273-43-31
Commercial Counselor 273-73-21
France
Nab. reki Moyki, 15 314-14-43
.... 312-11-30

Germany
Petra Lavrova ul., 39 273-55-98
.... 273-57-31
Hungary
Marata ul., 15 312-64-58
.... 312-67-53
Italy
Teatralnaya pl., 10 312-32-17
.... 312-28-96
Japan
Nab. reki Moyki, 29 314-14-18
.... 314-14-34
Poland
5-ya Sovetskaya ul., 12-14
.... 274-41-70
.... 274-43-51
Sweden
10-ya Liniya., 11 218-35-26
.... 218-35-27
United States
Petra Lavrova ul., 15 274-82-35
.... 274-85-68
.... 274-86-89

☎ CONSULTING FIRMS
КОНСУЛЬТАЦИОННЫЕ ФИРМЫ
BERATUNG
CONSULTATIONS, BUREAUX DE
KONSULTBYRÅER

See BUSINESS CONSULTANTS

☎ CONTACT LENSES
ЛИНЗЫ КОНТАКТНЫЕ
KONTAKTLINSEN
VERRES DE CONTACT
KONTAKT LINSER

Konkor
Dekabristov ul., 3 314-51-92
Closed Sunday
Kontakt-Servis-Optika
Izmaylovskiy pr., 23 251-12-62
Hrs: 9.30-19   Closed Sat. & Sun.
Lincor Kontakt
Krasnaya ul., 46 312-10-92
St.Petersburg Eye-Sight Correction Centre
Liteynyy pr., 25 272-32-13

☎ COPYING (PHOTOCOPYING)
КОПИРОВАЛЬНЫЕ РАБОТЫ
KOPIEREN (PHOTOKOPIEREN)
COPIEURS
KOPIERING

See PHOTOCOPYING,
BUSINESS SERVICES CENTERS.

☎ COSMETICS
КОСМЕТИКА
KOSMETIKA
PRODUITS DE BEAUTE
KOSMETIKA

See also HABERDASHERY DEPARTMENT
STORES *and* INTERNATIONAL SHOPS

*Cosmetics are sold in "parfumeriya"
(ПАРФЮМЕРИЯ), in haberdashery shops,
"galantereya" (ГАЛАНТЕРЕЯ)
(haberdashery) and in some special shops.
Proctor and Gamble is making a major
marketing effort to the Russian market
and their products are widely distributed
in Saint Petersburg. Most INTERNATIONAL
SHOPS sell western cosmetics and
personal hygiene products.*

Astoria Duty-Free
Astoria Hotel
Gertsena ul., 39 210-58-60
Baltic Star International Shopping
Pribaltiyskaya Hotel
Korablestroiteley ul., 14 ... 356-41-85
Bolgarskaya Roza
Finlyandskiy pr., 1 542-22-97
Bolgarskaya Roza
Nevskiy pr., 55 112-14-76
Debyut
Nevskiy pr., 54 312-30-26
Ives Rosher
Nevskiy pr., 61 113-14-96
Krasota
Nevskiy pr., 90 272-93-25

 **NAMES ARE CHANGING
IN SAINT PETERSBURG**

Street names are being
changed from
OLD "Soviet" names,
often to
"NEW" Tsarist names.
See our list of names
on pages 241, 242

LANCÔME
Nevskiy pr., 64 312-34-95

Neva Star International Shopping
at Moskva Hotel
Alexandra Nevskogo pl., 2
.... 274-00-24
Proctor & Gamble
at Grand Hotel "EUROPE"
Mikhaylovskaya ul., 1/7 ... 113-80-71
.... (ext. 458)
Rosgalantereya Obedinenie
Please call 166-25-40
Severnoe Siyanie
Nevskiy pr., 27 314-27-58

Salon "VANDA"
Nevskiy pr., 111 277-00-44
.... 279-43-29

☎ COURIER SERVICES
АВИАЭКСПРЕСС
EILBOTENDIENSTE
COURRIER, SERVICE DE
KURIR SERVICE

See EXPRESS MAIL/PARCEL SERVICE.

☎ COURSES
КУРСЫ
KURSE
COURS
KURSER

See also LANGUAGE COURSES,
BUSINESS INSTITUTES, EDUCATIONAL
PROGRAMS and UNIVERSITIES,
COMPUTER COURSES.

Obuchenie
Leninskiy pr., 149 293-13-35
Zagorodnyy pr., 58 292-38-61
*Language, cosmetics and
computer courses.*

Oktra Enterprise
Mayorova pr., 41 152-41-27
Open: 10-12, 19-20 Except Tues. and Wed.
*We offer courses in embroidery, rug
making and fabric painting*

☎ CREDIT CARD LOSS
КРЕДИТНЫЕ КАРТОЧКИ,
УТЕРЯННЫЕ
KREDITKARTENVERLUST
CARTES DE CREDIT,
PERTE DES
KREDITKORT, FÖRLORAT

See AMERICAN EXPRESS, page 40

☎ CRYSTAL & PORCELAIN
ХРУСТАЛЬ, ФАРФОР
KRISTALL UND PORZELLAN
CRISTAL ET PORCELAINE
KRISTALL OCH PORSLIN

Crystal and China
Stachek pr., 73 183-56-22
Crystal and China
Bolshoy pr., 92............... 234-93-65
Metro Petrogradskaya

GERA Porcelain Art
    Masterpieces on Porcelain
Vases, Plates, Tableware, Art Pieces
    Sculptures, Wall Hangings
Iskusstv pl., 3 352-18-18
Hrs: 12-22, closed Mon & Tues, rubles, English

Concern "Goryachev"
CRYSTAL & BRONZE
Fine Crystal Glassware, Vases & Pitchers
Chandeliers, Candlesticks, Chess Sets
    Signed Editions • Export
    Custom Orders and Wholesale
    Retail Stores & Display Rooms
Vereyskaya ul., 39............... 112-75-96
Utochkina ul., 7.................. 301-73-75
Fax 311-95-76
Hrs: 10-20, $, English

Farfor (Porcelain)
Nevskiy pr., 147............. 277-17-32
*The sales outlet of the Leningrad
Lomonosov Porcelain Factory*
The House of Porcelain and Crystal
"Torgovyy Dom "Farfor i Khrustal"
Nevskiy pr., 64.............. 312-18-81
.... 314-42-63

☎ CURRENCY EXCHANGE
ВАЛЮТА, ОБМЕН
GELDWECHSEL
DEVISES, CHANGE DE
VALUTAVÄXLING

See also TRAVELER'S CHECKS.

*While dollars circulate almost as a
second currency in some sectors of
society, most Russians use rubles and
most goods and services are still sold for
rubles, even to foreigners (although some
elements of the tourist industry demand
payments in dollars, and few refuse
payment in dollars). Other frequently*

used currencies include the Finnish mark,
and the German mark. Other currencies
are more difficult to use. Some
denominations ($1, 5, 10, 20) are useful
for purchases; $100 bills are preferred in
changing money. Traveler's checks can
be cashed only into rubles at selected
banks. Cash advances against your VISA
credit card are available at the Saint-
Petersburg Saving Bank (see ad).

There are now many more places
where you can change money officially
and get the proper receipts that may be
required to take some type of purchases
out of the country. Often, the banks
offer a good exchange rate tied to the
rates on the Moscow Currency Exchange,
which is currently higher than the official
rate. In June and July, the ruble/dollar
rate was rising. Note that exchange rates
can vary greatly for the purchase and sale
of hard currency and the service charges
vary from nothing to 5%. The rates on
the street vary according to supply and
demand and whether or not competing
banks are open. Thus, at night, on
holidays and weekends, the ruble/dollar
rate is lower. Changing large sums of
money on the street can be risky and is
not recommended.

In theory, all transactions after the 1st
of July should be carried out in rubles,
which simply means that the dollars will
have to be converted into rubles at the
very favorable market rates. As of June
30, 1992, there is considerable doubt
about the method and practicality of
implementing this law.

A Saint Petersburg currency exchange
has been registered and is expected to
start operations this fall.

BANK AND BANK OFFICES

**BANK
«SAINT
PETERSBURG»**

Bureau D' Exchange: 9:30 -12:00
Room 73
◇
Nab. Fontanki, 70/72...........................315-43-00
English spoken

Vneshterminal complex
Belinskogo ul., 11 275-61-61
.... 275-89-89
Vneshekonombank
Gertsena ul., 29 314-60-59

**CURRENCY EXCHANGE AT HOTELS
AND TERMINALS**

The following hotels have CURRENCY
EXCHANGE OFFICES or BUREAUX
D'EXCHANGE:

**Airport Pulkovo 1 Zone B "for ticketed
passengers"** and in Pulkovo-2
....No Phone
Hotel Astoria
Gertsena ul., 39 210-50-42
Grand Hotel Europe
by Vneshekonombank
at the American Express Office
Mikhaylovskaya ul., 1/7 and Nevskiy
Hotel Sankt-Petersburg
Nab. Pirogovskaya, 5/2.... 542-80-45
Hotel Moskva
Alexandra Nevskogo pl., 2
.... 274-21-27
Hotel Pribaltiyskaya
Korablestroiteley ul., 14 ... 356-38-03
Hotel Pulkovskaya
Pobedy pl., 1................. 264-51-47
closed
Hotel Sovetskaya
Lermontovskiy pr., 43/1
.... 259-25-63

☎ CUSTOMS
    ТАМОЖНЯ
    ZOLL
    DOUANE
    TULL

St.-Petersburg Customs
Administration
V.O., 9-ya Liniya, 10
Info 213-75-63
Secretary...................... 350-63-74
Trucking Department
Moldagulovoy ul., 7/6...... 224-67-55
Zaozernaya ul., 8............ 292-76-50
Vitebskiy pr., 3.............. 298-00-98
Airport   **Avia Department**
Pulkovo-1, Airport.......... 104-34-03
Pulkovo-2, Airport.......... 122-99-13
Sea Department
        Morskaya tamozhnya
Mezhevoy kan., 3, bldg. 2
.... 251-53-19

☎ CUSTOM CLEARANCE
    ТАМОЖЕННЫЕ ПОШЛИНЫ,
    ОСВОБОЖДЕНИЕ
    FOLLDEKLARIERUNG
    DEDOUANEMENT
    TULLDEKLARATIONER

BerSum
V.O., 17-ya Liniya, 54 213-65-74
Fax: 213-00-70
(Agent services, customs documents)

RUNO *Customs Clearance Service*
24 hours a day, holidays & weekends
P.S., Bolshoy pr., 22/24 233-67-18

Vneshterminal complex
Belinskogo ul., 11 275-61-61
.... 275-89-89
Hrs: 10 - 16, English

☎ CUSTOM REGULATIONS
    ТАМОЖЕННЫЕ ПРАВИЛА
    ZOLLVORSCHRIFTEN
    DOUANE, REGLEMENT DE
    TULLFÖRESKRIFTER

See also CUSTOMS CLEARANCE,
CUSTOMS.

*Customs regulations are being changed
frequently, and to our knowledge no complete up-to-date printed copy of the regulations were available in mid-July 1992. The
most recent revisions were on July 1, 1992.*
COMMERCIAL REGULATIONS: *Consult
a customs broker, or call or visit the*
CUSTOMS OFFICE.

St.-Petersburg Customs

Administration

V.O., 9-ya Liniya, 10

Information 213-75-63

secretary 350-63-74

TOURIST REGULATIONS

ARRIVING

Items allowed All items in reasonable quantities for personal use except those expressly limited (prohibited)

Limited   Spirits: 1 1/2 liters, Wine: 2 liters.

Forbidden items Illegal drugs, weapons, pornography, some fruits, vegetables and meats, and also rubles.

Currency

Any amount of almost any currency *except rubles* is allowed to be brought in if declared in your declaration (deklaratsiya, Декларация).

Procedure

Fill out "declaration" listing all currency including traveler's checks which you are bringing with you. You are suppose to include any other valuables, especially gold jewelry, precious stones, art works, icons and antiques, desktop computers, expensive cameras and other items that you want to take out again.

The purpose of this declaration is to prevent the illegal export of currency and valuables without permission so as to prevent sending capital abroad. KEEP THE STAMPED "DECLARATION" CAREFULLY WITH YOUR PASSPORT AND VISA.

LEAVING

Items allowed:

Anything you brought in and listed on declaration.

Item purchased in International Shops for hard currency with a proper receipt or from any art shop and other shops from which you have a receipt and the appropriate papers.

Restricted Items

If, however, you obtain an art work, manuscripts, musical instruments, coins, clothing, jewellry, antiques, old books or similar items as a gift or from the "market" that could have value as a "national cultural treasure", you must, according to the rules, get a permit from :

Department of Representative of the Ministry of Culture

Nab. kan. Griboedova, 107

.... 314-82-34

According to the Customs Regulations to be implemented on July 1st, 1992, all items purchased for rubles above the value of 300 rubles are to be subject to a 600% export tax payable in rubles at the airport. These rules were not available in print, so check before getting overly concerned.

For some paid advice on this subject, contact:

Vneshterminalkompleks

Belinskogo ul., 11 275-89-89

Hrs: 10 - 16, English.

☎ DACHA RENTALS

ДАЧИ, АРЕНДА
WOCHENDHAUS, VERMIETUNG
DATCHAS, LOUAGE
FRITIOSHUS, UTHYRES

Dacha is a country house or a cottage owned by individuals. It is possible to rent a house (or a room in a house) for a whole season or for a shorter time. People place information on dacha rentals in newspapers.

Dachas can be built of wood or brick and can be quite large. The bath facilities vary; luxurious occasionally, simple frequently. Running water in the house is a luxury, the toilet is often in a separate house in the yard, showers are a rarity, separate Russian-style bath houses are more frequent. Baths are usually in the nearest lake or river. The majority have electricity, telephones are few, heating comes from the stove. But they all are a special place to be in the summer.

Gardening is a major activity at the dacha and almost every respectable dacha has a large garden with flowers, berries, fruits and vegetables.

The most fashionable areas are on the Finland Gulf coast with better facilities, more stores, several hotels with restaurants, restaurants and better roads.

Dacha Service & Rentals

Nevskiy pr., 116/2 279-57-33

☎ DANCE INSTRUCTION
ТАНЦЫ ШКОЛА
TANZSTUDIOS, TANZSCHULEN
DANSE, STUDIOS DE
DANSSTUDIER/DANSLEKTIONER

There are many places to learn to dance in St. Petersburg. Call our advertiser for advice. There are dance courses in many "House of Culture" (Dom Kultury, Дом культуры) where you can take specialized courses for 1, 3, 6 months or even a year. A great way to meet people and learn Russian and dancing at the same time. There are discoteques also in many of the Houses of Culture listed below.

St. Pb Association of Ballroom Dance
Nab. reki Moyki, 94, kv. 95 .. 314-89-95
.... 166-38-23
Display Advertising at Int'l Dance Competitions

Gaza House of Culture
               Dom Kultury Gaza
Stachek pr., 72 184-35-83
Kirov House of Culture
            Dom Kultury im. Kirova
V.O., Bolshoy pr., 83 217-53-19
Lensoveta House of Culture
          Dom Kultury Lensoveta
Kirovskiy pr., 42 230-82-24

☎ DANCING
ДИСКОТЕКА
DISKOTHEKEN
DANSE
DANS

See RESTAURANTS, NIGHTTIME ENTERTAINMENT, DISCOTHEQUES, DANCE INSTRUCTION

Many restaurants have live music & a dance floor. Look for dancing in the display ads under RESTAURANTS. The young people dance at various discos.

☎ DATABASES
БАЗЫ ДАННЫХ
DATENBANKEN
DATABASES
DATABASER

The following firms have databases about the enterprises, banks, foreign firms and other organizations in St. Petersburg.

"Database of World's Tourist Firms"
10,000 Names, All countries, including Address, Phone, Fax, Telex.
191180, St.Petersburg, Russia,
Fontanka Embankment, 76, Apt. 34
.... 315-59-01
Fax 311-93-81
Leninformatika
Pushkinskaya ul., 10, office 13
.... 164-85-00
.... 164-53-60
Institute PROMSTROYPROEKT
Leninskiy pr., 160 295-40-94
"LIGA" International Agency
(Representation in St.-Peterburg)
Antonenko per., 3........... 319-99-72
.... 319-91-41
Fax 319-99-77
ASU-Impuls
(Representation in St.-Peterburg)
Please call..................... 246-20-22
"L I C"
Gertsena ul., 20............. 314-59-82
Fax 315-35-92

☎ DECORATING
КВАРТИРЫ, ДИЗАЙН, ДЕКОР
DEKORATION
DECORATION
HEMINREDNING

See INTERIOR DESIGNERS

☎ DELICATESSENS
КУЛИНАРИИ
FEINKOSTGESCHÄFTE
DELICATESSES
DELIKATESSAFFÄRER

The closest Russian equivalents of a delicatessen are the Kulinarii (Кулинарии). *Look at the one on Nevskiy. Many* INTERNATIONAL SHOPS *and the* FOOD STORES *selling for hard currency carry a selection of imported food.*

Gastronom No. 1
Nevskiy pr., 56. 311-93-23
The former Eliseevskiy'

Kulinarnyy magazin
Vladimirskiy pr., 2 314-00-48
Hrs: 10-15,16-20
Kulinarnyy magazin
Krasnaya ul., 18 314-99-32
Hrs: 10-15,16-20
Kulinarnyy magazin
Nevskiy pr., 120 277-29-14
Hrs: 10-15,16-20

Metropol
    Sadovaya ul., 22 310-18-75
        Hrs: 10-14,16-20

Neva
    Nevskiy pr., 46................ 110-40-55
        Hrs: 10-16,16-20

Kulinarnyy magazin Nevskiy
Nevskiy Delicatessen

At Entrance of Metro Mayakovskaya

Prepared Foods To Go • Microwave ready
Meats, Fish, Pizza, Baked Goods, Cakes
Pasteries, Vegetables, Fruit & Cereals

    Corner of Marata ul., 1 and Nevskiy 71
    Tel.............................. 164-85-81
        Hrs: 8 - 20, rubles, English

Tsentralnyy
    Malaya Sadovaya ul., 8.... 319-99-52
        Hrs: 10-13,14-20

☎ **DENTISTS**
    СТОМАТОЛОГИ
    ZAHNÄRZTE
    DENTISTES
    TANDLÄKARE

DENTAL POLICLINIC No. 3

Highly qualified experienced dentists
Extractions, fillings, root canal
Peridontal, checkups & dentures
Imported equipment & materials
24 hours emergency service available
Reasonable fees

V.O., 21-ya Liniya, 12 213-75-51
Night emergency care...... 213-55-50
    Hrs: 8-21 , English

NORDMED
A Private Dental Clinic
Specializing in
Bridges, Crowns & Root Canal
Filling, Extraction & Implants

Our staff graduated from the leading
dental schools, have trained in Europe &
now teach in leading institutes in St. Pb.

German & Finnish Equipment
Latest Western Materials

✉193124, Saint Petersburg, Russia
Tverskaya ul., 12/15

Tel....................................110-02-06
Duty Doctor Weekends & Evening 110-06-54
Fax 552-20-06
Hrs: 9-17:30, Thursday 9-20, English & German
Opening in September 1992

St. Petersburg Policlinic No. 2
An Independent Medical Group
Dental clinic *with highly trained dentists and*
Finish equipment
25 years serving diplomats and visitors
Clinic hours: M-F, 9:00 to 21:00
Sat. 9:00 to 15:00
Moskovskiy pr., 22 292-62-72

Dentist
    P.S., Bolshoy pr., 8, Clinic No. 83
    Kab. 13 238-40-68
Dentist
    Please call...................... 150-12-65
Dentist for children
    Mayorova pr., 34 314-25-65
Dentist
    V.O., 21-ya Liniya, 12 213-55-50
Dentist
    Moskovskiy pr., 122........ 298-56-13
DIKSI
    Liteynyy pr., 31 272-13-08
Medicon
    Borovaya ul., 55 168-32-06

Ulybka Koop
Salova ul., 37.................. 166-76-50
All types of Dental Treatment

NORDMED
DENTAL EQUIPMENT
Representative for
FINNDENT
Latest dental technologies and
equipment used worldwide
✉193124, Saint Petersburg, Russia
Tverskaya ul., 12/15
Tel.....................................110-02-06
Fax.................................552-20-06
Hrs: 9-17:30, Thursday 9-20, English & German
Opening in September 1992

☎ **DEPARTMENT STORES**
    УНИВЕРМАГИ
    KAUFHÄUSER
    GRANDS MAGASINS
    VARUHUS

The Russian equivalent to a Western
department store is called the
"Univermag" *(УНИВЕРМАГ). These*
resemble Western department stores and

have departments for clothing, coats & shoes, kitchen supplies, housewares, art supplies, sports goods, musical instruments, stationery, souvenirs, gifts, and electronics goods, etc. The best known ones are the Gostinyy Dvor, Apraksin Dvor, DLT & Passazh and the Univermag on Moskovskiy Prospect. Try the department stores first for things you need.

BEST   A DEPARTMENT STORE

1st Floor: Food Dept. with meats, dairy products, fruits, vegetables, and more.
2d Floor: Clothing, housewares, materials for interior decorating, appliances.
Our selection varies, so come back again.
Kupchinskaya ul., 15....... 261-64-53
METRO: Kupchino, hrs: 9-20, Ruble

Dom Leningradskoy Torgovli (DLT)
               Leningrad Trade House
Zhelyabova ul., 21-23...... 312-26-27
Children's goods, clothes, kitchen goods, souvenirs.
Hrs: 10-20 Mon-Fri, 10-18 Sat, Closed Sun

Gostinyy Dvor
The Major Department Store
In St. Pb. with many departments
Nevskiy pr., 35.............. 312-41-65
.... 312-41-74

The huge Gostinyy Dvor has many departments spread out over two floors. Location of a department is usually described by its "line" or side of the street: Sadovaya, Perinnaya, Nevskaya & Lomonovskaya. For example, "Raketa" department for watches, is on the Sadovaya Liniya on the ground floor. There are many "commercial shops" and even an INTERNATIONAL SHOP called Littlewoods selling the traditional mix of Western goods from cosmetics and clothes to jewelry and spirits.
Hrs: 10-21 Mon-Fri, 10-19 Sat, Closed Sun

Kalininskiy Univermag
Kondratevskiy pr., 40 540-29-35
.... 540-29-38
Hrs: 10-20 Mon-Fri, 10-18 Sat, Closed Sun
Kirovskiy Univermag
Stachek pr., 9 186-59-60
Hrs: 10-21 Mon-Sat, Closed Sun
Kupchinskiy Univermag
Slavy pr., 4, 12, 16, 30 ... 261-99-81
Hrs: 10-20 Mon-Fri, 10-17 Sat, Closed Sun

Moskovskiy Univermag
Moskovskiy pr., 205, 207 & 220
.... 293-44-55
Not far from Hotel Pulkovskaya.
Hrs: 10-21 Mon-Sat, Closed Sun

Narvskiy Univermag
Leninskiy pr., 120-138..... 255-84-29

Passazh (Passage)
Latest fashions, clothing, shoes, fabrics, sport clothing, lingerie, hats & handbags, electronics, cosmetics, watches, jewellery
Imported & domestic
Nevskiy pr., 48.............. 311-70-84
Hrs: 10-21 Mon-Fri, 10-18 Sat, Closed Sun

"Shopping Center"
            Tsentr Firmennoy Torgovli
The best domestic and imported goods
Specializing in apparel, footwear & electronics, furs, and cosmetics..
Nab. Novosmolenskaya, 1
.... 352-06-32
Hrs: 10-19 Mon, Wed; 10-20 Tues, Fri; 10-16 Sat, Closed Sun

Troika Mini-Market
Everything for the family and home
Imported food, clothing, shoes, TV & stereo, appliances
Just Opposite Troika Restaurant
Zagorodnyy pr., 28
Hrs: 10-19, $ & rbls, English, Between Metro Pushkinskaya, Vladimirskaya/Doestoyevskaya

Yubiley (Jubilee)
Department Store for Good Clothing, Coats, Furs, Wedding Dress & Gifts.
Nab. Sverdlovskaya, 60 ... 224-25-98
Hrs: 10-20 Mon-Fri, 10-18 Sat, Closed Sun
Yunost (Youth)
Novo-Izmaylovskiy pr., 4
.... 296-78-09
Hrs: 10-19 Mon-Fri, 10-16 Sat, Closed Sun

☎ DESKTOP PUBLISHING
НАСТОЛЬНАЯ ИЗДАТЕЛЬСКАЯ СИСТЕМА
DESKTOP PUBLISHING
DESKTOP PUBLISHING
DESKTOP PUBLISHING

See BUSINESS CARDS, PRINTING, PHOTOCOPYING and PUBLISHERS.

Desktop publishing thrives in St. Petersburg. Some firms listed under PUBLISHING and PRINTING are really desktop publishers.

☎ DIESEL FUEL
ДИЗЕЛЬНОЕ ТОПЛИВО
DIESELKRAFTSTOFF
DIESEL FUEL
DIESEL BRÄNSLE

Diesel Station
Primorskoe shosse, 18 km
.... 238-30-49
Diesel Station No. 45
Avangardnaya ul., 36 135-58-67

☎ DISCOTEQUES
ДИСКОТЕКИ
DISKOTHEKEN
DISCOTEQUES
DISKOTEK

See DANCE INSTRUCTION and
RESTAURANT

Santa (in hotel Kareliya)
Tukhachevskogo ul., 27, bldg. 2
.... 226-35-58

Nevskie Melodii
Nab. Sverdlovskaya, 62 ... 227-15-96
The liveliest disco in town.

☎ DOCTORS
ВРАЧИ
ÄRZTE
DOCTEURS
LÄKARE

See MEDICAL CARE *and* CONSULTATIONS
HOSPITALS *and* EMERGENCY MEDICAL
ASSISTANCE

☎ DOGS AND KENNELS
СОБАКИ, ПРОДАЖА
HUNDE UND HUNDEHÜTTEN
CHIENS, VENTE
HUNDAR OCH KENNLAR

St. Petersburg Dog-Breeding Club
V.O., 17-ya Liniya, 38 213-75-56
.... 213-75-60
Private 533-23-45

☎ DRUG STORES
АПТЕКИ
APOTHEKEN
PHARMACIES
APOTEK

See PHARMACIES
*There is no equivalent to the American
Drug Store in Russia. For medicine and
drugs, see PHARMACIES.*

☎ DRY CLEANING
ХИМЧИСТКА
CHEMISCHE REINIGUNGEN
NETTOYAGE A SEC
KEMTVÄTT

*Dry cleaning service (Khimchistka) is
provided in most major hotels, usually
payable in hard currency.*

Dry Cleaning (Highly recommended)
Salova ul., 57................. 166-13-28
We also dry clean rugs & furniture.
Rubles and Dollars

*The following are generic "Express Dry
Cleaners"*
Khimchistka
Hrs: 8-21, closed Sundays, Rubles
Izmaylovskiy pr., 12 292-33-47
Lermontovskiy pr., 1/44 ... 114-19-04
Nevskiy pr., 115 277-17-52
Metallistov pr., 73............ 540-19-35
Zanevskiy pr., 37............. 528-84-65
Razezzhaya ul., 12 164-77-01
Barmaleeva ul., 6 232-44-56

☎ DUTY-FREE SHOPS
ВАЛЮТНЫЕ МАГАЗИНЫ
DUTY-FREE-LÄDEN
DUTY FREE SHOPS
DUTY FREE SHOPS (TAX FREE)

See INTERNATIONAL SHOPS
*The only real duty free shops are the
Lenrianta shops in arrivals & departures of
the airports. The rest are really specialty
shops featuring imported goods and were
called "hard currency shops" ("valyuta
shops"). We list all such shops under
INTERNATIONAL SHOPS.*
*Many other shops, called
"COMMERCIAL STORES", however, now
sell a large variety of imported goods, too,
but for rubles.*

☎ EDUCATIONAL PROGRAMS
ОБРАЗОВАНИЕ, УЧРЕЖДЕНИЯ
WEITERBILDUNG
INSTITUTS EDUCATIFS
UTBILDNINGSINSTITUT

*These private organizations offer
education programs to Russian and
foreign students.*
See UNIVERSITIES AND INSTITUTES

Center for International Education
CIE

An Interdisciplinary Liberal Arts Study Center for Foreign Students in St. Pb.

In cooperation with and use of all the libraries and facilities of St. Petersburgs University

Design your own program from fields of study at St. Petersburg University from one month to one year.

Programs and lectures in English

Admission starting in September 1992

⊠ 190000, Saint Petersburg, Russia
Krasnaya ul., 60

☎ 227-60-78
☎ Fax........................... 143-85-21

St.-Petersburg International Management Institute - LIMI
Rastrelli pl., Smolnyy, entrance 9
P.B. 450......................... 273-41-48
Fax................................. 271-07-17

Soviet-Italian joint-venture

VNESHVUS-CENTRE

Business in Russia Seminars
Taxes, Laws, Banking, Privatization Seminars in English
Other Languages by Translation
Write to: Post Office Box 14
199226 Saint Petersburg Russia
V.O., Nab. Morskaya, 9.......... 356-99-05
Fax.. 355-69-87

☎ ELECTRICAL INSTALLATION
ЭЛЕКТРОТЕХНИКА
ELEKTROINSTALLATIONEN
ELECTRICITE(ELECTRIQUE, INSTALLATION)
EL INSTALLATION

See also EMERGENCY SERVICES.

Elektroproekt
Buharestskaya ul., 6........ 166-38-56
.... 166-38-52
Services for industry & agriculture

Khronotron Enterprise
Ans.mach....................... 315-68-79
Installation of electrical advertisements, ventilation & electrical equipment.

POLICE/MILITIA DIAL 02

☎ ELECTRICAL REPAIRS
ЭЛЕКТРОПРИБОРЫ, РЕМОНТ
ELEKTROGERÄTE, REPARATUR
ELECTRICITE(ELECTRIQUES, REPARATIONS)
ELEKTRIKER (ELEKTRISKA REP.)

See also EMERGENCY SERVICES.

Electrical Repair Shops
Bogatyrskiy pr., 10.......... 394-71-29
Bryantseva ul., 7............. 531-76-95
Lenina ul., 16................. 232-06-48
Tipanova ul., 29 299-87-51
"St. Petersburg Co" -
Nab. reki Fontanki, 116g, apt. 45
.... 259-50-11

☎ ELECTRICAL SUPPLIES AND GOODS
ЭЛЕКТРОТОВАРЫ
ELEKTROZUBEHÖR
ELECTRICITE(ELECTRIQUES, FOURNITURES)
ELTILLBEHÖR

Transformers can be bought at "Rubicon"
Lesnoy pr., 19................. 542-00-62
Abo
193167, P.O. 140........... 585-90-57
Electrical Goods
Kirovskiy pr., 18 232-78-22
Moskovskiy pr., 134........ 298-21-15
Zagorodnyy pr., 9 314-18-15
A/O 'LAIN'
V.O., 1-ya Liniya, 44 213-26-19
Elektrotovary No. 129
Liteynyy pr., 27 272-45-98
Elektrotovary No. 132
Sredneokhtinskiy pr., 48
.... 227-39-21
Elektrotovary No. 139
Pestelya ul., 10/23.......... 272-89-02
Elektrotovary No. 140
Grecheskiy pr., 27 271-21-74
Elektrotovary No. 143
Moskovskiy pr., 5 310-12-63
Elektrotovary No. 153
Moskovskiy pr., 134........ 298-21-15
Elektrotovary No. 164
Nevskiy pr., 65............... 311-04-45
Elektrotovary No. 37
Smirnova pr., 69............. 246-48-44
Elektrotovary No. 68
Karla Marksa pr., 40........ 542-57-11
Ogonek
Novocherkasskiy pr., 51
.... 211-14-12
Svet
Moskovskiy pr., 163........ 298-37-57

☎ ELECTRICITY
ЭЛЕКТРИЧЕСТВО
ELEKTRIZITÄT
ELECTRICITE
ELEKTRICITET

The electricity in St. Petersburg is
220 volt, 50 Hz.

Some newer appliances, laptop battery chargers and travel appliances automatically adapt to this voltage & cycles/herz. You still need a round two-pin plug adapter and a surge protector is recommended. Note that some Russians routinely unplug electronic equipment when not in use.

A transformer can convert from 220 volt to 110-130 volt without problems. It is not possible, however, to our knowledge to easily convert 50 Hz electricity to 60 Hz electricity, so be sure that your appliances or equipment can work with 110 volt, 50 hz power.

The small travel transformers are effective for small appliances & hair dryers, but not large motors, appliances and photocopiers. A 300 watt transformer weighs about 10 pounds and a 1,000 watt transformer about 30 pounds. They can be purchased, however, in Saint Petersburg. Most power sources are ungrounded.

☎ ELECTRONIC GOODS
(Stereos, Radio-TV's, VCR's, CD players)
ЭЛЕКТРОНИКА
ELEKTRONIK
ELECTRONIQUE, MATERIEL
ELEKTRONISKA APPARATER

See also COMPUTERS, OFFICE EQUIPMENT, TELEVISION SALES, VIDEO EQUIPMENT, PHOTOCOPIERS, INTERNATIONAL SHOPS.

There are now many shops, including some authorized dealers, selling a wide variety of western electronic goods from TVs & VCRs to computers & photo copiers.

The ALISA Trading House
Authorized Distributor
Phillips Electronics
Suvorovskiy pr., 2............ 277-01-25
V.O., 6-ya Liniya, 35b 218-34-33
.... 213-17-77
Electrionic goods & radios by Philips

The Electronics Store
at The Airport Shop
Pulkovo-1 Domestic Airport
Aviagorodok................... 104-34-92
.... 104-34-91
6 am to 12 midnight, $, CC, English

Argus
  Olminskogo ul., 6............ 567-26-10
Ajax Ltd (wholesale)
  Galernaya ul., 55 312-24-79
  Fax 314-39-45

Baltic Star International Shopping
  Pribaltiyskaya Hotel......... 356-41-85

Balteks
  Altayskaya ul., 1............. 293-29-67
  108-49-44
    Metro: Moskovskaya
East Market Co., Ltd
  Zhelyabova ul., 27, apt. 510
  312-88-39
  315-87-38
Elektronika
  Yuriya Gagarina pr., 12.... 299-38-49
Elektronika-Video
  Lesnoy pr., 22................ 542-36-54
Elke Electronics
  Bakunina pr., 29 271-31-61
Estoniya
  P.S., Bolshoy pr., 72 232-25-10
    Hrs :10-19
Records, Radio, Watchs No.13
    Gramplastinki, Radio, Chasy, No. 13
  Obukhovskoy Oborony pr., 81
  265-13-01
Iridan
  Zagorodnyy pr., 11 314-23-18
    Hrs: 10-19
Kvazar
  Kirovskiy pr., 5 233-40-33
Lek
  Mytninskaya ul., 19, apt. 20
  274-38-85
  271-14-29
Calkulators
    Mikrokalkulyatory, Store No. 3
  Vladimirskiy pr., 2........... 113-14-45
    Calculators
Calkulators
    Mikrokalkulyatory, Store No. 62
  Kirovskiy pr., 2 233-50-53
    Calculators
Microfornt
  Samoylovoy ul., 12 166-46-45

The City Code for Saint Petersburg
Dial ⑧①② + Number

Megapolis
   Smolnyy pr., 11 278-52-75
   Secretary 278-52-69
Ms-Audiotron
   4-ya Krasnoarmeyskaya ul., 4a
   310-48-01
   Fax 310-48-01

Neva Star International Shopping
   Moskva Hotel 274-00-24

Ortex
   Karla Marxa pr., 82 245-12-51
   245-21-25

   PROGRESS SERVICE
   Sales and service of video equipment
   Grivtsova per., 7 315-86-63
   Metro: Sennaya Ploshchad

Radiotekhnika
   Sverdlovskaya nab., 64
   224-04-57
   Hrs: 10-20
Raduga
   Yu. Gagarina pr., 18 299-14-86
Radios   Radiotovary
   Komsomola ul., 51 542-04-66
   Hrs: 10-19
Rigonda
   Moskovskiy pr., 171 298-08-40
Philips Electronics
            **Represented in St. Pb by the
            Alisa Trading House**
   Suvorovskiy pr., 2 277-01-25
Radiotovary Radiodetali, Store No. 46
   Lermontovskiy pr., 40/42
   251-48-80
   Radio, radio parts
RIK
   Nab. reki Monastyrki, 3 277-77-52
   274-38-88
   Fax 274-33-25
Rossa
   Morisa Toreza pr., 30 552-54-20
Sever
   Please call 567-00-86
Signal
   Nekrasova ul., 4 272-02-59
Sinus
   Morskoy pekhoty ul., 8, bldg. 1, apt. 4
   157-57-94
   electronic sales
   Hrs :10-19
Soneks
   Professora Popova ul., 7/8
   234-58-00
   Fax 234-55-04
Sovlyuks
   Orlovskiy per., 7/3 277-40-83
   277-34-29

Tekh Kompakt
   Moskovskiy pr., 181 108-48-65
   291-00-48
Vega Shop-Salon
   Lermontovskiy pr., 40 114-45-91
   Hrs: 10-19

☎ **ELECTRONIC GOODS
   REPAIR**
      ЭЛЕКТРОНИКА, РЕМОНТ
      ELEKTRONIK, REPARATUREN
      MATERIEL ELECTRONIQUE,
      REPARATION
      ELEKTRONISKA APPARATER,
      REPARATION

See ELECTRONICS GOODS, TELEVISION
REPAIRS, COMPUTER REPAIRS &
REPAIR SERVICES.

☎ **ELECTRONIC MAIL, E-MAIL**
      ЭЛЕКТРОННАЯ ПОЧТА
      E-MAIL, ELEKTRONISCHE
      NACHRICHTENÜBERMITTLUNG
      ELECTRONIQUE, COURRIER
      ELEKTRONISK POST

**NPK 'Masshtab'
Istok-K (Source-K)**
Electronic mail.
Payment in hard currency.
Kantemirovskaya ul., 6 245-51-65

Relcom
   V.O., 14-ya Liniya, 39 218-18-35

Sovam Teleport
*All International electronic mail services
(Bitnet, Internet, MCI, Mercury, Transpak, etc.)
Local access to international databases,
Express fax and telex links.
Short-term E-Mail Accounts for Visitors*
   Nevskiy pr., 30 311-84-12
   Fax 311-71-29
   Telex .... 158-230564 PETERS
   Int'l E-Mail: spbsovam@sovamsu.uucp

☎ **EMBASSIES**
      ПОСОЛЬСТВА
      BOTSCHAFTEN
      AMBASSADES
      AMBASSADER

*There are consulates but no embassies
in St. Petersburg. See CONSULATES for
the numbers & addresses of consulates in
Saint Petersburg.*

   EMBASSIES IN MOSCOW
   TELEPHONE DIAL 8-095 + #

Australia
   Kropotkinskiy per., 13 246-50-11
   246-50-16

Austria
Starokonyushennyy per., 1
.... 201-73-17
.... 201-73-79
Belgium
Stolovyy per., 7.............. 203-65-66
Bulgaria
Mosfilmovskaya ul., 66.... 147-90-00
.... 143-90-27
Canada
Starokonyushennyy per., 23
.... 241-58-82
.... 241-50-70
China, Peoples Republic of
Druzhby ul., 6 143-15-40
.... 143-15-43
Cshechoslovakia
Yuliusa Fucheka ul., 12/14
.... 250-22-25
Denmark
Ostrovskogo per., 9 201-78-60
.... 201-78-68
Estonia
Sobinovskiy per., 5 290-50-13
Kolashnyy per., 8............ 290-31-78
Finland
Kropotkinskiy per., 15/7
.... 246-40-27
France
Dimitrova ul., 43.............. 236-00-03
.... 231-85-01
Germany
Bol. Gruzinskaya ul., 17... 252-55-21
Greece
Skaternyy per., 25 291-62-83
Hungary
Mosfilmovskaya ul., 62.... 143-86-11
.... 143-86-12
Ireland
Grokholskiy per., 5.......... 288-41-01
Israel 238-04-63
Italy
Vesnina ul., 5.................. 241-15-33
Japan
Kalashnikov per., 12....... 291-85-00
Korea, Peoples Repulic of
Mosfilmovskaya ul., 72.... 143-90-58
Korea, South 938-28-08
Latvia
Chapygina ul., 3 925-27-03
Lithuania
Pisemskogo per., 10........ 291-16-98
.... 291-26-43
Mexico
Shchukina ul., 4 201-48-48
Netherlands
Kalashnikov per., 6 291-29-99
.... 291-29-48
New Zealand
Vorovskogo ul., 44 290-34-85
.... 290-12-77

Poland
Klimashkina ul., 4 255-00-17
Romania
Mosfilmovskaya ul., 64
.... 143-04-24
Spain
Gertsena ul., 50/8........... 202-21-61
.... 202-21-80
United Kingdom
Nab. Sofiyskaya, 14........ 231-85-11
United States
Chaykovskogo ul., 19/23
.... 252-24-59
Yugoslavia
Mosfilmovskaya ul., 46
.... 147-41-06

☎ **EMBROIDERY SHOPS**
ВЫШИВКА
STICKEREIEN
BRODERIE, MAGASINS DE
HANDARBETSAFFÄRER

Tyul (Lace) No. 77
Nevskiy pr., 124 277-30-21
Hrs: 11 - 20
Tyul, Kruzhevo
P.S., Bolshoy pr., 69 233-04-53

☎ **EMERGENCY MEDICAL CARE**
МЕДИЦИНСКАЯ ПОМОЩЬ
НЕОТЛОЖНАЯ
MEDIZINISCHE NOTVERSORGUNG
SOINS D' URGENCE MEDICAUX
AKUTSJUKVÅRD

 AMBULANCE 03

See also MEDICAL ASSISTANCES,
MEDICAL CARE CONSULTATIONS,
HOSPITALS

*In general, don't count on Western level
of emergency care from the extensive
EMT Service of Saint Petersburg. The
equipment, medications & standards have
suffered greatly from underfunding.*

*Good emergency medical care for
diplomats, high level officials & foreign
visitors is offered by several groups in
Saint Petersburg. The largest organization
with 25 years of experience is the now
independent medical group called Saint
Petersburg Policlinic No. 2 which has good
imported equipment, a new pharmacy
stocked with many Western pharmaceuticals.
It uses disposable dispensers & syringes in
medical treatment.*

They have their own well-staffed well-stocked ambulance and make emergency housecalls around the clock. Many doctors speak English and translators are available on short notice.

Emergency Wards
Gzhatskaya ul., 3............. 534-47-39
Nab. kan. Obvodnogo, 179
.... 251-09-24
Shaumyana pr., 51............. 221-23-32
Kosinova ul., 17 186-44-30
Krasnoy Konnitsy ul., 26
.... 274-76-55
Komsomola ul., 14............. 542-31-54
Pravdy ul., 18.................. 315-21-58
Sofi Perovskoy ul., 2 311-43-96

First-Aid Stations:

City Diagnostic Center No. 1
Sikeyrosa ul., 10............. 554-19-00
Hospital No. 9
Krestovskiy pr., 18.......... 235-20-58
Hospital No. 20
Gastello ul., 21............... 108-48-08
.... 108-48-10
Help
Please call 122-43-92
Medical Care
Bolshaya Podyacheskaya ul., 30
.... 310-45-25
Medical Care
Budapeshtskaya ul., 3 105-29-70
Medical Care
Nab. kan. Obvodnogo, 179
.... 251-09-24
Medical Care
Komsomola ul., 14 542-31-54
Medical Care
Engelsa pr., 37 554-25-59

Medical Care
Moskovskiy pr., 87 298-45-96
Medical Care
Nab. kan. Kryukova, 25 ... 114-52-98
Medical Care
Lva Tolstogo ul., 6/8 234-57-72
Medical Care
Liteynyy pr., 25 272-59-55
Medical Care
Mytninskaya ul., 25......... 274-43-84
Medical Care
V.O., Bolshoy pr., 85....... 217-02-82
Medtsentr DLT
P.S., Bolshoy pr., 29a...... 233-25-42
Polyclinic N2
Moskovskiy pr., 22 292-59-04
Casualty Station   Skoraya Pomoshch
Malaya Konyushennaya ul., 2
.... 311-43-96

☎ EMERGENCY SERVICES 24 HOURS/DAY
СЛУЖБЫ НЕОТЛОЖНЫЕ КРУГЛОСУТОЧНЫЕ
NOTDIENSTE
SERVICE D' URGENCE
AKUTMOTTAGNING DYGNET
RUNT

Round the clock, free of charge

FIRE..................................... 01
MILITSIYA (POLICE) 02
AMBULANCE 03
GAS LEAKS 04
EMERGENCY MEDICAL CARE
See *above*

AUTOMOBILIE ACCIDENTS
State Automobile Inspectorate (GAI)
Professora Popova ul., 42
.... 234-26-46
.... 234-26-52
EMERGENCY APARTMENT REPAIRS
Emergencies with your electricity, locksmith, sewers, heating, plumbing system, and water can be solved with help of Municipal Residential Repair Departments -"PREO" (ПРЭО) or "REU" (РЭУ). The emergency numbers below should be able to refer you to the proper local REU.

INFORMATION NUMBERS
Vasileostrovskiy.............. 356-96-14
Vyborgskiy..................... 550-29-78
Dzerzhinskiy................... 272-68-69
.... 272-43-65
Kalininskiy 524-26-18

Kirovskiy 252-65-23
Kolpinskiy 484-80-20
Krasnogvardeyskiy 227-48-49
.... 227-48-10
.... 227-48-98
Krasnoselskiy 130-65-32
Kuybyshevskiy 164-06-38
.... 164-05-92
Moskovskiy...................... 298-13-60
Nevskiy
(Left bank of Neva) 587-33-37
(Right bank of Neva) 588-78-53
Oktyabrskiy..................... 315-09-83
.... 315-74-10
Petrogradskiy 232-16-65
Petrodvortsovyy.............. 427-98-16
Primorskiy....................... 301-40-77
Smolninskiy 274-02-59
.... 274-25-54

GAS LEAKS

Lengaz (LenGas) Emergency Services
                                  Avariynaya Sluzhba
Sedova ul., 9/1............... 265-26-31

ELECTRICITY EMERGENCY

Information 311-15-00
.... 312-95-94

WATER UTILITY EMERGENCIES

Emergency Sanitary Technical Service
Zodchego Rossi ul., 1/3
.... 311-70-20

WATER PIPE BREAK & EMERGENCIES

Avariyanaya Sluzhba Vodoprovodnoy Seti
Krasnoy Konnitsy ul., 42
.... 274-10-95
Cold water..................... 230-83-17
Hot water 312-33-73

EMERGENCY STATIONS

Emergency Station of Kronshtadt
Vosstaniya ul., 17........... 236-39-00
Emergency Station of St. Petersburg
M. Sadovaya ul., 1
Secretary....................... 210-74-79
Emergency Station of Petrodvorets
Tolmacheva ul., 3 427-99-39
Information on accidents
.... 278-00-25
Police information
.... 315-00-19
Venerology center
.... 113-21-56

☎ EMPLOYMENT AGENCIES
БЮРО ПО ТРУДОУСТРОЙСТВУ
ARBEITSÄMTER
PLACEMENT, BUREAUX DE
ARBETSFÖRMEDLINGAR

Businesslink Company
V.O., 13-ya Liniya, 20 218-69-00
.... 355-92-57

BCG
Personnel - Recruitment
Russian-America J.V.
Gertsena ul., 23.............. 312-67-01
Fax: 312-53-68
*Official Representative
of HILL International*

Office of the Mayor Committee for Labor
& Employment
Krasnaya ul., 7 312-92-36
General Dept. 312-86-42
Hrs: 8 - 17
Employment Office for the Youth
            Molodezhnaya Birzha Truda
Smolnyy Sobor, entr. 9, apt. 3
Info............................... 278-52-01
Secretary....................... 274-15-62
Hrs: 10 - 18

INPREDSERVICE
EMPLOYMENT SERVICE
Let us find staff for your company.
Nab. Kutuzova, 34 272-15-00
Fax 279-50-24
*INPREDSERVICE is the Municipal Office for Service to
Foreign Representatives & their Staff*

SOVINFORM
Excellent employees guaranteed.
P.S. Kamennoostrovskiy pr., 42
Tel 230-80-04
Hrs: 9 - 21

☎ ENGINEERING CONSULTANTS
ТЕХНИЧЕСКИЕ КОНСУЛЬТАНТЫ
INGENIEURWESEN
INGENIEURS
INGENJÖRAR

See BUSINESS CONSULTANTS

Inzhener (Coop)
Dzerzhinskogo ul., 48 311-70-94
Skaner
Doblesti ul., 18, bldg. 2
.... 145-64-70

☎ ENTERTAINMENT ACTS
ТВОРЧЕСКИЕ КОЛЛЕКТИВЫ
VERANSTALTER
MANIFESTATIONS ARTISTIQUES
UNDERHÅLLNINGSFÖRMEDLING

Yuri Dimitrin
Librettist
Playwright, librettos, musicals, rock operas
Scripts for company presentations
Please call 164-79-51
Fax 164-79-51

Professional Movie Actors Guild
Actors, dancers, musicians, singers,
magicians, circus performers
from the leading theaters and studios of
Saint Petersburg available to perform in
video and films, advertising videos, movie
films, night club shows.
Nab. reki Fontanki, 11, apt. 8
Tel. & Fax 312-79-67

Advertise in the next edition of

THE TRAVELLER'S
YELLOW PAGES
SAINT PETERSBURG
& NORTHWEST RUSSIA
from Murmansk to Novgorod.
Winter-Spring 1993 (In Russian)
Closing October 1992

SAINT PETERSBURG & SUBURBS
with Special Supplement for
All Northwest Russia
Winter-Spring 1993 (in English)
Closing November 1993

NEW EDITIONS IN 1993

MOSCOW Winter-Spring 1993
KIEV Spring Summer 1993
BALTICS Spring Summer 1993

Write / Call for Closing Dates

Discounts for Advertisers
in Multiple Editions
Write / Call for Closing Dates
Published by
InfoServices International, Inc.
See page 237

PAVLOVSK PALACE
Private concerts in the Place of Paul 1st
Revolutsii ul., 20 470-29-61
.... 470-21-55

Investment Bankers
HOLDING
Saint Petersburg, Russia
General Sponsor of the

TEREM KVARTET
CLASSIC-MODERN-FOLK-ART
ST. PETERSBURG
"Unforgettable musical experience"
"Absolutely brilliant"
Exciting musical magic that's difficult to
capture in words
Modern, classical and folk music woven
into melodic Russian fantasy on ancient
instruments: Domra, Domra-Alt, Bayan,
and Balalaika-contrabas

The Saint Petersburg Conservatory
On Compact Disc THE TEREM QUARTET
Realworld/Virgin records CDRW23

Completing 26th European Tour, June '92

Looking for additional bookings in the
United States and Canada for their
1992/93 tours

Write: TEREM QUARTET, I. Kutyanskaya,
Director, Chaykovskogo ul., 75, kv. 9
Saint Petersburg 191000
Please Call 274-89-55
Fax 314-83-21
Telex..................... 121378 LFC SU

Torzhestvo
Lomonosova ul., 1 314-58-96

☎ EXCHANGES
БИРЖИ
BÖRSEN
BOURSES
BÖRS

See STOCK & COMMODITY EXCHANGES,
CURRENCY EXCHANGE

☎ EXCURSIONS
ЭКСКУРСИИ
AUSFLÜGE
EXCURSIONS
UTFLYKTER

See TOURS-SAINT PETERSBURG *and*
TOURS-RUSSIA

☎ EXHIBITION HALLS & GALLERIES, RENTAL
ВЫСТАВОЧНЫЕ ЗАЛЫ И ГАЛЕРЕИ
AUSSTELLUNGSRÄUME UND GALERIEN
EXPOSITIONS, SALLES D' ET GALLERIES A LOUER
UTSTÄLLNINGSLOKALER OCH GALLERIER

Exhibition Center for the Association of Artists of St. Petersburg
Organization of art exhibitions
Rental of art exhibit space
Gertsena ul., 38 314-64-32

Central Exhibition Hall
Isaakievskaya Ploshchad, 1
.... 314-88-59
.... 314-82-53
Hrs:11 - 19, Mon. 12 - 20, closed Thurs

Len_expo EXHIBITION CENTER
11 Modern Exhibitions Halls,
Exterior and marine display areas
Exhibits from 500 m to 20,000 m
Two conference halls, restaurants,
Conveniently located 15 min. from Center
Most experienced exhibition staff in St. Pb.
Bolshoy pr., 103 355-19-89
Other tel. lines................ 217-11-12
Fax: 355-19-85

Exhibition Hall of the Leningrad Regional Museum Administration
Liteynyy pr., 57 279-71-35
Hrs: 11 - 19, closed Mon
Leningrad Youth Palace
Professora Popova ul., 47
.... 234-97-13
Smolny Cathedral Concert & Exhibition Complex
Rastrelli pl., 3/1 311-35-60
Exibition Hall of the Union of Artists
Nab. Sverdlovskaya, 64 ... 224-06-33

Union of Architects
Conferences, Exhibitions, Presentations
in the beautiful 18th century residence
DOM ARKHITEKTORA
Two magnificent halls, exhibit gallery,
Oak, Bronze, White, Green, Velvet Rooms
Modern audio & presentation equipment
Gertsena ul., 52 312-04-00
....311-22-19

Dom Ofitserov
Liteynyy pr., 20 278-86-40
Direktsiya Inostrannykh Vystavok (Foreign Exhibits)
V.O., Bolshoy pr., 103..... 217-20-47
Tavricheskiy Palace
Voinova ul., 47............... 278-95-04

☎ EXHIBITION SERVICES
ВЫСТАВКИ, СЛУЖБЫ ПО ОРГАНИЗАЦИИ
AUSSTELLUNGSGESELLSCHAFTEN
EXPOSITION, SERVICES
UTSTÄLLNINGSSERVICE

The following organizations help to organize exhibitions in various fields. Some offer complete exhibition services from safe transportation to Saint Petersburg to setting up modern displays, publicity & translation services.

COMMERCIAL EXHIBITIONS

Alinter
Soviet-German joint venture
Nalichnaya ul., 6............. 356-37-21
Fax 356-24-14

Inex
Organization of exhibitions
Egorova ul., 18............... 292-50-13
Fax 108-10-30

Len_expo EXHIBIT SERVICES
Complete exhibition services
Transport of exhibits, space, set-up of exhibits, Western audio-visual equipment, interpreters, publicity, European display equipment, transportation and travel arrangements
11 Exhibitions Halls Conviently Located
Bolshoy pr., 103 355-19-89
Other tel. lines................ 217-11-12
Fax: 355-19-85

Leningrad Commercial Center of Lenglavsnab
Liteynyy pr., 57 272-26-77
Leningrad-Impex
Gertsena ul., 35.............. 310-94-41
Fax 319-97-09
Milena-Inform
Nab. kan. Griboedova, 34
.... 311-46-33
POLRADIS
Yuriya Gagarina ul., 1 297-85-36
Fax 297-86-74

EXHIBITIONS
ВЫСТАВКИ
AUSSTELLUNGEN
EXPOSITIONS
UTSTÄLLNINGAR

COMMERCIAL EXHIBITIONS

Saint Petersburg is an exhibition center with various exhibitions going on through out the year. Most large exhibitions are held on the grounds of LENEXPO on the bank of the Gulf of Finland.

NON-COMMERCIAL EXHIBITIONS

See also MUSEUM, ART GALLERIES. There are a large number of trade fairs & commercial exhibitions. Below are listed several permanent commercial & non-commercial exhibitions

Flowers Exhibition Hall
Potemkinskaya ul., 2 272-54-48
Closed Mon, Tue
Impekt
Gertsena ul., 35 310-94-41
Telex .... 121302 LIMEX SU
The House of Nature
Zhelyabova ul., 8 314-08-48
The Hothouses of the Botanical Museum
Aptekarskiy pr., 1 234-17-64
Hrs: 11 - 16 (11 - 14 Thurs), closed Fri

Len_{expo} EXHIBITION CENTER

11 Modern Exhibitions Halls,
Exterior and marine display areas
For new exhibitions, call
Bolshoy pr., 103 355-19-89
Other tel. lines................ 217-11-12
Fax:.............................. 355-19-85

Exhibition of musical instruments
Muzykalnykh Instrumentov
Isaakievskaya pl., 5......... 314-53-45

Rossiyskiy Fermer (Russian Farmer)
Pushkinskaya ul., 10, apt. 39
.... 112-32-78
Fax............................... 112-36-29
Telex ....121031 HEBA-TB

ARTS EXHIBITIONS

Art abounds in St. Pb and there are always art exhibitions displaying the works of today's artists going on somewhere in the city. Many art galleries have "permanent displays" as well as works of art for sale. In addition, the major art museums, The

Hermitage & the Russian Museum, have outstanding visiting exhibitions.

See ART GALLERIES & MUSEUMS.

Listed below are the organizations doing art exhibitions.

Exhibition Center for the Association
of Artists of St. Petersburg
Organizing art exhibitions
Rental exhibit space
Gertsena ul., 38.............. 314-64-32

The Hermitage
Nab. Dvortsovaya, 34...... 311-34-65
Palitra [The Palette]
Nevskiy pr., 166 277-12-16
Russian Museum
Inzhenernaya ul., 4.......... 314-41-53

☎ EXPORT-IMPORT FIRMS
ЭКСПОРТНО-ИМПОРТНЫЕ ФИРМЫ
EXPORT/IMPORT FIRMEN
EXPORTES-IMPORTES, SOCIETES
EXPORT/IMPORT FIRMOR

This heading includes firms looking for export markets and partners to develop technology and to provide new equipment and management.

Aveks Association of Foreign Trade
3-ya Krasnoarmeyskaya ul., 12
.... 292-48-37
Baltic Service
St.Pb., 189623, P.O. 4
.... 555-99-22
Sea products from South of Russia
Baltika-1
Profsoyuzov bul., 4 314-87-27
.... 314-12-87
Bosko Ltd.
Nevskiy pr., 8................. 219-18-56

Centre of Ultrasonic Technologies
Non-abrasive metal finishing using
ultrasonic technology
Production, licenses, technology exchange
Khalturina ul., 5.............. 110-62-30
Fax..............................311-62-16?
Hrs: 10-19, English ,German, French

TRANSPORT SIGNS

BUS   TRAM   TROLLEYBUS

St.-Pb. Chamber of Commerce
       Leningradskaya Torgovo-
       Promyshlennaya Palata
Chaykovskogo ul., 46/48
.... 273-48-96
.... 272-64-06
Telex .... 121324 SU

Impex
   Gertsena ul., 35 310-94-41
   Fax: 319-97-09
   Telex: .... 121302 LIMEX SU

Lenstroyinter
   Nevskiy pr., 1.................. 312-60-42
Lenvneshtorg
   Nab. Admiralteyskaya, 8
   312-42-54
   Fax.................................. 312-40-12
Shans Art
   Narvskiy pr., 15.............. 252-62-41

Tradex Ltd.
   Moskovskiy pr., 86 221-96-94
   221-46-84

Vneshenergomash
   Nab. reki Moyki, 67/69 311-09-88
   Fax.................................. 311-99-96
Vneshlenstroyservice
   Kalyaeva ul., 31.............. 272-58-28
   Fax.................................. 273-06-11
Vneshneekonomicheskaya Assotsiatsiya
                            Baltika
   Moskovskiy pr., 183........ 293-90-45

Saint Petersburg-Baltic Co.
An Import Export Firm
Vneshneekonomicheskaya Sankt-
Peterburga Baltika
Dimitrovskiy per., 3/5 164-60-08
.... 164-53-38

Vneshterminalkompleks
   Belinskogo ul., 11 275-61-61
Foreign Trade Publisher
                         Vneshtorgizdat
   Kuybysheva ul., 34 233-52-63

☎ EXPRESS MAIL
& PARCEL SERVICE
ЭКСПРЕСС-ПОЧТА
EILPOST/PEKETEILDIEMST
EXPRESS, COURRIER
EXPRESS BREV/PAKET SERVICE

Aero-Balt Service Company
Courier Service
Pilotov ul., 38.................. 104-18-12

Central Post Office
   Pochtamtskaya ul., 9....... 312-83-02
               Hrs: 9 - 21

Lenfinkom
    Gertsena ul., 3/4 314-00-60
    Fax.................................. 314-50-84

☎ EXTERMINATORS
ДЕЗИНФЕКЦИЯ
DESINFEKTION
EXTERMINATEURS
OHYREBEKÄMPNING

Exterminator
    Please call 524-20-24
Karelan
    Please call 521-77-27
        Hrs: 9 - 13
Len-Sof
    Aptekarskiy pr., 16 234-27-31
Private Exterminator
    Please call 314-86-07
    Pest control with imported chemicals

☎ EYE GLASS REPAIR
ОЧКИ, РЕМОНТ
BRILLENREPARTUR
LUNETTES, REPARATION
GLASÖGONREPARATIONER

See also OPTICIANS, CONTACT LENSES

Remont Ochkov I Oprav
    V.O., 9-ya Liniya, 32 213-57-93

☎ FABRICS
ТКАНИ
STOFFE
TISSUS
TYGER

*Russian fabrics and sewing notions are
bought in the numerous shops called
"cloth" (Tkani , ТКАНИ).*
Tkani
    Zagorodnyy pr., 21 164-93-66
Tkani
    Mira pl., 9...................... 315-90-45
Tkani
    Zanevskiy pr., 8.............. 528-16-89
Tkani
    Vladimirskiy pr., 4........... 113-13-36
Trikotazh (Knitting)
    Nevskiy pr., 136............. 277-08-96
        Metro: Vosstaniya pl.
Tkani
    Moskovskiy pr., 167........ 298-09-62
Tkani
    Nevskiy pr., 32............... 311-06-90

☎ FAIRS
ЯРМАРКИ
MESSEN
FOIRES
UTSTÄLLNINGAR, MÄSSOR

See EXHIBITIONS, FURS

☎ FARMERS' MARKETS
РЫНКИ,
        СЕЛЬСКОХОЗЯЙСТВЕННЫЕ
MÄRKTE
MARCHE AGRICOLE
LIVSMEDEL

See MARKETS

☎ FASHION SALONS
САЛОН МОД
MODESALONS
MODE, SALONS DE
MODESALONGER

See also DEPARTMENT STORES *and*
CLOTHING WOMEN'S

Atele Mod
    Nevskiy pr., 134 277-11-72

Dom Mod (House of Style)
P.S., Kirovskiy pr., 37...... 234-90-40
Dom Modeley (House of Models)
Nevskiy pr., 21............ 311-05-77
Dom Mode (House of Fashion)
Marshala Tukhachevskogo ul., 22
Show room 226-71-29
Director 226-86-20
Women clothing 225-18-18
Coats salon 225-19-19
Men 543-65-76
Knitted wear salon 543-90-02

Leningradskiy Dom Modeley Odezhdy

LDMO

*Most Fashionable Clothes
in Saint Petersburg*

Nevskiy pr., 21 311-44-48

"Kontinent"
Sedova ul., 37 560-99-58
"Palitra"
V.O., Sredniy pr., 55 213-48-21
Fax 274-09-11
Telex .... 121498 PAL SU

☎ FAST FOOD
КАФЕ-ЭКСПРЕСС
IMBISS STUBEN
FAST FOOD
SNABBMAT

See RESTAURANTS for complete listing.

The concept of "fast food" is catching on with "take out" and "stand up" restaurants. The following offer a quick stand-up snack. You can also try cafes.

"Around the corner and down the steps"
The CAFE "Bristol"
For a quick cup of good coffee and snack
Black & red caviar, pizza, & hachepuri
Nevskiy pr., 22 311-74-90
Hrs: 10-20, Ruble, English

PIZZA-EXPRESS

From 10 am to 24 pm,
*13 Varieties of Pizza, Steak,
Weiner Schnitzel, Pasta & Salad
Lapin Kulta Beer & European Wines*

Podolskaya ul., 23

7 minutes drive from center
Orders 292-26-66
Fax 292-10-39
$, CC, English, Finnish

Gino Ginelli
Nab.kan.Griboedova, 14
.... 312-21-20
"Polar Wagons" Fast Food
Hamburgers, Soft Drink, Beers
Locations:
●Moskovskiy pr., 220
●Corner of Gogolya ul. & St.Isaac pl.
●Metro: Elektrosila
●Ploshchad Iskusstv-Russian Museum
●Airport PULKOVO-1

Polarnoe Bistro
Nevskiy pr., 79 311-85-89

☎ FAX SERVICES
ФАКС-СЕРВИС
FAX-DIENSTE
FAX, SERVICE DE
FAX SERVICE

Faxes are now common in St. Pb. and can be sent from the BUSINESS SERVICES CENTERS.

AsLANTIS
A Consortium of Interpreters to Business
Fax & Phone Translation and Transmission
Tel............................... 213-76-81
Fax/Tel. 298-90-07
We can answer your call in English

Cellular Radio Telephone
In Saint Petersburg
Gateway to the World

Instant Access • Direct -Dial
Local and international phone & fax
From your home, office or car
Single calls & short-term rentals
Long-term subscriptions

Gertsena ul., 22.............. 314-61-26
Fax 314-88-37
.... 315-71-31
Fax. 275-01-90

Sovam Teleport
Low-cost 1 hour express text fax/telex
Nevskiy pr., 30 311-84-12
Fax 311-71-29

Central Telegraph & Telephone
Gertsena ul., 3/5............. 312-77-17
.... 311-00-23

☎ FERRIES
ПАРОМЫ
FÄHREN
FERRIES
FÄRJOR

Ferries leave for Sweden once a week on Monday at 12:00 midnight, for Germany once a week on Wednesday at 6 pm and to Finland 3 times per week, Tuesday and Thursday at 12:00 midnight and Sunday at 7 pm. They leave from the SEA PASSENGER SHIP TERMINAL. For information, call the following numbers.

Baltic Shiping Company at Sea Terminal
Baltiyskoe Morskoe Parokhodstvo
Morskoy Vokzal
Information on schedule of ferries
Morskoy Slavy pr., 1
.... 355-13-10
Tickets........................... 355-13-12

☎ FILM & FILM DEVELOPING
ФОТО И КИНОПЛЁНКА
FILME
FILM
FILM

See PHOTOGRAPHY - FILM & DEVELOPING

☎ FIRE
ПОЖАРНЫЕ
FEUERWENR
INCENDIE
BRAND

In case of Fire Call 01
The Russian word for "fire" is
POZHAR' (ПОЖАР)

☎ FIRST AID STATIONS
СКОРАЯ МЕД. ПОМОЩЬ
ERSTE HILFE
AMBULANCE
FÖRSTAHJÄLPEN STATIONER

See EMERGENCY MEDICAL CARE
In case of Medical Emergency
Call 03

☎ FISH STORES
РЫБНЫЕ МАГАЗИНЫ
FISCHGESCHÄFTE
POISSONNERIES
FISKHANDLARE

Okean-1
Sadovaya ul., 39/41 310-73-38
Okean-2
Shchorsa pr., 54/56 233-88-92

Okean-3
Leninskiy pr., 121 254-56-15
Ryba
Nevskiy pr., 132 277-29-27
Metro: Vosstaniya pl.
Ryba
Razezzhaya ul., 3............. 315-95-54
Ryba
Nevskiy pr., 43 319-98-51
Ryba
Nevskiy pr., 21 312-42-79

Baltic Service (wholesale)
Please call...................... 555-99-22
Fish products of high quality

☎ FISHING & HUNTING EQUIPMENT
ОХОТА И РЫБОЛОВСТВО, ТОВАРЫ
ANGEL- UND JADDGERÄTE
PECHE ET CHASSE, EQUIPEMENT
FISKE & JAKTURUSTNING

See HUNTING & FISHING EQUIPMENT and SPORTS EQUIPMENT

☎ FISHING & HUNTING
РЫБНАЯ ЛОВЛЯ И ОХОТА
FISCHGESCHAFTE
PECHE ET CHASSE
FISKE & JAKT (TURER)

See HUNTING & FISHING (TRIPS)

☎ FLOWER SHOPS
ЦВЕТОЧНЫЕ МАГАЗИНЫ
BLUMENGESCHÄFTE
FLEURISTES
BLOMSTERHANDLARE

The Russians love flowers. Always bring an odd number of flowers (1,3,5,7..) as a gift. Here is a list of florist shops. Flowers are also sold at markets. The best flowers are sold at Kuznetchnyi Market at Metro Vladimirskaya.

Bulgarian Flowers (Tzvety Bolgarii)
Beautiful Flowers.
Special bouquets on three days order
P.S., Kirovskiy pr., 5 232-46-85
Flora (Tsvety)
Voinova ul., 44............... 271-11-61
Hrs: 12 -20
P.S., Bolshoy pr., 86 232-84-07
Hrs: 8 - 20
No.24 Izmaylovskiy pr., 11
.... 251-61-28
No.47 Liteynyy pr., 38..... 273-72-42
Moskovskiy pr., 73 252-10-44
Moskovskiy pr., 194........ 298-42-42

Nevskiy pr., 110 273-42-28
Sadovaya ul., 46 310-08-63
V.O., Sredniy pr., 28 213-19-93
Suvorovskiy pr., 3 277-50-41
No. 6 Vladimirskiy pr., 3
.... 113-22-84
Zagorodnyy pr., 34 315-95-27
Zhukovskogo ul., 36 272-34-66

GERA

Gifts for Your Friends
FLOWERS, CHOCOLATES
Zhelyabova ul., 1 315-74-90

Hall of Flowers
Potemkinskaya ul., 2 272-54-48
Beautiful Flowers.
Special bouquets three days notice
Polish Bouquet
Nab. Morskaya, 15 352-20-75
Beautiful Flowers. Special bouquets.
Tsvety No. 5
Nevskiy pr., 5 312-64-37
Dzerzhinskogo ul., 8
(to order flowers) 312-16-26
Tsvety No. 25
Karla Marksa pr., 70 245-4619
Tsvety No. 26
Moskovskiy Railway Station
.... 168-4541

☎ FOOD DELIVERY
ПРОДУКТЫ, ДОСТАВКА
LEBENSMITTELLIEFERUNG
NOURRITURE, LIVRAISON
MATLEVERERING

Alexandr Popov "Gonar" Shop
Kakhovskogo per., 7 350-78-78
Alfa Express
.... 234-39-68
Food Delivery at any time
Pizza-RIF
.... 290-35-96
Food delivery from 7 p.m. to 8 a.m. $ & rbls

PIZZA-EXPRESS
Quick Home Delivery
From 10 am to 24 pm,
13 Varieties of Pizza, Steak,
Weiner Schnitzel, Pasta & Salad
Lapin Kulta Beer & European Wines
7 minutes drive from center
Orders 292-26-66
Fax 292-10-39
$, CC, English, Finnish

☎ FOOD MARKETS
РЫНКИ ПРОДОВОЛЬСТВЕННЫЕ
LEBENSMITTELGESCHÄFTE
SUPERMARCHES
LIVSMEDELSAFFÄRER,
MARKNADER

See MARKETS and FOOD STORES

☎ FOOD RADIOACTIVITY TESTING
ПРОДУКТЫ, ПРОВЕРКА НА
РАДИОАКТИВНОСТЬ
LEBENSMITTELKONTROLLE,
RADIOAKTIVITÄT
NOURRITURE, ESSAI RADIOACTIF
RADIOAKTIVITETSTESTPÅ, MAT

Radioactivity Tests for Food
4-ya Sovetskaya ul., 5 277-52-92

☎ FOOD STORES
ПРОДОВОЛЬСТВЕННЫЕ
МАГАЗИНЫ
LEBENSMITTELGESCHÄFTE
ALIMENTATION, MAGASINS D'
LIVSMEDELSAFFÄRER

See also FOOD DELIVERY
DELICATESSENS, BAKERIES, BABY FOOD,
MARKETS, INTERNATIONAL SHOPS.

Food is bought in a variety of shops. The modest self-serve supermarkets (called Universamy, Универсамы), have canned and packaged goods, juices, pots & tableware, soaps, paper products, dry goods, as well as meat, bread, fruits and vegetables. In a Gastronom (Гастроном) you usually buy meat, fish, conserves, diary products, and semi-prepared foods, but not dry goods. The farmers markets (called Rynki, РЫНКИ) have fresh vegetables, fruit, sausage, meat, cheese, flowers. See MARKETS. A variety of smaller shops, called "Products" (Producty ПРОДУКТЫ) have a smaller selection of groceries, sugar, and coffee. Other types of food stores include:

Diary	Moloko	Молоко
Bakeries	Bulochnaya	Булочная
Fruits	Fruckty	Фрукты
Vegetables	Ovoshchi	Овощи
Fish	Ryba	Рыба
Meat	Myaso	Мясо

Imported foods are bought in the food section of INTERNATIONAL SHOP and the shops listed below.

Universams   Универсамы
Universal self-service food stores

Gavanskiy, No. 14 near Metro Primorskaya
Nalichnaya ul., 42........... 350-17-08

Grazhdanskiy
Prosveshcheniya pr., 81
.... 531-54-44
Open: 8 - 21 (except during lunch 14-15)

Izmaylovskiy
Novo-Izmaylovskiy pr., 3
.... 296-51-45

Morskoy, No. 29 near Hotel Pribaltiyskaya
Korablestroiteley ul., 21 ... 356-86-59

Nevskiy
Bolshevikov pr., 6 588-30-13

Okhtinskiy No. 35 near Hotel Okhtinskaya
Nab. Sverdlovskaya, 62
.... 227-08-47

Pulkovskiy No. 24
Pulkovskoe shosse, 3....... 122-23-16

Severniy
Prosvescheniya pr., 72 558-52-01

Tallinnskiy
Veteranov pr., 89 150-78-71

Tulskiy, near Hotel Okhtinskaya
Tulskaya ul., 3 271-08-37
Open: 8-21 (except during lunch 14-15)

Vitebskiy
Dimitrova ul., 5............... 172-50-29
Open: 8-21 (except during lunch 14-15)

Vostochniy
Kollontay ul., 41, bldg. 1
.... 584-88-09
Open: 8-21 (except during lunch 14-15)

Vyborgskiy
Nauki pr., 23.................... 533-54-89
Open: 8-21 (except during lunch 14-15)

Yuzhnyy
Yaroslava Gasheka ul., 6
.... 176-10-13

Zapadnyy
Marshala Kazakova ul., 1
.... 157-01-55

Zvezdnyy
Zvezdnaya ul., 16 126-93-37

GASTRONOMS & OTHER FOOD STORES

Bakaleya, Myaso, Ptitsa
Nevskiy pr., 150............. 277-21-54

Gastronom No. 1 *"Eliseevskiy"*
Nevskiy pr., 54............... 311-93-23
Best gastronom

Gastronomiya no.14
Nevskiy pr., 128............. 277-14-31
Metro: Vosstaniya pl.

Torgovyy Dom "Minokhem"
Zamshina ul., 29............. 543-39-20

Moloko, Smetana
Nevskiy pr., 122............. 277-29-66
Metro: Vosstaniya pl.

Liteynyy Gastronom
Liteynyy pr., 12 272-27-91

Productovyy Magazine
Nevskiy pr., 105 277-06-31

Strela Gastronom
Izmaylovskiy pr., 16/30.... 251-27-09

COMMERCIAL & PRIVATE FOOD STORES

Troika Mini-Market

Everything for the family and home
Imported food, clothing, shoes, TV &
stereo, appliances
Just Opposite Troika Restaurant
Zagorodnyy pr., 28
Hrs: 10-19, $ & rbls, English, Between Metro
Pushkinskaya, Vladimirskaya/Dostoevskaya

OTHER COMMERCIAL STORES

Donon (Commercial shop)
Ligovskiy pr., 5 279-18-45

Elf (Commercial shop)
Gertsena ul., 25/11 314-64-43

Kooperator
Nevskiy pr., 120 277-59-05
    Metro: Vosstaniya pl.

FRUIT & VEGETABLES STORES

Frukty, Ovoshchi (fruits, vegetables)
Nevskiy pr., 132 277-21-63
Metro: Pl. Vosstaniya
    Hrs: 9 - 21

Gdansk products from Poland
Leninskiy pr., 125 255-80-45

Gdynya products from Poland
Zanevskiy pr., 20 528-27-08
    fruit & vegetables

Kooperator
Moskovskiy pr., 36-38 292-16-65

Ovoshchi - Fructy
Nevskiy pr., 127 277-26-33
Sadovaya ul., 56/45 315-59-20
Sredniy pr., 34 213-10-43
Zagorodnyy pr., 45 113-52-01
    vegetables & fruit

Sopot products from Poland
Sredniy pr., 25 218-49-75

Yablonka
Nevskiy pr., 65 164-98-72

☎ **FOREIGN CONSULATES**
КОНСУЛЬСТВА
KONSULATE
CONSULATS, ETRANGERS
UTLÄNDSKA KONSULAT

See CONSULATES

☎ **FOREIGN FIRMS**
ФИРМЫ, ИНОСТРАННЫЕ
FIRMEN, AUSLÄNDISCHE
COMMERCE EXTERIEUR,
SOCIETES DU
UTLANDSKA FFARSAKTIEBOLAG

AMEREX INTERCONTINENTAL
Kamenoostrovskiy pr., 37
"Dom Mod" 3rd floor 233-87-31

American Express
in "Grand-Hotel Europe" ... 315-74-87
.... 315-52-15

ASEA Brown Boveri Zurich/Mannheim
V.O., Bolshoy pr., 10 213-78-71
.... 350-49-10
Telex: .... 121510 HDDTW SU
Fax: 350-29-11

Arthur Andersen Frankfurt/Main
V.O., Bolshoy pr., 10 213-78-74
.... 350-48-13
.... 350-49-84

A. J. EST S.U
Profsoyuzov bul., 4, Entr. 6
.... 110-64-96
Telex .... 121732 CGTT SU

AT&T - Dalnaya Svyaz
Liflyandskaya ul., 4 186-29-37

Badische Anilin - and Sodafabrik - BASF
                        Ludwigshafer
V.O., Bolshoy pr., 10 218-53-81
.... 350-72-56

Cameron Associates 558-96-17

Carl Zeib Jena GmbH
V.O., Bolshoy pr., 10 213-78-73
.... 350-48-35
Telex: 121564
Fax: 213-78-73

Cheryl Ann Sigsbee 109-69-14

Coca Cola Representation:
Nab. Obvodnogo kan., 93a
.... 315-76-32
.... 113-31-60
.... 210-17-27

Contact Businesslink 355-92-57

Delta Airlines
Gertsena ul., 36 311-58-20
Pulkovo-2 Airport 104-34-38

Delta Telecom - U.S. West 275-41-49
Gertsena ul., 22 314-61-26
Fax 314-88-37
Fax. 275-01-30

DHL
Nab. kan. Griboedova 5, Office 51
.... 311-96-82
Fax 314-64-73

Dialog Invest
Dostoevskogo ul., 19 164-89-56

Deutche Lufthansa
V.O., Bolshoy pr., 10 314-49-79
.... 314-59-17
Fax: 312-31-29

ECO Stahl AG Eisenhuttenstadt
V.O., Bolshoy pr., 10 218-17-84
.... 350-48-06
Fax: 218-17-84

Export Industries. 122-57-16

Elegant Logic Inc.

Sells computers, office electronics,
consumer goods, food.
Technological equipment.
Barter.
Real estate property.

Nab. reki Fontanki, 46 312-38-86
Fax: 311-04-52

Ford Europe (TDV auto, dealer)
Kommuny ul., 16 521-46-13
Inter Marco Import - and Export
                                    GmbH Hamburg
V.O., Bolshoy pr., 10 350-46-56
Gillette at Petersburg Products Int.
.... 298-68-87
Hotel Development Corp.
Nab. kan. Griboedova, 5
.... 312-35-57
.... 311-04-71
Kamennyy Ostrov
Kamennyy Ostrov, Polevaya alleya, 6
.... 234-10-11
Otis Sankt Petersburg
Khimicheskiy per.,12 252-36-94
Proctor and Gamble
Grand-Hotel Europe, Brodskogo ul., 1/7
......................113-80-71 (Ext. 458)
Ben & Jerry's - Petrazavodsk
.... (81400) 74108

CONSULTING/REAL ESTATE FIRMS/LAWS/ADVERTISING

A and A Relocation.............. 312-76-88
Arthur Anderson ....
Coopers Lybrand ....
Gertsena ul., 39, Hotel "Astoria",
Rm. 528........................ 210-55-28
DRT Inaudit
.... (095) 281-55-20
Florman Information Russia
Kamennoostrovskiy pr., 14b
.... 233-76-82
Fax: 232-80-17
Telex: 121609
Sharon Deeney, Attorney 356-69-90
Ernst & Young 116-01-67
IMIM 311-24-27
International Group 277-64-05
InterOccidental Inc.
Ryleeva ul., 33 273-43-23

Invest-Develop Stern-Kersh & Co.
Nevskiy pr., 104 275-45-87
Petrograd Expedition 597-71-02
Russian-American Law Firm
.... 277-53-98

Telinfo "The *Traveller's* Yellow Pages"
Nab. reki Moyki, 64......... 315-64-12
.... 315-98-55
Fax 315-74-20
.... 312-73-41

OFFICES OPENING SOON

Baker McKenzie
Moscow............... (095) 200-49-06
Batterymarch Financial Management

☎ FREIGHT FORWARDING AGENTS
ДОСТАВКА, АГЕНСТВА
SPEDITION
COMMISSIONNAIRES
EXPEDITEURS
EXPEDITÖR

See SHIPPING AGENTS

☎ FUNERALS/UNDERTAKERS
ПОХОРОННЫЕ БЮРО
BESTATTUNGSINSTITUTE
POMPES FUNEBRES,
BUREAUX DES
BEGRAVNING

In case of a death at home, in a hotel or almost anywhere, it is necessary to call a doctor for determination of the cause of death. As a rule, the same ambulance that brought the doctor can take the body to the morgue of the "on-duty" hospital, where a pathologist examines the body and perhaps does an autopsy. Births, deaths, weddings and divorces are registered at the ZAGS. See MARRIAGE BUREAU.

Information about funerals 067
Funeral Parlors & Undertakers
1-aya Sovetskaya ul., 8 ... 278-40-67
.... 277-53-05
Spetservices
Mayorova pr., 25, Flr. 3, Rm. 32-33
.... 315-50-32
                    Hrs: 9-13, 14-18

Flowers, wreaths, funeral clothes, caskets and similar items can be bought at a small Funeral Department at the ZAGS or at the following funeral shops.

Funeral Shop   Pokhoronnye Magazin
Tipanova ul., 29 299-39-83
.... 299-79-27
                    Hrs: 8-20, Sunday 8-19

Store No. 1
Dostoevskogo ul., 9/8 314-51-86
.... 164-24-01
Information 113-25-34

☎ FURNITURE STORES
МЕБЕЛЬНЫЕ МАГАЗИНЫ
MÖBELGESCHÄFTE
MEUBLES, MAGASINS DE
MÖBELHANDLARE,
MÖBELAFFÄRER

Furniture is sold in stores called
'"Furniture" (Mebel, Мебель)

Bon Servis
V.O., Bolshoy pr., 63 217-31-37

BETAC
Lva Tolstogo ul., 6/8 265-17-61
Furniture from bamboo

Delfin
Gagarina pr., 8 264-79-14

Drezden
Morisa Toreza pr., 40/1 ... 552-47-52

Concern "Goryachev"
Fine Furnishings

Furniture, Reproductions, Chandeliers,
Decorative Wood Wall Paneling
National Handicrafts & Costumes
Objects from Crystal, Bronze, Fine Woods

Custom Orders and Wholesale

Retail Stores & Display Rooms
Vereyskaya ul., 39............... 112-75-96
Utochkina ul., 7.................. 301-73-75
Fax 311-95-76

Hrs: 10-20, $, English

Klen
Slavy pr., 2, bldg. 1 260-18-33

Klen
Kommunarov pl., 6.......... 113-81-86

Lenkomplektmebel
Tsiolkovskogo ul., 9 251-39-00

Lenraumamebel JV
Mebelnaya ul., 5 246-09-12

Mebel
Dibunovskaya ul., 37....... 239-44-64
Domestic Furniture.......... 239-84-34

Mebel
Leninskiy pr., 137 255-00-97
.... 254-21-45

Mebel
Novocherkasskiy pr., 22/15
.... 221-03-88

Stroitel
Chkalovskiy pr., 56 234-39-27

Novosel
Nalichnaya ul., 40, bldg. 7
.... 350-59-84

Salon "Karnisy"
Nab. reki Fontanki, 73 310-88-62

ZIM
Boytsova per., 4 272-11-18
.... 567-11-97

☎ FURS
МЕХА
PELZE
FOURRURES
PÄLSAR

See also DEPARTMENTS STORES,
FASHION SALONS *and*
CLOTHING-WOMEN'S

Baltic Star at Pribaltiyskaya Hotel,
Korablestroiteley ul, 14 356-41-85

Dom Firmennoy torgovli
Nab. Novosmolenskaya, 1
.... 352-11-34

LENA
FINE FURS
SAINT PETERSBURG

ЛЕНА
LENA
Vosstaniya ul., 23............273-75-42
LENA at **DOM MOD**
P.S., Kirovskiy pr., 37.....233-85-17
LENA FUR SALON
P.S., Bolshoy pr., 29A.....233-85-17

Custom Orders, Design, Exports
Tel: 310-23-22   Fax: 310-36-15

Hrs: 10-19, $ & rubles, English

Lenkomissiontorg Shop
Kirovskiy pr., 2
.... 233-51-53
Open Mon-Sat 11 - 14, 16 - 20
Liteynyy pr., 32/34
.... 273-08-32
Open Mon-Sat 11 - 14, 16 - 20

Neva Star at Moskva Hotel,
Alexandra Nevskogo pl., 2
.... 274-00-24
.... 274-00-12
Rot Front Retail Shop
Gertsena ul., 34 311-73-57
Atele Mod
Nevskiy pr., 139 277-56-33
Atele
Rubinshteyna ul., 9 113-23-26
Gostinyy Dvor
Nevskiy pr., 35 312-41-65
.... 312-41-74
Passazh
Nevskiy pr., 48 311-70-84
Fur Auction "Pushnoy auktsion"
Moskovskiy pr., 98 298-46-36
Fur auctions in January, July, October

☎ GARDENS
САДЫ
PARK
JARDINS
TRÄDGÅRDAR

Botanical Garden of Academy
of Sciences Institute
Botanicheskiy Sad Instituta Academii Nauk
Professora Popova ul., 2
.... 234-17-64
Summer Garden and Palace of Peter the I
Letniy Sad i Dvorets Petra I
.... 312-96-66
Garden of the Anichkov Palace
Sad Leningradskogo Dvortsa Pionerov
Nevskiy pr., 39 314-72-81
Tavricheskiy Garden
Tavricheskiy Sad
Saltykova-Schedrina ul., 50
.... 272-60-44

☎ GAS - PROPANE
ТОПЛИВО, ПРОПАН
PROPANGAS
PROPANE
BENSIN

Polyustrovskiy pr., 77 245-54-19
Sedova ul., 9 265-17-35

☎ GAS SERVICE
ГАЗ, СЛУЖБА
STADTGAZ
GAZ, SERVICE
BENSINSERVICE

GAS EMERGENCY, CALL......04
For initiation and termination of
service, billing information, for installation
and service of gas lines, call.
.... 265-14-79
.... 265-26-31

To install or repair:
Dzherzhinskiy District 277-03-82
Kalininskiy District.......... 557-70-64
Krasnoselskiy District 130-36-51
Leninskiy District 292-25-39
Moskovskiy District......... 297-05-02
Nevskiy District 265-12-51
Oktyabrskiy District......... 311-25-39
Petrogradskiy District....... 233-18-82
Primorskiy District 239-28-60
Vyborgskiy District.......... 550-08-65

☎ GAS STATIONS/PETROL
АВТОЗАПРАВОЧНЫЕ СТАНЦИИ
TANKSTELLEN
ESSENCE, POSTE A
BENSINSTATIONER

The petrol/gasoline situation improved
dramatically with the opening of the 3 Neste
Petro Service stations in St. Petersburg.
Also, note those gas stations carrying Au-
93, A-95 gas/petrol, especially the
Sovavtointerservice stations.

Nakhimova ul., 18 356-93-30
Au-93m, oil

City Center
Teatralnaya pl................. 312-21-35

Park imeni V.I. Lenina 1
232-45-23
Au-93, Au-95

Nab. reki Fontanki........... 251-38-71
Tavricheskiy per., 18....... 273-49-62
City North
Vyborgskoe shosse, 4 553-45-54
Primorskiy pr., 56........... 239-09-45
Nepokoryonnykh pr., 15
.... 534-17-16
Polyustrovskiy pr., 73..... 245-23-51
Suzdalskiy pr., 12 531-89-95
Rustavelli ul., 40............. 249-42-57
Primorskoe shosse, 18 km
(Olgino) 238-30-49

Savushkina ul., 87............ 239-04-15
Au-93, oil

Ekaterininskiy pr., 11 225-70-60
City South
Vitebskiy pr., 9............... 225-70-60

Yuriya Gagarina pr., 32.... 293-72-10
Au-93, oil

Pulkovskoye shosse, 27	293-47-80
Au-93, diesel	
Pilotov ul., 6a...............	122-96-00
Narodnogo Opolcheniya pr., 16	
....	254-37-48
Tallinskoe shosse., 10 km	
(Krasnoe Selo)	132-14-22
Matyushenko ul., 3	567-17-46
Sovetskiy pr., 37	262-44-60
Moskovskoe shosse, 35	
....	293-24-19
Moskovskiy pr., 100.......	293-24-19

NESTE
Petro Service

GASOLINE and LUBRICANTS
ACCESSORIES • MINI-SHOP

24 HOURS A DAY
MAJOR CREDIT CARDS ACCEPTED
Gasolines: 76, 92, & 95 oct. & leadfree
98 oct. for catalytic converter equipped
cars, automotive oils, fluids & accessories.
Cigarettes, soft drinks, food & travel
needs

3 LOCATIONS IN ST. PB.

STATION NO. 3 NEAR MOSCOW GATE
Moskovskiy pr., 100...... 298-45-34
STATION NO. 29 ON VASILIEVSKIY ISLAND
Malyy pr., 68 355-08-79
STATION NO. 49 ON ROAD TO
PULKOVO AIRPORT
Pulkovskoe shosse, 43 .. 122-03-01
DIESEL FUEL AT THIS LOCATION
MAIN OFFICE:TEL: 296-54-49, FAX: 296-81-72

SERVICE

Service, parts, gas, oil & repairs
specializing in Volvo, Mercedes, VW, Opel
& other foreign cars.
Service centers throughout Russia
Service Center in Saint Petersburg
Predportovyy Proyezd, 5.... 290-15-10
(Next to Hotel Pulkovskaya)
Daily, 9 am - 8 pm, Eng, $ & Rbl.
For other services, call
Malodetskoselskiy pr., 24 .. 292-77-18
Fax 292-00-28
Telex .... 121412 LTOS SU

☎ GIFT SHOPS, SOUVENIRS
ПОДАРКИ
GESCHENKARTIKEL
CADEAUX
SOUVENIRER, PRESENTAFFÄRER

See also CRYSTAL and PORCELAIN,
ART GALLERIES and HANDICRAFTS
FLOWER, ALCOHOL

It is customary to bring a small gift or
flowers when you go visiting. Gifts are
sold in shops called "Gifts" (Podarki,
Подарки).

Alivekt
Nevskiy pr., 22/24 315-59-78
Artistic Products
        Khudozhestvennye Promysly
Nevskiy pr., 51 113-14-95

GERA
Gifts for Your Friends

Open 24 hours a day for last minute gifts
Exquisite Porcelain Gifts Imported Liquors
Flowers, Chocolates & Cigarettes

Zhelyabova ul., 1 315-74-90
Open 24 hrs/day (except 9-10, 15-16)
Metro: Nevskiy Pr.
On V. O., visit our other shop
V.O., Zheleznovodskaya ul., 9
☎ 350-74-98
Hrs: 11-19, Closed Sat & Sun
Metro: Primorskaya

The Globe/Globus
  Nevskiy pr., 78............... 272-95-98
Slide-film, slides, prints & posters on St. Pb.
Khudozhestvennyy fond
  Nevskiy pr., 45 311-21-96
Leningradskiy Khudozhik, Salon
  Nevskiy pr., 31 314-80-81
   Paintings, ceramics, accessories.
Nasledie
  Nevskiy pr., 116 279-50-67
Gifts   **Podarki No. 1**
  Nevskiy pr., 54 314-18-01
Gifts   **Podarki No. 2**
  P.S., Bolshoy pr., 51 232-20-92
  Nevskiy pr., 92 279-42-79
Gifts   **Podarki No. 3**
  Kosygina pr., 26 520-73-36
Pole Star   **Polyarnaya Zvezda**
  Nevskiy pr., 158 277-09-80

Russkoe Iskusstvo
Saltykova-Shchedrina ul., 53
.... 275-69-68
Glass, ceramics, wood & lamps.

Sankt Petersburg
Petra Lavrova ul., 42 273-03-41

Yubiley
Nab. Sverdlovskaya, 60
.... 224-25-98

☎ GOLF
ГОЛЬФ
GOLF
GOLF
GOLF

Please send information to Telinfo about golf in the St.-Petersburg area.

☎ GOVERNMENT
ПРАВИТЕЛЬСТВО
REGIERUNG
GOUVERNEMENT
REGERING

See CITY COUNCIL & MAYOR OFFICE

☎ GRILL BARS
ГРИЛЬ-БАРЫ
GRILL-IMBISS
GRILL BARS
GRILLBARER

See RESTAURANTS

☎ GROCERY STORES
БАКАЛЕЯ
LEBENSMITTELGESCHÄFTE
EPICERIE
LIVSMEDELSAFFÄRER

See FOOD STORES

☎ GYMS
СПОРТИВНЫЕ ЗАЛЫ
TURNHALLEN
GYMS
GYM

Baltika Sports Center
Pertrovskiy pr., 16 235-51-64

Dinamo Sports Center
Dinamo pr., 44. 235-58-87

Elektrosila Sports Club
Moskovskiy pr., 156........ 297-17-44

Mototrek Rowing Club
Zhaka Dyuklo ul., 67 553-70-15
.... 553-70-11

Sport Center
Vyborgskoe shosse, 34 ... 553-32-03
Acrobatics & bicycling

Spartak Rowing Sport Center
Nab. Bolshoy Nevki, 24 ... 234-36-22

Yubileynyy Sports Palace
Dobrolyubova pr., 18....... 238-41-22

Zenit Sport Palace
Butlerova ul., 9............... 534-86-55

Zimniy Stadium
Manezhnaya pl., 2 315-57-10

☎ HABERDASHERY
ГАЛАНТЕРЕЯ
KURZWARENGESCHÄFTE
MERCERIE
ASSESSEDARER, KLÄDER

At the so-called HABERDASHERY *shops, (Galantereya, Галантерея), you can buy personal accessories, such as neckties and belts, needles & thread, bags, and often cosmetics, perfumes and toiletries. You also can buy these personal accessories at* DEPARTMENT STORES *and* COMMERCIAL SHOPS. *You can also buy neckties at Necktie shops, called (Galstuki, Галстуки). See also* COSMETICS.

Pierro Guidi v Rossii
Nevskiy pr., 54............... 314-25-38

Galantereya Parfumeriya
Nevskiy pr., 139 277-15-89

Mens Haberdashery
Muzhskaya galantereya
P.S., Bolshoy pr., 57 232-93-85

The Shaving Shop
Tovary dlya britya
Nevskiy pr., 112 272-74-21

☎ HAIR CUTTING
ПАРИКМАХЕРСКИЕ
FRISEURSALONS
COUPE DE CHEVEUX
HÅRKLIPPNING

There are hundreds of haircutting salons in St. Petersburg. called (Parikmakherskie, ПАРИКМАХЕРСКИЕ) for women (zhen-shchin, ЖЕНЩИН) and men (mushchin, МУЖЧИН). Most large hotels, listed below, also have haircutting salons and may speak English. There are a growing number of private shops. Wella is one of the best for women and Pari one of the best for men.

IN THE HOTELS:
Astoria
Gertsena ul., 39............... 210-58-35

Grand Hotel Europe
Brodskogo ul., 1/7 315-45-61

Karelia
Tukhachevskogo ul., 27
.... 226-30-38

Morskaya
Morskoy Slavy pl., 1........ 355-13-21

Moskva
Alexandra Nevskogo pl., 2
.... 274-20-97

Oktivian (forman Gavan)
V.O., Sredniy pr., 88 356-85-04

Oktyabrskaya
Parikmakherskaya No. 310
Ligovskiy pr., 10............. 277-62-93

Pribalstiyskaya
Korablestroiteley ul. 14 356-28-02

Pulkovskaya
  Pobedy pl., 1 264-51-15
Saint Peterburg
  Nab. Vyborgskaya, 5 542-91-70

HAIRDRESSER/BEAUTY SALONS:
WOMEN HAIRDRESSER/BEAUTY SALONS:

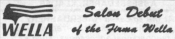

Salon Debut
of the Firma Wella

WELLA

Finest hair stylists in Saint Petersburg
Featuring well known imported hair products
  Nevskiy pr., 54 312-30-26
Hrs: 9-21, Clsd. Sun, $, English and German

Parikmakherskaya No. 1
  Nevskiy pr., 3 312-60-78
Parikmakherskaya No. 82
  Kazanskaya ul., 6 221-42-92
Parikmakherskaya No. 24
  Babushkina ul., 131 267-33-40
Parikmakherskaya No. 32
  Vosstaniya ul., 19 279-02-79
Parikmakherskaya No. 35
  Ligovskiy pr., 63 164-55-39
Parikmakherskaya No. 302
  Nevskiy pr., 168 277-41-09
Parikmakherskaya No. 341
  Nab. Fontanki, 5 314-00-80
Salon Zhenskikh Prichesok No. 22
  Nevskiy pr., 22/24 311-40-34
Salon Zhenskikh Prichesok No. 209
  P.S., Kirovskiy pr., 9 232-42-46
Salon Zhenskikh Prichesok No. 217
  P.S., Bolshoy pr., 53 233-29-23
Salon Zhenskikh Prichesok
  Bolshoy pr., 22/24 235-28-84
Salon Zhenskikh Prichesok
  Nevskiy pr., 29 314-24-35
Salon Zhenskikh Prichesok
  Nevskiy pr., 140 279-44-37
Salon Zhenskikh Prichesok "Glorya"
  Nevskiy pr., 168 277-41-09
Salon Zhenskikh Prichesok "Nadyezhda"
  Liteynyy pr., 61 273-50-43
Studiya "M"
  Morisa Toreza pr., 30 557-78-47

MEN'S BARBERS, HAIR SALONS:

Parikmakherskaya No. 56
  Finlyandskiy Vokzal
  (Finland Railway Station).. 542-38-08
Parikmakherskaya No. 284
  Karla Marksa pr., 92 245-24-03
Parikmakherskaya No. 309
  Nevskiy pr., 156 277-08-59
Parikmakherskaya No. 331
  Vosstaniya ul., 20 273-13-94
Parikmakherskaya No. 337
  Liteynyy pr., 8 272-49-40
"Pari" Barber's Salon for Men
          Salon myzhskikh Prichesok No. 18
  Vladimirskiy pr., 3 113-12-09
          Best Men's Salon
Salon Muzhskikh Prichesok No. 19
  Nevskiy pr., 50 312-40-32

Salon Muzhskikh Prichesok No. 108
  Gertsena ul., 25 314-75-21
Salon Muzhskikh Prichesok No. 221
  P.S., Bolshoy pr., 10 232-18-88
Salon Muzhskikh Prichesok No. 325
  Liteynyy pr., 43 273-29-71
Parikmakherskaya No. 19
  Nevskiy pr., 50 312-40-32

CHILDREN'S BARBER/HAIRDRESSER:

Parikmakherskaya No. 176
  Moskovskiy pr., 190 298-31-38
Parikmakherskaya
  Nevskiy pr., 129 277-19-77
Parikmakherskaya No. 124
  Ligovskiy pr., 91 164-15-11

HAIRDRESSER-UNISEX WOMEN, MEN & CHILDREN SALONS:

Parikmakherskaya No. 351
  Izmaylovskiy pr., 22 251-32-09
Parikmakherskaya No. 353
  Izmaylovskiy pr., 31 251-00-65
Parikmakherskaya No. 399
  Veteranov pr., 16 156-66-61

☎ HARD CURRENCY SHOPS
      ВАЛЮТНЫЕ МАГАЗИНЫ
      VALUTALÄDEN
      MAGASINS EN DEVISES
      HARDVALUTA AFFÄRER

See INTERNATIONAL SHOPS

☎ HARDWARE
      СКОБЯНЫЕ ТОВАРЫ
      EISENWAREN
      QUINCAILLERIES
      JÄRNHANDLARE

See BUILDING SUPPLIES

Khozyaystvennye tovary
  Yakornaya ul., 1 224-38-03
  Yakornaya ul., 2 224-34-86
Stroitelnye Tovary
  Moskovskiy pr., 4 310-17-33

☎ HATS
      ГОЛОВНЫЕ УБОРЫ
      HÜTE
      CHAPEAUX
      HATTAR

You can buy hats also at DEPARTMENT STORES and FASHION SALONS or specialized shops called Atelier of Headgear (Atele golovnykh uborov, Ателье головных уборов), where you can buy ready-made hats or have a hat made to order.

Atelier of Headgear
                Atele golovnykh uborov
  Vernnosti ul., 10, bldg. 2
  535-75-95
          women only
  Moskovskiy pr., 20 292-78-20
          women only
  Nevskiy pr., 98 279-33-30
          men and women

Nevskiy pr., 107 277-11-55
women only

DOM MOD
Kirovskiy pr., 37 234-93-63
for men and women
Marshala Tukhachevskogo ul., 22
.... 226-71-29
for men and women

☎ HEALTH CARE
ЗДРАВООХРАНЕНИЕ
GESUNDHEITSWESEN
SOINS MEDICAUX
SJUKVÅRD

*See EMERGENCY MEDICAL CARE,
MEDICAL CARE AND CONSULTATIONS,
HOSPITAL, OPTICIANS, HEARING AIDS,
DENTISTS, WATER, PHARMACIES,
WHAT-TO-BRING.*

SOME HEALTH INFORMATION

Body Temperature:
98.6 = 37° C   Normal
102 = 39° C   High

Normal Pulse Rate:
60 - 90 per minute

☎ HEALTH CLUBS
ШЕЙПИНГ, ФИЗКУЛЬТУРНЫЕ
ЦЕНТРЫ
FITNESSCENTER
SPORT FITNESS, CLUB DE
HÄLSOKLUBBAR

*Most large hotels have Western-style
health clubs with universal equipment,
saunas, and massage. There are now a
number of Russian health clubs as well.*

BAST Sports Centre
The Place to Relax
Tennis courts, sport halls, exercise room,
Sauna & massage
Raevskogo proezd, 16 552-55-12
Fax 552-39-36
Open 24 hours/day, English & Spanish

World Class ®
Fitness Center
At The Astoria Hotel
Sauna, Pool, Gym, Solarium, Massage
Gertsena ul., 39 210-58-69
*Hrs: Mon-Fri:7:30-10:00; 15:00 - 22:00
Sat, Sun: 9:30-21:00 $, English
A Swedish-Russian Firm*

Shaping Association
6-ya Krasnoarmeyskaya ul., 14
.... 110-18-87

Shaping
Lenin Stadium, Petrovskiy Ostrov
.... 235-49-64
Federation of Shaping of Russia
Petrovskiy Ostrov, 2-g 235-64-87
.... 235-51-80
Fax 558-01-39
Intersport
Moiseenko ul., 22/17 271-36-21
Laun-Tennis Sport Center
Metallistov pr., 116, Stadium Krasnyy
Vyborzhets 540-75-21
.... 540-74-21
Fitness, aerobics, martial arts

World Class ®
Health Club
At The Grand Hotel Europe
Sauna, Pool, Gym, Solarium,
Massage, Hairdresser
also includes "Nike" Sportswear Shop
Mikhaylovskaya ul, 1/7 312-00-72, x-6500
*Hrs: Mon-Fri:7:00-22:00,
Sat, Sun: 9:00-21:00 $, English
A Swedish-Russian Firm*

Lena 559-36-55
Hrs: 10 - 22
Olymp Co-operative
Plekhanova ul., 41 311-57-34
Workout room, sauna, minipool
Rossiya
Chernyshevskogo pl., 11
.... 296-72-21
*The culture and fitness center attached to
the Hotel Rossiya, Body shaping*
Solyaris
Nab. kan. Obvodnogo, 203
.... 251-36-41
*Sport & fitness complex:
workout room & sauna*

Sport Class Cooperative
Kirovskiy pr., 26/28 232-75-81
*Sports & fitness complex, workout room,
solarium, massage & beauty parlor, bar*

TYP

*TRAVEL IN LUXURY
LIMOUSINES AND TAXIS*
See LIMOUSINE
page 142

☎ HEALTH RESORTS/SPA
КУРОРТЫ
KURORTE
STATIONS CLIMATIQUES
HÄLSOHEM

Dyuny Health Spa
Sestroretsk, Primorskoe shosse, 38 km
.... 237-44-38

☎ HEARING AIDS
СЛУХОВЫЕ АППАРАТЫ
HÖRGERÄTE
APPAREILS, ACOUSTIQUES
HÖRSEL HJÄLP

Meditsinskaya Apparatura
V.O., 15-ya Liniya, 32 213-06-09

Slukh
Krasnaya ul., 55 210-94-65

☎ HOLIDAYS
ПРАЗДНИКИ
FEIERTAGE UND FERIEN
FETES
HÖGTIDER, FERIER

*Holidays are in considerable flux. Note,
that if a holiday falls on Thursday, then
Friday and Saturday may also be holidays.*

1	Jan—	New Year's Day
7	Jan—	Russian Orthodox Christmas
8	March—	International Women's Day
	March/April—	Easter (Paskha)
1 & 2	May—	International Labor Day
9	May—	Victory (1945) Day
19	May—	St.Petersburg Day
12	June—	Independence Day for Russia
7	Oct—	Constitution Day
7 & 8	Nov—	Undetermined status Holidays are changing.

SCHOOL & SUMMER VACATIONS

Schools start September 1 and finish
May 31 with a week vacation in
November, two weeks in January at the
New Year and one week in March.

Universities usually start the fall
semester about September 1 and finish
classes about the 20th of December
followed by an exam week in January.
Winter break is from the 25th of January
to 8th of February. Spring semester starts
on the second week of February. Classes
end around the end of May followed by
exams ending about the 25th of June.

Most workers are entitled to 24 days
of paid vacation and most people take
their vacation in the summer at the dacha.

☎ HONEY
МЕД
HONIG
MIEL
HONUNG

Dary Lesa
Poltavskaya ul., 4 279-42-30
Pchelovodstvo
Liteynyy pr., 46 273-70-74

☎ HORSEBACK RIDING
ЛОШАДИ, КАТАНИЕ
REITEN
EQUITATION
RIDNING

Kirov Stadium
Krestovskiy octrov, Morskoy pr., 1
.... 235-18-51
Konen
Marata ul., 86 164-07-22

 PROSTOR-PARK RIDING SCHOOL & STABLES

Horseback Riding & Carriages
Horseback Riding in Primorskiy Park
On the banks of the Neva River
By the hour or by the day
Instruction in Dressage & Jumping
Famous Horseback Stunt Riders
Available for Film & TV Production

Boarding of Horses • Carriages
Purchase and sale of horses.

Inquire about our summer Horse Camp
and Horseback Tours at Lake Ladoga

Fox hunting with Russian wolfhounds
Krestovskiy Ostrov, 20.....230-39-88
Fax................................310-67-56
Hrs: 9-20, $ & rubles, English

Skachki A/O *(Horseback riding)*
Partizana Germana ul., 3
.... 136-73-83

☎ **HOSPITALS**
　БОЛЬНИЦЫ
　KRANKENHÄUSER
　HOPITAUX
　SJUKHUS

There are at least 40 hospitals in St. Pb. The level of care varies from very good to poor. The hospitals listed below have a good reputation. Unfortunately, they are often short of supplies and staff with the current economic conditions.

HOSPITALS IN MEDICAL INSTITUTE

Psychoneurological Institute
　　　　Psykhonevrologicheskiy Institute
　　　　　　　　im Bekhtereva
Bekhtereva ul., 3 265-24-30
Institute of 1st aid
　　　　　Institut Skoroy Pomoshchi
Fuchika ul., 3 105-29-70
Toxicology, cardiology, liver diseases.
Burn Treatment
Neuro Institute
　　　　　　　Institut Neirokhirurgii
Mayakovskogo ul., 12 272-81-35
Institute of Onkology named after Petrov
　　　　　Institut Onkologii im. Petrova
Pesochnyy poselok,
Leningradskaya ul., 68
.... 237-89-94
Trauma and Orthopedic Institute
　Institut Travmatologii i Ortopedii im Vredena
Akademika Baykova ul., 8
.... 556-08-31

CITY HOSPITALS

Clinic General Hospital Mechnikova
　　Klinicheskaya Bolnitsa im. Mechnikova
Piskarevskiy pr., 47......... 543-94-46
Reception 543-03-01
No. 1 General Hospital Lenin
　　　　　Gorodskaya Bolnitsa No.1
V.O., Bolshoy pr., 85....... 217-26-31
Reception 217-54-98
No. 3 General Hospital
　　　　　Gorodskaya Bolnitsa No.3
Vavilovykh ul., 14........... 556-77-22
No. 4 General Hospital Karl Marks
　Gorodskaya Bolnitsa No.4 im. Karla Marksa
Severnyy pr., 1............... 511-99-63
No. 10 Hospital for Emergency Medicine
　　　　　Bolnitsa Skoroy Pomoshchi
Pionerskaya ul., 16.......... 235-71-13
No. 14 General Hospital Volodarsky
　　　　　Gorodskaya Bolnitsa No.14
　　　　　　im. M.M. Volodarskogo
Kosinova ul., 19 186-76-76
No. 15 General Hospital
　　　　　Gorodskaya Bolnitsa No.15
Avangardnaya ul., 4 135-96-97
No. 16 General Hospital Kuybyshev
　　　　　Gorodskaya Bolnitsa No.16
　　　　　　im. V.Y. Kuybysheva
Liteynyy pr., 56 278-89-24
No. 20 General Hospital
　　　　　Gorodskaya Bolnitsa No.20
Gastello ul., 21 108-48-08

MATERNITY HOSPITALS

ITUS Clinic & Maternity Hospital
Clinic Specializing in
Gynecology and Obstetrics
Large Modern Maternity Facilities
Outstanding Medical Staff
Tambasova ul., 21 130-27-13
Fax 130-27-14

Maternity Ward No.1　　Rodilnyy Dom
14-ya Liniya,19, Vasileostrovskiy District
Information 213-21-46
Maternity Ward No. 11　　Rodilnyy Dom
Lesozavodskaya ul., 10, Nevskiy District
Information 262-42-12
Maternity Ward No. 12　　Rodilnyy Dom
Kanonerskaya ul., 12, Oktyabrskiy District
Information 114-15-69
Maternity Ward No.13　　Rodilnyy Dom
Kostromskaya ul., 4, Smolninskiy District
Information 275-68-65
Maternity Ward No. 16　　Rodilnyy Dom
M. Balkanskaya ul., 54
Information 178-75-62
Maternity Ward No.2　　Rodilnyy Dom
Petra Lavrova ul., 36, Dzerzhinskiy District
Information 273-37-43

Maternity Ward No. 3   Rodilnyy Dom
Shchorsa pr., 13, Petrogradskiy District
Information 235-11-51

Maternity Ward No. 4   Rodilnyy Dom
Nab. Sverdlovskaya, 36,
Kalininskiy District
Information 225-06-86

Maternity Ward No. 5   Rodilnyy Dom
Marshala Govorova ul., 4, Kirovskiy
District
Information 183-55-00

Maternity Ward No. 6   Rodilnyy Dom
Mayakovskogo ul., 5, Kuybishevskiy
District
Information 272-47-24

Maternity Ward No. 7   Rodilnyy Dom
Tambasova ul., 21, Krasnoselskiy District
Information 130-84-65

Maternity Ward No. 9   Rodilnyy Dom
Ordzhonikidze ul., 47, Moskovskiy District
Information 126-87-31

OPHTHALMOLOGY HOSPITAL

No. 7 Ophthalmology General Hospital
Gorodskaya Oftalmologicheskaya
Bolnitsa No. 7
Mokhovaya ul., 38 272-35-80

MEDAKS
Kultury pr., 4................... 558-93-55
.... 558-97-21
.... 558-86-66

Center of Eye Microsurgery
Tsenter Mikrokhirurgii glaza
Yaroslava Gasheka ul., 3
.... 178-85-44
Liteynyy pr., 25 272-59-55

PSYCHIATRIC HOSPITAL

No. 2 Psychiatric General Hospital
Gorodskaya
Psikhiatricheskaya Bolnitsa No. 2
Nab. Reki Moyki, 126 114-10-83

SKIN AND VENEREAL HOSPITAL

No. 6 Skin and Venereal Disease
No. 6 Gorodskaya
Kozhno Venerologicheskaya Bolnitsa
Vosstaniya ul., 45........... 272-79-34

TRAVMA HOSPITAL

No. 31 Travmatology General Hospital
No. 31 Gorodskaya Bolnitsa
Krestovskiy Ostrov, Dinamo pr., 3
.... 235-12-02

TUBERCULOSIS HOSPITAL

No. 2 Tuberculosis
Gorodskaya Tuberkulyoznaya Bolnitsa
Toreza pr., 93 553-37-24

CHILDRENS CITY HOSPITALS
Detskie Gorodskie Bolnitsy

No. 1 Children's Hospital
(Highly recommended)
Detskaya bolnitsa No. 1
Avangardnaya ul., 14 135-12-07

No. 2 Children's Hospital Krupskoy
Detskaya bolnitsa No. 2 im. N.K.Krupskoy
V.O., 2-ya Liniya, 47 213-29-37

No. 6 Children's Hospital
Detskaya bolnitsa No. 6
Chaykovskogo ul., 73 273-38-66

No. 19 Children's Hospital Raukhfus
Detskaya bolnitsa No. 19 im. Raukhfusa
Ligovskiy pr., 8 277-79-00

☎ HOTELS
ОТЕЛИ
HOTELS
HOTELS
HOTELL

See also BED & BREAKFAST, MOTELS

For information and reservations, call the front desk, but if you have a problem, usually it is necessary to talk to the "Manager on duty", called the "Administrator".

Russian hotels vary greatly in quality and service. The Russian rating system for hotels is not the same as the Western system. A four star hotel rated in Russia is definitely a solid hotel but has a very different quality than a four-star hotel in London or Paris.

ASTORIA HOTEL

★★★★

A Very Elegant Hotel in the Old Tradition
In the heart of Saint Petersburg

Angleterre Bar, Angleterre Restaurant
Restaurant Christopher Columbus
Astoria Restaurant
Winter Garden Restaurant
Astoria Night Bar

InNis *Car Rentals, Fitness Center*
Sauna & Pool, Business Center,
Elegant **Astoria** *Shop*
The Astoria **International Shop**

Hairdresser's, bureau de change, clothing &, shoe repair, train & plane tickets, theater tickets, excursions.

Right on Saint Isaac's Square

Gertsena ul., 39 311-42-06
Astoria A...210-50-10
Astoria B...210-50-20
Fax 315-96-68
Telex ....121213 ASTOR SU
Restaurants.....................................210-59-06

Hrs: restaurant: 8-11:30, 12-11; grill bar: 8-11; sauna &
pool: 8-12, 3-8, night bar: 11-6
$, English, German,

Hotel Helen ★★★

On the beautiful Fontanka Canal
Convenient to center of city
Next to the Hotel Sovietskaya

Lermontovskiy prospect, 45/1

Restaurant Sovetskiy
The Night Bar at Hotel Helen
International Shop
Business Center & Communications

Administrator 251-61-01
Telex .... 121349 Helen, SU
Fax 113-08-59

Rest. Sovetskiy 12-23:30, rubles, Night Bar Helen
10- 2, $ & CC, English & Finnish

A Finnish-Russian Management Firm

International Seaman's Club
Nab. Griboedova, 166 114-54-52

KARELIYA

Tukhachevskogo ul., 27, bldg. 2

Inquiries Office 226-35-15
Restaurant 226-35-56
Director 226-32-77

*Restaurants, discotheque,
sauna, bureau de change. Beriozka shop, train &
plane ticket desk, clothing & shoe repairs, florist.*

Kievskaya

Dnepropetrovskaya ul., 49
St. Pb. 192007

Tel 166-04-56
Restaurant, clothing repairs, hairdressers.

Ladoga
Shaumyana pr., 26 528-56-28
*Restaurant, hairdressers
Metro: Krasnogvardeyskaya*

A Saint Petersburg Council for Tourism Hotel

Hotel Losevskaya

A Small Resort Hotel
on the beautiful Vuoksa Lakes
in Losevo Natural Park Reserve
on the Karelia Peninsula
"A vacation secret for nature lovers"
Pick berries & mushrooms and hike among
the birch & pine forests. Boat, kayak,
swim & fish on our lakes & rivers.

Hunting and fishing trips with skilled local
guides-interpreters
Boat excursions to Lake Ladoga
Restaurant, Bar, Sauna, Service Bureau
Less than two hours from St. Pb.

✉ 188724, Leningrad Oblast, Russia
Priozerskiy Rayon, Pos. Losevo
Tel ....(279) 6-72-29
English & Finnish, $ & Rubles

Hotel Mercury

A small fashionable hotel

Located near Tavricheskiy Park
and Smolnyy Cathedral

Favorite of executives & professionals
for its cozy homelike atmosphere

Large, comfortable 1 to 3 room suites

Bar-Restaurant & Winter Garden,
Two beautiful banquet rooms
All international communications
Audi cars & Ford mini-vans with drivers.

Tavricheskaya ul., 39 278-19-77
Fax 278-19-77

$, English

Mir (Tourist)
Gastello ul., 17, St. Pb. 196135
Director and Secretary 108-51-69
Administrator 108-51-66
Restaurant 108-51-62

Morskaya

Morskoy Slavy, 1
at the Head of the Harbor

Administrator 355-14-17
Service bureau................ 355-14-05

*Sauna, hairdresser, massage & make-up rooms,
clothing & shoe repair, dry-cleaning, hard-currency
Beriozka shop, theater ticket desk, excursion desk,
train & plane ticket desk.*

Moryakov
Gapsalskaya ul., 2
Info & Administrator........ 251-43-68
Director and Secretary 251-09-71

MOSKVA

Alexandra Nevskogo pl., 2
★★★

•**Plovdiv Restaurant and Bar,**

Director 274-21-00
Secretary 274-21-15
Inquiries 274-20-52
Restaurant 274-20-65
Business center 274-21-30
Tel. porter....................... 274-20-51
Telex .... 121669 INTER SU
Fax 274-21-30

*Sauna, currency exchange, duty-free shop,
clothing & shoe repairs, hairdresser's,
dry-cleaning, car rental, train & plane ticket desk,
theater ticket desk, excursion desk.
Metro: Pl. Aleksandra Nevskogo*

Na Sadovoy
Sadovaya ul., 53............. 314-43-88
Director 310-65-37

Neva
Chaykovskogo ul., 17
Information 278-05-04

Pulkovskaya
★★★★

• Meridian & Turku Restaurants & Bar

Pobedy pl., 1.................. 264-51-17

.... 264-50-22

.... 264-51-22

Telex ....121477 PULKA SU

Cafeteria, saunas, hairdresser's, duty-free shop, bureau de change, clothing & shoe repairs, dry-cleaning, florist, fax facilities, photocopying, car rental, train & plane ticket desk, excursion desk, theater ticket desk

Metro: Moskovskaya

Rechnaya

Obukhovskoy Oborony pr., 195

.... 267-31-96

Restaurant, hairdresser's, clothing & shoe repairs.
Metro: Proletarskaya

The Fural at the Hotel Rechnaya
A modest comfortable hotel

Obukhovskoy Oborony pr., 195

director 273-99-25

administrator.................. 262-84-00

Night Bar 17-23, Rubles and $

Russian-Liechtenstein Management Firm

Rossiya

Chernyshevskogo pl., 11

On Moskovskiy pr.

.... 296-76-49

.... 296-73-49

Restaurant, cafe, hairdresser's, clothing & shoe repairs, train & plane ticket desk, theater ticket desk, excursion desk.
Metro: Park Pobedy.

RETUR — Motel

On the beautiful Gulf of Finland

Cozy motel-hotel with 30 double rooms, TV, bath & phones

Comfortable 2-rm. cottages with bath

Breakfast, bar & restaurant, sauna, Russian baths

Heated swimming pool, tennis, Auto & caravan camping with hot showers 29 km from center on St. Pb.- Helsinki highway

Primorskoe Shosse, 29 km

.... 237-75-33

Fax................................ 273-97-83

Open 24 Hrs, $, English, German, Finnish

ST. PETERSBURG
★★★★

• Just across The Neva River from Summer Garden

• Restaurants (Petrovskiy & Zerkalnyy)

• Three night clubs, two pools, sport hall, Nab. Pirogovskaya, 5/2

Inquiries................................542-91-23

Secretary..............................542-91-01

Administrator 542-94-11

Restaurant 542-91-55

.... 542-91-21

.... 542-90-43

Fax................................... 542-90-42

Bars, hard-currency Beriozka shop, sauna, chauffeur-driven car for hire, bureau de change, duty-free shop, train & plane ticket desk, florist, clothing & shoe repair, dry-cleaning, theater ticket desk, concert hall, 2 conference halls.

Metro Station: Ploshchad Lenina.

Sovetskaya

Lermontovskiy pr., 43/1 ... 259-20-70

.... 259-25-52

.... 259-26-56

Restaurant, cafe, hairdresser's, clothing & shoe repairs, train & plane ticket desk, excursion desk.
Metro: Baltiyskaya

Hotel Sportivnaya

Deputatskaya ul., 34 235-02-36

HOTEL SPUTNIK
Most reasonable hotel in St. Pb.

A small, cozy, well-kept hotel In the NW quiet green zone

All rooms with bath, telephone, satellite TV
Restaurant, bar, Finnish Sauna
Small Conference Hall
Business Center
Single, double, & deluxe
Convenient to Metro.

Morisa-Toreza pr., 34 552-56-32

Fax 552-80-84

TELEX.......................... 121702 SAP SU

Rubles, English German

Turist Hotel

Sevastyanova ul., 3......... 297-81-93

Victoria Hotel   Victoriya-Otel

Khalturina ul., 22 ....No phone
Russian-American Joint Venture

Vyborgskaya
Torzhkovskaya ul., 3

Inquiries 246-23-19
Director......................... 246-36-22
Duty Administrator.......... 246-91-41
Restaurant..................... 246-91-19
*Restaurants, bar, clothing & shoe repairs,
hairdresser's, bureau de change, train & plane
ticket desk, theater ticket desk, car rental.
Metro: Chernaya rechka.*

Hotel Yuzhnaya
Rasstannaya ul., 26 166-10-88

☎ HOURS, SHOPS, WORK
ВРЕМЯ, ПРИЕМНЫЕ ЧАСЫ
ÖFFNUNGSZEITEN
HEURES
ÖPPETTIDER, AFFÄRER

See also HOLIDAYS and SCHOOLS

*Most organizations and institutes work
from 9 or 10 am to 6 pm and are usually
closed Saturdays and Sundays, although
some work Saturdays.*

*Most shops and many organizations
close for one hour in the middle of the
day for a lunch break (called "pereryv",
перерыв).*

*Many shops and public institutions,
such as museums, close one day per
month in addition to their regular closing.*

Shops: hours and days closed.

Bakeries
 Open every day, some closed Sunday
 Hrs: 7-8 am to 8 pm
Commercial Shops
 Closed Sunday and often Monday
 Hrs: 11 am to 8 pm
Gastronoms
 Closed Sunday
 Hrs: 9 am to 7-9 pm, break 1-2 pm
Milk, Fish, Meat
 Closed Sunday, some closed Saturday.
 Hrs: 9-10 am to 7-8 pm, break 1-2 pm
Shops selling clothing
   and manufactured goods
 Closed Sunday, some closed Monday.
 Hrs: 10-11 am to 7-8 pm, break 2-3 pm
Univermag
 Closed Sunday, some closed Monday.
 Hrs: 11 am to 8 pm
Universam
 Closed Sunday
 Hrs: 8 am to 9 pm, break 1-2 pm
International Shops
 See ads in INTERNATIONAL SHOPS

☎ HOUSE CLEANING
КВАРТИРЫ, УБОРКА
GEBÄUDEREINIGUNG
APPARTEMENTS, NETTOYAGE
STÄDNING, HUS

See APARTMENT CLEANING

☎ HOUSEWARES
ТОВАРЫ ДЛЯ ДОМА
HAUSHALTSWAREN
MENAGE, MARCHANDISES POUR
HUSHÅLLSARTIKLAR

See DEPARTMENT STORES

Metallicheskaya posuda
Nevskiy pr., 97 277-17-81

☎ HUNTING & FISHING
EQUIPMENT
ОХОТА И РЫБОЛОВСТВО, ТОВАРЫ
JAGEN UND FISCHEN
CLUBS DE CHASSE
JAKT OCH FISKEFORENINGAR

Hunting No. 1   Okhota
Liteynyy pr., 26 272-60-47
Fishing No. 12   Rybolovstvo
Moskovskiy pr., 37 292-58-33
Hunting and Fishing No. 17
     Okhota i Rybolovstvo
Nevskiy pr., 60 311-01-19
Fishing   Rybolov
Kirovskiy pr., 4 232-08-52

☎ HUNTING & FISHING
EXCURSIONS
ОХОТА И РЫБОЛОВСТВО,
ЭКСКУРСИИ
JAGD-UND ANGELVEREINE
CHASSEURS ET DE PECHEURS,
SOCIETES DE
JAKT OCH FISKEFÖRENINGAR

Hunting and Fishing Association of
    Leningrad voennyy okrug
Nab. reki Fontanki, 32......... 219-23-74
Buses 2,22,100; Trams 31,33,42

Leningrad Regional Council
DINAMO Society

Dinamo pr., 44 235-35-59
Buses; 71, 71A; Trams; 12,17,21,26,33,34

✦ ✦ VERSAM ✦ ✦

Game hunting and fishing
on beautiful Kolskiy Peninsula
400 km NW of St. Pb.

*Salmon, gorbushi, kymzhi, trout,
waterfowl, elk and bear in season*

Comfortable cabins in the wilderness
English speaking guides
✉ VERSAM, Rizhskaya ul., 16
Saint Petersburg, 195196, Russia
☎. 221-24-89
FAX ☎ 223-58-23

Baltic Service
St. Pb., 189623, P.O. 4 ... 555-99-22
Hunting & fishing trips near Rostov-upon-Don

Turbus
Sapernyy per., 16 273-00-67
Hunting in Leningrad region

☎ ICE CREAM
МОРОЖЕНОЕ
EISCAFÉS
GLACE
GLASS

Ice cream is popular in St. Petersburg and is sold on the street as well as in numrous ice cream cafes (cafe morozhenoe, кафе мороженное).

BASKIN-ROBBINS
Thirty-one flavors of ice cream
American Ice Cream
Nevskiy pr., 79 164-64-56
Hrs: 10-21, Rubles.

Chayka
Nab. kan. Griboedova, 14
.... 311-05-62
Gino Ginelli
Nab. kan. Griboedova, 14
.... 312-46-31
Kafe - Morozhenoe
Kirovskiy pr., 44 232-91-41
Kafe - Morozhenoe
Kirovskiy pr., 41 232-53-89
Kafe - Morozhenoe
Bukharestskaya ul., 31 174-41-68
Kafe - Morozhenoe
Blagodatnaya ul., 35 297-25-83
Kafe - Morozhenoe
Beloostrovskaya ul., 27 ... 245-51-11
Kafe - Morozhenoe
Ligovskiy pr., 57 164-83-49
Kafe - Morozhenoe
Dzerzhinskogo ul., 11 314-66-14
Kafe - Morozhenoe
Nevskiy pr., 100 279-33-11
Kafe - Morozhenoe
Nevskiy pr., 3 312-65-45
Kafe - Morozhenoe
Sredneokhtinskiy pr., 25
.... 224-08-95
Kafe - Morozhenoe
Sadovaya ul., 97 114-39-37
Kafe - Morozhenoe
V.O., 9-ya Liniya, 18 213-08-41
Kafe - Morozhenoe
Sadovaya ul., 33 310-82-31
Kafe - Morozhenoe
Potemkinskaya ul., 7 272-91-57

Kafe - Morozhenoe
Sadovaya ul., 27 310-06-38
Kafe - Morozhenoe
Nevskiy pr., 54 312-24-60
Kafe - Morozhenoe
Nevskiy pr., 154 277-07-25
Kafe - Morozhenoe
Nevskiy pr., 24 311-00-71

☎ INSTITUTES-RESEARCH
ИНСТИТУТЫ, НАУЧНО-
ИССЛЕДОВАТЕЛЬСКИЕ
FORSCHUNGSINSTITUTE
INSTITUTS
FORSKNINGSINSTITUT

See also UNIVERSITIES
St. Petersburg is a research center of Russia with almost 100 research institutes. In this category we list only those attached to the St. Pb. State University. For information on other institutes, call the Russian Academy of Sciences.

Russian Academy of Sciences
Rossiyskaya Akademiya Nauk
Nab. Universitetskaya, 5
.... 218-37-87

Religions Academy and Seminary
Dukhovnaya Akademia and Seminariya
Nab. kan. Obvodnogo, 17
.... 277-33-50
St. Petersburg State University Institutes and Facilities
Astronomy Observatory
Petrodvorets,
Bibliotechnaya pl., 2 428-71-29
Research Institute of the Mathematics Faculty
Petrodvorets,
Bibliotechnaya pl., 2 428-69-97
Research Institute for Applied Mathematics & Process Control
Petrodvorets,
Bibliotechnaya pl., 2 428-71-79
Research Institute for Physics
Petrodvorets,
Ulyanovskaya ul., 1 428-72-00
Research Institute for Mathematics and Applied Mechanics
Petrodvorets,
Bibliotechnaya pl., 2 428-69-44
Research Institute for Geography
V.O., Sredniy pr., 21 218-79-04
.... 213-90-23
.... 213-90-14
Earth's Crust Research Institute
Nab. Universitetskaya, 7/9
.... 218-97-75
Research Institute for Sociological Studies
Krasnaya ul., 60 311-84-45
Research Institute for Physiology named after Ukhtomskiy.
Nab. Universitetskaya, 7/9
.... 218-95-85

Research Institute for Chemistry
Petrodvorets,
Universitetskiy pr., 2 428-67-70
Research Institute for Biology
Petrodvorets
Oranienbaumskoe shosse, 2
.... 427-97-79
Scientific Construction Technological
               Bureau "Radiophisics"
Petrodvorets, Ulyanovskaya ul., 1, bldg. 1
.... 428-72-89

☎ INSURANCE
СТРАХОВАНИЕ
VERSICHERUNGEN
ASSURANCE
FÖRSÄKRINGAR

Asko-Petersburg Insurance Company
Gagarina pr., 1 297-83-33
.... 297-85-00
All types of Insurance for your needs.
Gosstrakh *All types of Insurance*
Zodchego Rossi ul., 1/3
.... 110-42-07
Ingosstrakh *Insurance in Hard Currency*
Kalyaeva ul., 17.............. 272-06-28
Progress
Vosstaniya ul., 18........... 275-61-70

ROSSIYA INSURANCE Co., Ltd.
Saint Petersburg Branch
Affiliate of Rossiya Insurance
Company, Ltd., Moscow
All forms of insurance
Automobile, medical, property & liability,
exhibition, transport & cargo insurance
for residents and foreigners.
Coverage in rubles and hard currency
Reinsurance with Francona, München
Rückversicherungs & others
Leninskiy pr., 115 153-91-08
.... 153-91-09
Fax.............................. 153-91-10
Hrs: 9:30- 17, English and German
Colonia (Germany) and leading Russian banks and
companies are our shareholders.

Rosmedpolis *Medical insurance*
Please call 130-27-13
Rus *Property and Life Insurance*
Smolnyy, Entrance 4, rm. 429
.... 278-11-16
.... 278-16-94

☎ INTERIOR DESIGNERS
ДИЗАЙНЕРЫ ПОМЕЩЕНИЯ
INNENAUSSTATTER
LOGEMENT AMENAGEMENT
HEMINREDNING

Decorative Arts Centre
Our master craftsmen will decorate your office,
exhibit, hotel or business interior with tapestry,
ceramics and more.
From single item to complete interior.
Morisa Toreza ul., 98 .. 553-98-50

Concern "Goryachev"
Interior Decorating
Designers & Producers
Furniture & Period Reproductions Chandeliers,
Decorative Wood Wall Paneling
Objects from Crystal, Bronze, Fine Woods

Retail Stores & Display Rooms
Vereyskaya ul., 39............... 112-75-96
Utochkina ul., 7.................. 301-73-75
Fax 311-95-76
Hrs: 10-20, $, English

Ecopolis
Interior Designers
Design and construction of interiors.
Contemporary, Saint Petersburg & Russian
International Fashion Center, Moscow, 1992
Saint Petersburg Radio & Television Centre
Designs for offices and apartments.
Zanevskiy pr., 32, Bldg. 2, No. 3528-26-66

Decorative Design Center
Rimskogo-Korsakova ul., 24/135
.... 114-37-66
Lenfor Enterprise
.... 554-47-00
Interior renovation of apartments & offices.
Malakhit
Bolshevikov pr., 33, bldg. 1
.... 586-63-88

ROSDESIGN
Custom works in colored glass by renown artists
at Baron Shtiglits Art Institute. Interior decorating
& custom pieces in metal, ceramics, & textiles
Solyanoy per., 13............. 279-41-96

☎ INTERNATIONAL SHOPS
ВАЛЮТНЫЕ МАГАЗИНЫ
VALUTALÄDEN
BOUTIQUES INTERNATIONALES
INTERNATIONELLA AFFÄRER,
VALUTAAFFÄRER

    International shops include those
shops that usually sell a selection of
imported goods only for hard currency.
The "hard currency only" status of many
of these shops is uncertain pending
implementation of the "transactions in
rubles only" rule on July 1. Increasingly,
shops sell imported goods for rubles as
well as dollars because of the increasing
legal convertibility of the ruble.
    Here we list those generalized
international shops selling everything from

souvenirs and cigarettes to liquors, imported foods, T-shirts and electronics in one shop.
We do NOT include here some specialized shops, such as PHARMACIES, RESTAURANTS, FOOD STORES, COMPUTERS, OFFICE EQUIPMENT, PHOTOCOPIERS, STATIONERY and ELECTRONICS shops, that may also sell only for hard currency. Please look under the category of goods or service that you want.

Aer Rianta International Ireland.
Fine international stores in St. Pb
AIRPORT SHOPS, ASTORIA FRONTIER SHOP, INTERNATIONAL SHOP/ASTORIA, BALTIC STAR NEVA STAR, SKYSHOP

The Alisa Trading House
Featuring Phillips electrical goods, radios and Televisions
Suvorovskiy pr., 2 277-01-25
Hrs: 10 a.m.-9 p.m.

The Astoria
The finest Russian porcelain, crystal and china, perfumes, elegant scarves, amber and gold jewelry, beautiful clothing
An Aer Rianta Store Block A.
At the Astoria Hotel
Gertsena ul., 39 210-63-51
Daily: 9.-21, $, MC, V, Amex, English

"BOSKO International Shop"
Imported clothing, electronics & food
Two locations in St. Petersburg
Nevskiy pr., 8 219-18-56
Zhukovskogo ul., 20 273-70-92
Hrs: 11-20. Rubles & $

The CASTOR Shop
Imported foods & delicacies clothing, shoes, TV, Stereos VCR
Nab. Makarova, 30 213-71-61
Metro: Vasileostrovskaya Hrs: 10-17, $, English

Gallery 102
Nevskiy pr., 102 273-68-42

The International Shop
at the Astoria
Selection of Stereo, TV, & Tape Players
Fine Liquors, Delicatessen, Candy
Conveniently located on St. Isaac's Sq.
An Aer Rianta Shop
At the Astoria Hotel Block B
At corner of Gogolya ul. & Isaakievskaya pl..
Tel 210-58-60
Daily: 9-21, $, English

Baltic Star
International Shopping
at the Pribaltiyskaya Hotel
Specializing in fashion, Levi's, electronics, cameras, film, tobacco, liquor, perfumes, jewelry, watches, gifts, confectionery, travel goods, toiletries, Russian champagnes, caviar, vodkas & souvenirs.
An Inturianta Shop
Korablestroiteley ul., 14
Hotel Pribaltiyskaya 356-41-85
Daily 8-23, $, CC, English

Beriozka Shops
Featuring the best Russian Handicrafts, Vodka, Cognac, and Souvenirs
Wide selection of imported goods.
Ten locations in St. Petersburg
Open: 10 a.m. - 19 a.m. Closed Sunday
• Gertsena ul., 26 314-66-37
   315-46-47
• Malookhtinskiy pr., 6 528-63-16
• Nevskiy pr., 7/9 315-51-62
• Nab. Morskaya, 15 (Opposite
   Hotel Pribaltiyskaya) 355-18-75
• Nab. Morskaya, 9 356-55-98
• Nalichnaya ul., 35/1 351-74-57
• At Kareliya Hotel
   Marshala Tukhachevskogo ul., 27
   226-32-37
• At Olgino Hotel and Campsite
   Primorskoe shosse, 59 ... 238-31-98
• At Sovetskaya Hotel
   Lermontovskiy pr., 43 . Please Come

Intershop
This is the Store Where You Can Find Absolutely Everything.
Pulkovskaya Hotel, Pobedy pl., 1
.... 264-51-15

Elka
Bakunina pr., 29 271-31-61
Fax 274-78-89

The Frontier Shop
At the Finnish-Russian Border. The shop offers a wide range of goods including liquor, perfumes, tobacco, soft drinks, delicatessen, leisure wear, fashion accessories, cameras and film, watches, jewelry, gifts and souvenirs
Town of "Torfyanovka"
on the Helsinki-St. Petersburg Road
Aer Rianta-Vyborg Town JV
Open: 8 am -12 pm daily

TRAVEL SHOP

Imported from Germany and Holland.
Sports clothing, leather jackets, shoes,
packaged foods, cosmetics, beer, liquor,
drinks, cigarettes, thermos, coffee
makers, small refrigerators, radios, etc.
Moskovskiy pr., 73 296-57-90
Metro: Frunzenskaya,
Hrs. 10-7 (Closed Sun & Mon), English, $

S V I T

Finest quality European shoes for family
Wholesale and retail
Sofiyskaya ul., 30 269-65-62
Hours: 10-19, Closed Sun. & Mon.

☎ **INTERPRETERS**
ПЕРЕВОДЧИКИ
ÜBERSETZERDOLMETSCHER
INTERPRETES
TOLKAR

See TRANSLATION SERVICES

☎ **INTOURIST**
ТУРИСТИЧЕСКИЕ АГЕНТСТВА
REISBÜROS
VOYAGES, AGENGES DE
INTOURIST

See TRAVEL AGENCIES

☎ **INTRODUCTION SERVICE**
ЗНАКОМСТВ, СЛУЖБА
BEKANNTSCHAFTEN
RENCONTRES, SERVICE DE
KONTAKTFÖRMEDLING

This category refers to Russian "dating
services" for singles to meet each other,
similar to those in Western countries.

NEVSKIE ZORI (Neva Dawns)
Partners for life.
Furmanova ul., 30 279-76-49
Hrs: 9-21

Noolis
Kamennoostrovskiy pr., 42
.... 230-75-35
Hrs: 9-21

Sintez 271-09-69

☎ **INVESTMENT BANK**
ИНВЕСТИЦИОННЫЙ БАНК
ANLAGEBANKEN
INVESTISSEMENTS, BANQUE D'
INVESTERINGSBANK

HOLDING
Investment Bankers
Saint Petersburg

• •

Investments
Industrial Plants
Office Buildings
Oil Refineries
New Companies
Conversion of
Military Plants
Marketing & Consulting
Services
Representation of
Foreign Companies
Establishment of Authorized
Dealers & Distributors

• •

Saint Petersburg 198188
Zaytseva ul., 41

Tel 184-68-66
Tel 184-68-88
Fax 184-89-23
Telex .... 621103 WNESH SU

☎ **INVESTMENT COMPANIES**
ИНВЕСТИЦИОННЫЕ КОМПАНИИ
ANLAGEGESELLESCHAFTEN
INVESTISSEMENTS,
COMPAGNIES D'
INVESTERINGSBOLAG

SCORPION
A FINANCIAL INVESTMENT COMPANY

Dealers in Investments ✦ Loans
Moscow & St. Pb Currency Exchanges
St. Petersburg Stock & Commodity Exchange

Founded by Bank Saint Petersburg
Sberbank and Unicombank
Nab. reki Fontanki, 70/72 219-80-37
.... 277-47-37
Fax 315-83-27

☎ **JAZZ**
ДЖАЗ
JAZZ
JAZZ
JAZZ

Jazz Philharmonic Hall

(Formerly Jazz Club)
David Goloshchekin's jazz band
Nightly programs starting at 8 pm
Jam sessions past midnight
on Friday & Saturday
Sunday matinee " Jazz for the Children"
Zagorodnyy pr., 27 164-85-65
.... 113-53-31

BUS 30, TRAMS 11,28,34, TROLLEYS 3,8,9,16, from
METRO: VLADIMIRSKAYA

Kvadrat Jazz Club
Pravdy ul., 10................. 164-56-83
Evening jazz concerts: call for schedule
Metro: Vladimirskaya

☎ **JEWELLERY**
ЮВЕЛИРНЫЕ ИЗДЕЛИЯ
JUWELIERE
BIJOUTERIES
SMYCKEN

RUSSIAN JEWELLERY ART

ANANOV

THE ANANOV COLLECTION
GOLDSMITHS

Jewellery in the Faberge Style

The Grand Hotel Europe
Mikhaylovskaya ul., 1/7 and Nevskiy
Daily from 10:00 to 20:00

Collection/Store........... 312-00-72, Ext./ 6522
Office/Secretary.............................235-42-51
Fax...230-17-18

$, English and French

Almaz
Veteranov pr., 87 150-82-38
Ametist
P.S., Bolshoy pr., 64 232-01-02

Aquamarine (Akvamarin)
Nab. Novosmolenskaya, 1
.... 352-07-66
Biryuza
Nevskiy pr., 69............. 312-21-76
Bramepton
Khalturina ul., 8.............. 311-88-51
Daimon
Utkin proezd, 8.............. 528-07-89
Granat
Bukharestskaya ul., 72, bldg. 1
.... 268-22-75
Iskorka
Ivanovskaya ul., 26........ 560-35-31
Izumrud (second hand shop)
Moskovskiy pr., 184........ 298-32-42
Jewellery hand made
P.S., Barmaleeva ul., 6 232-17-67
Polyarnaya Zvezda
Nevskiy pr., 158............. 277-09-80
Rubin
Stachek pr., 69 183-51-39
Russkie Samotsvety
Utkin proezd, 8.............. 528-06-31
Salon-skupka
Karla Marksa pr., 92........ 245-36-51
Sapfir
Engelsa pr., 15 550-00-88
Yakhont
Gertsena ul., 24.............. 314-64-47
Zhemchug
Slavy pr., 5.................... 261-37-20

☎ **KEROSENE**
КЕРОСИН
KEROSIN/PETROLEUM
KEROSENE
GASOL

*Kerosene is used in dachas and sold in
the suburbs. Try the local Russian
equivalent of a hardware-paint-dry goods
store (Khozyaystvennye tovary
Хозяйственные товары). Otherwise try
this store.*

Kerosene Store No. 90, Suburb of Pargolovo
Vokzalnaya ul., 2 594-89-69

☎ **KIOSKS**
КИОСКИ
KIOSKE
KIOSQUES
KIOSKER

*Outdoor kiosks are shops in small
cabins on the sidewalks, squares, markets
and around the metros of St. Petersburg
which sell almost anything from food and
drinks, and especially beer and vodka to
books and clothing. Russian newspapers
and some magazines are sold largely in
kiosks on the street and in hotels.
Magazines are usually sold in
Soyuzpechat, now called "Rospechat"*

See NEWSPAPERS, MAGAZINES

☎ KITCHEN APPLIANCES
БЫТОВЫЕ ПРИБОРЫ, КУХОННЫЕ
КÜCHENGERÄTE
CUISINE, INTRUMENTS DE
KÖKSAPPARATER

*For fans, small kitchen appliances,
vacuum cleaners, small appliances try*
ELECTRICAL GOODS SHOPS, HARDWARE
STORES *and* DEPARTMENT STORES.
*Large appliances (refrigerators, stoves,
freezers) are sold in special stores called
(Kholodilniki* Холодильники). *Imported
and Russian appliances are also available
in* COMMERCIAL STORES *and some*
INTERNATIONAL SHOPS. *Previously,
appliances had long waiting lists, but now
with higher prices, the availability has
improved. Air conditioners are scarce.*

*For information on cost and availability
of refrigerators in various appliance stores
in Saint Petersburg* 184-98-14

Kholodilniki No. 44
Dostoevskogo ul., 22 164-94-07
Kholodilniki No. 47
Karla Marksa pr., 80........ 245-27-68
Kholodilniki No. 48
Moskovskiy pr., 208........ 293-14-00
Kholodilniki No. 50
9-ya Sovetskaya ul., 11/13
.... 271-21-61

REPAIR OF REFRIGERATORS
Vera-Servis
Bukharestskaya ul., 116
.... 106-88-42
Repair & installation of refrigerators

☎ KITCHENWARE
ПРЕДМЕТЫ ДЛЯ КУХНИ
GESCHIRR
CUISINE, ARTICLES POUR
KÖKSTILLBEHÖR

*This category includes tableware, pots
& pans, dishes, teapots, etc. Most of these
items can be bought in the Russian
equivalent of a* HARDWARE *store and now in
some* COMMERCIAL STORES. *These are
specialized shops for tableware and small
appliances.*

Household goods
Domashnie prinadlezhnosti
Dzerzhinskogo ul., 45/38
.... 310-07-34
Khozyaystvennye tovary
Yakornaya ul., 1 224-38-03
Yakornaya ul., 2 224-34-86
Tableware and cookware
Metallicheskaya posuda
Nevskiy pr., 97............... 277-17-81
Tableware and cookware
Metallicheskaya Posuda
P.S., Bolshoy pr., 57 232-72-57
Hrs 10 - 19

Tableware & Chemicals (soap, cleaners)
Posuda, Khimiya
V.O. Bolshoy pr., 40/8..... 355-81-96
Hrs 10 - 19
Tableware **Posuda**
Mayorova ul., 18 314-81-48

☎ LANGUAGE COURSES
КУРСЫ ИНОСТРАННЫХ ЯЗЫКОВ
SPRACHKURSE
LANGUES, COURS DE
SPRÅKKURSER

*There are many opportunities to learn
languages in St. Pb. Private instructors
are hesitant to give their names and
addresses, but they have all been called.
Try them for private tutoring. The large
advertisers here are very professional firms.*

A. J. EST S.U.
Russian Language Tours
St. Petersburg, Moscow, Odessa
Profsoyuzov bul., 4, Entry. 6
.... 110-64-96
Telex.................. 121732 CGTT SU

AsLANTIS
A Consortium of Language Faculty
Flexible Programs with University Instructors
Let us arrange your Visa Support,
Accommodation and Cultural Program
⊠P.O. Box 398 St. Petersburg 196105
Tel 297-26-14
Fax/Tel. 298-90-07
We can answer your call in English.

Baltika Enterprise
Please call...................... 310-37-34
Courses in English, Finnish and French.
Company
Please call...................... 350-51-33
.... 350-45-42
Learn English in just 4 weeks.
Dar *Russian for foreigners*
Boytsova per., 4 273-51-28
Fax 113-58-96
Dialogue *Russian for foreigners*
Avangardnaya ul., 20, bldg. 1, apt. 31
.... 136 00 99
Globus
Kirovskiy pr., 21, rm. 122
.... 232-89-83
.... 232-31-31
Courses of foreign languages
(Including Russian)
Kursy inostrannykh yazykov
Moskovskiy pr., 173........ 242-07-27
LS- Language School
Moskovskiy pr., 1 310-58-28
Structured Courses

St. Petersburg State University
Russian Language Center
Nab. Universitetskaya, 7/9.
.... 213-32-56

Language Courses
P.S., Bolshoy pr., 73 232-00-26
Language Courses
Vitebskiy pr., 49 299-63-21
Language Courses
V.O., 14-ya Liniya, 29 218-44-62
Mercury School
Please call 298-19-53
OMIS
Mytninskaya ul., 19/48.... 233-17-85
Obuchenie
Zagorodnyy pr., 58 292-40-05
.... 292-38-61

SAINT PETERSBURG TRANSIT
Translators and Interpreters
English & European & Oriental Languages
Personalized Instruction in Russian
Let our staff introduce you to St. Pb.
Dumskaya ul., 3.................. 314-89-84
Tel. 555-55-54
Hrs: 10-22, Rbl. & $

Sileks
Volodi Ermaka ul., 9....... 290-62-61
.... 219-75-87
Fax................................ 110-68-82

Teks Center for Foreign Languages
Mayorova pr., 6.............. 315-73-88
Open: 10-19
2 to 3 month courses offered in English, German,
Swedish and Spanish.

VNESHVUS-CENTRE 〰

Russian Language Courses
Special courses for business & academics
Survival Russian in Two Weeks
Large library for teaching
Write to: Post Office Box 14
199226 Saint Petersburg Russia
V.O., Nab. Morskaya, 9.................356-99-05
Fax 355-69-87
English, German, Finnish & Others

☎ **LAUNDROMATS**
СТИРАЛЬНЫЕ АВТОМАТЫ
WASCHAUTOMATEN/
WASCHMASCHINEN
LAVOIRS
TVÄTTOMATER

St. Petersburg has had Laundromats
with self-service for years. See below.

☎ **LAUNDRY/DRY CLEANING**
ПРАЧЕЧНЫЕ, ХИМЧИСТКА
WÄSCHEREIEN/CHEM. REIN.
BLANCHISSERIE
NETTOYAGE A SEC,
TVÄTT/KEMTVÄTT

See also DRY CLEANING. Laundry can
be a problem for travelers. Do it yourself
like many Russians, ask at hotel, or entrust it
to the 210 "municipal laundries" listed in
the Short Leningrad Telephone Book 1991.
There are also three self-service laundromats
and dry-cleaning in St. Petersburg. For an
update on Laundromats, call the Central
Administration of Laundries at
.... *239-41-69*
One laundry with an excellent reputation
in the diplomatic community is the following:

Dry Cleaning
Moiseenko ul., 24 271-29-06
Metro: Pl. Vosstaniya

Laundry & Dry Cleaning
Tramvaynyy pr., 14......... 254-83-41

Laundries with self-service laundromats &
dry-cleaning: Hrs: 8-21, M-F, some Sat.
Izmaylovskiy pr., 12 292-33-41
Metallistov pr., 73........... 540-19-35
Zanevskiy pr., 37............. 528-84-19

☎ **LAW COURTS**
СУДЫ
GERICHTE
PALAIS DE JUSTICE
RÄTTSSAL

City Court of Saint Petersburg
Gorodskoy Sud
Nab. reki Fontanki, 16
Secretary....................... 273-07-52
Regional Court of Leningrad Oblast
Oblastnoy Sud
Nab. reki Fontanki , 16
Chief Judge 273-08-26

☎ **LAW FIRMS & LAWYERS**
ЮРИДИЧЕСКИЕ ФИРМЫ И
ЮРИСТЫ
RECHTSANWÄLTE UND NOTARE
NOTAIRES
ADVOKATBYRÅ, ADVOKAT

There are many types of lawyers in
Russia. In particular jurists who provide
legal advice, register firms and draw up
contracts, and advokats who try cases
before a court of law. There are many
new private lawyers and law firms as well
as the traditional "official legal consultation
groups". We have listed Russian law
firms and lawyers, the legal consultation
groups, western law firms, and selected
western law firms in Moscow.

Russian law firms & Lawyers

ABC
Sadovaya ul., 55/57, rm. 505
.... 310-84-36
.... 315-77-14

AVIL law firm
P.S., Bolshoy pr., 64, flr. 5
.... 235-66-15
Fax............................... 235-66-15

Arnold
Novgorodskaya ul., 27..... 271-20-21
Fax............................... 312-43-74
Telex .... 121345 PTB SU ARNOLD

The Law Firm "AZ St. Petersburg"
Alekseev and Zagaraev
Complete registration of new enterprises
Legal consultation and contracts
Representation in arbitrage and courts
Krasnoputilovskaya ul., 5
.... 275-45-64

English Spoken

Balfort
Bolshoy Smolenskiy pr., 36
.... 568-04-91
.... 568-04-93

BAZIS
Legal advise given to those who form
companies, corporations and joint ventures.
Nab. reki Fontanki, 44 ... 310-39-59
Open: 11-17

Inaudit AKG
Rakova ul., 33................ 311-19-49
.... 310-53-11
.... 311-61-53
Fax............................... 310-53-33

Konkord
Antonenko per., 2, apt. 10
.... 314-05-54

Kokuroshnikov, Evgeniy Vladislavovich
Private specialist of law
Please call 557-96-14
Hrs: 8-20, German

Legal Consultation
Toreza pr., 2/40.............. 247-60-01
.... 550-16-05

TYP *FOR AN EXCITING EVENING OUT*
Look under
NIGHTTIME ENTERTAINMENT
Page 156

LEGIS law firm
Legal consulting
Experienced in registration of firms
Nab. reki Moyki, 48........ 311-60-95
Fax............................... 312-42-16
Telex....................... 121638 KIT SU
German

Onega
Liteynyy pr., 62, apt. 3.... 168-68-84
Mon - Wed 10-12; Thurs - Fri 15-17

NEVINPAT
St. Petersburg International
Patent
and Trade Mark Agency
Complete assistance with
patent, trademark, and design
Registration, Searches
Patent & Trademark Infringement
Ligovskiy pr., 87 164-45-91
Fax...164-74-04
English, German, Finnish
A Russian-Finnish Law Firm

Poverennyy
Moskovskiy pr., 18
.... 292-31-27
Fax............................... 296-67-45
Correspondent relations with leading law firms
in Western Europe and North America.
Arbitrage, Contracts, Registration
Court Representation

Prizma
Primorskiy pr., 6, rm. 9 239-97-59
Fax 239-97-58

Lawer Michael S. Aksenov
Please call....................... 427-78-09

Lawer Alexander V. Savochkin
Please call....................... 225-00-71

NATARI
Business law consultants
Contract law, tax advice & customs
Full registration with all documents
Antonenko per., 5........... 315-93-82

Regionalnoe Ekspertnoe Agenstsvo
Sofi Perovskoy ul., 14 315-96-30

ROSINTEX INTERNATIONAL Ltd.
Specializing in Business Law
Full registration of new firms • Ownership
Privatization • Taxation • Export-import • Contracts
Nab. kan. Obvodnogo, 93A, rm. 54
Tel...210-13-96
Fax...210-13-96
Hrs: 9:30-18:00, Closed Sat & Sun, English

Sodruzhestvo
  Rubinshteyna ul., 3 315-18-34

Yuriskon
  Plekhanova ul., 36 312-78-92
  Fax 311-78-50
IKR
  Please call 235-39-14
Yurisconsult
  Please call 275-05-55
          Hrs: 10-18
Romviks
  Admiralteyskiy pr., 6, apt. 415 ....
  312-86-10

SEMI-OFFICIAL LEGAL ORGANIZATIONS
Foreign Legal Colloquium
Kollegiya Inostrannaya Yuridicheskaya
  Pushkinskaya ul., 13 112-02-61
  112-08-39
  112-16-79
Presidium Of The City Court
  Nab. reki Fontanki, 16 272-61-73
Kollegiya Advokatov
  Nevskiy pr., 53 113-15-89
Kollegiya Advokatov
  Nevskiy pr., 16 312-81-36
Saint-Petersburg Bar Association
  Sadovaya ul., 32/1,
  enter on Apraksin per. 315-85-10
CITY LEGAL CONSULTATION OFFICE
Yuridicheskaya Konsultatsiya
  Ligovskiy pr., 31 277-54-32
          For Foreign Customers. English
Yuridicheskaya Konsultatsiya
  Moiseenko ul., 2 271-74-74
Yuridicheskaya Konsultatsiya
  P.S., Bolshoy pr., 33-a..... 232-41-11
Yuridicheskaya Konsultatsiya
  Obukhovskoy Oborony pr., 90
  567-54-82
Yuridicheskaya Konsultatsiya
  Moskovskiy pr., 127........ 298-70-55
Yuridicheskaya Konsultatsiya
  Gogolya ul., 9 312-24-95
Yuridicheskaya Konsultatsiya
  Nevskiy pr., 74............... 273-56-52
Yuridicheskaya Konsultatsiya
  Sredneokhtinskiy pr., 12.. 224-05-90
Yuridicheskaya Konsultatsiya
  Baltiyskaya ul., 3 252-63-67
Yuridicheskaya Konsultatsiya
  Komsomola ul., 10 542-22-87

Yuridicheskaya Konsultatsiya
  Karla Marksa pr., 88....... 245-89-82
Yuridicheskaya Konsultatsiya
  Kolpino, Vokzalnaya ul., 14
  484-50-90
Yuridicheskaya Konsultatsiya
  Bolshoy pr., 61 213-50-00
Yuridicheskaya Konsultatsiya
  Truda pl., 4.................... 219-82-58
Yuridicheskaya Konsultatsiya
  Zagorodnyy pr., 22 164-96-26
Yuridicheskaya Konsultatsiya, No. 10
  Liteynyy pr., 33 272-82-56
Yuridicheskaya Konsultatsiya, No...... 17
  Mayorova pr., 41 314-80-27

Western Law Firms in Moscow

APCO .... (095) 333-90-70
Baker and McKenzie
  Bolshoy Gnezdnikovskiy pr., 7
  .... (095) 200-49-06
  .... (095) 200-61-67
  Fax .... (095) 200-02-03
Chadbourne & Parke
  Krasnopresnenskaya ul., 12
  Mezhdunarodnaya ul., II, apt. 1421
  .... (095) 253-14-21
  Fax .... (095) 253-16-00
Coudert Brothers
  Petrovka ul., 15, apt. 19-20
  .... (095) 928-78-38
  .... (095) 923-93-30
  Fax .... (095) 200-02-68
Leboeuf, Lamb, Leiby & Macrae,
c/o USCO
  Chaykovskogo ul., 5
  .... (095) 135-13-02
  Fax .... (095) 230-21-01
Steptoe and Johnson
  c/o USCO .... (095) 255-48-48
White & Case
  Tverskaya ul., 7, entre 7
  .... (095) 201-92-92
  .... (095) 201-92-96
  Fax .... (095) 201-92-84
Vnesheconomservis
  Ilinka ul., 6............. (095) 259-37-53
Inyurcollegiya
  Tverskaya ul., 5...... (095) 203-68-64
Moscow Legal Collegium
  Pushkinskaya ul., 6, 7
  .... (095) 229-90-33
  .... (095) 229-90-07

☎ **LEATHER GOODS**
   КОЖАНЫЕ ИЗДЕЛИЯ
   LEDERWAREN
   CUIR, ARTICLES DE
   LÄDERVAROR

See LUGGAGE.

☎ LIBRARIES
БИБЛИОТЕКИ
BIBLIOTHEKEN
BIBLIOTHEQUES
BIBLIOTEK

See also UNIVERSITIES

Academy of Sciences Library
Birzhevaya Liniya, 1 218-35-92
Agricultural Library
Gertsena ul., 42 314-49-14
Library of the Blind
Shamsheva ul., 8............ 232-71-07
Library of the Academy of Arts
Nab. Universitetskaya, 17
.... 213-65-29
.... 213-71-78
Lunacharskiy Theater Library
Zodchego Rossi ul., 2.... 311-08-45
Mayakovskiy Central City Library
Nab. reki Fontanki, 44 311-30-26
Medical Scientific Library
Lunacharskogo pr., 45..... 592-71-43
Pushkin Central City Children's Library
Gertsena ul., 33 232-41-29
Russian National Library
Sadovaya ul., 18 310-28-56
.... 310-71-37
St. Petersburg State
University Libraries
Nab. Universitetskaya, 7/9
.... 218-27-51
*Each department (Faculty) has its own
specialized library. Call the department.*
Hrs: 11 - 17, Closed Sat, Sun

☎ LIGHTING FIXTURES/ BULBS
ОСВЕЩЕНИЕ/ЛАМПЫ
LAMPEN/BELEUCHTUNG
FIXATION D'ELIATRAGE
LYSE/LAMPOR

See also ELECTRONIC GOODS.

*Remember that electricity is 220 volt,
50 Hz and is not compatible with US
standards. The following shops are
centrally located and usually have a good
selection of lamps and lighting fixtures.*

OGONEK (A little light)...........Огонёк
Novocherkasskiy pr., 51 221-14-12

Svet (Light)
Moskovskiy pr., 163........ 298-37-57

Elektrotovary No. 139
Pestelya ul., 10/23.......... 272-89-09
Elektrotovary No. 129
Liteynyy pr., 27.............. 272-45-98
Elektrotovary "Luch" No. 132
Sredneokhtinskiy pr., 48
.... 227-39-21
Elektrotovary No. 164
Nevskiy pr., 65............... 311-04-45

☎ LIMOUSINE SERVICE
ЛИМУЗИНЫ
LIMUSINENDIENST/
AUTOVERMIETUNG
LIMOUSINES, SERVICE DE
LIMOUSINESERVICE

See also AUTOMOBILE RENTAL and TAXI.

*All levels of comfort and luxury in
chauffeured automobiles are readily
available at all in St. Petersburg. Service
is offered by private individuals with a
little old Moskvich and by firms with
elegant stretch Volvos & Mercedes. Most
car rentals in St. Pb. come with a driver.*

INTERAUTO - Hertz Int.Lic.
*Large selection of cars & minibuses with
or without drivers. Reservations at the
Grand Europe & Moscow Hotels*
Ispolkomovskaya ul., 9/11 277-40-32
Complete 24 hrs service $, English

MATRALEN
TAXI & LIMOUSINE
At the Hotel Pulkovskaya
Featuring FORD automobiles & mini-vans
Lyubotinskiy proezd, 5..... 298-36-48
.... 298-12-94
Fax................................ 298-00-73
Telex............... 121028 MATRA SU
24 Hours Daily, $, English, German

Concern SOPPOL
LIMOUSINE & TRANSPORT
Transport of passengers & valuable cargoes
Experienced drivers with modern mini-vans
anywhere in Russia, Baltics & CIS
Within 24 hour notice
2-ya Krasnoarmeyskaya ul., 7
Tel..110-12-09
24 hours/day, $ & rubles, English

TAXI
At Pribaltiyskaya Hotel
Taxi and Limousine Service
24 Hours/Day,
Featuring Fords
Korablestroiteley ul., 14
Dispatcher 356-93-29
Director......................... 356-10-74
Fax................................ 356-00-94
Fax................................ 356-38-45
$, English, German, Finnish

☎ LINENS
БЕЛЬЕ, МАГАЗИНЫ
LEINENWÄSCHE
LINGES
LINNE

See DEPARTMENT STORES

☎ LINGERIE
БЕЛЬЕ ДЛЯ ЖЕНЩИН
DAMENUNTERWÄSCHE
LINGERIE
UNDERKLÄDER, DAM

See also DEPARTMENT STORES and
CLOTHING WOMEN'S

☎ LIQUOR/SPIRITS
КРЕПКИЕ НАПИТКИ
ALKOHOLISCHE GETRÄNKE
ALCOOL
ALKOHOL

See ALCOHOL/OFF-LICENSE

☎ LOCKSMITHS
СЛЕСАРНЫЕ РАБОТЫ
SCHLOSSEREIEN
SERRURIER
LÅSSMEDER

See also APARTMENT REPAIR.

Locksmith service is proved by municipal organizations called PREO and REU (ПРЭО и РЭУ) which provide a variety of repair services such as plumbing, electrical, redecorating and locksmithing to a very specific region of the city. Service is variable. There are a number of other organizations and private cooperatives providing such services also.

Elton
   Please call 538-24-26
   260-51-88
Bikar
   Mayorova pr., 16 274-42-91
Petersbuskie Zori (municipal)
   Nevskiy pr., 93............... 277-17-17
   277-45-47
Slesarnye raboty
   Nekrasova ul., 60 279-26-76
Usluga
   Lermontovskiy pr., 1 114-49-01

☎ LOST PROPERTY
СТОЛЫ НАХОДОК
FUNDBÜROS
OBJETS TROUVES, BUREAU DES
FÖRLORAD EGENDOM

Stol Nakhodok
   Sredniy pr., 70 213-00-39
Stol Nakhodok
   Kalyaeva ul., 19............. 278-36-90

☎ LUGGAGE
БАГАЖ
GEPÄCK
BAGAGE
RESVÄSKOR

See also DEPARTMENT STORES and
SPORTS EQUIPMENT

Luggage, briefcases and leather goods are bought in special TRAVEL SHOPS, DEPARTMENT STORES, SPORT EQUIPMENT SHOPS and in DLT, Tsentr Firmennoy Torgovli.

Gostinyy Dvor
   On the 1st floor on the Sadovaya Line and Perinnaya Line.

Tovary v dorogu (Travel Shop)
   Nevskiy pr., 114 273-31-38
Tourist (goods for travelers)
   Nevskiy pr., 122 277-02-79
   Kondratevskiy pr., 33 540-13-94

☎ MAGAZINES
ЖУРНАЛЫ
ZEITSCHRIFTEN
MAGAZINES
MAGASIN, VECKO-OCH
MÅNADSTIDNINGAR

WHERE TO BUY FOREIGN MAGAZINES

Imported magazines and newspapers are sold in hotels, bookstores and selected kiosks, often for foreign currency.

WHERE TO BUY RUSSIAN MAGAZINES

Russian newspapers are sold largely in kiosks on the street and in hotels. Magazines are sold in Rospechat, (Роспечать) stores.

You can receive information on any newspaper or magazine of Rospechat by calling:
   Commercial Department... 315-44-78
The following shops specialize in selling Russian periodicals.

Rospechat No. 2
   Suslova ul., 15 152-00-91
Rospechat No. 6
   Nab. kan. Griboedova, 27
   311-70-58

Rospechat No. 7
Ligovskiy pr., 107 164-34-83
Rospechat No. 8
Nauki pr., 42 249-09-00
Rospechat No. 11
Bukharestskaya ul., 72, bldg. 1
.... 268-08-57
Rospechat No. 12
Ligovskiy pr., 34 164-66-24
Rospechat No. 13
Veteranov pr., 78 150-61-48
Rospechat No. 17
Dekabristov ul., 36 114-48-28
Rospechat No. 23
Moskovskiy pr., 73 252-64-08
Rospechat No. 28
Ligovskiy pr., 171 166-11-51
Rospechat No. 27
Nab. reki Moyki, 32 312-77-25
Rospechat No. 18
Mayakovskogo ul., 23 272-80-65
Rospechat
Zhukovskogo ul., 4 273-65-18
Rospechat No. 5
V.O., Bolshoy pr., 72 217-25-22
Rospechat No. 19
Mira pl., 5 315-60-80
Rospechat No. 21
Rubinshteyna ul., 10 311-44-12
Rospechat No. 24
Razezzhaya ul., 16/18 312-95-00

Economic press

MAGAZINES WITH OFFICES IN ST. PB.

The following magazines have offices in St. Petersburg.

Ars
Nevskiy pr., 179 274-36-64
.... 274-25-20
Amour
Pochtamtskaya ul., 5/30 311-63-19
Aurora
Khalturina ul., 4 312-13-23
Literary, artistic, social & political

Florman Information Russia
Publisher
Saint Petersburg News
Kirovskiy pr., 14 B 233-76-82
Fax 232-80-17
Telex 121609

Lenizdat
Nab. reki Fontanki, 59 310-53-72
Leningradskaya Panorama
Nevskiy pr., 53 113-15-23
.... 113-13-28

Lvinyy most
Ligovskiy pr., 253, apt. 2
.... 166-37-96
Neva
Nevskiy pr., 3 312-65-37
New Times international
Pochtamtskaya ul., 5/30
.... 311-63-19

Delovye Lyudi Press-Contact
Business in Russia
M. Novikova ul., 10/1, rm. 11
Moscow 333-33-40
Fax 330-15-68

Petersburg News
Kirovskiy pr., 14 B 233-76-82
Russkaya Literatura
Nab. Makarova, 4 218-16-01
Shop-talk
Pochtamtskaya ul., 5/30 .. 311-63-19
St. Petersburg
Pestelya ul., 4 275-64-06
Sudostroenie (Shipbuilding)
Promyshlennaya ul., 14a
.... 186-16-09

SANTA LTD Advertising Agency
Publisher of
St. Petersburg
Today & Tonight
For visitors to Saint Petersburg
Quarterly in English and German
Nab. Makarova, 30 279-73-29

Top-Shyly (for children)
Pushkinskaya ul., 10, apt. 123
.... 164-57-07
Zvezda (Star)
Mokhovaya ul., 20 272-89-48

☎ **MAP SHOPS**
КАРТЫ, МАГАЗИН
LANDKARTEN
CARTES, MAGASINS DE
KARTOR
КАРТЫ
LANDKARTEN
MAGASINS DE CARTES
KARTHANDLARE

Several good maps of St. Petersburg in Russian are available at street kiosks There is an inexpensive "Tourist Map of "Leningrad", list Maps and a "One Day in St. Petersburg" map for dollars in some hotels. The best map in English (and German) is our map "The Travellers Yellow Pages City Map of Saint Petersburg 1992", described below.

Dom Knigi
Nevskiy pr., 28 219-94-45

☎ MARKETS
(Farmer's Markets, Kolkhoz Markets)
РЫНКИ
MÄRKTE
MARCHES
LIVSMEDELSÄFFARER

See also FOOD STORES
The lively farmers' markets, sometimes referred to as "collective farm markets or kholkhoz markets", have fruits, vegetables, meat, sausage, cheese, milk, honey, eggs, jams, preserves, and flowers, baked goods and more. Locally they are called a "rynok" (РЫНОК).

All St. Petersburg's Markets Are Open 8:00 To 19:00 (except Monday)

Kirovskiy Rynok (market)
Stachek pr., 54 184-84-01
Metro: Kirovskiy zavod

Kondratevskiy/Kalininskiy Rynok (market)
Polyustrovskiy pr., 45...... 540-30-39
Metro: Ploshchad Lenina
Kuznechnyy Rynok (market)
Kuznechnyy per., 3 312-41-61
Metro: Vladimirskaya
Moskovskiy Rynok (market)
Reshetnikova ul., 12........ 298-11-89
Metro: Elektrosila
Nekrasovskiy Rynok (market)
Nekrasova ul., 52............ 279-25-83
Metro: Ploshchad Vosstaniya
Nevskiy Rynok (market)
Obukhovskoy Oborony pr., 75a
.... 265-38-89
Sennoy Rynok (market)
Moskovskiy pr., 4/6 310-02-17
Metro: Ploshchad Mira
Sytnyy Rynok (market)
Sytninskaya pl., 3/5 233-22-93
Metro: Gorkovskaya
Torzhkovskiy Rynok (market)
Torzhkovskaya ul., 20 246-83-75
Metro: Chernaya Rechka
Vasileostrovskiy Rynok (market)
V.O., Bolshoy pr., 16....... 213-66-87
Metro: Vasileostrovskaya

☎ MARRIAGE BUREAU (ZAGS)
ЗАГСЫ
STANDESÄMTER
MARIAGE, BUREAU DE L'ETAT CIVIL
ÄKTENSKAP, REGISTRERING

These "Marriage Bureaus" are really "Registration Offices of Vital Statistics: Marriages, Births, Deaths and Divorces". But the registration of marriages gives them their image as a marriage bureau.

Marriage Bureau No. 1
Nab. Krasnogo Flota, 28
.... 314-98-48
Marriage Bureau No. 2
Petra Lavrova ul., 52 273-73-96
Marriage Bureau No. 3
(only ZAGS for foreigners)
Nab. Petrovskaya, 2........ 232-82-37
.... 233-07-43

☎ MASSAGE
МАССАЖ
MASSAGE
MASSAGE
MASSAGE

See also MEDICAL CARE & CONSULTATIONS and HEALTH CLUBS.
The health clubs in most hotels offer massage.
Massazh
Kositskaya Mariya Alekseevna
please call...................... 350-28-83
all types of massage

☎ MAYOR'S OFFICE
МЭРИЯ
BÜRGERMEISTERAMT
MAIRIE
BORGMÄSTARADMINISTRATIONEN

See ST. PETERSBURG CITY
GOVERNMENT, THE MAYORS OFFICE

☎ MEASURES
РАЗМЕРЫ (Единицы измерения)
MASSEINHEITEN
MESURAGE
ENNETER MÄTNINGEN

For TABLES OF MEASURES, WEIGHTS
and SIZES, *see pages 242-245.*

☎ MEDICAL ASSISTANCE
МЕДИЦИНСКАЯ СКОРАЯ
ПОМОЩЬ
ERSTE HILFE
MEDECINE, ASSISTANCE
MEDICALE
SJUKVÅRD

See EMERGENCY MEDICAL CARE,
MEDICAL CARE AND CONSULTATIONS,
HOSPITALS, DENTISTS, MEDICAL
INSTITUTES.

AMBULANCE................. 03

☎ MEDICAL CARE & CONSULTATIONS
ЗДРАВООХРАНЕНИЕ И
МЕДИЦИНСКИЕ
КОНСУЛЬТАЦИИ
ARZTBESUCHE,
MEDIZINISCHEVERSORGUNG
SOINS MEDICAUX
CONSULTATIONS MEDICALES
SJUKVÅRD, MEDICINSKA
KONSULTATIONER

See also DENTISTS, EMERGENCY
MEDICAL CARE, HOSPITALS,
MEDICAL INSTITUTES.

*Medical consultations are at Policlinics
similar to an "official" medical group for
outpatient care. The best known is
Policlinic #2, which used to be the clinic
for foreign diplomats, visitors and Russian
officials and executives. There are now a
large number of cooperative medical
groups, and newly independent hospitals
and policlinics offering similar services.*

TESTS
AIDS Test
    Mirgorodskaya ul., 3........ 277-56-71
Radioactivity Tests of Food
    4-ya Sovetskaya ul., 5-a
    277-52-92

PHYSICIANS AND DOCTORS

Sergey Victorovich Melnik, MD
Specialist in Internal and Family Medicine
At Your Home or Hotel
Asafeva 2, Bldg. 2, Apt. 38
Tel...................... 513-25-35
Hrs: 8-24, German & English

Family Doctor
    Please call...................... 513-25-35
    Heart diseases, lungs, gastroenterology
Neuropathologist for children
    Belousova Nina Vasilyevna
    Please call...................... 273-71-68
Family Doctor
    Pozdnyakova Ludmila Vasilevna
    Please call...................... 135-09-67
Pediatrician
    Surovtseva Alla Pavlovna
    235-18-20
Professor- Neuropathologist
    Please call...................... 552-79-50
    247-25-39
    Consultations, advice's, new methods
Registered Nurse & Massage
    Please call...................... 350-28-83
        All types of Massages
Urologist
    Please call...................... 157-13-32
Consultations, treatment in office & at home

OBSTETRICS AND GYNECOLOGY

ITUS Clinic & Maternity Hospital

*Clinic Specializing in
Gynecology and Obstetrics
Large Modern Maternity Facilities
Outstanding Medical Staff*
    Tambasova ul., 21 130-27-13
    Fax 130-27-14

Lider
    Kostyushko ul., 2 293-80-65
WOMEN'S CLINICS

Zhenskaya Konsultatsiya No. 2
    Pestelya ul., 25 272-82-23
Zhenskaya Konsultatsiya No. 3
    Nab. reki Fontanki, 155 ... 114-29-58
Zhenskaya Konsultatsiya No. 30
    Mayakovskogo ul., 5 272-00-69
Zhenskaya Konsultatsiya No. 35
    2-ya Sovetskaya ul., 4..... 273-42-58

MEDICAL GROUPS AND CLINICS

Center for Microsurgery
Saint Petersburg
A private medical group

Hand surgery, plastic & reconstructive surgery. treatment of trauma and limb illnesses, fractures, battle injuries

Modern equipment, latest techniques, Highly experienced orthopedic and microsurgeons

Stay in private & semi-private rooms in one of the best hospitals in St.-Pb.

⊠ Kultury pr., 4, St. Pb. 194291

Duty Doctor	558-88-71
Chief Surgeon	558-85-17
Fax	559-9673

MEDELEN
Dialysis center
for patients on holiday
in Saint Petersburg

L. Tolstogo ul., 17	234-50-01
Fax	234-54-78

St. Petersburg Policlinic No. 2
An Independent Medical Group
World renown for its 25 years of service to diplomats & visitors to St. Pb.
Leading medical specialists in internal medicine, cardiology, urology, surgery, pediatrics, orthopedics, gynecology, & other fields.

Complete Western Pharmacy
Wide selection of Western drugs, antibiotics, cortisone, vitamins, personal hygienic products.

Modern x-ray, EKG, & labs

Dental clinic *with highly trained dentists and Finish equipment*

Highest sanitary standards *with all disposable syringes, etc.*

Clinic hours: M-F, 9:00 to 21:00
Sat. 9:00 to 15:00

24-hour emergency coverage
House calls at your home or hotel
Well-equipped ambulance

Moskovskiy pr., 22	292-62-72
24 hours around the clock	
	110-11-02
Fax	292-59-39

New Way

Rentgena ul., 4	232-41-60
	234-47-08

SPORTS MEDICINE CLINIC
Physical Therapy Specialists
Personal programs for injury rehabilitation, therapy and physical fitness.

Cardiac and physical fitness evaluation

Swedish and Eastern Massage, Hydrotherapy, ultrasound & electrotherapy

Neck and Back Therapy Programs

Facilities include swimming pools, universal exercise & weight room,

Large Experienced Staff of MD's, PT's & Chiropractors

Rentgena ul., 12	232-25-49
	232-43-85

Hrs: 9-16, $ & Rubles, English, German, Spanish

MEDIKORT
MEDICAL GROUP
Gynecology, Internal Medicine, Nervous Disorders, Ears, Nose, Throat
General & Urgent Surgery
New German Equipment
Comfortable Well-Run LOMO Hospital
Specialists From
Military Medical Institute, 1st Medical Institute, Institute for Post-Graduate Studies in Medicine

1st Surgical Department, LOMO Hospital, Chugunnaya ul., 46

	248-56-68
	248-55-68

A Russian-German Medical Firm

Eye Microsurgery Center

Y. Gasheka ul., 21	178-85-44
	177-34-20
	178-32-22

LenFin Med

Nab. reki Fontanki, 77	310-96-11

$, English, German, Finnish
A Russian-Finnish Firm

Children's City Hospital

Chaykovskogo ul., 73	273-38-66

Experienced Pediatricians.

Cosmetic Center (Plastic surgery)
(Diagnostics & Medical Treatment)

Dzerzhinskogo ul., 6	312-58-15

Emergency surgery

Severnyy pr., 1	511-09-61
Fax	511-81-02

Kosmeticheskiy Kabinet No. 329

Liteynyy pr., 28	273-19-69

Lecheniye bez Lekarstv (coop).
Treatment without Medicine
Call please 584-09-76
Medaks
Kultury pr., 4.................. 558-93-55
.... 558-97-21
.... 558-86-66
Medical Center Deviz
Moskovskiy pr., 95/3....... 299-72-55
General Practitioners, Gynecologists,
Physical therapists
Medical Consultation
Nalichnaya ul., 19........... 217-06-19
Medical Consultation
Stremyannaya ul., 4........ 113-21-56
Medical Consultation
Varshavskaya ul., 104..... 293-29-73
Medical Consultation
Nevskiy pr., 111............. 277-00-44
Medical Group
Home consultation
Please call... 520-60-20
.... 529-86-97
Medicon
Borovaya ul., 55. 166-47-62
Cosmetic surgery at reasonable cost.
Nadezhda Medical Center
Specialists in Gynecology. Choice of doctors.
V.O., Bolshoy pr., 49/51 .. 218-51-36
Open: 10-19; Sat.: 10-13
St. Petersburg Oblastnaya
Klinicheskaya bolnitsa
Lunacharskogo pr., 45-47
.... 594-26-02
.... 594-29-34
Plastic surgery. Burn Specialists.
Plasticheskaya khirurgiya
Clinics of the Military Medicine Academy
Zagorodnyy pr., 47 292-20-66
.... 259-52-76
.... 292-38-88
Polimed
Nastavnikov pr., 22......... 521-46-33
.... 521-46-34
Lenskaya ul., 8/2........... 521-10-93
Professor's Medical Group
Kirishskaya ul., 5, bldg. 3
.... 532-18-18
.... 531-79-61
Open: 9-20 Clsd. Sun. Metro: Grazhdanskiy pr.
Prognoz
3-ey Pyatiletki ul., 30 100-83-15
Metro: Rybatskoe
Reabilitatsiya Center
Izmaylovskiy pr., 2.......... 552-17-68
Medical consultations of all types
"Romashka"
Chernyakhovskogo ul., 17
.... 164-81-78
Russian folk methods of medicine.
Tonus (coop)
Podvoyskogo ul., 14, bldg. 9
.... 588-25-07

Vanga-Medika
3-ya Sovetskaya, 6 271-09-00
.... 271-08-20
Ultra sound procedures; gynecologists,
oncologists, gastroentrologists.
Veronika (gynecologists)
Nab. Vyborgskaya, 65 246-28-91
Vinmed Servis
Veteranov pr., 89, bldg. 3
.... 150-75-10
.... 155-91-66
Vrachebno- Kosmeticheskiy Salon "Vanda"
Nevskiy pr., 111 277-00-44
White way   "Belyy Put"
Traditional and non-traditional Medical care
Zverinskaya ul., 15.......... 233-11-08
.... 232-33-09
Zdorove
Litovskaya ul., 2 542-88-58
Znakhar Center
Komsomola ul., 6............ 542-53-12
Hrs: 12-19 Mon., Thurs., Wend.

☎ **MEDICAL EQUIPMENT**
МЕДИЦИНСКОЕ ОБОРУДОВАНИЕ
MEDIZINISCHE
AUSRÜSTUNGGERÄTE
MEDECINE, ÉQUIPEMENT MEDICAL
SJUKVÅRDSMATERIAL

ALMED (Diamond-Instrument)
Koly Domchaka ul., 24, bldg. 2
.... 298-65-36
.... 298-24-61

☎ MEDICAL INSTITUTES
МЕДИЦИНСКИЕ ИНСТИТУТЫ
MEDIZINISCHE INSTITUTE
MEDECINE; INSTITUT DE
SJUKVÅRDSINSTITUT

The leading specialists are associated with the medical institutes. Here are the major medical institutes in St. Petersburg. One of the few CAT scanners in St. Petersburg is found at the Institute of Oncology.

1st Medical Institute
                         1yy Meditsinskiy
  Lva Tolstogo ul., 6/8
  Secretary...................... 238-71-34
  Information 234-54-48

Institute of Hematology and
               Blood Transfusion
  2-ya Sovetskaya ul., 16
  Information 277-47-08

Institute of Emergency Medicine
  Budapeshtskaya ul., 3
  Information 174-86-75
  Cardiology, toxicology, burn Unit.

Institute of Cardiology
               Institut Kardiologii
  Parkhomenko ul., 15
  Information 557-75-47

Institute of Children's Infections
          Institut Detskikh Infektsiy
  Prof. Popova ul., 9
  Information 234-10-29

Institute of Children's Orthopedics
       Ortopedicheskiy Detskiy Institut
  Pushkin, Parkovaya ul., 64/68
  Information 465-34-31

Institute of Dental Cosmetics
          Institut Protezirovaniya
  Bestuzhevskaya ul., 50
  Information 544-21-89

Institute of Epidemiology & Microbiology
     Institut Epidemiologii i Mikrobiologii
  Skorokhodova ul., 15
  Donors dept. 232-20-96

Institute of Neurosurgery
           Institut Neyrokhirurgii
  Mayakovskogo ul., 12
  Information 272-81-35

Institute of Obstetrics and Gynecology
     Institut Akusherstva i Ginekologii
  V. O., Mendeleevskaya Liniya, 3
  Information 218-98-59

Institute of Oncology
              Institut Onkologii
  Pesochnyy poselok,
  Leningradskaya ul., 68
  Information 237-89-94

Institute of Orthopedics
     Institut Travmatologii i Ortopedii
  Akademika Baykova ul., 8
  Information 556-08-31

Institute of Pediatrics
          Pediatricheskiy Institute
  Litovskaya ul., 2
  Information 542-93-57

Institute of Radiology
     Rentgeno-Radiologicheskiy Institut
  Pesochnyy, Leningradskaya ul., 70/4
  Information 237-56-29

Pediatrics Medical Institute
     Meditsinskiy Pediatricheskiy Institut
  Litovskaya ul., 2
  Secretary...................... 542-39-83

Bechterev Psychoneurology Institute
  Bekhtereva ul., 3 567-89-97
  265-24-30
  567-54-06

Sanitary and Hygiene Institute
      Sanitarno-Gigienicheskiy Institut
  Piskarevskiy pr., 47
  Information 543-19-80

☎ MEETING ROOMS
ПОМЕЩЕНИЯ ДЛЯ
ПЕРЕГОВОРОВ ,ВСТРЕЧ
SITZUNGSSALE
REUNIONS, SALLES
MÖTESRUM/AFFÄRSSERVICE

See CONFERENCE ROOMS

☎ MEN'S CLOTHING
ОДЕЖДА ДЛЯ МУЖЧИН
HERRENBEKLEIDUNG
HOMMES, VETEMENTS POUR
HERRKLÄDER

See CLOTHING, MEN'S

☎ METRO
МЕТРО
U-BAHN
METRO
TUNNELBANA

St. Petersburg Subway (Underground), called the Metro (Метро) *for "Metropoliten", has 51 stations and operates from 5:30 in the morning to 1:00 in the morning. The trains run at intervals of 2-3 minutes during rush hours and of 4-6 minutes at other times. In June, 1992, it cost 1 ruble. To use the metro, you must now buy "tokens" (Zhetony, жетоны) at the entrance of the Metro. For long visits and greater convenience, buy a monthly ticket. In July this ticket cost 40 rubles for the metro alone and 75 rubles for all the city transport. It pays in time alone.*

St. Petersburg Metro
       St. Peterburgskiy Metropoliten
  Moskovskiy pr., 28
  251-66-68
  Metro: Tekhnologicheskiy Institut

☎ MILITIA - POLICE
МИЛИЦИЯ
POLIZEI
MILICE
MILITÄR

Many of the daily functions of police in Western countries are performed in Russia by the militia (militsiya, МИЛИЦИЯ) and the related "traffic police," called "GAI" (ГАИ), which stands for the "State Automobile Inspectorate" .The militia respond to emergencies, keep public order and do preliminary investigation of crimes. The GAI are traffic police and enforce traffic rules. Here are the district headquarters of the militia.

Militia Headquarters (Main Office)
Liteynyy pr., 4 02

Militia Headquarters (Dzerzhinskiy District)
Chekhova ul., 15
Emergency Duty 272-02-02
Militia Headquarters (Frunzenskiy District)
Rasstannaya ul., 15
Emergency Duty 166-02-02
Militia Headquarters (Kaliniskiy District)
Mineralnaya ul., 3
Emergency Duty 540-02-02
Militia Headquarters (Kirovskiy District)
Stachek pr., 18
Emergency Duty 252-02-02
Militia Headquarters (Kolpinskiy District)
Truda ul., 6
Emergency Duty 484-02-02
Militia Headquarters (Krasnogvardeyskiy)
Krasnodonskaya ul., 14
Emergency Duty 224-02-02
Militia Headquarters (Krasnoselskiy District)
Avangardnaya ul., 35 136-02-75
Militia Headquarters (Kronshtadt District)
Lenina pr., 20................ 236-02-02
Militia Headquarters (Kuybyshevskiy District)
Krylova pr., 3 310-02-02
Militia Headquarters (Leninskiy district)
Sovetskiy pr., 9 292-02-02
Militia Headquarters (Moskovskiy District)
Moskovskiy pr., 95 298-02-02
Militia Headquarters (Nevskiy District)
Krupskoy ul., 30 560-02-02
Militia Headquarters (Petrogradskiy District)
Skorokhodova ul., 20 233-02-02
Militia Headquarters (Primorskiy District)
Generala Khruleva ul., 15
.... 394-02-02
Militia Headquarters (Smolninskiy District)
Mytninskaya ul., 3 271-02-02
Militia Headquarters (Vasileostrovskiy District)
V.O., 19-ya Liniya, 10 213-02-02

Militia Headquarters (Vyborgskiy District)
Lesnoy pr., 20................ 542-02-02
KGB
Liteynyy pr., 4 278-71-10

☎ MONEY CHANGING
ВАЛЮТА, ОБМЕН
GELDWECHSEL
DEVISE CHANGE DE
VALUTA VÄXLING

See CURRENCY EXCHANGE

☎ MOTELS
МОТЕЛИ
MOTELS
MOTELS
MOTELL

See also HOTELS, BED & BREAKFAST, APARTMENTS

Motel OLGINO
Primorskoe shosse, 18 km.
Info in English 238-35-53
Info in Russian................ 238-34-89
Fax 238-39-54
$, English, German, Finnish, Swedish, French.

☎ MOTORCYCLES
МОТОЦИКЛЫ
MOTORRÄDER
MOTOS
MOTORCYKLAR

Motolyubitel
Apraksin Dvor, bldg. 1, apt. 57
.... 310-01-54

☎ MOUNTAINEERING
ГОРНЫЙ ТУРИЗМ
BERGSTEIGEN
ALPINISME
BERGSKLÄTTRING

St. Petersburg's Tourist Club
Zhelyabova ul., 27 311-45-17
Fax.............................. 314-63-70
Telex .... 121345 TURKLUB SU
Organized alpinist tours
Petrogradskiy Tourist Club
Please call 230-80-21
"Wilderness" tourism.

☎ MOVIES
КИНОТЕАТРЫ
KINOS
CINEMA
BIOGRAFER

See CINEMAS.

☎ MOVING COMPANIES
ПЕРЕВОЗКИ ГРУЗОВЫЕ
MÖBELSPEDITIONEN
FRETS, COMPAGNIES DE
FLYTTBOL, SE ÄVEN SHIPPING

See also SHIPPING AGENTS

Agency
Please call 238-42-41
Inner-city Moving Services
Enterprise
Please call 108-47-60

Lentransagentstvo
Vatutina ul., 19 540-90-05

Lenvneshtrans
Mezhevoy kan., 5 251-41-97
Fax 186-28-83
Telex..................... 121511 SVT SU
Declaration Points:
Moldagulovoy ul., 6......... 224-04-94
Pulkovo-2, Shturmanskaya ul., 32
.... 104-34-98
V.O., 9-ya Liniya, 6.......... 218-31-72
Naydenov & Company
Telezhnaya ul., 7/9.......... 530-25-23
Hrs: 13-21

☎ MUSEUMS
МУЗЕИ
MUSEEN
MUSEES
MUSEER

Most museums close one day each week and also the last Wednesday or Thursday or Friday of each month (indicated by "last"). These hours and days can change, especially in fall and winter, so check.

Academy of Arts Museum
Nab. Universitetskaya, 17
.... 213-64-96
Hrs: 11-17, Closed: Mon. & Tues.
Anna Akhmatova Literary Museum
Nab. reki Fontanki, 34 272-58-95
Hrs: 10:30 - 18:30 Closed Mon.
& last Wed. Metro Vladimirskaya
Applied Arts Museum
Solyanoy per., 13 273-32-58
Hours: 11-17, Closed: Sun., Mon.
Artillery Museum
Park Lenina, 7 232-02-96
Hrs: 11-17, Closed Mon., Tues., last Thursday.
Metro: Gorkovskaya
Museum of the Arctic & Antarctic
Marata ul., 24a.............. 311-25-49
Hours: 10-17, Closed: Mon., Tues.
Metro: Vladimirskaya, Mayakovskaya
Blok House
Dekabristov ul., 57.......... 113-86-16
Hours: 11 - 17, Closed Wed.
Botanical Museum
Professora Popova ul., 2
.... 234-84-70
"Orangery" 234-17-64
Hours: 10 - 17 Orangery Closed Fri.
Museum closed: Mon., Tues., Thurs., Fri.
Brodskiy House   *Closed for repair*
Iskusstv pl., 3 314-36-58
Circus Art Museum
Nab. reki Fontanki , 3...... 210-44-13
The Cruiser Aurora
P.S., Nab. Petrogradskaya, 4
.... 230-52-02
Hrs: 10:30. - 16, Closed: Mon., Fri.
Metro: Ploshchad Lenina; Gorkovskaya
The Museum of the Defense of Leningrad
Solyanoy per., 9 275-72-08
Hours: 10-17, Closed: Wed., last Thurs.
Metro: Chernychevskaya

Dostoevskiy Literary Museum
    Kuznechnyy per., 5/2 164-69-50
    Hours: 10.30-17.30, Closed Mon., last Wed.
                Metro: Vladimirskaya

Museum of Ethnography of the
                    Peoples of the USSR
    Inzhenernaya ul., 4/1 219-11-74
        Hours: 10-17, Closed: Mon., last Fri.
                Metro: Gostinyy Dvor

Ethnograpy
    Nab. Universitetskaya, 3
    218-14-12
    Hours: 11 - 17, Closed: Fri., Sat., last Thurs.

Exhibition Halls of the Union of
                    Artists of the RSFSR
    Nab. Sverdlovskaya, 64 ... 224-06-33
    Gertsena ul., 38 211-82-19
        Hours: 12-18, Closed: Mon.

The Hermitage
    Nab. Dvortsovaya, 34...... 311-34-20
    219-86-25
Hours: 10.30-18, Closed: Mon. Metro: Nevskiy pr.

History of Leningrad Museum
    Nab. Krasnogo Flota, 44
    (Red Fleet Embankment),
    past Lt. Shmidt Bridge
    311-75-44
    Hrs: 11-17, Closed: Wed., last Tues.
                Metro: Vasileostrovskaya

History of St. Petersburg Museum
    Peter-Paul Fortress pl. 3... 238-46-13
    238-45-11
        Hours: 11 - 17, Closed: Wed.
                Metro: Gorkovskaya

Isaakievskiy Sobor
    Isaakievskaya pl., 1......... 315-97-32
        Hours: 11-18, Closed: Wed.

Kazan Cathedral
    (Museum of Religion & Atheism)
    Kazanskaya pl., 2 311-04-95
    Hours: 11-17, Sun. 14-18 Closed: Wed. & last Thurs.
                Metro: Nevskiy Prospekt

Kirov House
    Kirovskiy pr., 26/28......... 233-38-22
        Hours: 11-18, Closed Wed.

Letniy Sad........................... 314-03-74
Park open 8 to 23. Building open 11-18, Closed Tues.
        Hours: 11-18, Metro: Gostinyy Dvor

Literatorskie Mostki ("Literary Plot"
            of the Volkovskoe Cemetery)
    Rasstannyy per., 30 166-23-83
        Hours: 11-19, Closed Thurs.
                Metro: Ligovskiy Prospekt

Lomonsov Museum
    Nab. Universitetskaya, 3.. 218-12-11
        Hours: 11-19, Closed :Fri. and Sat.
                Metro: Nevskiy Prospekt

Lomonosov Museum and Parks
    See LOMONOSOV, Hrs: 11-17, Cls: Tue

Manege Central Exhibition Hall
                Exhibits vary
    Isaakievskaya pl., 1......... 314-88-59
    Hours: 11-18, Closed: Tues. Metro: Nevskiy Prospekt

Mendeleev House
    Universitetskaya Nab., 7/9
    218-97-44
            Closed: Sat., Sun.

Menshikov Museum-Dvorets
    Nab. Universitetskaya, 15
    213-11-12
        Hours: 10.30-16.30, Closed: Mon.

Museum of Military Medicine
    Lazaretnyy per., 2 113-52-15

Museum of Musical Instruments
    Isaakievskaya pl., 5......... 314-53-45

Museum of Town Sculpture
    Alexander Nevskiy Lavra
    Alexandra Nevskogo pl., 1 277-17-16
        Hours: 11-17, Closed: Thurs.

Naval Museum
    Pushkinskaya pl., 4 218-25-01
    Hours: 10.30-17.30, Closed: Mon. ,Tues.

Nekrasov House
    Liteynyy pr., 36 272-01-65
        Hours: 11-17, Thurs. 13-19
            Closed: Tues. & last Fri.

Oreshek Fortress
    Schlisselburg 238-47-20
            Hours: 10.00-17.00

Pavlovsk Museum and Parks
See PAVLOVSK. Hrs: 9.00-17.30, Closed Fri.

Peter and Paul Fortress
    P.S., Revolyutsii pl., Zayachiy Isd
    238-45-40
    Hours: 11-17, Closed: Wed. Metro: Gorkovskaya

Peter the Great's Cottage
    Nab. Petrovskaya, 6 232-45-76
    Hours: 10.30-18.00, Closed: Tues. & last Mon.
                Metro: Gorkovskaya

Petrodvorets Museum and Parks
    See PETRODVORETS Hrs: 11-18, Cls: Mon.

Piskarevskoe Cemetery
    Nepokorennykh pr., 74 247-57-16
    Hours: 10.00-18.00 Metro: Pl. Muzhestva

Planetarium
    Park Lenina, 4 233-31-53
        Hours: 12-18, Daily Metro: Gorkovskaya

Popov's House
    Professora Popova ul., 5 .. 234-59-00

Pushkin House
    Nab. reki Moyki, 12......... 311-35-31
    Hours: 10.30 - 18.00, Closed: Tues. & last Fri.

Pushkin Museum and Parks
    See PUSHKIN Hrs: 10-17, Cls: Tue

Railway Museum
    Sadovaya ul., 50............. 315-14-76
    Hours: 11.00-17.30, Closed: Fri., Sat., last Thurs.
                Metro: Ploshchad Mira

Razliv (Barn Museum)
    Razliv, Emelyanova ul., 3 . 237-29-37

Repin Museum (Penaty)
Repino, Primorskoe shosse, 411
.... 231-68-28
Hours: 10-16, Closed: Tues.

Rimskiy-Korsakov House
Zagorodnyy pr., 28, fl. 3.. 113-32-08
Hours: 11-18, Closed: Mon., Tues., last Fri.
Metro: Vladimirskaya

Russian Museum
Inzhenernaya ul., 4.......... 314-34-48
.... 314-41-53
Khalturina ul., 5/1 (Department)
.... 312-91-96
Hours: 10 - 18, Closed: Tues.
Metro: Nevskiy Prospekt

Russian Political History Museum
Kuybysheva ul., 4 233-70-50
.... 233-70-52
Hours: 10.00-17.30, Closed : Thurs.
Metro: Gorkovskaya

Shalyapina House
Graftio ul., 26 234-26-98
Closed: Mon., Tues.

Smolny Institute
Rastrelli pl., 3/11 311-36-90
Hours: 11-17, Closed: Thurs.

Theater Museum
Ostrovskogo pl., 6 311-21-95
.... 312-36-23
Hours: 11-18, Wed. 13-18, Closed: Tues.
Metro: Gostinyy Dvor

Yelagin Palace
Kirov Central Park of Culture and
Rest, Yelagin Ostrov, 1
.... 239-11-30
Hours: 10.00 - 18.00, Closed: Mon., Tues.

Yusupov Palace
Nab. reki Moyki, 94........ 314-98-83
.... 311-53-53
Hours: 12.00-20.00, Cld: Sun.
Metro: Ploshchad Mira

Zoological Museum
Nab. Universitetskaya, 1 .. 218-01-12
Hrs: 11-17, Closed: Fri.

☎ **MUSIC SCHOOLS**
МУЗЫКАЛЬНЫЕ ШКОЛЫ
MUSIKSCHULEN,
MUSIKUNTERRICHT
MUSIQUE, ECOLES DE ET COURS
MUSIKSKOLOR OCH
UNDERVISNING

Children's Music School
Sadovaya ul., 32 310-04-62
Music School
Ogorodnikova pr., 8 251-33-73
Music School
Kirovskiy pr., 5 233-94-61
Music School
Sedova ul., 32................ 568-02-63
Music School
Marata pr., 68................ 315-03-63
Music School
Nab. Leytenanta Shmidta, 31
.... 355-74-52

Music School
Nekrasova ul., 4/2.......... 273-69-86
Rimskiy-Korsakov Conservatory
Matveeva per., 1-a.......... 114-16-22

☎ **MUSIC SHOPS**
МУЗЫКАЛЬНЫЕ МАГАЗИНЫ
MUSIKGESCHÄFTE
MUSIQUE, MAGASINS DE
MUSIKAFFÄRER

See also RECORDS, COMPACT DISKS

House of Music and Radio
         Dom Muzyki i Radio
Grazhdanskiy pr., 15, bldg. 1
.... 535-03-14
Melodiya
Moskovskiy pr., 34/36..... 292-35-05
Melodiya
Nevskiy pr., 32/34 311-74-55
Music Shop
V.O., 7-ya Liniya, 40 213-35-88
Music Store
Novocherkasskiy pr., 41/14
.... 528-16-90
Muzyka
Sredniy pr., 48 213-41-88
Muzykalnaya Mozayka (coop)
Ligovskiy pr., 141 164-05-79
Muzykalnyy Salon (coop)
Zhelyabova ul., 7 312-86-05

Rapsodiya
Zhelyabova ul., 13 314-48-01
Hrs: 10-19

☎ **MUSICAL INSTRUMENTS**
МУЗЫКАЛЬНЫЕ ИНСТРУМЕНТЫ
MUSIKINSTRUMENTE
MUSIQUE, INSTRUMENTS DE
MUSIKINSTRUMENT

See also PIANOS

Concern **"Goryachev"**
Fine Grand Pianos
Custom-built elegant fine pianos
Vereyskaya ul., 39.............. 112-75-96
Fax 311-95-76
Hrs: 10-20, $, English

Apraksin Dvor
Komissionnyy magazin No. 29
.... 310-31-34
Ilmera, A/O
6-ya Krasnoarmeyskaya ul., 7
.... 292-27-77
Musical Instruments (Two shops)
         Muzikalnye Instrumenty
V.O., Sredniy pr., 48 213-41-88
Grazhdanskiy pr., 15 535-03-14
Univermag "Gostinyy dvor"
Nevskiy pr., 35................ 110-53-66

Univermag DLT
  Zhelyabova ul., 21/23...... 312-26-27

☎ MUSICIANS
  МУЗЫКАНТЫ
  MUSIKANTEN
  MUSICIENS
  MUSIKER

See ENTERTAINMENT ACTS

☎ NEWS AGENCIES
  АГЕНСТВА НОВОСТЕЙ
  NACHRICHTENAGENTUREN
  NOUVELLES, AGENCES DE
  NYHETSBYRÅER

*These News Agencies are based in
Moscow. See* NEWSPAPERS *for
newspapers in St. Petersburg.*

NBC (USA)
  Gruzinskiy per., 3 ..... (095) 230-26-75
CBS (USA)
  Sadovaya-Samotechnaya ul., 12/24
  .... (095) 200-29-92
United Press International (USA)
  Kutuzovskiy pr., 4 .... (095) 243-68-29
Associated Press (USA)
  Kutuzovskiy pr., 7/2 . (095) 230-28-45
CBC (Kanada)
  Gruzinskiy per., 3 ..... (095) 250-52-65
RAI (Italy)
  Mira pr., 74 .... (095) 280-76-89
`Times` (GBR)
  B. Dorogomilovskay ul., 14
  .... (095) 230-24-57
BBC (GBR)
  Sadovaya-Samotechnaya ul.,12/24
  .... (095) 200-20-27
ABC (USA)
  Kutuzovskiy pr., 13 .. (095) 243-05-72
New York Times (USA)
  Sadovaya-Samotechnaya ul.,12/24
  .... (095) 230-25-03
Time (USA)
  Kutuzovskiy pr., 14 .. (095) 243-15-11
Newsweek (USA)
  Kutuzovskiy pr., 14 .. (095) 243-17-73
Welt (Germany)
  Kutuzovskiy pr., 7/4 . (095) 253-97-07
DPA (Germany)
  Kutuzovskiy pr., 7/4 . (095) 243-97-90
Zuddeutsche Zeitung (Germany)
  Kutuzovskiy pr., 7/4 . (095) 230-25-09
France-Press (France)
  Sadovaya-Samotechnaya ul., 12/24
  .... (095) 292-31-75
Swenska Dagbladet (Sweden)
  Kutuzovskiy pr., 9/2 . (095) 243-67-47
Radio France et Television Francais
  Gruzinskiy per., 3 ..... (095) 250-25-05

☎ NEWSPAPERS & MAGAZINES
  ГАЗЕТЫ, ЖУРНАЛЫ
  ZEITUNGEN/ZEITSCHRIFTEN
  JOURNAUX/MAGAZINES
  TIDNINGAR/VECKOTIDNINGAR

See also MAGAZINES

*Russian newspapers are found at many of
the kiosks found on street corners.
Foreign language newspapers are available
at the Grand Hotel Europe, Pribaltiyskaya,
Okhtinskaya, Astoria and other hotels.*

**WHERE TO BUY AND SUBSCRIBE
         TO FOREIGN NEWSPAPERS**

BUREAU "INPRESS"

**Distributors of 27 foreign newspapers
and over 40 foreign magazines in St. Pb.**
including *Wall St. Jrnl, Int. Herald, Die Welt,
Le Monde, & Corr. della Sera* and 22 others.
Available at Grand Hotel Europe, Pribaltiyskaya,
Okhtinskaya, Astoria and other fine hotels.
Subscriptions (short-term and long-term)
Pochtamtskaya ul., 9 312-82-91

**Where and how to subscribe to
         Russian Publications.**
  *If the magazine or journal is sold by
Rospechat (formerly Soyuzpechat) (see*
MAGAZINES*), you can subscribe and pay
for these magazines at any* POST OFFICE.
*Or send the post card or form in the
magazine to the publisher.*

NEWSPAPERS IN ST PETERSBURG

Aktsioner [Stock-holder]
  A newspaper on economics of Russia.
  Shpalernaya ul., 52, apt. 19
  Tel................................. 272-96-76
  Fax 275-76-11
Business-Inform
  Moscow:
  Narodnogo Opolcheniya ul., 31
  .... (095) 197-56-30
Business-Shans
  Nab. reki Fontanki, 59 210-84-57
  Advertisement newspaper printed in color
Chas Pik [Rush Hour] *(weekly)*
  Nevskiy pr., 81.............. 277-13-40
24 Chasa [24 Hours]
  Digest of the Russian and foreign press
  Rimskogo-Korsakogo ul., 9
  310-45-61
Commersant ℀
  St. Petersburg Representative
  Nevskiy, 3, apt. 25 314-62-52
  In Moscow:
  Vrubelya ul., 4........ (095) 943-97-68
  .... (095) 943-97-10

Economic Life
             Economicheskaya Gazeta
  St. Petersburg Representative
             See Nevskiy Vestnik
Evening Petersburg
             Vecherniy Petersburg
  Daily evening newspaper of Lensovet
  Nab. reki Fontanki, 59 312-06-38
  Editorial Office................ 311-88-75
  310-45-55
             Hrs: 10-15
Everything for you (PROFIT)
  Pochtamtskaya ul., 5/30
  311-63-19
Izvestiya
  St. Petersburg correspondent office
  Nevskiy pr., 19............... 311-85-06
  311-87-33
Kinonedelya Sankt-Peterburga
             [Film week St. Petersburg]
  Nab. reki Fontanki, 59
  Editorial Office................ 310-44-54
Komsomolskaya Pravda
  St. Petersburg correspondent office
  Khersonskaya ul., 12....... 274-06-63
Krasnaya Zvezda [Red Star]
  St. Petersburg correspondent office
  Liteynyy pr., 20.............. 272-58-25
5 Uglov [5 Corners]
  Editorial Office
  Nab. reki Fontanki, 59 310-41-11
Literaturnaya Gazeta [Literary News]
  St. Petersburg correspondent office
  Voynova ul., 18, apt. 21.. 279-08-73
Moscow News [Moscow Business Week
             Russian Press Service]
  In Moscow:
  Tverskaya ul., 16/2 . (095) 209-17-49
  .... (095) 209-05-60
  In St. Petersburg:
  Pochtamtskaya ul., 5/30
  311-63-19
Moscow News Business
  Moscow:
  Tverskaya ul., 16/2
  .... (095) 200-08-68

┌─────────────────────────────────────┐
Nevskoe Vremya [Neva Times]
             Independent newspaper
  Gertsena ul., 47 314-21-34
  312-16-82
  312-40-40
             three times a week
└─────────────────────────────────────┘

Neva Magazine
  Nevskiy pr., 3................. 312-70-35
  312-64-78
  312-65-37
Neva News
  Pravdy ul., 10 164-47-65
  Published in English specially for tourists

Nevskiy Vestnik
  Nab. reki Fontanki, 59 315-84-65
  Editorial Office................ 315-61-74
Niva [Cornfield]
             Illustrated weekly
  Nab. kan. Griboedova, 15. 311-02-03
Omega
  Khersonskaya ul., 12....... 274-07-04
  Fax: 312-79-31
Reklama-Shans
  Nab. reki, Fontanki, 59 210-84-41
             Weekly newspaper for private
             advertisement and information
This day from morning till night
             3 utra do vechera segodnya
  Khersonskaya ul., 12....... 274-08-57

┌─────────────────────────────────────┐
  St. Petersburg Business News
  Antonenko per., 6, apt. 40
  314-62-52
  Fax: 312-62-17
  Telex:........................121465 LSWS
  E-mail:........................... aag@cfera
  Business, commercial and other information by
  E-mail, both in this country & abroad Dealers in
             USA, Canada, Europe.
└─────────────────────────────────────┘

Sankt-Peterburgskie Vedomosti
  Nab. reki Fontanki, 59 310-45-61
  Editorial Office................ 314-71-76
             Daily
Smena [Shift]
  Nab. reki Fontanki, 59 210-84-63
Soroka [Magpie]
  Proletarskoy Diktatutry pl., 6, apt. 424
  278-14-08
  Fax 271-16-82
Sotsialisticheskaya Industriya
             [Socialist Industry]
  St. Petersburg correspondent office
  Lenina ul., 20................. 233-12-05
Sovetskaya Rossiya   [Soviet Russian]
  St. Petersburg correspondent office
  Khersonskaya ul., 12....... 274-06-51
Sovetskiy Sport   [Soviet Sport]
  St. Petersburg correspondent office
  Lomonosova ul., 22......... 314-24-17
Sport. Chelovek. Vremya.
             [Sport. Men. Time.]
  Editorial Office................ 310-43-70
Televidenie, Radio   Television Radio
  Editorial Office
  Nab. reki Fontanki, 59 310-57-75
  310-57-26
             Program of radio and telecasting
Trud [Labor]
  St. Petersburg correspondent office
  Truda pl., 4...................314-94-17n
Vesti [News]
  Millionnaya ul., 30........... 314-19-85
  314-19-86
             Three times a week

☎ NIGHT TIME ENTERTAINMENT
РАЗВЛЕЧЕНИЯ НОЧНЫЕ
UNTERHALTUNG/
    VERANSTALTUNGEN, ABENDS
DIVERTISSEMENT NOCTURNE
NÖJESSTÄLLEN, NATTLIV

See also THEATER/BALLET,
RESTAURANTS, BARS, CINEMAS,
DISCOTHEQUE, CASINOS, BOATS
*Night time entertainment abounds in
St.-Pb. from concerts, cultural evenings
and THEATER to the elaborate variety
shows at the big RESTAURANTS and
intimate dancing at the late NIGHT BARS.*

NIGHT RESTAURANT VOSTOK
"NIGHT RESTAURANT ORIENT"
Indian & European Cuisine
One of the best kitchens in the city
In beautiful Primorskiy Park Pobedy
New variety shows & orchestra
Primorskiy Park Pobedy.... 235-59-84
Hrs: 12-4:30 am, $ & rubles, English

Galspe at Palanga
Galspe invites you to bingo, casino, disco,
Spanish restaurant, bar & Spanish
confectionery
Leninskiy pr., 127 254-88-12
.... 254-21-92
Fax 255-51-60
$, rubles, CC, English, Spanish

THE NIGHT BAR ASTORIA
At the Hotel Astoria, Bldg. B
Music and Dancing
to the Wee Hours of the Morning
Gertsena ul., 39 210-59-06
Hrs: 11 to 6, $, CC, English

THE NIGHT CLUB
at the Hotel Pribaltiyskaya
Dinner and Dance
Jazz and Contemporary Music
Korablestroiteley ul., 14 356-44-09
Hrs: 20-early am, $, English

LEADER
A PETERSBURG DESSERT
AN ART CONCERT AT THE PALACE
With internationally recognized musicians

An evening of chamber music & art
with "a la fourchette" supper and drinks
at the 19C Malyutka Palace

Exhibition-sale of paintings & applied arts
by famous painters & artists in St. Pb.

At P. Lavrova ul., 58
For schedule and reservations
Tel. 238-81-48
Call hrs: 10-14, $ & rubles, English

TROIKA

✦✦✦✦✦
The International-Russian Variety Show
Chorus Line, Song, Dance & Variety
"Moulin Rouge of Saint. Petersburg"
A Great Show
✦✦✦✦✦
Zagorodnyy pr., 27 113-53-43
Hrs: 7-24, $ & rbls, English
A Russian-Swiss Company

SCHWABSKI DOMIK
SCHWABEN HÄUSLE
Come join us for
Schnitzel, Wurst and German Beer
The German Gaststätte-Pub in St. Pb
International & German Cooking
Great selection of European Wines
Music and Folklore Ensemble

Just ten minutes drive from center city
Krasnogvardeyskiy pr., 28/19
.... 528-22-11
.... 528-06-69
Take the Metro: Krasnogvardeyskaya,
Hrs: 11 am to 2 am $, English and German

☎ NOTARY PUBLIC
НОТАРИАЛЬНЫЕ УСЛУГИ
NOTARIATE
NOTARIAT
NOTARIER

Many forms must be notarized by an official NOTARY BUREAU (Notarialnaya Kontora, Нотариальная контора). Often they must be translated or reviewed by an officially approved translator.

Notarialnaya Kontora
              (Notary Public of Kronshtadt)
  Surgina ul., 15 236-27-53
Notarialnaya Kontora No. 1
  Nevskiy pr., 109 277-40-38
Notarialnaya Kontora No. 3
  Nevskiy pr., 44 110-50-44
Notarialnaya Kontora No. 4
  Leninskiy pr., 130 255-31-52
Notarialnaya Kontora No. 9
  Zagorodnyy pr., 14 164-73-11
Notarialnaya Kontora No. 13
  Serebristyy bulv., 22, bldg. 1
  393-45-95
Notarialnaya Kontora No. 14
  Karla Marksa pr., 108 246-07-71
Notarialnaya Kontora No. 15
  Manezhnyy per., 13 279-02-55
Notarialnaya Kontora No. 18
  Plovdivskaya ul., 9 108-19-17

☎ OBSTETRICIANS
АКУШЕРЫ-ГИНЕКОЛОГИ
FRAUENARZT
OBSTETRICIENS
GYNEKOLOGER

See HOSPITALS, MEDICAL CARE & CONSULTATIONS

☎ OFFICE EQUIPMENT
ОФИСЫ, ОБОРУДОВАНИЕ
BÜROEINRICHTING
OFFICES, EQUIPEMENT
KONTORSUTRUSTNING

See also COMPUTER STORES

Commark Ltd
  Sablinskaya ul., ... 233-30-08

LenPoliGraphServis
  Primorskiy pr., 35a 239-68-84

Ortex
  Karla Marksa pr., 84 245-12-51
      Office equipment

Dzhekob
  Sadovaya ul., 53 310-67-17
Tekhnopost
  Marii Ulyanovoy ul., 4 292-25-62
      Repairs fax.
Trionix
  Povarskoy per., 8 321-38-44
  131-03-33

TYP *NEED TO GET WESTERN MEDICINES* Look under PHARMACIES

TYP *NEED A TIRE* Look under AUTOMOBILE PARTS and TIRES

☎ OFFICE SPACE RENTALS
ОФИСЫ, АРЕНДА
BÜROVERMIETUNG
OFFICES, BAIL
KONTORSLOKALER ATT HYRA

See also APARTMENTS and REAL ESTATE AGENTS

☎ OFFICE SUPPLIES
КАНЦЕЛЯРСКИЕ ТОВАРЫ
BÜROARTIKEL
BUREAUX, FOURNITURE
KONTORSMATERIAL

See STATIONERY

☎ OPERA
ОПЕРА
OPER
OPERA
OPERA

See THEATER/BALLET

☎ OPHTHALMOLOGISTS
ОФТАЛЬМОЛОГИ
AUGENÄRZTE
OPHTAMOLOGISTES
ÖGONLÄKARE

See HOSPITALS, MEDICAL CARE & CONSULTATIONS, OPTICIANS and CONTACT LENSES

☎ OPTICIANS
ОПТИКИ
OPTIKER
OPTICIENS
OPTIKER

See also CONTACT LENSES and MEDICAL CARE AND CONSULTATIONS

Atele Optiko-Mekhanicheskikh Priborov
  Nevskiy pr., 20............... 311-05-78
Diamon
  Kultury pr., 4.................. 559-96-63
  558-89-14
Lincoln-Kontakt
  Krasnaya ul., 46 312-10-92
    Contact-lense prescriptions
         Hrs: 9 - 21 Daily
Konkor
  Krestovskiy pr., 18
  Information 235-73-75
         Closed Sun
Kontakt-Servis-Optika
  Izmaylovskiy pr., 23
  Information 251-12-62
       Contact Lense Center
    Hrs: 11 - 19 ,Sunday 14 - 15
Optika
  Zhukovskogo ul., 6
  Administrator 272-57-66
    Hrs: 11-14 , 15-19, closed Sat, Sun
Optika
  Nab. kan. Griboedova, 18
  Administrator 314-31-63
    Hrs: 11-14 , 15-19, closed Sat, Sun
Optika
  Nevskiy pr., 13
  Administrator 311-45-88
    Hrs: 11-14, 15-19, closed Sat, Sun
Optika
  Chaykovskogo ul., 36
  Administrator 273-64-54
Optika
  12-ya Krasnoarmeyskaya ul., 3
  Administrator 251-52-22
    Hrs: 10 - 14, 15- 19 Clsd Sat. & Sun.
Optika-Atele
  V.O., 15-ya Liniya, 32
  Administrator 213-68-51
    Hrs: 10-14, 15-19, closed Sat, Sun
Optika-Atele
  Maklina pr., 29
  Administrator 114-49-41
    Hrs: 10-14, 15-19, closed Sat, Sun
J.V. "VISOR" (Russian-British)
  Liteynyy pr., 30
  Administrator 272-76-42
    Hrs: 10-14, 15-19, closed Sat, Sun
Optika-Atele
  V.O., 9-ya Liniya, 32
  Administrator 213-57-93
    Hrs: 10-14, 15-19, closed Sat, Sun
Optika-Atele
  Kirovskiy pr., 57
  Administrator 234-93-10
    Hrs: 10-14, 15-19, closed Sat, Sun
Optika-Atele
  Kuybysheva ul., 32
  Administrator 233-46-84
    Hrs: 10-14, 15-19, closed Sat, Sun
Optika-Atele
  Zagorodnyy pr., 39
  Administrator 113-59-41
    Hrs: 10-14, 15-19, closed Sat, Sun

Optika Centre of eyes correction
  Pushkin, Leningradskoe shosse, 13/1
  466-20-59
         Hrs: 10 - 21

☎ ORCHESTRAS
  ОРКЕСТРЫ
  ORCHESTER
  ORCHESTRES
  ORKESTRAR

Dmitriev's Academic Symphony Orchestra
  Brodskogo ul., 2 311-73-33
Symphony-Orchestra
  Please call.................... 219-96-02
         Open: 6-24
Timirkanov's Academic Symphony Orchestra
  Please call..................... 110-42-26

☎ PAINT SUPPLIES
  КРАСКИ, ЛАКИ
  FARBEN UND LACKE
  PEINTURE, FOURNITURE
  FÄRGHANDLARE

    See also BUILDING SUPPLIES *and*
              HARDWARE

Laki. Kraski. Skobyanye Tovary
  Nevskiy pr., 146 274-02-84
         Metro: Pl. Vosstaniya
Building Materials
                      Stroitelnye materialy
  Zamshina ul., 31 543-31-77
  Kultury pr., 29, bldg. 1
  559-93-88
  Stachek pr., 34 186-77-22
  Nab. Chernoy rechki, 6
  239-84-90
Novosel
  Yakornaya ul., 1 224-38-03

☎ PARKING LOTS
  АВТОСТОЯНКИ
  PARKPLÄTZE
  PARKINGS
  PARKERINGSPLATSER

  These are for cars. For trucks and buses, see TRUCK PARKS. *The Hotel Astoria and other hotels also have watched car parks.*

Supervised Car Parks for foreign vehicles
  Varshavskaya ul., 42 296-58-20
Agro
  Utkin proezd, 11, apt. 6
  528-69-59
Municipal Parking Lots
                          Avtostoyanka
Avtostoyanka
  Rustavelli ul., 71............. 532-53-59
Avtostoyanka No. 3
  Vosstaniya ul., 7b........... 236-16-83
Avtostoyanka No. 5
  Piskarevskiy pr., 23......... 541-29-30

Avtostoyanka No. 8 (Garage)
    Kronshtadtskaya ul., 19... 183-51-67
Avtostoyanka No. 20 (Parking Lots)
    Kronshtadtskaya ul., 19... 184-48-86
Avtostoyanka No. 29
    Airport Pulkovo.............. 291-88-06
Avtostoyanka No. 35
    Birzhevoy per., 2............. 218-21-01
Avtostoyanka No. 42
    M. Balkanskaya ul.,........ 177-41-35
Avtostoyanka No. 51
    Varshavskaya ul., 42....... 296-58-20
Avtostoyanka No. 53
    Zvezdnaya ul., 2............. 127-24-69
Avtostoyanka No. 68
    M. Balkanskaya ul........... 178-26-28
Avtostoyanka
    Sirenevyy Bulvar, 1 599-97-64
Avtodelo
    Zemledelcheskaya ul., 3... 245-50-21
    275-91-96

High Security   AUTO PARK
Cars, Trucks, Buses
Varshavskaya ul., 42....... 296-58-20
Near the Russia Hotel
Daily 24 hrs English, $ & rbl

Sovtransavto
    Vitebskiy pr., 3.............. 298-46-50
    298-10-50
    Fax................................ 298-77-60

☎ **PARKS**
    ПАРКИ
    PARKANLAGEN
    PARCS
    PARKER

See also GARDENS.

St. Petersburg has a variety of parks
for a Sunday afternoon excursion. They
are especially nice for children and some
have rides.

Botanical Gardens
    Professora Popova ul., 2
    Museum 234-84-70
    Greenhouse 234-17-64
        Hrs: 11 - 16 Clsd. Fridays
Kirov Central Park (TZPKO)
Entertainment programs, dances for young
people, discotheques, side-shows, boats
for hire & rock concerts
Elagin Ostrov (Elagin Island), 4
    239-09-11
    Director.......................... 239-10-10
        Hrs: 10 - 20, Bus 71, Trams 12, 17, 26

Moscow Victory Park
                    Park Pobedy Moskovskiy
    Kuznetsovskaya ul., 25
    Director 298-08-81
            Metro: Park Pobedy
Coastal Victory Park
                    Primorskiy Park Pobedy
    Side-show, rides and tennis courts
    Krestovskiy pr., 21 235-21-46
    230-04-19
    Buses 71, 71A, Trolley 9, Trams 21, 33, 34
Sosnovka
    Manchesterskaya ul., 18
    554-32-23
Summer Gardens   Letniy Sad
    Park open all year, Statues: May 1 to first frost.
    Pestelya ul., 2 314-03-74
    312-96-66
Tavricheskiy Sad
    Saltykova-Shchedrina ul., 50
    Director 272-60-44
    Also has a small amusement park
    for children and a little lake.
            Metro: Chernyshevskaya
Tikhiy Otdykh
    Kamennoostrovskiy pr., 1
    234-49-45
Yuzhno-Primorskiy Park
    Petergofskoe shosse, 27
    151-52-85

☎ **PASSPORT PHOTOS**
    ФОТО ДЛЯ ДОКУМЕНТОВ
    PASSFOTOS
    PASSEPORT, PHOTOS POUR
    PASSFOTO

See also PHOTOGRAPHERS

The following shops will take photos for
passports and other documents.

Bukharestskaya ul., 31/1 174-70-06
Kondratevskiy pr. 540-60-47
Liteynyy pr., 23................. 273-21-53
Moskovskiy pr., 34.............. 292-38-47
Nevskiy pr., 22/24.............. 312-01-22
Nevskiy pr., 103................. 277-06-30
Nevskiy pr., 156................. 277-14-61
Vladimirskiy pr., 3 113-16-77

☎ **PAWN SHOPS**
    ЛОМБАРДЫ
    PFANDHÄUSER
    MONT-DE- PIETE
    PANTBANKER

Lombard, Headquarters
    Pushkarskaya ul., 20 232-52-40
Lombard
    Vladimirskiy pr., 17 164-99-81
Lombard
    Nab. reki Moyki, 72......... 314-95-92
Lombard
    V. O., 8-ya Liniya, 25 213-10-46

☎ PET STORES
ЗООМАГАЗИНЫ
TIERHANDLUNGEN
ANIMALERIE
DJURAFFÄRER

You can buy birds, dogs, fish, cats, and other pets at the Kondratevskiy Pet Market in the Vyborgskiy Rayon.

Kondratevskiy Pet Market, also called the Polyustrovskiy Pet Market
 Polyustrovskiy pr., 45...... 540-30-39
 Trolley Bus: 12, 3, 43 Tram: 30, 12
 Nearest Metro: Ploshchad Lenina.
 Daily except Sun & official holidays.
Zoo Magazin No. 2
 Ligovskiy pr., 63............. 164-76-74
Zoo Magazin No. 7(under renovation)
 Akademika Lebedeva ul., 19
 542-04-11
Zoo Magazin No. 9
 Ligovskiy pr., 79............. 164-74-77
Zoo Magazin No. 1 (Filial)
 Karla Marksa pr., 81........ 245-78-11

☎ PHARMACIES
(DRUG STORES)
АПТЕКИ
APOTEKEN
PHARMACIES
APOTEK

Until recently there was no equivalent to western pharmacies or drug stores, fully stocked with the latest medicine, and personal hygiene products. However, the situation is rapidly improving as can be seen from the two ads in this section. The standard Russian apothecary is an "apteka" (АПТЕКА) with a limited & uncertain supply of medicines & related products. Most Western medicines & personal items, such as antibiotics, antifungals, sanitary napkins & good quality condoms, are still NOT WIDELY available and you may not be able to refill your prescriptions. Now associated with the well-known Policlinic No. 2 is a well stocked western-style pharmacy with a full variety of imported medicines, personal care products & infant care needs.

KNOLL, AG
Producer of Pharmaceuticals
 ⊠ 199034 Saint Petersburg, Russia
 V.O., Bolshoy pr., 10
 ☎...................................... 218-53-81
 ☎ Fax 350-72-56
 Subsidiary of BASF

The Pharmacy Damian
Of St. Petersburg Policlinic No. 2
Wide selection of Western medicines, antibiotics, cortisone, vitamins, personal hygienic products baby equipment and cosmetics
Pharmacy: M-F, 9:00 to 20:00

 Moskovskiy pr., 22 110-17-44
 Fax................................ 292-59-39
 English, Finnish, German

Pharmacy Panacea
 Primorskiy pr., 37............ 239-59-50
 New! in St. Petersburg.

The following state APTEKA stores are open daily 8-21:
Drug Store
 Nevskiy pr., 5.................. 312-70-78
Drug Store
 Nevskiy pr., 22............... 311-15-44
Drug Store
 Nevskiy pr., 50............... 311-44-98
Drug Store
 Nevskiy pr., 66............... 314-56-54
Drug Store
 Nevskiy pr., 83............... 277-79-79
Drug Store
 Nevskiy pr., 111............. 277-29-31
Drug Store
 Suvorovskiy pr., 48......... 274-66-83
Drug Store
 Vosstaniya ul., 30........... 272-39-41
Drug Store
 Zagorodnyy pr., 21 315-96-36
Imported medicines and products, $, Rbl.
Drug Store
 V.O., 7-ya Liniya, 16...... 213-62-68

☎ PHONE
ТЕЛЕФОН
TELEFON
TELEPHONE
TELEFON
See TELEPHONE

☎ PHOTOCOPIERS, SERVICE & SUPPLIES
ФОТОКОПИРОВАЛЬНАЯ ТЕХНИКА
FOTOKOPIER AUSRÜSTUNGEN
PHOTOCOPIEURS, EQUIPEMENT
FOTOKOPIERING UTRUSTNING

Canon   Technical Centre
CANON PHOTOCOPIERS
Authorized Sales and Service
For St. Pb. & NW Russia
Branches: Pskov, Arkhangelsk, Petrozavodsk
 Volkovskiy pr., 146/3 269-05-04
 Fax................................ 166-36-24
Hrs: 9-17, Closed Sat, rubles & $, English

Commark Ltd.
Sablinskaya ul., ... 233-30-08

LenPoliGraphServis
Primorskiy pr., 35a 239-68-84

MINOLTA
World Famous Photocopiers & Electronics
Antonenko per., 6 319-93-44

RANK XEROX

World leader in Photocopiers

For Sales, Service & Supplies

Regional Office
Obvodnyy kan., 93a 315-76-70
Fax 315-77-73

Our authorized dealers in
Saint Petersburg

Commark Ltd.
Sablinskaya st., ... 233-30-08
LenPoliGraphServis
Primorskiy pr., 35a 239-68-84
SKIF
Vosstaniya ul., 32 275-41-60

SKIF

AUTHORIZED RANK XEROX DEALER

See our ad under OFFICE EQUIPMENT
Vosstaniya ul., 32 275-53-45

SKIF, office equipment

AUTHORIZED RANK-XEROX DEALER
SALES & SERVICE IN NW RUSSIA
Photocopiers A4-A0 and typewriters,
fax, laser printers, paper & supplies
Personal computers sales & rental
Photocopier Rentals & Stationery
Vosstaniya ul., 32 275-53-45
.... 275-47-53
Fax 275-58-71
Telex .... 621110 SKIF SU
Hrs: 9-18, $ or rubles, English, French

☎ PHOTOCOPYING

ФОТОКОПИИ
FOTOKOPIEREN
PHOTOCOPIEURS
KOPIERING

Most BUSINESS CENTERS *listed under*
BUSINESS SERVICES CENTERS *have photocopying services. Here are some others.*

Charter Kommercheskiy Tsentr
S. Perovskoy ul., 14 312-03-39
Hrs: 11 - 20

Copy-Centre
Morisa Toreza pr., 30 552-54-20
Closed: Saturday, Sunday
Express-print
Pushkinskaya ul., 20 113-18-08

Informatika
Nab. reki Moyki, 64/1 314-06-32
The least expensive photocopies in St. Petersburg. Reduction and enlargement. Good quality paper on Xerox equipment. All sizes up to A3

Inmarkon
Bekhtereva ul., 3/2 265-38-50
Kopiya
Izmaylovskiy pr., 12 292-04-96
Photocopying Center - Copy-Centre
Morisa Toreza pr., 30 552-54-20
Hours: 10 - 19, Closd. 13.30-14.15
Complete photocopying services
Lengiprotorg
Avtovskaya ul., 20 183-34-24
Photocopying and Binding
Marine Computer Systems
Babushkina ul., 80 568-39-48
.... 568-39-50
Optima office
Chaykovskogo ul., 36 273-78-82
Fax 279-79-60
Poligrafiya
Kuybysheva ul., 10 230-81-35
Sever
Olminskogo ul., 13 567-00-86
.... 567-19-93
Fax 567-16-08
Sintez
Rubinshteyna ul., 8 110-66-76
.... 112-56-33
Hrs: 11-18; Clsd. Sat, Sun.

SKIF, Photocopies

Complete Photocopying Service
Xerox Equipment A4-A3
Full Color Photocopying
Coming in September
Vosstaniya ul., 32 275-53-45
.... 275-47-53
Fax 275-58-71
Hrs: 9-18, $ or rubles, English, French

Sinus
Morskoy Pekhoty ul., 8, bldg. 1
.... 157-57-94

☎ PHOTOGRAPHERS, PHOTOS

ФОТОГРАФЫ, ФОТОАТЕЛЬЕ
FOTOGRAFEN, FOTOSTUDIOS
PHOTOGRAPHES
FOTOGRAFER

Alenmax
Liteynyy pr., 20, rm. 14 ... 278-86-81
Fax 114-36-52
We speak both English and Finnish

Anichkov Most Photoservice
Nab. reki Fontanki, 23 314-49-36
.... 314-39-72
Fotoavtomat (Automatic)
Nevskiy pr., 128 277-31-32
Fotografiya
P.S., Bolshoy pr., 33 232-44-35
Fotografiya
Volodarskogo ul., 14 237-21-62
Fotografiya
Veteranov pr., 140 135-45-46
Fotografiya
Krasnoputilovskaya ul., 9
.... 184-64-76
Fotografiya
Karla Marksa pr., 75 245-00-94
Fotografiya
Kronshtadt, Lenina ul., 13
.... 236-21-65
Fotografiya No. 2
S. Perovskoy ul., 7 311-80-20
Specializing in children
Fotografiya No. 27
Nevskiy pr., 22/24 312-01-22
Fotografiya No. 5
Sadovaya ul., 27 310-06-35
Fotografiya No. 52
Chernyshevskogo pr., 17
.... 279-52-33
Fotografiya No. 6 (Fast Photo)
Liteynyy pr., 23 273-21-53
Fotografiya No. 60
Novocherkasskiy pr., 22/15
.... 221-22-87
Fotografiya No. 67
Gagarina pr., 24 264-60-34
Fotografiya No. 8 (under renovation)
V. O., Sredniy pr., 49 213-12-63

KITEZH

Professional photographers
Art, architecture and folk art
Illustration of art books & calendars
Custom work & museum slides
Write: Box 216, St. Pb., 199034
Telephone in St. Pb: 213-65-96

Photographer
Sedova ul., 154 262-49-27
Photographers for the Weekend
Private Photographer
.... 235-65-49
Photos in your home
Studio Photographer
Nauki pr., 38 249-07-64
Artistic photos and other Photo services

☎ **PHOTOGRAPHY
CAMERAS & SUPPLIES**
ФОТОГРАФИЯ - АППАРАТУРА И
ПРИНАДЛЕЖНОСТИ
FOTOAPPARATE UND ZUBEHÖR
PHOTO-CAMERAS ET
FOURNITURES
FOTO, KAMEROR OCH TILLBEHÖR

See also shops listed under
PHOTOGRAPHY-FILM & DEVELOPING.
Fotokinotovary
P.S., Bolshoy pr., 63 232-19-02
Foto
Moskovskiy pr., 192 298-17-47

☎ **PHOTOGRAPHY - FILM
& DEVELOPING**
ФОТОГРАФИЯ - ПЛЕНКА И ЕЕ
ПРОЯВЛЕНИЕ
FOTO, FILME UND ENTWICKLUNG
PHOTO-PELLICULE
FOTO, FILM OCH FRAMKALLNING

See also INTERNATIONAL SHOPS

A wide selection of 110-size and 35 mm print and slide (Ektachrome) films are available in most hotels, INTERNATIONAL SHOPS, Pyotr Velikiy, Achminov Most and the new Agfa shop on Nevskiy.

Quick film processing using imported chemicals is now available for Kodak (Kodak C41 process and Ektachrome E6 process), Fuji and Agfa. Russian-made film is supposedly compatible with Agfa process only, but it is best processed in Russia.

You can drop your film off for overnight developing at the following hotels: ASTORIA, SAINT PETERSBURG and GAVAN (now Octivian)

1 HOUR PHOTO
Nevskiy pr., 20 311-99-74
Film Processing (including movie)
Nevskiy pr., 54 311-08-38
*Hrs: 11 - 14, 16 - 20 Clsd. Sunday
(& Saturday in Summer)*

SOME HISTORICAL DATES

1689-1725	*Reign of Peter The Great*
16 May 1703	*St.-Petersburg founded by Peter the Great*
1712	*St.-Petersburg made capital of the Russian Empire*
1700-1721	*Northern War between Sweden and Russia over access to the Baltic Sea*
1725	*Peter the Great died.*

Fotoeffekt
Prosveshcheniya pr., 87
.... 530-09-04
24 hour service.
*Film developing of Kodak, E-6, G-41 and
other types of films. Filming in photo
studios.*

Kinolaboratoriya
Sofi Perovskoy ul., 7 311-02-45

Fuji Film and Processing

ANICHIKOV MOST'
PHOTOGRAPHY SHOP
1 HOUR FUJI PROCESSING
FUJI PHOTO SUPPLIES
Nab. reki Fontanki, 23 314-49-36

Kino-Photo repair
Nevskiy pr., 92 273-89-01
Hrs: 10 - 19

Kino-Photo
Sredniy pr., 27 213-18-56

Pyotr Velikiy, photography shop

Kodak
EXPRESS

KODAK *EXPRESS* SERVICE
All Kodak Paper, Chemicals, & Equipment
Enlargements to 28 by 36
Drop-off your film at night, back in the morning
at Astoria & St. Petersburg, Gavan
Two shops in Saint Petersburg
• Sofi Perovskoy ul., 7 *Metro: Nevskiy prospekt*
....110-64-97
   Fax...292-42-79
• Leninskiy pr., 138....................110-61-97
In the Narvskiy Univermag at the Metro: Leninskiy pr.
Hrs: 10-20, $, English

Obektiv
Sofii Perovskoy ul., 7 110-64-97
Fax 292-42-79
Hrs: 10 - 20 $, Rbls

☎ **PHOTOGRAPHY - REPAIRS**
ФОТОАППАРАТЫ, РЕМОНТ
FOTO, REPARATUR
APPAREILS DE PHOTO,
REPARATION
KAMEROR, REPARATION

Camera Repairs (including movie)
Atele Po Remontu Kinofotoapparatury
Nevskiy pr., 168.............. 277-58-18
Orders for repair of foreign equipment
Hrs: 10 -19, Clsd. Sun.
Camera Repairs
Nevskiy pr., 20............... 315-49-88
Hrs: 9 - 20, Mon. & Sat. 8 - 18 Clsd. Sun.
Nevskiy pr., 168.............. 277-58-18
Hrs: 9 - 17 Clsd. Sun

Fotokinotovary No. 58 (repair)
Nevskiy pr., 92.............. 273-89-01

☎ **PIANOS**
ПИАНИНО
KLAVIERE
PIANO
PIANO

Concern **"Goryachev"**
Fine Grand Pianos
Custom-built elegant fine pianos
Vereyskaya ul., 39............... 112-75-96
Fax 311-95-76
Hrs: 10-20, $, English

☎ **PIZZERIAS**
ПИЦЦЕРИИ
PIZZERIEN
PIZZERIAS
PIZZERIOR

Allegro
Moskovskiy pr., 73 298-95-52
Hrs: 12 - 23

PIZZA-EXPRESS
Quick Home Delivery
From 10 am to 24 pm,
13 Varieties of Pizza, Steak,
Weiner Schnitzel, Pasta & Salad
Lapin Kulta Beer & European Wines
Visit our restaurant
          at Podolskaya ul., 23
7 minutes drive from center
Orders........................... 292-26-66
Fax 292-10-39
$, CC, English, Finnish

Pizzeria
Rubinshteyna ul., 30 314-57-18
Gino Ginelli
Nab. kan. Griboedova, 14
.... 312-21-20
Musa Cafe - "Pizza Express" *Pizza*
Ogorodnikova pr., 48....... 251-17-24

☎ **PLANETARIUM**
ПЛАНЕТАРИЙ
PLANETARIUM
PLANETARIUM
PLANETARIUM

Planetarium
Park Lenina, 4 233-31-53
Metro: Gorkovskaya

☎ POLICE
ПОЛИЦИЯ
POLIZEI
POLICE
POLIS

See MILITIA

Call...........................02

☎ PORCELAIN
ФАРФОР
PORZELLAN
PORCELAINES
PORSLIN

See CRYSTAL & PORCELAIN

☎ PORTS
ПОРТЫ
HÄFEN
PORTS
HAMNAR

See SEA TERMINALS
and RIVER TERMINALS

☎ POSTAL ADDRESSES
ПОЧТОВЫЕ ПРАВИЛА
POSTANSCHRIFT
REGLES POSTALES
POST ADRESS

*Addresses on international mail into
and out of Russia may be written in
English and in standard western format.
The usual order of writing an address
WITHIN Russia is the following:*
   Country
   Six digit postal code, City or Town
   Street Name
   Name of Addressee
followed below by the return address

☎ POSTAL RATES
ПОЧТОВЫЕ РАСЦЕНКИ
POSTGEBÜHREN
PRIX POSTAL
POST, AVGIFTER

*Postal rates are changing quickly.
Consult the post office to check rates.
Currently inland (domestic) postal rates
are used for the Commonwealth countries
(CIS, СНГ) but not the Baltics and other
totally independent republics.*

TYP *WANT TO BUY CLOTHING
AND DON'T KNOW THE
RUSSIAN SIZES.*
**Look at our TABLE OF SIZES
Page 245**

DOMESTIC POSTAL RATES

(Inland incl. CIS):

   Letters to 20 grams .... 80 kop.
   Postcards .... 50 kop.
   Books to 20 grams .... 2.25 rbl.
   Each additional 20 grams of
   letters and books.................. 25 kop.
   Packages vary according to weight
   and distances. For each 500 grams:

Distance	Cost in Rubles
< 600 km...........................	680
601-2000 km.........................	1040
2001-5000 km........................	1220
5000-8000 km........................	1340
> 8000 km...........................	1480

EXPRESS MAIL RATES (RUBLES)

JV "EMC Garant Post"
   at Main Post Office, (till autumn)
   Pochtamtskaya ul., 9....... 312-26-93
   Starting in the autumn at new address
   Bul. Profsoyuzov, 4 311-11-20

Zones: I Europe, II Japan, III Canada,
   Germany, Israel, NZ, USA

	Zone I	Zone II	Zone III
Documents: (Rubles)			
0 - 100 g	1375	1540	1750
100 g - 1 kg	1980	2200	2475
over 1 kg	+330	+550	+660
Goods: (Rubles)			
0 - 250 g	2475	2750	3025
250 - 500 g	2750	3025	3300
500g - 1 kg	3080	3575	4070
over 1 kg	+330	+550	+770

INTERNATIONAL POSTAL RATES

Letters (Rubles)	Air	Surface
0 ÷ 20 g	5.00	3.60
20 ÷ 100 g	16.00	8.60
100 ÷ 250 g	39.00	17.30
250 ÷ 500 g	80.00	32.00
Postcards (Rbl.):	3.50	2.50
Books (Rubles):		
20 ÷ 100 g	38.50	28.00
100 ÷ 250 g	70.50	42.00
250 ÷ 500 g	124.00	65.00
500 g ÷ 1 kg	217.50	101.00
1 ÷ 2 kg	392.00	167.00
2 ÷ 3 kg	567.50	229.00

Packages by surface mail

(Rubles):	Germany	Israel	USA
1 kg	1865	2040	1460
10 kg	3565	4755	5280

☎ POST OFFICES
ПОЧТА
POSTÄMTER
POSTE
POSTKONTOR

See also EXPRESS MAIL/PARCELS SERVICE

Outbound airmail to the UK & USA takes about three weeks and is reliable. Inbound mail is less reliable and can take three weeks or more. Express Mail is part of the international express mail service and works rather well. Use better envelopes than those supplied by the post office.

There are about 700 post offices in St. Petersburg which sell stamps. Many handle international mailings of letters and books. To mail packages and express mail abroad, however, you must still go to the Main Post Office called the Glav Pochtamt (Глав Почтампт). Packages are wrapped at the post office. There also were post office counters in the following hotels: Astoria, Kareliya, Leningrad, Moskva, Pribaltiyskaya, and Pulkovskaya.

Main Post Office (Glav Pochtamt):
Stamps, express mail, packages, magazine and newspaper subscriptions, telegraph, philately.
    Pochtamtskaya ul., 9....... 312-83-05
                Daily: 9 - 21
DISTRICT POST OFFICES
Open from 9 am to 9 pm, lunch break 2-3
Dzerzhinskiy Post Office
    191187, Furmanova ul., 17
    Information 272-75-13
Frunzenskiy Post Office
    192282, Bukharestskaya ul., 23, bldg.1
    Information 105-44-35
Kirovskiy Post Office
    198095, Stachek pr., 18
    Information 252-28-32
Krasnogvardeyskiy Post Office
    195253, Energetikov pr., 42
    Information 225-60-82
Krasnoselskiy Post Office
    198259, Tambasova ul., 32
    Complaints..................... 130-49-07
Moskovskiy Post Office
    196084, Moskovskiy pr., 75
    Information 292-08-01
Petrogradskiy Post Office
    197198, Olega Koshevogo ul., 10-a
    Information 232-13-13
Pochta 24-ye otdelenie
    Nevskiy pr., 148
    Insurance Dept. 277-13-81
    Telegraph 277-05-37
        Metro: Ploshchad Vosstaniya

Sestroretskiy Post Office
    189640, Kommunarov ul., 2/4
    Information 237-37-73
Smolninskiy Post Office
    193167, Perekupnoy per., 11/15
    Information 274-06-27
Vyborgskiy Post Office
    194223, Orbeli ul., 25
    Information 244-09-06

☎ POST RESANTE
ПОЧТА ДО ВОСТРЕБОВАНИЯ
POSTLAGERNDE SENDUNGEN
POSTE RESTANTE
POSTE RESTANTE

See also EXPRESS MAIL/PARCEL SERVICE.

Most post offices have a "general delivery" called "post restant" where you can pick up mail from the post office. Foreigners can use the following. But don't rely on it for highly critical items.

    Russia:
    19044, St. Petersburg
    Nevskiy Prospekt 6
    Poste Restante
    Name of Addressee
But you can address it to any post office "Post office" by using the correct postal code, street address, including the words Pochta Do Vostrebovaniya, (Почта до востребования) and your name. Try having mail sent to your hotel or the American Express Company, located in the Grand Hotel Europe (for card holders only); mail will be held for two months.

☎ PRINTING
ТИПОГРАФИИ
DRUCKEREIEN
IMPRIMERIE
SKRIVA

Alcor Technologies Inc.
Stepana Razina ul., 8/50 310-44-01
    Fax 310-44-70

ECS, USA
    Nevskiy pr., 147/149....... 277-15-90
    277-68-70
Ego
    Dzerzhinskogo ul., 6........ 219-11-94
    315-27-73
    Fax 312-92-84

Leningradskiy Kombinat Tsvetnoy Pechati
(Color Printing)
Obukhovskoy Oborony pr., 110
....262-20-77

Rikki-Tikki-Tavi
Dekabristov ul., 62..........219-76-92
....114-19-20
Book printing, calendars, albums, etc.
Sileks
Volodi Ermaka ul., 9........219-75-87
Smart
Admiralteyskiy pr., 8/1 110-66-55
Fax.................................314-34-35
Telex ....121 432 SMART SU
Tayny veka
Sadovaya ul., 53 310-65-37
Tipografiya im. Ivana Fedorova
Zvenigorodskaya ul., 11
....164-45-29
Tipografiya No. 4
Sotsialisticheskaya ul., 14
....164-87-06

☎ **PROPANE**
ПРОПАН
PROPANGAS
PROPANE
PROPAN (GAS)

Lenavtoremont Enterprise
Saltykovskaya doroga, 15
....226-67-26
Installation servicing of propane-gas equipment
Propan
Polyustrovskiy pr., 77
...............................245-54-19
Sedova ul., 9............265-17-35

☎ **PSYCHIATRISTS**
ПСИХИАТРЫ
PSYCHIATER
PSYSCHIATRES
PSYKIATER

See MEDICAL CARE *and* CONSULTATIONS

☎ **PUBLISHERS**
ИЗДАТЕЛЬСТВА
VERLAGE
EDITEURS
FÖRLÄGGARE

Albor
Kalyaeva ul., 25, apt. 38
....275-49-10
....275-75-29

Byuro - 2
Povarskoy per., 9, apt. 10
.... 542-87-03
Detskaya Literatura [Children's Literature]
Nab. Kutuzova, 6............ 273-48-24
.... 279-08-78
Izobrazitelnoe Iskusstvo [Graphic Arts]
Sadovaya ul., 89 114-69-62
Iskusstvo-SPb [Art-Saint Petersburg]
Nevskiy pr., 28................ 219-94-72

KIFA ORTHODOX CENTRE

Publishers for Russian Orthodox Church
Literature & Icons
Library of Russian Church Literature
Meetings of the Russian Orthodox

Leninskiy pr., 135........... 255-60-81
.... 225-59-28
Fax...................... 470-43-62
Hrs: 10-19, Closed Sundays

Khudozhestvennaya Literatura
[Art Literature]
Nevskiy pr., 28................ 311-32-51
.... 219-90-10
Khudozhnik Rossii [Artists of Russia]
Bolsheokhtinskiy pr., 6, bldg. 2
.... 224-06-37
.... 224-06-39

L I C

Information & Publishing Agency, Ltd.

Publisher of the
St.Petersburg Business Guide

Gertsena ul., 20 314-59-82
Fax................................ 315-35-92

Lenizdat [Len Press]
Nab. reki Fontanki, 59 210-84-11
.... 311-14-51
Meditsyna [Medicine]
Nekrasova ul., 10 273-55-10
Muzyka [Music]
Ryleeva ul., 17 279-01-75
.... 279-02-52
Mysl [Idea]
Nab. kan. Griboedova, 26
.... 314-33-45
Isdatelskaya firma vserossiyskogo
obedineniya "Nauka" [Science]
Mendeleevskaya Liniya, 1
.... 218-39-12
.... 218-40-11
Nedra
Farforovskaya ul., 18....... 560-40-65
Palitra [Palette]
Perekupnoy per., 15/17 ... 274-45-18
Fax: 274-09-11

Rossiyskoe isdatelskoe obedinenie
"Sankt-Peterburg"
Gertsena ul., 45.............. 314-09-21
.... 311-15-95

ROTAR, publishers

A private company of Gorokhovskiy

Design and publication of
Newspaper "Aktsioner", books,
brochures & advertising materials
Design of Business Stationery
Shpalernaya ul., 52, apt. 23
Tel................ 275-31-12
Fax................ 275-31-12
Telex.............121745 GARDA SU

SANTA LTD Advertising Agency

Publisher of

St. Petersburg
Today & Tonight

Information magazine

For visitors to Saint Petersburg

Four times per year • English & German

Printed in Finland, 20,000 copies

Nab. Makarova, 30 279-73-29

Smart
Admiralteyskiy pr., 8 110-66-34
.... 110-66-55
Fax: 110-65-70
Telex:.................121432 Smart SU
Rossiyskiy Pisatel [Russian writer]
Liteynyy pr., 36 279-03-36
Transport
Dekabristov ul., 33.......... 114-52-32

VNESHVUS-CENTRE

Publishers

with Ivan Feodorov Printing House
Books & catalogues
Postcards, brochures, & calendars
Translated & published in any language.
Write to: Post Office Box 14
199226 Saint Petersburg Russia
V.O., Nab. Morskaya, 9.................356-99-04
Fax.......................................355-69-87
English, German, Finnish & Others
Inter'l Centre for Research, Education & Commerce

Yuridicheskaya Literatura [Legal literature]
Nevskiy pr., 28................ 219-94-65

☎ QUALITY CONTROL
КОНТРОЛЬ ЗА КАЧЕСТВОМ ПРОДУКЦИИ
QUALITÄTSKONTROLLE
QUALITE DE LA PRODUCTION, CONTROLE
KVALITETSKONTROLL, LAB

Metrolog (Coop)
Please call 213-44-06
Quality control for polished metal surfaces.

☎ RACING
БЕГА, СКАЧКИ
WETTRENNEN, RENNEN
COURSES
RACING, (HÄST, KAPPLÖPNING, BILRACING

There is no official horse racing in St. Pb. buy they are building a racetrack. For automobile racing, try the following to get information on competitions or participate in them.
Automotosport in St.Petersburg
.... 274-66-53
.... 274-22-56
Mototrek
Zhaka Duklo ul., 67......... 553-17-61
.... 553-70-11
Director......................... 553-70-15
.... 553-70-11

The track in Yukki is used for international competitions on auto and motorcycles. The Mototrek track at Zhaka Duklo is also used for international competitions.

☎ RADIO STATIONS
РАДИОСТАНЦИЯ
RADIOSENDER
RADIO, STATIONS DE
RADIOSTATIONER

A small multi band radio with FM, MW (AM), short-wave and long wave bands with a nice sound for music is a good companion on any trip to listen to local stations and occasionally to tune into BBC, MOXAS and Voice of America. The Russians and Europeans sometimes use "wavelength" in meters rather our "kilohertz" and "megahertz".

What to listen to in Saint Petersburg. There are three official stations and a growing number of commercial radio stations in Saint Petersburg. Many old Russian radios have one to three buttons to select the stations, because historically many apartments were wired for three-channel

inexpensive radios. New radios can tune in a variety of programs on fm, short-wave, middle wave and long wave.

AM (Middle Waves)

KHz	Mtrs	Station, type, hours
549	550	MAYAK, *Music and news* *4 am -24.00*
684	460	RADIO ALA, *Music and news* *4 am -3 am*
747	401	RADIO BALTICA *Music and news* *7 am-24.00*
800	375	RADIO ST.-PETERSBURG *News, music, St.-Pb.* *current events*
873	345	RADIO ROSSII *Music, news, commentary* *5 am-3 am*
1053	285	OTKRYTYY GOROD *St.-Pb. Current Events* *7.30 am-22*
1125		ORFEY *Classical music* *6 am-24.00*
1260		GOLOS NADEZHDY (VOICE OF HOPE) *Religious programs, music* *Daily 2 pm-3 am* *7 am-9 am on* *Tues., Wed., Sat., Sun.*
1271	234	RADIO-I, *Music and news* *6 am -1 am*
1494	190	RADIO ALA, *Music and news* *1 am-7.30 pm*

FM

67.45	MAYAK *Music and news* *5 am-3 am*
66.3	RADIO ROSSII *Music, news, commentary* *5 am-am*
69.47	ST.-PETERSBURG *News, music and local* *classified advertising* *5 am-1 am*
71.24	RADIO BALTICA *Music and news*
100.5	EUROPA PLUS, Popular *Music*
102.0	RADIO ROX, Popular *Music*

Europa Plus
Inquiries 234-40-80
Prof. Popova ul., 47 234-98-60
The Best of the West

Radio stations studios in Saint Petersburg.
Advertising on St. Petersburg Radio
Commercial Advertising Board of
Leningrad Radio
Rakova ul., 27................ 219-96-85
Radioveshchanie
Rakova ul., 27
Information 219-96-16

☎ RAIL INFORMATION
ЖЕЛЕЗНОДОРОЖНАЯ ИНФОРМАЦИЯ
ZUGAUSKUNFT
INFORMATION FERROVIERE
TÅGINFORMATION

Railway Information:........ 168-01-11

The length of time for railroad trips:

Abroad:
Berlin - 34 hours, Warsaw - 23-26 hours, Helsinki - 6.5 hours.

Domestic:
Moscow: 6- 8.5 hours (15 times daily), Pskov 4-5 hours, Tallinn 7-8 hours, Riga 9-10 hours

☎ RAILWAY STATIONS
ЖЕЛЕЗНОДОРОЖНЫЕ ВОКЗАЛЫ
BAHNHÖFE
GARES, FERROVIERE
TÅGSTATION

🚂 Baltic Station
Балтийский **Baltiyskiy**
Mainly for suburban trains
Nab. Obvodnogo kan., 120
Information 168-01-11
Metro: Baltiyskaya
Buses: 10, 49, 60, 67, 109
Trolleys: 3, 24
Trams: 1, 2, 19, 29, 34, 35, 43

🚂 Finland Station
Финляндский **Finlyandskiy**
Trains to Helsinki
Lenina pl., 6
Information 168-01-11
Container Service
Mineralnaya str., 25 168-72-72
Metro: Ploshchad Lenina
Buses: 2, 28, 37, 47, 49, 78, 104,
106, 107, 36, 137, 262
Trolleys: 3, 8, 12, 19, 23, 38, 43
Trams: 6,17, 19, 20, 23, 25, 30, 32,
38, 51

🚂 Moscow Station
Московский **Moskovskiy**
Trains to Moscow, Far North, Crimea, Georgia, Central Asia
Vosstaniya pl., 2
Information 168-01-11
Metro: Ploshchad Vosstaniya,
Mayakovskaya
Buses: 3, 7, 22, 26, 27, 44, 74, 174
Trolleys: 1, 5, 7, 10, 14, 16, 22, 42
Trams: 10, 16, 19, 25, 44, 49

🚂 Warsaw Station
Варшавский **Varshavskiy**
Trains to Baltics, Pskov, Lvov and Eastern Europe

Nab. Obvodnogo kan., 118
Information 168-26-11
Freight collection 168-26-55
Metro: Baltiyskaya
Buses: 10, 60
Trolleys: 15,17,24
Trams: 1, 2, 15, 16, 19, 29, 34, 35, 43

🚂 Vitebsk Station
Витебский **Vitebskiy**
Trains to Smolensk, Belorus, Kiev, Odessa and Moldavia
Zagorodnyy pr., 52
Information 168-53-90
Small international freight packages
.... 168-57-93
Freight office.................. 314-02-35
Metro: Pushkinskaya
Trolleys: 3,8,9,15
Trams: 11,28, 34

☎ REAL ESTATE AGENTS
АГЕНТЫ ПО КУПЛЕ-ПРОДАЖЕ
MAKLER, IMMOBILIEN
ACHAT ET VENTE, AGENTS D' FASTIGHETSMÄKLARE

Antaks-Tur
Metallistov pr., 119, rm. 28
.... 540-50-26

DOM PLUS
A G E N C Y

We buy, sell and rent commercial, industrial and residential properties.
Full service agency providing assistance with negotiations and documents.
Kanal Griboedova, 3 312-11-32
Fax 312-83-51

Ecopolis
Real Estate Development
Real Estate Consulting for Foreign Companies
Purchase, Renovation, Sale & Lease
Buildings in center & suburbs of St Pb.
Zanevskiy pr., 32, Bldg. 2, No. 3528–26–66

Interpolice
Plekhanova ul., 49 314-07-97
Lenalp
Bolshoy Smolenskiy pr., 2
.... 567-09-84
.... 567-95-50
Peterburgskiy Auktsion
Grivtsova per., 5, rm. 34-37
.... 311-06-56
.... 311-01-92
Fax 311-06-01

Rubezh
  Pionerstroya ul., 14, bldg. 1
  138-72-51
  138-72-47
  Fax 138-72-45

☎ RECORDS
ПЛАСТИНКИ СМ. МУЗЫКАЛЬНЫЕ
    МАГАЗИНЫ
SCHALLPLATTEN
DISQUES
SKIVOR

See also MUSIC SHOPS.

Records, tapes, and CD's can be bought in many department stores and in special shops.

Dom Muzyki i Radio
      House of Music and Radio
  Grazhdanskiy pr., 15, bldg. 1
  ....,,,,,, . 535 03-14
  534-42-18
  Metro: Akademicheskaya
  Hrs: 10-19 Tu-Sat

Melodiya
  Wide selection of the best modern
  Russian and Western popular music
  Classical music department.
  Nevskiy pr., 32/34 311-74-55
  Metro: Nevskiy prospekt Hrs: 11-20 Mon-Sat

☎ REFRIGERATORS
ХОЛОДИЛЬНИКИ
KÜHLSCHRÄNKE
REFRIGERATEURS
KYLSKÅP

See KITCHEN APPLIANCES &
    DEPARTMENT STORES.

Russian freezers and refrigerators are basic solid appliances without many features. Consider buying one from a specialty store called "Refrigerators" (Kholodilniki, ХОЛОДИЛЬНИКИ) or a Univermag department store.

☎ RENTALS
(furniture, bicycles, TVs)
ПРОКАТ ОБОРУДОВАНИЯ,
    ТЕЛЕВИЗОРОВ
VERLEIH
LOUAGE DE T.V., D' EQUIPMENT
UTHYRNING, MÖBLER, CYKLAR,
    TV-APPARATER ETC.

The Russians rent a number of items, such as TVs, coffee pots, furniture, and bicycles. Try the official rental stores in the nearest "rental point" (punkt prokata, Пункт проката).

Dzerzhinskiy District (Punkt Prokata)
  Volynskiy per., 8/19 314-42-10
  Chernyshevskogo pr., 13
  273-23-61

Frunzenskiy District
  Dimitrova ul., 20 (TV's)
  172-53-46
  Kupchinskaya ul., 32 (Furniture)
  176-77-45
Kalininskiy District
  Grazhdanskiy pr., 92 555-11-12
  Timurovskaya ul., 8 557-66-83
  Akademika Lebedeva ul., 15
  542-11-34
Kirovskiy District
  Avtovskaya ul., 32 184-20-38
  Leninskiy pr., 117 157-76-18
Krasnogvardeyskiy District
  Novocherkasskiy pr., 22/15
  221-22-82
  Novocherkasskiy pr., 12
  520-94-83
Kuybishevskiy District
  Kolokolnaya ul., 2 113-38-82
  Dzerzhinskogo ul., 36 310-88-53
Leninskiy District
  Uglovoy per., 5 292-79-38
Moskovskiy District
  Novo-Izmaylovskiy pr., 28
  295-43-06
  Leninskiy pr., 147 295-63-67
Nevskiy District
  Dybenko ul., 25 585-42-80
  Narodnaya ul., 1 263-60-23
  Narodnaya ul., 2 263-74-00
Oktyabrskiy District
  Lermontovskiy pr., 24 114-22-87
  Sadovaya ul., 49 314-82-47
  Bolshoy pr., 19 232-48-58
Rentals
  Torzhkovskaya ul., 1 246-17-21
Rentals
  Veteranov pr., 141 144-33-75
Rentals of Petrogradskiy District
  Kirovskiy pr., 52 234-54-76
  Vokzalnaya ul., 17 237-64-02
Primorskiy District
  Shkolnaya ul , 56 239-01-20
Smolninskiy District
  Tverskaya ul., 7 271-97-12
Vasileostrovskiy District
  Nab. Morskaya, 17 356-98-83
  Nalichnaya ul., 11 356-54-15
Vyborgskiy District
  Gavrskaya ul., 4 553-88-48
  Neyshlotskiy per., 23 542-30-03

TYP
BUYING TICKETS TO
THE THEATER
Check our SEATING PLANS
Page 246 - 251

☎ REPAIR SERVICES
РЕМОНТ КВАРТИР, СЛУЖБА
RENOVIERUNG
REPARATION, SERVICE DE
REPARATIONER

APARTMENT REPAIR
See APARTMENT REPAIR

COMPUTERS
See COMPUTER REPAIR:

ELECTRICAL APPLIANCES:
Minsk Repair Center
Baltiyskaya ul., 3 186-12-06
Refrigerators repair and services
Ravenstvo
Promyshlennaya ul., 19.... 252-92-89
*Repair of precision instruments, optical
and mechanical equipment.*
Vera-Servis
Grazhdanskiy pr., 33 535-04-88
Bukharestskaya ul., 116
.... 106-88-42
We repair all types of refrigerators.

ELECTRONICS:
Electrical Repairs
Budapeshtskaya ul., 15, bldg. 2, apt. 64
.... 174-33-34
Repairs of electrical equipment

OFFICE SUPPLIES:
Kantstovary, Pishushchie Mashinki,
Kalkulyatory
Nevskiy pr., 130............ 277-07-30
Metro: Vosstaniya pl.

PHOTOCOPIERS:

RADIO/TELEVISION:
"Hitachi"
Representative at Gavan,
Lenexpo, please call
Nalichnaya ul., 6............. 355-33-42

SEWING & KNITTING MACHINES:
See SEWING MACHINE REPAIR

TYPEWRITERS:
Bait
Zastavskaya ul., 26........ 531-26-11
Remont i Regulirovka Pishushchikh Mashin
Grazhdanskiy pr., 31 535-73-13
Typewriter service and repair.

☎ RESTAURANTS & CAFES
РЕСТОРАНЫ И КАФЕ
RESTAURANTS
RESTAURANTS
RESTAURANGER

*See also CAFES, FAST FOOD, PIZZA,
FOOD DELIVERY, DELICATESSENS
and ICE CREAM.*

Saint Petersburg has over 1000 eating establishments from the numerous very basic, inexpensive cafeterias (stolovaya, столовая, and cafeteriy, кафетерий) to the most elegant restaurants in old palaces and hotels. Here we include only those establishments offering something substantial to eat, from sandwiches, soup, pizzas and good pancakes to steaks and great fish. Cafes (КАФЕ) serving only drinks, pastries and ice cream are listed under cafes.

The English word "restaurant" has a much wider meaning among Westerners than in Russia. The Russians themselves make a sharp distinction between the concept of "restaurant" and all other places to eat. "Restaurant" means high-class, good-quality, expensive with a special cuisine and often an orchestra, variety show and music with champagne, wine and vodka. This is the "classic Russian restaurant".

But there are many other places to eat in Saint Petersburg and the food, while simpler, can be quite good, especially at some of the cafes. Some special places to eat are the "Blinnaya" (БЛИННАЯ) which serve Russian blinyes and baked pastries, "cafe-morozhenoe" (КАФЕ-МОРОЖЕНОЕ), which serve ice cream, coffee, chocolate sweets, champagne and cognac, "pyshech-naya" (ПЫШЕЧНАЯ), which serve coffee and a Russian-style donuts-puffs. A beer bar (pivnoy bar, ПИВНОЙ БАР) serves beer and appetizers, a beer restaurant has a more extensive menu. A "grill bar" is more expensive and serves drinks, grilled meats and "shashlyk".

"Light snacks" usually means open-faced sandwiches with cheese, meat, caviar, some baked goods, some juices, cognac & champagne.

Hotel restaurants tend to be large restaurants, often with orchestra and "variety", although some have small dining rooms and quiet corners (as noted).

"Rubles" means only rubles, $ means hard currency only, and "$ and rubles" can mean three things: a ruble menu with a more limited selection (or even in a different section) than for $, or drinks are paid in hard currency and the meal is paid in rubles, or an entrance fee is paid in $ and the rest in rubles.

Reservations are recommended, especially for the large restaurants and hotels. To make reservations, call and ask for the "ADMINISTRATOR" or MAITRE D'HÔTEL.

"Music" usually means recorded music. Look for "Orchestra" or "Chamber Music" or "Band" for live music. "Variety show" usually means singing of contemporary music, dance line and comedy. A "cultural evening" may include classic music, poetry and Russian romantic ballads.

"Folklore" and "gypsy" are usually in national costume and feature folk and national songs.

* * * * * * * * * * * * * * * * * *

ADMIRALTEYSKIY
Gertsena ul., 27 314-45-14
Russian Cuisine, Hrs: 12-23, Rubles

AnnA

A SPECIAL DINING EXPERIENCE
FOR
YOUR TOURISTS' GROUPS & SYMPOSIA
BREAKFAST, LUNCH & DINNER
TO ORDER
Please call to arrange
Khlopina ul., 5 247-24-02
Fax 247-28-57
Hrs: 12-24, rubles & $, English

"ARAGVI"
Tukhachevskogo ul., 41 225-03-36
Georgian Cuisine, Hrs: 12-23, rubles

THE ASTORIA
Fine Dining at the Hotel Astoria
European and Russian Cuisine
Gertsena ul., 39 210-59-06
Hrs: 12- 24, $, CC, English

THE ASTORIA GRILL
FINE GRILLED SPECIALTIES
At the Hotel Astoria, Bldg. B
Gertsena ul., 39 210-59-06
Hrs: 12- 24, $, CC, English

THE ANGLETERRE
RESTAURANT
At the Hotel Astoria, Bldg. B
Meet for lunch or dinner
At St. Isaac's Square
Gertsena ul., 39 210-59-06
Hrs: 12- 1, $, CC, English

THE ATRIUM MEZZANINE CAFE
AT THE GRAND HOTEL EUROPE
MEET AT THE ATRIUM CAFE FOR
A CUP OF COFFEE WITH FINE PASTRY OR GLASS
OF WINE WITH A GOURMET SANDWICH

Mikhaylovskaya ul., 1/7 & Nevskiy
☎ ....312-00-72, Ext. 6340
Daily 11-23, Sunday 3-11, $, English

AUSTERIA
RUSSIAN & INTERNATIONAL CUISINE
AT THE Peter and Paul Fortress,
In the Joannovskiy Ravelin
.... 232-75-80
.... 238-42-62
Hrs: 12-24, rubles

AKHTAMAR
Budapeshtskaya ul., 33
.... 260-74-94
Russian & Georgian, 11-23, rubles

ALENUSHKA
Moskovskiy pr., 78 292-29-96
Russian cuisine , 12-23, rubles

AVTOMAT CAFE
Nevskiy pr. 45 311-15-06
Coffee and Snacks

BALTIKA
Restaurant & Nightclub • Russian Cuisine
Mira pl., 4/1 310-21-08
Administrator 310-71-21
Hrs: 12 to 5 am, rubles

BELYE NOCHI W H I T E N I G H T S
Fancy Russian Restaurant
Orchestra & Great Dance Music
Mayorova pr., 41 314-84-32

BELAYA LOSHAD
A Russian Beer Restaurant
Chkalovskiy pr., 16 235-11-13
Hrs: 12-23:30, rubles

BISTRO, coffee & sandwiches
Michurinskaya ul., 12 232-34-93
Hrs: 10-20

BUKHARA,
Nepokorennykh ul., 74 249-34-81
Cuisine from Middle Asia, Hrs: 12-23, rubles

THE BRASSERIE
IN SAINT PETERSBURG
BEST HAMBURGERS IN TOWN
EUROPEAN WINE CELLAR
AT THE GRAND HOTEL EUROPE
Mikhaylovskaya ul., 1/7 (& Nevskiy)
☎ ....312-00-72, Ext. 6340
Daily 11-23, Sunday 15-23, $, English

Brigantina
Dvinskaya ul., 3 259-08-15
European & Russian Cuisine
Variety Show Manhattan

"Around the corner and down the steps"
The CAFE "Bristol"
For a quick cup of good coffee and snack
Black & red caviar, pizza, & khachapuri
Nevskiy pr., 22............... 311-74-90
Hrs: 10-20, Ruble, English

RESTAURANT
CHRISTOPHER COLUMBUS
ITALIAN CUISINE
At the Hotel Astoria, Bldg. B
Gertsena ul., 39 210-59-06
Hrs: 12- 24, $, CC, English

CHAYKA
Nab. Griboedova, 14 312-21-20
$, German

DADDY'S STEAK ROOM
The Best Steaks in Saint Petersburg
Moskovskiy pr., 73 298-95-52
Hrs: 12-23, $, CC, English & German & Finnish
Pizza Express , A Russian Finnish Firm

DEMYANOVA UKHA
Demyan's fish soup
The place for seafood in Saint Peterburg
Maksima Gorkogo pr., 53
.... 232-80-90
Hrs: 12 - 23, rubles

DADIS
Moskovskiy pr., 73 252-77-44
.... 298-95-52
$, English, Finnish
DIANA Grill-bar
Sadovaya ul., 56 310-33-22
Hrs: 12 - 24

DIAMOND JACK
Bubnovyy valet
Telephones at your table for your convenience.
Relaxing piano music to accompany the outstanding
Russian Cuisine.

Petrogradskaya Storona
Lenina (Shirokaya) ul., 32
.... 230-88-30
Hrs: 12-24, $ & rbl, English, French, German
A Russian-German Firm

DOM ARKHITEKTORA
The Place for Classic Russian Cuisine
In the beautiful turn-of-the century hall
A favorite of St. Petersburg
RESERVATIONS REQUIRED
Gertsena ul., 52 311-45-57
Hrs: 12 - 23

DAUGAVA
An Intimate Restaurant
At the Hotel Pribaltiyskaya
Serving Grilled Meat Specialities
Classic & Folk Music Trio
Korablestroiteley ul., 14.... 356-44-09
Hrs: 8-24, rubles

DRUZHBA CAFE
For Lunch and Supper
Video-Discotheque 7 - 11 pm
Nevskiy pr., 15. 315-95-36
Lunch & Supper Hrs: 11-23.

DR. OETKER NEVSKIY 40
A Bar - Pub in the German Style
Essen, Trinken, Geniessen
Eating, Drinking and Enjoyment
Imported German Beers & Good Food
NEVSKIY PR., 40 311-90-66
Hrs: 12 - 24 $, English and German

Galspe at Palanga
Galspe, the new Spanish restaurant,
invites you to bingo, casino, disco, bar &
Spanish confectionery
Leninskiy pr., 127 254-88-12
.... 254-21-92
Fax............................... 255-51-60
$, rubles, CC, English, Spanish

GERA
A small quiet restaurant serving
good Slavic cuisine.
Ideal for before & after theater
Masterskaya ul., 4...................352-18-18
Near Theater Square
Hrs: 18 - 2 am

"FREGAT" CAFE
   *Good Traditional Russian Cuisine.
   No Smoking, Live Music at Night.*
   V.O., Bolshoy pr., 39 213-49-23
GARGANTUA *Russian Cuisine*
   Prosveshcheniya pr., 23
   597-72-10
GINO GINELLI *Ice cream & Snacks*
   Nab. kan. Griboedova...... 312-21-20
GOLUBOY DELFIN
   Sredneokhtinskiy pr., 44
   227-21-35
   Seafood Restaurant

GRILL BAR
   Mokhovaya ul., 41 273-53-79
GRILL BAR
   Nalichnaya ul., 5............ 356-55-24
   Hrs: 12-23, rubles
GRILL BAR
   Bolshaya Pushkarskaya ul., 30
   232-10-30
   Hrs: 12-23, rubles
   Metro: Gostinyy Dvor, Nevskiy Prospekt
GROT CAFE   *Drinks, coffee & snacks*
   Peter & Paul Fortress....... 238-46-90
   Hrs: 10-23, rubles
GRILL BAR "KARAVELLA"
   Leni Golikova ul., 27 152-52-68
   A Russian Grill-Bar, Hrs: 11-21, rubles

HOTEL RESTAURANTS
   *Here is a list of restaurants at selected
hotels in Saint-Petersburg.
See ads for more information. Most hotels
serve:
- Breakfast from 8:00 am often with a
"Swedish Table Smorgasbord" and
- Hot dishes from 12 noon to 11 pm*
   ASTORIA
      Winter Garden, Angleterre, Astoria
   GRAND HOTEL EUROPE
      Europe, The Brasserie, Sadko's,
      Atrium Cafe,
   PULKOVSKAYA
      Meridian, Turku
   PRIBALTIYSKAYA
      Neva, Daugava, Leningrad
      Pribaltiskiy (groups)
      Swedish Table for brealfast
      Night Club/Panorama
   SAINT-PETERSBURG
      Saint-Petersburg
      Other restaurants in renovation
IMERETI
   Karla Marksa pr., 104 245-50-03
   *Georgian & Caucasian Restaurant
   Hrs: 12-23.30*
IVERIYA CAFE
   Marata ul., 35 164-74-78
   Georgian & Caucasian Restaurant
IZMAYLOV
   6-ya Krasnoarmeyskaya ul., 22
   292-68-38
THE KARELIA at the Hotel Karelia
*Breakfast, Lunch & Dinner Classic Russian
   Cuisine Discotheque & Dancing*
   Tukhachevskogo pr., 7/2
   226-35-49
   Hrs: 7 - 23, $ & rubles, English
KINGSWOOD TRUST RESTAURANT
   at Hotel Kingswood (formerly. H. Druzhba)
   Russian Cuisine, Dance Orchestra
   Chapygina ul., 4 234-37-94
   Hrs: 12-23, $ & rubles, CC, English
KLONDIKE at the Hotel Kareliya
   Good Russian Food, Discoteque from 8 -12
   Tukhachevskogo pr., 27/2
   226-35-49
   7:00-24:00, $ & rbls, English
KHACHAPURI
   Georgian & Caucasian Cuisine
   6-ya Krasnoarmeyskaya ul., 13/18
   292-73-77
   Hrs: 13-23, rubles

KLASSIK
Ligovskiy pr., 202 166-01-59
Russian Cuisine, Music, Hrs. 11-20

KOLOBOK, cafe-konditerei
Kominterna ul., 27 476-62-55
Hrs: 8-20

KOLOMNA CAFE, Grilled meats
Nab. kan. Griboedova, 162
.... 144-32-32
Hrs: 11-22, rbls, Russian Cuisine

KOELGA
Good Russian Cuisine & Dancing
Narodnaya ul., 15 263-18-93
Metro: Lomonosovskaya, Hrs: 21-6:00 am

La Trattoria

at the Grand Hotel Europe

Delicious Italian Cooking

The Place for Lunch and Supper

Mikhaylovskaya ul., 1/7

☎ ..... 312-00-72, Ext. 6391

Hrs: 1-23, $, English

The LENINGRAD RESTAURANT

A favorite in Saint Petersburg
At the Hotel Pribaltiyskaya
Orchestra and Dancing
Cabaret and Variety Show
356-44-09

Hrs: 8-23, $$ rubles, English

Breakfast, Lunch, & Dinner for Groups

LUKOMORE CAFE
Soups & Cutlets, Desserts & Coffee
V. O., 13-ya Liniya, 2/19
.... 218-59-00
Hrs: 12-23, rubles

THE LITERARY CAFE

Elegant Cafe-Restaurant
in the Old Tradition
Fine Russian Cuisine
Classical Music, Literary Readings
Poetry & Good Conversations
Nevskiy Prospekt, 18 312-85-36
.... 312-85-43
Hrs: 12-17, 19-23, rubles

The MERIDIAN

At the Hotel Pulkovskaya
A Classic Russian Restaurant
Great Russian Cuisine
Orchestra and European Cabaret
Breakfast at the Swedish Table
Pobedy pl., 1 264-51-77
Seating for 800, Hrs: 8 - 24, $ & r, CC, Eng.

THE METROPOL

Outstanding Russian Cuisine
In a Beautiful Restaurant
Elegant Old World Decor
Orchestra and Dancing
A Favorite with Saint Petersburg
Sadovaya ul., 22 310-19-33
.................................310-22-81
Hrs: 12-24, rubles, English

MINUTKA (Bistro)
Nevskiy pr., 20 311-24-19

MORSKOY (at the Sea Terminal)
Morskoy Slavy pl., 1 355-14-46
*Status of this popular restaurant is uncertain.
It was sold to "Montana" and may be
closed for renovation. Check.*

The MOSKVA Restaurant at the Hotel Moskva
Russian Cuisine
Large Orchestra & Variety Show Dancing
Alexandra Nevskogo pl., 2
.... 274-95-03
*Hrs: Swedish Table 8-11, Restaurant 12-23:30
Metro: Ploshchad Alexandra Nevskogo*

"MUSE" CAFE-PIZZA EXPRESS

Ogorodnikova pr., 48 251-17-24
.... 251-33-52
Phone reservations accepted
Hrs: 12-18 & 19-23 Daily

NA FONTANKE

*A quiet intimate restaurant
Pelmeni and other Russian classics
Light dinner music*

Nab. reki FONTANKI, 77 310-25-47
Hrs: 13-17, 19:30-23:30, rbl, drinks for $, English

NAIRI

Armenian Cuisine & Music to Order
Dekabristov ul., 6 314-80-93
Hrs: 12-23, rubles

NEPTUN
Stachek pr., 25a 186-61-10
Under renovation, Russian Cuisine, Hrs: 12-23

NEVA
*Russian & European Cuisine Orchestra,
Variety, & Dancing*
Nevskiy pr., 46
Administrator 311-36-78
Administrator 110-59-80
Hrs: 12-24, rubles, English

THE NEVA RESTAURANT
at Hotel Pribaltiyskaya
A Small Intimate Russian Restaurant
With Russian Folk Orchestra
Korablestroiteley ul., 14 356-44-09
Hrs: 8 - 23:30, $ & rbls, CC, English & German

NEVA STARS
See Nevskie Zvezdy
NEVSKIE ZVEZDY Russian Cuisine
Babushkina ul., 91 262-54-90
Under Renovation to early July

restaurant
NEVSKIY

Classic Russian Dining Experience
With first-class service

The Winter Garden for
        Russian-European Cuisine

The St. Petersburg Gallery for
        A Great Variety Show

The Nevskiy Room For
        A Pleasant Lunch and Supper

Great for small intimate parties or
the largest banquets with orchestra

Nevskiy pr., 71 311-30-93

At Metro Mayakovskaya
Hrs: 12-23, rubles, English

NEVSKIE MELODII
Russian Cuisine, Disco, Bar.
Nab. Sverdlovskaya, 62 ... 227-15-96
.... 227-26 76
Fax 227-15-96
Hrs: 12-18 for rubles, 18-1 $ & rbls, $ for drinks.,
discotheque 21-1, CC, English, German, French

THE NIGHT CLUB
at the Hotel Pribaltiyskaya
Dinner and Dance
Jazz and Contemporary Music
Korablestroiteley ul., 14 356-44-09
Hrs: 20-early am, $, English

OKEAN *Sea Food Restaurant*
Primorskiy pr., 31b 239-28-77
Hrs: 12 -24, Rubles, Music

OKHOTNICHIY KLUB
Russian Cuisine, Music
Dzerzhinskogo ul., 45 310-07-70
Metro: Ploshchad' Mira, Hrs: 12-24

OKOLITSA, A small Russian restaurant
Good Russian Cuisine In a Russian Setting
On the road out of St. Pb. to Helsinki
Primorskiy pr., 15 239-69-84
Hrs:11-23, rubles. Metro: Chernaya Rechka

"OKTIVIAN"(FORMERLY "GAVAN") AT
"OKTIVIAN"(FORMERLY "GAVAN") HOTEL
Sredniy pr., 88 356-12-06
Hrs: 7-22:00,$ & rubles,

OKTYABRSKIY *Russian Cuisine*
Ligovskiy pr., 10 277-67-38
Hrs: 12-23, $ & rubles, English, German
ORESHEK (under renovation)
Podolskogo ul., 22 583-01-02
Dessert Restaurant
PALANGA A simple Russian restaurant
Leninskiy pr., 127 255-64-17
Hrs: 12:30-23:30

PANORAMA
Overlooking the Gulf of Finland
from the 15th floor
of the Hotel Pribaltiyskaya
Breakfast, Lunch & Dinner
Russian & European Cuisine
Russian Folk Music
At the Hotel Pribaltiyskaya
Korablestroiteley ul., 14 ...., 356-44-09
Hrs: 8-23:30, rubles, English

PETROSTAR
Bolshaya Pushkarskaya ul., 30
.... 232-40-47
Russian Cuisine, Hrs. 12-23, rubles

PETROVSKIY
The Floating Restaurant at the
Embankment near Peter & Paul Fortress
Borshch, Shchi, Bliny with Caviar &
traditional Russian specialties
Nab. Mytninskaya, 3 238-47-93
Bar Hrs: 12-24 (Except 16-17)

PETROVSKIY ZAL At the Hotel St. Petersburg
IN RENOVATION
Traditional Russian Specialties with Panoramic Views of City
Nab. Vyborgskaya, 5/2 542-91-55

PIZZERIA, a small cafe
Serving pizza & meat specialties
Rubinshteyna ul., 30 314-57-18
Hrs: 12-20, rubles
PIZZUNDA CAFE, a small cafe
Kirovskiy pr., 12. 232-24-77
Russian cuisine, Hrs: 12-23, rubles
Pogrebok
Gogolya ul., 7 315-53-71
Little Restaurant with Simple Good Food
Hrs: 11-22, rubles, music

PRIMORSKIY, Russian cuisine
P.S., Bolshoy pr., 32 235-70-20
Hrs: 12-24, rubles
PULKOVO-1 Airport Restaurant
Pulkovo-1, Domestic Airport
.... 104-37-69

Railway Station (Vokzal)
Restaurants
All are open from 12 to 23, rubles
Baltiyskiy Vokzal Restaurant
Nab. Obvodnogo kan.
.... 252-77-42
Finlyandskiy Vokzal Restaurant
Lenina pl., 5.................... 542-27-36

Moskovskiy Vokzal Restaurant
Nevskiy pr., 85............... 277-30-31
Varshavskiy Vokzal Restaurant
Nab. Obvodnogo kan., 118
.... 259-45-33
Vitebskiy Vokzal Restaurant (Closed)
Zagorodnyy pr., 52 314-02-43
Rechnoy Vokzal Restaurant
at the River Terminal
Orchestra & Variety Show
Obukhovskoy Oborony pr., 195
.... 262-89-38
Hrs: 12-23:30

ROSSIYA restaurant
At the Hotel Rossiya
A RUSSIAN RESTAURANT WITH ORCHESTRA &
DANCE FLOOR
Chernyshevskogo pl., 11 296-75-49
Hrs: 12-24, $ & rubles, English

The "Rus" Restaurant
A new restaurant
serving classic Russian cuisine
Veteranov pr., 53............ 152-19-45
.... 152-19-11
Hrs: 12-23:30, rubles

RUSSKIE SAMOVARY
A Very Simple Russian Blinnaya
Popular for blinyes.
Sadovaya ul., 49............. 314-82-38
Hrs: 10 - 20, rubles

RYABINUSHKA *a konditerei-cafe*
For a cup of coffee & some pastries
Oskalenko ul., 11............. 239-40-80
Dessert Restaurant, Hrs: 7 - 17

SAIGON-NEVA
Vietnamese Restaurant
Plekhanova ul., 33 315-87-72

TÊTE À TÊTE

"Among the very best in St. Petersburg"
Elegant, Intimate. Excellent
Light Dinner Music
Reservations required
P.S., Bolshoy pr., 65 232-75-48
Hrs: 12-23:30, rubles, English

∽ TBILISY ·∾

Fine Georgian & Caucasian Cuisine
Georgian Songs and Music
Reservations Required
Sytninskaya ul., 10 232-93-91
Hrs: 12-23:30, Rubles, $ for drinks

TROIKA

A LUXURIOUS RUSSIAN STYLE
RESTAURANT

From Salmon & Chicken a la Kiev
to Troika Roulade, Champagne & Caviar
✦✦✦✦✦
The International-Russian Variety Show
Chorus Line Song, Dance & Variety
"Moulin Rouge of Saint. Petersburg"
A Great Show
✦✦✦✦✦
Great Vodkas & European Wine Cellar

Zagorodnyy pr., 27 113-53-43
Hrs: 7-24, $ & rbls, English
A Russian-Swiss Company

TURKU Restaurant
At the Hotel Pulkovskaya
Russian cuisine
Orchestra, Dancing & Folklore
Pobedy pl., 1 264-57-16
Hrs: 7-16, 17-23:30, rbl & $, CC, Eng & German

U Kazanskogo restaurant cafe
Nevskiy pr., 26 314-27-45
Russian Cuisine, Hrs: 11-22, rbls, music

Cafe *U Bobrinskikh*
Excellent Russian Home Cuisine
Delicious French Pastry
Krasnaya ul., 60 311-04-51

U Petrovicha
An Intimate "Merchant's-Style
Restaurant" from the 19th Century
Fish & fowl & venison & bear
Black, red & trout caviar
Light dinner music and dancing
Sredneokhtinskiy pr., 44 .. 227-21-35
Hrs: 12-17, 18-24, $ & rbls, English

U PRICHALA (in Renovation)
V.O., Bolshoy pr., 91 217-44-28

U SAMOVARA *CAFE & KONDITEREI*
Piskarevskiy pr., 52 538-30-95
Coffee and Pastries, Hrs: 10-19:30, rbls

UNIVERSAL restaurant
Russian "Kukhnya" from a Good Kitchen
Many intimate dining rooms
Nevskiy pr., 106 279-33-50
Hrs: 10 am -1 am, rubles, English

URARTU
Armenian, Georgian & Caucasian Dining
Rudneva ul., 25 558-69-19
Hrs: 12-23, rubles, Georgian

VENETSIA
Italian cuisine and pizza
Korablestroiteley ul., 21
.... 353-20-54
.... 352-14-32
Hrs: 12-23, $ & rbl, CC, English & Italian
Rimilen (Italian-Russian Firm)

VERONIKA GRILL-BAR
Nevskiy pr., 87 279-67-33
HRS: 10:00-4:00 RUBLES

"THE **VICTORIA** RESTAURANT"
FAVORITE OF THE COGNOSCENTI IN ST. PB.
EUROPEAN-RUSSIAN CUISINE
"A REALLY GOOD KITCHEN"
Kirovskiy pr., 24 232-51-30
Hrs: 12-24, rbls, English,
Metro: Petrogradskaya

VISLA
Dzerzhinskogo ul., 17 315-87-87
Hrs: 12-23:30, rbls, music
Russian cuisine

VOLKHOV
Liteynyy pr., 28 273-20-79
.... 273-47-36
Hrs: 12-24, rbls Russian Cuisine

NIGHT RESTAURANT VOSTOK
"NIGHT RESTAURANT ORIENT"

Indian & European Cuisine
One of the best kitchens in the city

In beautiful Primorskiy Park Pobedy
New variety shows & orchestra
Primorskiy Park Pobedy.... 235-59-84
Hrs: 12-4:30 am, $ & rubles, English

VOLSHEBNYY KRAY "Pyshechnaya"
Coffee and pastry
Bolshoy pr., 15/3............. 233-32-53
Hrs: 10-20, rbls

VYBORGSKIY Restaurant
Torzhkovskaya ul., 3 246-99-23
banquet hall.................... 246-99-23
Hrs: 9-24, For Tourist Groups, rbls

WINTER GARDEN
ZIMNIY SAD

Elegant Dining At the Hotel Astoria
in the beautiful Winter Garden
Classic Russian Cuisine
Bliny with Caviar, Borshch, Pelmeni
Gertsena ul., 39............................. 210-59-06
Hrs: 8-23.30, $ and rbls, English

ZASTOLE restaurant
Nevskiy pr., 74.............. 272-90-17
A Russian kitchen, Hrs: 12-24, rubles

ZERKALNYY (MIRROR) (in renovation)
Hotel St. Peterburg
Nab. Vyborgskaya, 5 542-91-55

ZURBAGAN RESTAURANT

Good Home Style Russian Cuisine

Prepared especially for your group
Private parties and dinner meetings
Advanced Reservation Only

P.S., Ordinarnaya ul., 21 235-29-09

SOME HISTORICAL DATES

1762-1796	*Reign of Catherine The Great*
1764	*Hermitage collection started at the Winter Palace*
1796-1801	*Reign of Paul I*
1801-1825	*Reign of Alexander I*
1819	*St.-Petersburg University was founded*

The following are restaurants located in the suburbs:

PETRODVORETS

RESTAURANT
PETERHOF
A Fine Restaurant in Petrodvorets

For Lunch and
Dinner

In a small congenial restaurant
International and Russian cuisine from
steak & french fries to bliny & caviar
German beers & fine European wines

At the entrance to the lower Park
in the Peterhof - Petrodvorets

427-98-87 & 314-49-47

Hrs: 10-22,$ & rubles, German & English

PUSHKIN

"ADMIRALTEYSTVO"
Ekaterininskiy Park 465-35-49

SESTRORETSK

cafe BY THE LAKE
U ozera
Music & European Cuisine
Primorskoe shosse, 352 237-48-17
hrs: 11-24, $, English, Swedish
Russian - Swedish Cafe

SOLNECHNOE

Gorka
Primorskoe shosse, 371
.... 237 40-60
Hrs: 14-23, $ & rbls, English

ZELENOGORSK

OLEN
Primorskoe shosse, 549
.... 231-47-70
Russian Cuisine

OLGINO

OLGINO
Variety Show & Russian Cuisine
Olgino Campsite,
Primorskoe shosse, 18 km
.... 238-36-74
Hrs: 8 - 24, Rubles & $, English

VOLNA   ВОЛНА
On the road to Vyborg
"Excellent food and service."
Fodor's '92
Kronshtadt,
Internatsionala ul., 13...... 236-37-65

☎ RESTROOMS
ТУАЛЕТЫ
TOILETTEN
TOILETTES
TOALETTER

Restrooms frequently have no toilet paper or use recycled newspaper. It is strongly recommended to carry a couple of small packs of tissue (Kleenex) in your purse or bag.

* Kirovskiy pr., 37b
* Krestovskiy pr., 18
* Nab. reki Fontanki, 40
* Nab. reki Moyki, 37
* Nevskiy pr., 20, 39, 50/13, 88
* Moskovskiy pr., 205
* Muchnoy per., 9
* Nab. Petrogradskaya, 10
* Lva Tolstogo pl., 2
* Dobrolyubova ul., in the garden
* Nepokorennykh pr., 68
* Stachek pr., 9
* Sadovaya ul., 69
* Nab. Sverdlovskaya , 62, 64
* Dumskaya ul., 13
* Gogolya ul., 9
* Marata ul., 4
* Nekrasova ul., 21
* Plekhanova ul., 6
* Rubinshteyna ul., 3
* Saltykova-Shchedrina ul., 2
* Sofi Perovskoy ul., 12
* Vosstaniya ul., 1
* V.O., 8-ya Liniya

☎ RIVER BOAT EXCURSIONS
ЭКСКУРСИИ, РЕЧНЫЕ
BOOTSAUSFLÜGE
EXCURSION EN BATEAU
BÅTTURER, KANAL

See BOAT EXCURSIONS

☎ RIVER TERMINALS
ВОКЗАЛЫ, РЕЧНЫЕ
FLUSSHÄFEN
GARE FLUVIABLE
FLODTERMINALER

See also SHIP TERMINAL and
BOAT EXCURSIONS

Wharves / Docks
Pristan "Ermitazh" (Hermitage)
In St.-Petersburg............. 311-95-06
Pristan "Kronshtadt" (In Kronstadt)
Kronshtadt.................... 236-33-17

Pristan "Petrodvoterts" (In Petrodvorets)
Petrodvorets.................. 427-72-12

River-Passenger Terminal
РЕЧНОЙ ПАССАЖИРСКИЙ ВОКЗАЛ
Departures for river passenger trips leave from this terminal.
Obukhovskoy Oborony pr., 195
Information 262-13-18
.... 262-02-39
METRO: PROLETARSKAYA, BUSES 11,

☎ ROCK/POP MUSIC CLUBS
РОК И ПОП КЛУБЫ
ROCK-/POPMUSIK-CLUBS
ROCK/POP MUSIC CLUBS
ROCK/POPMUSIKKLUBBAR

See also Jazz Clubs

Rock Club
Best of the West
Rubinshteyna ul., 13 314-96-29

☎ ROWING CLUBS
ГРЕБНЫЕ КЛУБЫ
RUDERVEREINE
CANOTAGE, CLUBS DE
RODDKLUBBAR

Department for Sports Facilities of
Leningrad City Committee for Sports
& Physical Culture
Tolmacheva ul., 9 314-49-54
Nab. Bolshoy Nevki, 24.... 234-36-22
Club "VOLNA"
Petrodvorets,
Krylova ul., 17................ 427-64-65

☎ RUGS & CARPETS
КОВРЫ И ДОРОЖКИ
TEPPICHE UND LÄUFER
TAPIS
MATTOR

Buy rugs in large DEPARTMENT STORES
Skif
Sadovaya ul., 42............. 310-13-15
Kovry No. 2
Pogranichnika Garkavogo ul., 4
.... 144-82-83

☎ RUSSIAN LANGUAGE COURSES
КУРСЫ РУССКОГО ЯЗЫКА
RUSSISCHE SPRACHKURSE
LE RUSSE
RYSKA, KURSER

See LANGUAGE COURSES

⚓ SAILING
ЯХТЫ, АРЕНДА И ПРОДАЖА
SEGELN
NAVIGATION
SEGLING

See YACHT CLUBS

⚓ SAUNAS
САУНЫ
SAUNA UND FITNESSCENTER
SAUNAS
BASTU/BAD

See also HEALTH CLUBS, BATHS,
SWIMMING

SAUNAS in the HOTELS
hard currency only

Hotel Astoria
Gertsena ul., 39 210-58-69
Hotel Gavan *(under renovation)*
V. O., Sredniy pr., 88...... 356-96-46
Only for hotel clients
Hotel Kareliya
Marshala Tukhachevskogo ul., 27/2
.... 226-35-17
Hotel St. Petersburg
Nab. Pirogovskaya, 5/2.... 542-37-98
Hotel Pribaltiyskaya
Korablestroiteley ul., 14 ... 356-17-92
Hotel Pulkovskaya
Pobedy pl., 1................. 264-58-09
Hotel Rossiya
Chernyshevskogo pl., 11
.... 296-31-44

Other saunas

Intursport, *Saunas, Gyms, Massage*
Moiseenko ul., 22/17 271-36-21
Metro: Pl. Vosstaniya
Fonarnye
Nab. reki Moyki, 82......... 312-56-55
Nevskie
Marata ul., 5/7 311-14-00

☎ SCHOOLS/PUBLIC, PRIVATE
ШКОЛЫ, ГОСУДАРСТВЕННЫЕ И
ЧАСТНЫЕ
SCHULEN, STAATLICHE UND
PRIVATE
ECOLES D'ÉTAT ET PRIVÉES
SKOLOR, ALLMÄNNA OCH
PRIVATA

*There are about 600 primary schools
(grades 1-3), lower middle schools (grades
4-9) and middle school (equal to
secondary school or high school grades
10-11) in Saint Petersburg. Children enter
primary school when they are six years
old. Sometimes, they go to private or
state kindergartens. Education lasts
usually 9 or 11 years.*

*Some schools, specialize in certain
areas such as mathematics, physics,
foreign languages and humanities. These
elite schools require a special exam and
interview and are being renamed as
gymnasiums, colleges or lyceums.*

*There are four quarters in the school
year: the first from 1 September to 1
November followed by a one week
vacation; the second from November 10
to end of December followed by a two-
week New Year vacation; the third term
from mid January to mid-March is
followed by a one week vacation. The
spring term starts in late March and ends
May 31 followed by the three month
summer vacation.*

Committee for Education of the Office of
the Mayor
.... 319-91-79

Humanitarian Lyceum
Please call...................... 279-04-73
Krasnoselskiy Business Lyceum
Please call...................... 143-87-79
Physics and Mathematics Lyceum
Please call...................... 272-96-68

PRIVATE SCHOOL
VZMAKH

For children 6-17

*Small individualized classes
Languages, music, arts, mathematics
Introduction to commerce & economics
College-educated teachers with post-
graduate training in pedagogy*

Dmitrovskiy per., 16........ 311-80-19
Fax 526-66-24

⚓ SEA TERMINALS
ВОКЗАЛЫ МОРСКИЕ
SEEHÄFEN
GARES MARITIMES
HAMNTERMINAL

See SHIP TERMINALS

☎ SECOND HAND SHOPS
КОМИССИОННЫЕ МАГАЗИНЫ
SECOND-HAND-LÄDEN
OBJETS D' OCCASION,
MAGASINS
ANDRAHANDSAFFARER

See COMMISSION STORES and
COMMERCIAL STORES.

☎ SECRETARIAL SERVICES
СЕКРЕТАРСКИЕ РАБОТЫ
BÜRODIENSTLEISTUNGEN
SECRETARIAT, SERVICE
SEKRETERARSERVICE

See also TEMPORARY HELP

EKOS
Specializing in temporary help
Trained secretaries & translators
English, German and other languages
V.O., 13-ya Liniya, 12 355-91-51

Typewriting Works
Liteynyy pr., 28 272-45-80
Hrs: 9-20, closed Sat, Sun
Stenography and typewriting
Ligovskiy pr., 63 164-77-74
.... 164-53-11
Optimum (Coop)
Kosmonavtov pr., 18 106-69-25
Hrs: 12-17

SAINT PETERSBURG TRANSIT TEMPORARY PERSONNEL
Trained secretaries, Interpreters
Experienced with computers
English, German, Swedish, French
Spanish, Finnish, & Japanese
Inquire about other languages.
Dumskaya ul., 3 314-89-84
Tel. 555-55-54
Hrs: 10-22, Rbl & $

☎ SECURITY
СИСТЕМЫ БЕЗОПАСНОСТИ
SICHERHEIT(SYSTEME)
SECURITE
SÄKERHET

See also LOCKSMITHS
and ALARM SYSTEMS
*These firms provide a variety of
security services from armed bodyguards
and transport to installation of fire alarm
systems, metal doors, and secure
warehouses.*

Alex Security Ltd.
Members of Int'l Detective Association
Leading Private Security Firm in Russia

Security for hotels, stores, offices & firms
Residential & insured cargo security
Bodyguards (armed & unarmed)
Warehouse security & canine patrols
Well-trained professional staff with
knowledge of English & German

Please call 150-49-39

Amfion
Rossiyskiy pr., 5, P.O. 445
.... 113-55-15
We specialize in locks & metal doors.
Bikar
Mayorova pr., 16 274-42-91
Fax 315-56-18
Telex 121353
*Electronic security installation for offices,
museums & stores*
Enterprise
Ans. Mach 294-04-75
Alarm System "Contact", coded locks
Kontak
Moskovskiy pr., 182 298-86-35
Automobile Security
Leader
Malaya Posadskaya ul., 30
Please call 238-81-48
Small Enterprise
Govorova ul., 43 252-14-40
Various types of security equipment.

Concern SOPPOL
Security and Alarms
Security guards for
banks, firms, major hotels, offices
Trained security officers for
personal security, meetings & exhibitions.
Alarm systems for
Offices, banks, stores & sound, motion &
fire detectors, TV surveillance systems.
Secure fireproof storage for
valuable equipment, personal belongings,
and documents with 24 hour guards
Armed transport of valuables
to any region of Russia, Baltics and CIS

2-ya Krasnoarmeyskaya ul., 7

Tel 110-14-32
24 hours/day, $ & rubles, English

Strazha Enterprise
5-ya Sovetskaya ul., 28 ... 274-38-48
Security Services for Enterprises
Trans Kontinental Servis
Mayakovskogo ul., 5 273-69-04
Zashchita
Dobrolyubova pr., 13 233-82-62

☎ SEATING PLANS
ПЛАН МЕСТ В ТЕАТРЕ
THEATERPLATZANORDNUNG
PLAN DE THEATRE
KARTA ÖVER SITTPLATSER,
TEATER

See also THEATER SEATING PLANS

*Seating plans of Mariinskiy Theater of
Opera and Ballet, Malyy Theater of Opera and
Ballet, Russian Academic Drama Theater,
Bolshoy Philharmonic Hall, Cappella Glinka
(Choir) Hall, and Bolshoy Concert Hall
October are on page 246-251.*

☎ SEWING MACHINE REPAIR
РЕМОНТ ШВЕЙНЫХ МАШИН
NÄHMASCHINENREPARATUR
MACHINES A COUDRE,
REPARATION
SYMASKINSREPARATIONER

Bait
Zastavskaya ul., 26......... 531-39-89
Podolsk-Sokol
Razezzhaya ul., 12.......... 315-36-63
Sewing Machine Repairs

☎ SHIPPING
МОРСКАЯ ДОСТАВКА
SEETRANSPORTE
TRANSPORT MARITIME
BÅTSPEDITION

See also TRUCKING, AIR CARGO,
SHIPPING AGENTS,
EXPRESS MAIL/PARCELS SERVICE.

*This listing includes only companies
with ships or that handle cargo to and
from ships. To book passenger tickets,
see* SHIP TERMINALS

Baltic Shipping Company
Mezhevoy kanal, 5.......... 251-07-42
Ship arrivals.................. 251-12-38
Fax 186-85-44
Telex 121501

INFLOT St. Petersburg Ltd.
*The most complete in-port service,
liner, tramp agency
over 50 years experience
in the port of Saint Petersburg*

Gapsalskaya ul., 10......... 251-73-26
Director:........................ 251-12-38
Fax: .... (812) 186-15-11
Telex: .... 121505 /A,B,C/

Kron-flot
Volodarskogo ul., 1......... 422-46-04

 **MCT EUROPE**

*HANDLING & DELIVERY OF CARGOES
VIA PORT OF ST. PETERSBURG
CONTAINER STORAGE IN ST. PB.*

MEZHEVOY KANAL, 5 251-86-62
FAX .... (812)186-83-44
TELEX .... 121691 MCT SU

Neva
Narodnaya ul., 95 266-41-92
.... 266-33-53

North-western River Shipping Company
Severo-Zapadnoe rechnoe parokhodstvo
Gertsena ul., 37.............. 312-01-45
Fax.............................. 312-03-59
Telex............................ 121038
River & sea transport in Russia & Europe

The Sea Shipping Company

*First private shipping company in
Russia. All types of cargo from
45 to 50,000 mtr to ports in
Baltic, Europe and the world*
Gorokhovaya ul., 22........ 314-06-59

SOVMORTRANS
St. Petersburg Branch
*Freight Forwarding & N.V.O.C.C.
Liner Agent for SEA-LAND SERVICE, INC.
Port Agents
Container trucking*
In Saint Petersburg.......... 252-75-81
Telex................... 121115 SMTL SU

Sovavto-Leningrad Shipping Company
Vitebskiy pr., 3............... 298-55-56
Sovmortrans
Dvinskaya ul., 8, bldg. 2
.... 252-75-81
.... 114-24-67
.... 259-89-94
at harbor 259-83-32
Fax.............................. 259-09-94
Telex................... 121115 SMT SU
Shipping Company
Please call...................... 520-07-89
SILVUS-BELGIUM
Please call...................... 277-00-13
Shipping cargos by sea to Europe and back

☎ SHIPPING AGENTS,
FREIGHT FORWARDERS
МОРСКИЕ АГЕНТСТВА, ДОСТАВКА
SEESPEDITIONEN
AGENTS MARITIMES, EXPEDITEURS
HAMN SPEDITÖRER, EXPEDITÖR

See AIR CARGO, SHIPPING, TRUCKING,
EXPRESS MAIL/PARCELS SERVICE.

INFLOT St. Petersburg Ltd.
*The most complete in-port service,
liner, tramp agency
over 50 years experience
in the port of Saint Petersburg*

Gapsalskaya ul., 10......... 251-73-26
Director:........................ 251-12-38
Fax: .... (812) 186-15-11
Telex:................... 121505 /A,B,C/

SOVMORTRANS
St. Petersburg Branch
Freight Forwarding & N.V.O.C.C.
Liner Agent for SEA-LAND SERVICE, INC.
Port Agents
Container trucking
In Saint Petersburg.......... 252-75-81
Telex .... 121115 SMTL SU

☎ SHIP TERMINALS
МОРСКИЕ ВОКЗАЛЫ
SCHIFFDOCKS
GARES MARITIMES
HAMNSTERMINALER, FARTYG

See also RIVER TERMINALS

Passenger Ocean Ship Terminal
Morskoy passazhirskiy vokzal
МОРСКОЙ ПАССАЖИРСКИЙ ВОКЗАЛ
The Passenger Ocean Ship Terminal is located on the Gulf of Finland near the end of Bolshoy prospect on Vasilevskiy Island. The Hotel Morskaya, bar, kiosks, and cruise ship and ferry terminal are located there.
Morskoy Slavy pl., 1
Information 355-13-10
Hotel 'Morskaya' 355-14-16
Take BUSES 128,151,152 or Trolley 10A from METRO PRIMORSKAYA

River Passenger Terminal
Rechnoy passazhirskiy vokzal
РЕЧНОЙ ПАССАЖИРСКИЙ ВОКЗАЛ
Departures for river passenger trips leave from this terminal.
Obukhovskoy Oborony pr., 195
Information 262-13-18
METRO PROLETARSKAYA, BUSES 11,

The following organizations run the St. Petersburg and other ports.

Association of Russian Commercial Sea Ports
Gapsalskaya ul., 4, Lenmortorgport
Director 186-68-22

St. Petersburg Commercial Sea Port
St.-Peterburgskiy Morskoy Torgovyy Port
Mezhevoy kanal, 5 259-81-70

☎ SHIPS
КОРАБЛИ, КУПЛЯ-ПРОДАЖА
SCHIFFE
NAVIRES
BOKHYLLOR

Poul Christensen (Russia) Ltd.
A Danish Company
Shipbuilding/Purchase & Sale of Ships
in the Russian market
Leninskiy pr., 161/2 108-49-32
Fax 293-52-49
Telex................ 121665 PCRUS SU

☎ SHOE REPAIRS
РЕМОНТ ОБУВИ
SCHUHGESCHÄFTE
CHAUSSURES, RÉPARATION DES
SKOAFFÄRER

There are many little shoe repair shops called remont obuvi (Ремонт обуви), or instant shoe repair in the little kiosks.

Fast Shoe Repair Ремонт обуви
Kolomenskaya ul., 29 164-29-47
Metro: Ligovskiy pr. Hrs: 10 - 20

Fast Shoe Repair
Nevskiy pr., 19 315-41-97
Hrs: 10 - 19

Fast Shoe Repair
Vosstaniya ul., 23........... 272-77-23
Hrs: 11 - 19

Fast Shoe Repair
Nevskiy pr., 153 277-30-27
Hrs: 11 - 14, 15 - 19

Shoe Repair
Razezzhaya ul., 12 164-92-92
Hrs: 9 - 19

☎ SHOE STORES
ОБУВНЫЕ МАГАЗИНЫ
SCHUHMACHER
CHAUSSURES, MAGASINS DES
SKOMAKARE

Try DEPARTMENT STORES and Lenwest for stylish women's shoes and good winter boots. Imported sneakers and sport shoes (often copies) and dress shoes are sold everywhere including

COMMERCIAL STORES *and even outdoor* MARKETS.

Gorizont
Shelgunova ul., 4 262-02-67
.... 262-41-78
Hrs: 10 - 19

Lenwest, shoes

For the latest models and best selection

The Lenwest Shoe Salon

At Nevskiy pr., 119 277-06-35

The best place to buy shoes in St. Pb.

Dress shoes for men, women & children
Wet weather and winter footwear
Stylish boots for women

Outstanding footwear produced with the best
materials and German technology
designed by world-renown Salamander

Nevskiy pr., 119 277-06-35
Nevskiy pr., 11 314-73-17
Suvorovskiy pr., 36 275-22-28
Sofiyskaya ul., 57 108-62-03
Varshavskaya ul., 120 123-01-09

Hrs: 10-14, 15-19, Rubles, English

Orthopedic Shoes
Soyuza Pechatnikov ul., 14
.... 114-17-52

Shoe House
Krasnogvardeyskaya pl., 6
.... 224-06-83
Hrs: 10 - 19

Shoes
Nevskiy pr., 116 279-57-64
Hrs: 10 - 19

Shoes For Men & Women
Moskovskiy pr., 153 298-27-63
Men's Shoe Dept. 298-27-73
Hrs: 10 - 19

Shoe Store
Vosstaniya ul., 24 273-36-48
Hrs: 10 - 19

Vityaz
Narodnaya ul., 6 266-56-62
Hrs: 10 - 20

☎ SHOOTING RANGES
ТИРЫ
SCHIEBSTÄNDE
TIR, CLUB DE
SKJUTBANOR

Gorodskoy Strelkovyy Tir
P.S., Aptekarskiy pr., 14
.... 234-35-62

Tir No. 8 (under repair)
Zagorodnyy pr., 36 315-31-54

Tir No. 53
V.O., 6-ya Liniya, 29 213-08-52

Tir No. 83
Nevskiy pr., 20 311-68-29

☎ SHOPS
МАГАЗИНЫ
GESCHÄFTE
MAGASINS
AFFÄRER

We have tried to include at least 3 or 4 shops for each category. One purpose of the Traveller's Yellow Pages is to help travelers shop in Saint Petersburg. With perseverance most products and services can be bought. There are four basic types of stores in St. Petersburg.

- *Department store*
  (Univermag - Универмаг)
- *Supermarkets*
  (Universam - Универсам)
- *Markets (Rynok - Рынок)*
- *Shops (Magazin - Магазин)*

The Russians still make a strong distinction between the low-priced "state" shops and the "commercial" shops and "commercial departments" which charge much higher prices which most Russians cannot afford to pay.

See COMMERCIAL STORES, DEPARTMENT STORES

☎ SIGNS
ВЫВЕСКИ
AUSHÄNGESCHILDER
ENSEIGNES
SKYLTAR, TILLVERKNING

Komposit
Narodnaya ul., 8 274-12-87
.... 278-91-34

Obelisk
Signs on metal & glass.
Saltykova-Shchedrina ul., 53
.... 275-69-60
.... 275-69-68

☎ SIGHTSEEING
ЭКСКУРСИИ, ОБЗОРНЫЕ
AUSFLÜGE
EXCURSIONS
SIGHTSEEING

See also TOURS-SAINT PETERSBURG & TOURS-RUSSIA

☎ SIZES
РАЗМЕРЫ
GRÖSSE
TAILLE, POINTURE
STORLEKAR

See pages 242-244.
Tables of Measures, Weights and Size.

☎ SKATING
КАТАНЬЕ НА КОНЬКАХ
SCHLITTSCHUHLAUFEN
PATINAGE
SKRIDSKOÅKNING

Skating
V.O., 15-ya Liniya..............No Phone
Central Park of Culture and Rest
Yelagin Ostrov, 4............ 239-09-11
Tavricheskiy Sad,
Katok Gorodskogo Detskogo Parka
Saltykova-Shchedrina ul., 50
.... 272-60-44
Katok Moskovskogo Parka Pobedy
Kuznetsovskaya ul., 25.... 298-34-11
.... 298-08-81
Letniy Sportklub LVO
Nab. reki Fontanki, 112 ... 292-20-81
.... 291-90-21
.... 292-21-28
Summer Skating Rink

☎ SKIN & VENEREAL
DISEASES
КОЖНО-ВЕНЕРОЛОГИЧЕСКИЕ
ДИСПАНСЕРЫ
HAUT- UND VENERISCHE
KRANKHEITEN
PEAU, MALADIES DE
HUD OCH KÖNSSJUKDOMAR

See MEDICAL CARE & CONSULTATIONS,
HOSPITAL *and* MEDICAL ASSISTANCE

☎ SOUVENIRS/GIFTS
СУВЕНИРЫ, ПОДАРКИ
SOUVENIRE/GESCHENKARTIKEL
SOUVENIRS/CADEAUX
SOUVENIRER/PRESENTAFFÄRER

See ART GALLERIES, ARTS &
HANDICRAFTS, JEWELLERY, PORCELAIN
& CRYSTAL, FURS, INTERNATIONAL
SHOPS, GIFTS SHOPS.

☎ SPORTS CLUBS
СПОРТИВНЫЕ КЛУБЫ
SPORTVEREINE
SPORT, CLUBS
SPORTKLUBBAR

See also ROWING CLUBS, SAILING,
TENNIS, MOUNTAINEERING, HUNTING,
VOLLEYBALL, SWIMMING, BICYCLING.
Sportservis
Petrovskiy ostrov, 21 238-40-54
Billiard Club
Vindavskaya ul., 2 251-15-61
24 hours a day
"Zenit" Football Club (Soccer Club)
Butlerova ul., 9.............. 535-01-71

☎ SPORTS EQUIPMENT
СПОРТИВНОЕ ОБОРУДОВАНИЕ
SPORTAUSRÜSTUNGEN
SPORT, EQUIPEMENT
SPORTUTRUSTNING

Sport equipment is bought in
DEPARTMENT STORES, *in the special*
"Sport Equipment" shops (Sporttovary,
Спорттовары), and HUNTING AND FISHING
EQUIPMENT, DEPARTMENT STORES
Apraksin Dvor
Sadovaya ul,. 310-20-03
Section 85-95 310-36-29
.... 310-30-58
.... 310-73-50
Hrs: 10 - 20
Sporttovary
Kondratevskiy pr., 33 540-13-94
Sporttovary
Liteynyy pr., 57 272-67-51
Sporttovary
Moskovskiy pr., 37 292-58-33
Sporttovary
Nevskiy pr., 122 277-02-79
Hrs: 11 - 14, 15 - 20 Metro: Vosstaniya pl.
Yunost
Babushkina ul., 111 262-49-48

☎ SPORTS FACILITIES
СПОРТИВНЫЕ СООРУЖЕНИЯ
SPORTANLAGEN
SPORT, ACTIVITES
SPORTHALLAR

See also STADIUMS, TENNIS, HEALTH
RESORTS, SAILING, BICYCLING, HEALTH
CLUBS, HUNTING & FISHING, RACING

BAST Sports Centre
The Place to Relax
Tennis courts, sport halls, exercise room,
Sauna & massage
Raevskogo proezd, 16 552-55-12
Fax............................... 552-39-36
Open 24 hours/day, English & Spanish

Mototrek (Mototrek racing)
Zhaka Duklo ul., 67......... 553-70-11
.... 553-70-15
Palace of Sport Games "Zenit"
Butlerova ul., 9............. 535-01-71
Football, Gymnastics
Sport-Klass (Coop)
Kirovskiy pr., 26/28......... 232-75-81
Yubileynyy Sports Palace
Dobrolyubova pr., 18....... 238-41-22

☎ STADIUMS
СТАДИОНЫ
STADIEN
STADES
ARENOR/STADIOS

Kirov Stadium
Krestovskiy Ostrov, Morskoy pr., 1
Deputy Director 235-00-78
Box Office 235-54-94

Lenin Sport & Concert Center
Called Sport & Concert Complex
named after Lenin
Gagarina pr., 8 298-48-47
.... 298-46-59
Advertising Dept............. 298-24-90

Lenin Stadium
Petrovskiy Ostrov, 2-g 238-40-03
Director......................... 233-17-52

Zimniy Stadium
Manezhnaya pl., 2 315-57-10
Administrator 210-48-65

☎ STAMPS/SEALS
ШТАМПЫ И ПЕЧАТИ
STEMPEL UND SIEGEL
EMPREINTES ET CACHETS
FRIMÄRKEN, SIGILL

Interstartservices
V.O., 2-ya Liniya, 25, apt. 15
.... 350-93-58

L-T Shtamp
Lermontovskiy pr., 24...... 114-22-87

Roderic Ltd.
Please call 314-69-05

Tecknolog
Krasnaya ul., 22 219-82-69
.... 315-27-83

☎ STATIONERY
КАНЦТОВАРЫ
SCHREIBWAREN
BUREAUX, FOURNITURES
PAPPERSHANDLARE

See also COMPUTER SUPPLIES,
PHOTOCOPIERS & ART SUPPLIES.

Private stores stocking Western European stationery goods are quickly opening up in St. Petersburg. Existing state shops, usually called Kantselyarskie Tovary (Канцелярские товары), *are opening "commercial" departments where it is also possible to buy imported stationery supplies. Good quality photocopy paper, both imported and domestic is available. Note that it is virtually impossible to buy stationery supplies, especially paper, for the American standard letterhead.*

Chelovek, stationers
IMPORTED STATIONERY
Wholesale and Retail
Large Selection from Germany
Nab. Makarova, 10.............213-18-66
Hrs: 10-18, Closed Sun, rubles, English

SKIF
AUTHORIZED **RANK XEROX** **DEALER**
Stationery & photocopier supplies
Vosstaniya ul., 32........... 275-53-45

S & A Stationery Co.
Established by Statfall Inter'l, Ltd.
Supplier of imported office products and stationery
to businesses & visitors in St. Petersburg

*Full line of 3M, Stabilo, Staedtler, Pelican,
High-quality Finnish paper*
Wholesale & retail, delivery, ask for price list.

Located in central St. Petersburg.
Konyushennaya ul., 27, rm. 3
(Formerly Zhelyabova ul.)

☎................................. 311-87-20
Hrs 9-18, Closed Sun., English, Deutsch, $ & rbl.

Avtoruchki, Store No. 22 *Pens*
Nevskiy pr., 69 314-62-37
Kantselyarskie Tovary Store No. 19
Nevskiy pr., 130 277-07-30
Kantselyarskie Tovary Store No. 20
Sadovaya ul., 31............. 310-82-49
Kantselyarskie Tovary Store No. 28
P. S., Bolshoy pr., 69 232-79-06
Kantselyarskie Tovary Store No. 28
P. S., Bolshoy pr., 72 232-01-26
Kantselyarskie Tovary Store No. 40
Pionerstroya ul., 4........... 144-44-64
Kantselyarskie Tovary Store No. 48
Chernyshevskogo pr., 9 ... 273-34-91
Kantselyarskie Tovary Store No. 56
Kirovskiy pr., 6............... 233-34-43
Kantselyarskie Tovary Store No. 61
Liteynyy pr., 36 273-66-02
Kantstovary Store, No. 31
Suvorovskiy pr., 24 279-37-16
Kantstovary, Store No. 53
Novo-Izmaylovskiy pr., 40
.... 295-39-26
Drafting Supplies
Otkrytka (Greeting Card)
Liteynyy pr., 63 273-48-97
Open: 10-19
Student, Store No. 7
Nevskiy pr., 102 279-32-79
School Supplies

☎ STOCK & COMMODITY EXCHANGES
БИРЖИ, ТОВАРНЫЕ И ФОНДОВЫЕ
WARENBÖRSE
WERTPAPIERBÖRSE
BOURSE DES VALEURS ET DES MARCHANDISES
AKTIEMARKNAD

There are many so-called "Stock and Commodity Exchanges" in St. Petersburg now, some with very similar names. Note, in particular, the older and larger Stock and Commodity Exchange St. Petersburg and the smaller St. Petersburg Stock and Commodity Exchange.

Stock & Commodity Exchange St. Petersburg
199026, Saint Petersburg
V.O., 26-ya Liniya, 15
Tel. 217-44-92
Brokers 217-53-90
.... 355-68-67
Fax............................... 355-68-62
Fax 355-68-63
Fax 355-68-59

St. Petersburg Stock Exchange.
197061, Saint Petersburg, Russia
Skorokhodova ul., 19
Tel 232-55-00
Fax 232-18-86

Alisa Commodity Exchange
Branch of Moscow Commodity Exchange
Trading in construction materials.
Zanevskiy pr., 6. 221-86-83
.... 221-87-83
.... 221-47-01

Interlesbirzha
Wood and paper
195009, Saint Petersburg, Russia.
Mikhaylova ul., 17 541-87-50
Fax............................. 542-64-01

St. Petersburg Freight Exchange.
193015, Saint Petersburgs
Kavalergardskaya ul., 6
Tel 271-81-59
Fax 274-29-66

North-West Agricultural Products Exchange
195252, Saint Petersburg, Russia
Rustaveli ul., 31 538-16-54
Fax 184-63-36

Baltika Marine Exchange
Stachek pr., 18 292-95-18
Fax 252-15-15

Computer Exchange
Compyuternaya birzha
Moskovskiy pr., 98 292-40-20

Ladoga
Ochakovskaya ul., 7........ 274-76-54
Fax................................. 274-69-93

Medical Section of St. Petersburg, Stock & Commodity Exchange
Veteranov pr., 56........... 156-96-67

Neva Construction Exchange
Liteynyy pr., 22 272-25-62
.... 273-49-02
brokers........................... 273-49-02

Rossiyskaya bumaga v SPb
Sestroretskaya ul., 8 239-78-28
.... 239-56-28
.... 234-50-58
.... 234-52-15

Russo-Balt
Morskoy Slavy pl., 1....... 355-47-47
.... 355-43-40
.... 355-14-12
Fax 355-47-48
Telex.................... 121585 MRW SU

Resurs
Kirovskiy pr., 5 233-83-69

Sfinks Construction Exchange
Nab. reki Moyki, 76......... 319-92-93

St. Petersburg Stock & Commodity Exchange
Zhelyabova ul., 25 164-38-49
Fax .... (812) 315-17-01
Telex........................121221 ETAP

☎ STORAGE
СКЛАДСКИЕ ПОМЕЩЕНИЯ
LAGERHÄUSER
ENTREPOTS
LAGER

See WAREHOUSES

MCT EUROPE

CONTAINER STORAGE IN ST. PB.

MEZHEVOY KANAL, 5 251-86-62
FAX .... (812)186-83-44
TELEX ....121691 MCT SU

Concern **SOPPOL**

Secure fireproof storage for
valuable equipment, personal belongings,
and documents with 24 hours guards

2-ya Krasnoarmeyskaya ul., 7

Tel 110-14-32
24 hours/day, $ & rubles, English

Baltimor
Sadovaya ul., 53 310-67-47
Interservice
Liteynyy pr., 35 275-35-61
.... 275-35-57
Kirovspec
Stachek pr., 47 183-82-75
Duty Operator 183-67-38
Fax 252-17-30
Kronverk
Gertsena ul., 56 311-84-27
Poliservis
Tsimlyanskaya ul., 6........ 222-94-88
Open: 10-20
Stroyagroservis
Favorskogo ul., 12 534-01-94
Sever Co., Ltd.
4-ya Predportovaya ul., 5
.... 122-44-09
Transkontinentalservis
Mayakovskogo ul., 5 272-14-24

☎ STREETCARS, TRAMS
ТРОЛЛЕЙБУСЫ, ТРАМВАИ
STRAßENBAHNEN, O-BUSSE
TRANSPORTS EN COMMUN
SPÅRVAGNAR

See TRAMS

☎ ST. PETERSBURG CITY GOVERNMENT

CITY COUNCIL
ГОРОДСКОЙ СОВЕТ
STADTRAT, ST. PETERBURG
COMITE EXECUTIF DE
ST.PETERSBOURG
STATSFULLMÄKTIGE

*All the Commissions of the City
Council listed below are in the City
Council Building on St. Isaac's Square
unless otherwise noted.*

City Council
190107, Isaakievskaya pl., 6
Telex: .... 121575 LSUWS SU
Fax: 310-47-76
Information 319-04-05
Head of the City Council
BELYAEV, Alexander Nikolaevich
.... 310-00-00

Vice-Head of the City Council
MOISEEV, Boris Alexandrovich
.... 319-47-49

DEPARTMENTS:
External relations
Upravlenie vneshnikh svyazey
Apt. 357 319-97-06
External Relations Commission
Komissiya po vneshnim svyazyam
Rm. 360 319-95-81
Conversion Commission
Komissiya po konversii
Rm. 326 319-94-61
Ecological Commission
Komissiya po ekologii
Rm. 335 319-95-04
Economic Reforms Commission
Komissiya po Ekonomicheskim reformam
Plekhanova ul., 36, Rm. 509
.... 310-12-84
Commission on Planning, Budget and Finance
*Planovo i byudzhetno
finansovaya komissiya*
Rm. 100 314-41-56
Transportation Commission
Komissiya po Transportnomy kompleksu
Rm. 383 319-90-56
Legislation & Legal Commission
*Komissiya po voprosam zakonnosti,
pravoporyadka i raboty
pravookhranitelnykh organov*
Rm. 303 319-98-19
Medical Health Commission
*Komissiya po meditsinskomy
obespecheniyu*
Rm. 246 319-98-04
Property Management Fund
Fond imushchestva
Rm. 102 310-46-45

☎ ST. PETERSBURG CITY GOVERNMENT
THE MAYOR'S OFFICE
МЭРИЯ
ST. PETERBURG,
BÜRGERMEISTER
MAIRE DE PETERSBURG
BORGMÄSTARE

*The Mayor's Offices are now located in
Smolnyy Institute at Proletarskoy
Diktatury pl. 1. The Mayor is Anatoliy
Alexandrovich Sobchak, Prof. of Law at
the St. Petersburg State University.*

Mayor's Office at Smolnyy Institute
Information 315-98-83
Office info. 278-19-68

.... 278-69-68
Info. for appointments 278-13-46
.... 278-22-46
Fax................................. 274-10-26
From Metro Chernyshevskaya, take Trolley Bus: 15, 18, & 49 or Bus: 22, 27 136.
From Metro Ploshchad Vosstaniya, take Trolley bus 5 & 7, or Bus 22 & 27

Economic Development Committee
Komitet po ekonomicheskomu razvitiyu
Smolnyy, Rm. 382
Reception 278-11-68
.... 278-61-69
Deputy Mayor 273-48-93
.... 273-21-36

City Property Management Committee
Komitet po upravleniyu gorodskim imushchestvom
Smolnyy, Rm. 260 (reception)
.... 278-15-57
Deputy Mayor, Rm. 262, . 278-15-37

Social Welfare Committee
Komitet po sotsialnym voprosam
Smolnyy, Rm. 368 (reception room)
.... 278-13-81
Deputy Mayor 278-15-37

Foreign Relations Committee
Komitet vneshnikh svyasey
Antonenko ul., 6............. 319-91-02

Foreign Humanitarian Relations
Upravlenie mezhdunarodnykh gumanitarnykh svyasey
Smolnyy, Rm. 123 278-12-24

Regional International Relations
Regionalnye mezhdunarodnye svyazi
Smolnyy......................... 319-92-38

Development of International Humanitarian Relations Department
Otdel razvitiya mezhdunarodnykh gumanitarnykh svyazey
Smolnyy......................... 278-13-78

Foreign-Economic Relations Administration
Upravlenie vneshneekonomicheskikh svyasey
Antonenko ul., 6, Rm. 22. 314-73-69

Foreign Companies Representations in Saint Petersburg Committee
Upravlenie po obsluzhivaniyu inostrannykh predstavitelstv, akkreditovannykh v Sankt-Peterburge
Nab. Kutuzova, 34 272-50-24
.... 272-15-00

Free-Trade Zone Committee
Komitet po upravleniyu Zonoy Svobodnogo Predprinimatelstva
Smolnyy, Rm. 288 278-16-78

Transport and Communications Committee
Komitet po transportu i svyazi
Smolnyy, Rm. 252 278-15-16
.... 278-23-62

Public Improvements and Roads Committee
Komitet po blagoustroystvu i dorozhnomu khozyaystvu
Smolnyy, Rm. 233 278-18-42

Municipal Services and Energy Committee
Komitet zhilishchnogo khozyaystva i energetiki
Smolnyy 312-58-11

Legislation Committee
Yuridicheskiy komitet
Smolnyy, Rm. 341 278-16-51

Requests and appeals Committee
Komitet po obrashcheniaym i zhalobam
Smolnyy, Rm. 345 278-12-57

Press and mass media Committee
Komitet po pechyati i sredstvam massovoy informatsii
Smolnyy, Rm. 274 273-41-02
.... 278-12-61

☎ SUBWAY(Underground)
МЕТРО
U-BAHN
METRO
TUNNELBANA

See METRO

☎ SUPERMARKETS
УНИВЕРСАМЫ
SUPERMÄRKTE
SUPERMARCHES
STORKÖP

See FOOD STORES, MARKETS & DELICATESSENS.

☎ SWIMMING
ПЛАВАНИЕ
SCHWIMMBÄDER
NATATION
BAD/SIM HALLAR/PLATSER

Try some of the pools listed under HEALTH CLUBS or this entry. If you are going to visit a swimming pool in St. Petersburg, please phone and ask when you can go. Some may require you to have a medical clearance, which can be obtained from a physician.

Army Sport Club
Litovskaya ul., 3 542-01-62
Administration................ 245-27-75
Open: 6-20

Baltic Sea Fleet
Nevskiy pr., 22/24 311-46-89
Open: 6-24

Delfin
Dekabristov ul., 38.......... 114-20-54
Open: 6-24

Dinamo
Dinamo pr., 44 235-29-44
Open: 6-24

Lokomotiv Swimming Pool
Konstantina Zaslonova ul., 23
.... 164-46-10

Naval Sports Club Swimming Pool
Krasnogvardeyskiy pr., 5a
.... 528-73-28

Popular Education Committee
Bolshaya Raznochinnaya ul., 20
Duty 235-38-77
Open: 6-24

Spartak Swimming Pool
Konstantinovskiy pr., 19 .. 235-05-83

Yunost
Pravdy ul., 11................. 315-01-17
Open: 6-24

☎ SYNAGOGUES
СИНАГОГИ
SYNAGOGEN
SYNAGOGUES
SYNAGOGER

Choral Synagogue
Please call 114-00-78
Synagogues
Lermontovskiy pr., 2 206-00-78
Alexandrovskoy Fermy pr., 66
.... 262-04-47

☎ TAILOR/SEAMSTRESS
ПОРТНЫЕ
SCHNEIDER
TAILLEUR/COUTURIER
SKRÄDDARE/SÖMMERSKOR

There are many skilled tailors and seamstresses in St. Pb. working in "Atele". There are three categories of quality: 2nd, 1st and "Lux". There are even more private tailors & seamstresses. Ask at the House of Fashion or your friends.

Atele No. 3
Nevskiy pr., 95............... 277-19-22
Atele
Nevskiy pr., 12............... 312-73-51
Lux
Moskovskiy pr., 125........ 298-30-92
Liteynyy pr., 27.............. 272-65-51
Private tailor
Please call 159-47-34

```
┌─────────────────────────────────────┐
│  The City Code for Saint Petersburg  │
│       Dial  812 + Number             │
└─────────────────────────────────────┘
```

☎ TAX CONSULTING
КОНСУЛЬТАЦИОННЫЕ ФИРМЫ
ПО ВОПРОСАМ БИЗНЕСА И
ФИНАНСОВ
STEUERBERATER
IMPOTS, SERVICE DES
REVISORER OCH
HANDELSKONSULTER

See ACCOUNTING & AUDITING FIRMS
& BUSINESS CONSULTANTS

☎ TAXIS/LIMOUSINES
ТАКСИ
TAXIS
TAXI/LIMOUSINE
TAXI

See also AUTOMOBILE RENTAL,
LIMOUSINE, AIRPORT TRANSPORTATION.

There is little real distinction between renting a car by the hour or day with a driver and a taxi, except that taxis are for specific destinations and car rentals are for time. Taxis can also be hired by the hour.

There are three types of taxis: official taxis, private taxis, and private cars.

Official (and private) taxis can be identified by a small green light on the windshield. Official taxis also have the distinctive T and checkered emblem is on doors and may have yellow lights on the roofs.

Many private cars will also stop to pick up passengers, often by drivers going to work or on business. A reasonable contribution "for gas" is usually expected and appreciated. The cost of keeping a car is now very expensive for the average car owner. Taking private cars for taxis can be risky and is only for the adventure some who know some Russian. Travel in twos and avoid being picked up by cars with two people.

The OFFICIAL TAXI RATE is now some MULTIPLE OF THE RUBLE RATE ON THE METER. In June 1992 it was 40 times the amount on the meter, or, if no meter, between 30 and 200 rubles depending on the time of day and the distance to be traveled. Or about 200 to 300 rubles for an hour. Rates are higher late in the evening. Rates are rising rapidly.

Note that there is often one price for when you negotiate in English and a lower price when you negotiate in Russian. For foreigners the standard rate in the front of hotels is around $5 to most places, and more to more distant places, such as $15 to/from the airport. Ruble taxis can be found if you walk a block or two from a hotel. Getting a reasonably priced taxi at the airport can be difficult because of some tough price fixing by local drivers.

Arrange for a ride or call for an official cab to pick you up.

When hailing a taxi, you tell the driver where you are going and ask the price. It will usually be higher than normal. If they quote an outrageous price in dollars, you can bring the price down if you say that it is too much and begin to walk away. There usually will be another taxi. Unless, of course, it is 2 AM in the morning and pouring rain. The market works here.

<u>Ordering an official taxi</u>
Ordering an official taxi usually works quite efficiently, at least in the center of the city during the day. Officially they ask for two hour advanced notice, but often they come more quickly.

<u>OFFICIAL TAXI</u> (FOR RUBLES)
Orders: 312-00-22
Inquiries:.............................. 315-11-17

<u>PRIVATE TAXI</u> (FOR $)

MATRALEN
TAXI & LIMOUSINE
At the Hotel Pulkovskaya
Featuring FORD automobiles & mini-vans
Lyubotinskiy proezd., 5.... 298-36-48
.... 298-12-94
Fax................................. 298-00-73
Telex .... 121028 MATRA SU
24 Hours Daily, $, English, German

 TAXI

At Pribaltiyskaya Hotel
Taxi and Limousine Service
24 Hours/Day,
Featuring Fords
Korablestroiteley ul., 14

Dispatcher 356-93-29
Director........................ 356-10-74
Fax................................ 356-00-94
Fax................................ 356-38-45
$, English, German, Finnish

INTERAUTO - Hertz Int. Lic.
Large selection of cars & minibuses with or without drivers. Reservations at the Grand Europe & Moscow Hotels
Ispolkomskaya ul., 9/11 277-40-32
Complete 24 Hrs service $, English

☎ **TECHNICAL INSTITUTES**
ИНСТИТУТЫ ТЕХНИЧЕСКИЕ
TECHNISCHE INSTITUTE
INSTITUTS TECHNIQUES
TEKNISKA INSTITUT

See UNIVERSITIES & INSTITUTES for *educational institutions and* INSTITUTES RESEARCH *for research institutes.*

Education and research are major industries in St. Petersburg and it has one of the best educated populations.

☎ **TECHNOLOGY TRANSFERS**
ТЕХНОЛОГИИ, ОБМЕН
TECHOLOGIETRANSFER
TECHNOLOGIES, TRANSFERT DES
TEKNISK ÖVERFÖRING

See EXPORT-IMPORT FIRMS
& BUSINESS CONSULTANTS, CENTERS.

Many firms and research institutions are offering "technology" and are looking for partners.

Akater SP (Russian-Finnish JV)
Zemledelcheskaya ul., 7, bldg. 2
.... 242-34-10
Alba (Russian-American JV)
V.O., 3-ya Liniya, 52 213-30-58
Alcor Technologies Inc.
　　　　　　　(Russian-American JV)
Stepana Razina ul., 8/50
.... 310-44-01
Alinter (Russian-German JV)
Nalichnaya ul., 6............. 356-37-21
Alpiya (Russian-Australian JV)
Voskova ul., 6................ 233-82-74
Aluma System Monolitstroy Corp.
　　　　　　(Russian-Canadian Enterprise)
Ryleeva ul., 29 273-26-46
DAB International (Russian-American JV)
Obukhovskoy Oborony pr.,295
Director.......................... 262-24-22
Konsofin
Ogorodnikova pr., 58....... 259-91-06
LST-Metall (Russian-German JV)
Doroga na Petroslavyanku, 5
Director.......................... 267-08-24
Nauchnyy Interkontakt
Vladimirskiy pr., 2.......... 319-93-61
**Mineral Processing Engineers
(Russian-Finnish JV)**
V.O., 21-ya Liniya, 8-a 213-99-86
Project-Engineering JV (Russian-French)
Zaozernaya ul., 1 259-67-17
Laser Technology Center (Russian-German)
Politekhnicheskaya ul., 29
.... 535-52-47
Fokon
Sablinskaya ul., 14.......... 238-85-53
**Assoc. for Foreign Economic Cooperation
Assotsiatsiya Vneshneekonomi-
cheskogo Sotrudnichestva**
Khalturina ul., 27, apt. 49
.... 315-86-27
**Leningradintekh
Vneshneekonomicheskaya Assotsiatsiya**
Chkalovskiy pr., 52 234-92-23
Sigmatech
Nab. Krasnogo Flota, 8 315-62-02
Patents & technology sales military complex

☎ TELEGRAM
ТЕЛЕГРАММЫ
TELEGRAMME
TELEGRAMME
TELEGRAM

See COMMUNICATIONS, TELEPHONE & BUSINESS SERVICES CENTERS.

You can send internal telegrams from most post offices and telegram posts. You can send international telegrams from several post offices in each district including the main post office in each region. See POST OFFICES.

Telegraph
    Nab. Sinopskaya, 14 265-27-50
    Nab. Sinopskaya, 14 066
       To send telegrams by credit.
St. Petersburg Telegraph Office
    Pochtamtskaya ul., 15 312-97-51

☎ TELEPHONE BOOKS
ТЕЛЕФОННЫЕ КНИГИ
TELEFONBÜCHER
DIRECTOIRES TELEPHONIQUES
TELEFONKATALOGAR

See also BUSINESS PUBLICATION
Contrary to common knowledge, there are telephone books for Saint Petersburg. The Leningrad Telephone Company published two telephone books in the last 4 years: Telephone Book of Leningrad 1988 *(Telefonyy spravochnik Leningrada 1988 (Телефонный справочник Ленинграда 1988)* and an updated and better organized* Short Telephone Book of Leningrad 1991 *(Kratkiy Telefonnyy spravochnik 1991, Краткий Телефонный справочник Ленинграда 1991). They are a combination of non-residential white pages and "yellow pages" without any informational advertising.*

From the viewpoint of the Western readers, the principal problems are that the books are in Russian, they are hard to find, very incomplete, out-of-date and they are very poorly organized for the Western user accustomed to the Western-style Yellow Pages. They are basically organized by type of organization and institution rather than by category of goods and services. Thus, they still have no "Yellow Pages". Our Travellers Yellow Pages is the first for Saint Petersburg. A second, more comprehensive, but less convenient Yellow Pages will be published in the autumn by another company.

There are other phone directories about Saint Petersburg. See BUSINESS PUBLICATIONS.

☎ TELEPHONE EQUIPMENT
ТЕЛЕФОННОЕ ОБОРУДОВАНИЕ
TELEFON-ZUSATZ GERÄTE
TELEPHONE, EQUIPEMENT
TELEFONUTRUSTNING

Western telephones can be bought at most ELECTRONIC SHOPS. *Be sure they work on "Pulse" as well as "Touch-Tone". Don't buy the cheapest; they burn out from the voltage fluctuations. Good Western phones can be installed by rewiring the plug. Easier yet, bring along an adapter outlet to rewire into the Russian outlet and just plug in the phone. They work.*
Alcatel
    Gertsena ul., 16.............. 315-89-38
DELTA TELECOM
    Gertsena ul., 22.............. 314-61-26
    Fax.............................. 314-88-37

XXI Vek
    V.O., 17-ya Liniya, 12-a
    213-22-12

Lizsey Radioelektroniki
    P.S., Bolshoy pr., 18 235-06-18
    Inter-office and Intercoms

☎ TELEPHONE INFORMATION
СПРАВКИ ПО ТЕЛЕФОНУ
TELEFONAUSWEISE
INFORMATIONS TELEPHONIQUE
TELEFONINFORMATION

The phone company has a list of "free information numbers" and "paid information numbers." In Russian!
FREE INFORMATION
    FIRE............................ 01
    MILITIA (POLICE) 02
    EMERGENCY MEDICAL 03
    GAS EMERGENCY.............. 04
    TELEGRAPH.................... 066
    INTERCITY CALLS............. 07
    EXACT TIME 08
    PHONE COMPANY 09
PAID INFORMATION
    001 Weather
    009 Telephone number or address of subscribers
    061 Address of resident of Leningrad oblast (name and birth date)
    062 Ship arrivals, monthly weather forecast, Lotto results, Program of TV, theaters, cinemas.
    063 Address & numbers of organizations, hours and days of museums, postal codes.
    006 Aeroflot
    007 Conditions about intercity telephone network
Information on Moscow telephone numbers.............................. 314-73-52
Look in the Short Leningrad Telephone Book 1991 *for a more extensive listing.*

☎ TELEPHONE- INTERCITY CALLING
ТЕЛЕФОНЫ МЕЖДУГОРОДНИЕ
TELEFON, FERNGESPRÄCHE
TELEPHONE INTERURBAIN
ТЕЛЕФОН /INTERCITY/

You can dial most cities in Russia directly from St. Petersburg. Simply dial the INTERCITY CODE listed below followed by the number. There is a special service for calling people without telephones called the "07" service. You "order a call for a specific date and time and length of call, the person called is notified and comes to the "Telephone Post" to talk with you.

If you don't know the telephone code or telephone number in the distant city, call Information "07". For a more complete listing of codes, see the Short Leningrad Telephone Book 1991, *pp. 475-488*

Intercity Code
Leningrad region

Boksitogorsk	266
Volosovo	273
Volkhov	263
Vsevolozhsk	270
Vyborg	278
Gatchina	271
Kingisepp	275
Kirishi	268
Kirovsk	262
Lodeynoe Pole	264
Luga	272
Podporozhie	265
Priozersk	279
Slantsy	274
Sosnovyy Bor	269
Tikhvin	267
Tosno	261

Intercity Code
Northwest Russia

Arkhangelsk	818
Murmansk	815
Novgorod	816
Pertozavodsk	814
Pskov	81122
Syktyvkar	82122
Vologda	81722

Intercity Code
Other Major Cities in Russia, CIS, Baltics and former USSR

Alma-Ata*	3272
Ashkhabad*	3632
Baku*	8922
Bishkek*	3312
Brest	01622
Bryansk	0832**, 08322

Bukhara	36522
Cheboksary	8352
Chelyabinsk	3512
Cherepovets	820
Chernovtsy	03722
Chita	30222
Gomel	0232**, 02322
Dnepropetrovsk	0562
Donetsk	0622
Dushanbe*	3772
Dzhambul	3262**, 32622
Fergana	37322
Ivanovo	0932**, 09322
Irkutsk	3952
Kazan	8432
Kaliningrad	0112
Kaluga	0842**, 08422
Karaganda	3212
Kaunas	0127
Khabarovsk	81732
Kharkov	0572
Kherson	055
Kiev*	044
Kirov	833
Kishinev*	0422
Klaypeda	01261
Krasnodar	8612
Krasnoyarsk	3912
Kursk	071
Lipetsk	0742
Lvov	0322
Mineralnye vody	86531
Minsk*	0172
Mogilev	0222
Moskva*	095
Narva	01435
Nizhniy Novgorod	8312
Nikolayev	051
Novosibirsk	3832
Odessa	0482
Omsk	3812
Palanga	01236
Panevezhis	01254
Penza	8412
Perm	3422
Pyatigorsk	86533
Riga*	0132
Rostov-na-Donu	8632
Ryazan	0912
Samara	8462
Samarkand	3662
Saratov	8452
Sverdlovsk	3432
Sevastopol	069
Simferopol	0652
Smolensk	081
Sochi	8622
Suzdal	09231
Sukhumi	88122
Tallinn*	0142
Tashkent*	3712
Tbilisi*	8832

Termez	37622
Tver	08222
Tomsk	3822
Tula	0872
Ulyanovsk	8422
Ufa	3472
Urgench	36222
Vilnus*	0122
Vinnitsa	04322
Vitebsk	0212**, 02122
Vladikavkaz*	86722
Vladimir	09222
Volgograd	8442
Vorkuta	82151
Voronezh	0732
Yaroslavl	0852
Yerevan*	8852
Zaporozhe	0612**, 06122
Zhitomir	0412

*Bold letters are capitals of the republics or former republics of the USSR.

**First code is used with telephone with 6 numbers; the second code is used with telephones with 5 numbers.

☎ TELEPHONE INTERNATIONAL CALLS
МЕЖДУНАРОДНЫЙ ТЕЛЕФОН
AUSLANDSGESPRÄCHE
TELEPHONE INTERNATIONAL
UTRIKES SAMTAL

INTERNATIONAL CALLING

Placing international calls is much easier now than a few years ago. Here are some suggestions.

1. DIRECT DIAL. Since June 1 you can direct dial to United States, Germany and many East European countries from many homes & offices (depending on your exchange). Dial "8", wait for second dial tone and then dial "10", the country code and telephone number. Here are some international codes from St. Petersburg.

Bulgaria	8-10-359-( )-
Sophia	8-103592
Varna	8-1035952
Czechoslovakia	8-10-42-( )-
Prague	8-10422
Bratislava	8-10427
Brno	8-10425
Germany	8-10-37-( )-
Berlin	8-10372
Dresden	8-103751
Rostock	8-103781
Hungary	8-10-36-( )-
Budapest	8-103611
Poland	8-10-48-( )-
Warsaw	8-104822
Gdansk	8-104858
USA	8-10-1-( )-
Yugoslaviya	8-10-38-( )-
Belgrade	8-103811

For a more complete listing of international codes, see the 1991 Short Leningrad Telephone Book, pp. 489-491.

Often the international lines are busy, so that you still may want to try the traditional ways described below.

To call most other countries in the world, you must :

2. ORDER A CALL IN ADVANCE

The traditional way to place an international call, is to order a call in advance. You can "order" an international call for a specific time and day, up to two days in advance. You must give them the number you are calling when you order the call (although you can change it before the call is placed).

To call home from a private phone, you can place a reservation with the overseas operator after 9 am, often two days in advance. Dial 315-00-12 and ask for an English speaking operator. Explain that you want to place an international call, and when you want to call, they will tell you dates and times available. Give the number you are calling and the number you will be at the time of the call. You will be called back when the call is placed. Occasionally, you can get through immediately, especially to the USA, which now costs 260 rubles/minute instead of the former 16 rubles per minute.

Prices are rising rapidly. As of late June, it cost the following per minute: 4.5 rubles to call Finland, 9 rubles to call Albania, Bulgaria, Hungary, Mongolia, Poland, Rumania and Czechoslovakia, 27 rubles to call Germany, Yugoslavia, Sweden, France and Switzerland. Calling Israel costs 54 rubles per minute, calling the USA cost 260 rubles per minute. The latest tariffs are also available from 315-00-12.

In a hotel, they will assist you in ordering a call, but you may still have to wait. Book in advance for calls in rubles.

3. PLACE A DIRECT CALL AT TELEPHONE STATION

Try going to the "long-distance and international communication point" at Gertsena ul., 3/5, daily from 9-17 to place a call directly. Expect to wait in line and pay rubles.

4. PLACE AN IMMEDIATE DIRECT CALL BY SATELLITE AND BY LEASED LINES.

For immediate calls via satellite, go to one of the "BUSINESS SERVICES CENTERS" or DELTA TELECOM, or a COMMUNICATION company or a hotel that lists "phone or satellite phone". It costs between $8-25 per minute, but it is quick.

*6. SUBSCRIBE TO YOUR OWN
INTERNATIONAL ACCESS SERVICE.
Several of the firms listed under
COMMUNICATIONS and CELLULAR
PHONE provide the instant access to
international lines from your office or
home phone. These are ideal for business
& industries that want their own instant
access to international lines, from office,
home or car.*

☎ TELEPHONE REPAIRS INSTALLATION
ТЕЛЕФОНЫ, УСТАНОВКА, РЕМОНТ
TELEFONINSTALLATION,
REPARATUR
TELEPHONE, INSTALLATION
TELEFONINSTALLATION

*To get your phone repaired or to check
on interruption of service, it is best to call
the service number for your "phone
exchange" which are too many to list
here. They are listed in the back of the
most recent 1991 edition of the "Short"
Leningrad Telephone Book 1991. Or try
these numbers (in Russian) to find out the
repair number to call for your exchange:*

  Vyborgskiy telefonyy uzel 054
  Moskovskiy telefonyy uzel..........055
  Nekrasovskiy telefonyy uzel........053
  Petrogradskiy telefonyy uzel 052
  Tsentralniy telefonyy uzel..........051

ALPHA
.... 132-43-91
.... 132-62-26
*Assembling, installation & service of telephone
station ALPHA.*

☎ TELEPHONE SERVICE
ТЕЛЕФОННОЕ ОБСЛУЖИВАНИЕ
FERNSPRECHDIENSTE
TELEPHONE
TELEFON

*See also TELEPHONE-INTERNATIONAL;
TELEPHONE-INTERCITY; TELEPHONE
REPAIRS AND INSTALLATION,
TELEPHONE EQUIPMENT AND CELLULAR
TELEPHONES*

*The telephone situation is rapidly
improving in Saint Petersburg as the
Leningrad Telephone Company works with
Western telephone companies to improve
service and as more firms enter the
market to supply telephones and
telephone services. Official prices are
rising rapidly also, especially for
immediate installation in offices and
enterprises and for long distance calls.
There are long waits for domestic service,
but things can be speeded up under
certain circumstances.*

Alcatel
  Gertsena ul.,16............... 315-89-38
**Leningrad City Telephone Network
Leningradskaya gorodskaya
telefonnaya set**
Leningrad Central Telephone Station
  Gertsena ul., 3-5............. 311-70-01
Telephone information (in Russian)
.... 09
Intercity Telephone Calls & Station
.... 07
  "Mezhdugorodnyy" 274-93-83
International Communications Point
*To make immediate phone calls
abroad, go to Gertsena ul., 3-5, daily
from 9 am - 5 pm*
International telephone
Requests from hotels
  "Mezhdunarodnyy".......... 314-47-47
International telephone
requests from homes and business
  "Mezhdunarodnyy".......... 315-00-12
Leningrad City Telephone Board
  Gertsena ul., 24.............. 314-37-57
Telephone repair service
See TELEPHONE REPAIR

**Cellular Radio Telephone
In Saint Petersburg
and the World**

For businesses and individuals.
See our ad under cellular phones
Gertsena ul., 22.............. 314-61-26
Fax............................... 314-88-37
Fax. 275-01-30

Lenfinkom, JV
  Gertsena ul., 3-5............. 314-00-60
  Fax:.............................. 314-50-84
*Automatic international telephone lines
Electronic mail ($), English*

☎ TELEVISION - CABLE
ТЕЛЕВИДЕНИЕ КАБЕЛЬНОЕ
KABELFERNSEHEN
TELEVISION DE CABLE
TV, KABEL

*Cable TV first appeared in St. Petersburg
about three years ago. One of the best
centers, "Pyotr Velikiy", has 5 channels.
There is also the local cable TV for
separate city areas and even for individual
apartment buildings.*

Kabelnoe Televidenie (Cable TV)
Mokhovaya ul., 17 273-51-39
Kabelnoe Televidenie
Advertisement agency
Sadovaya ul., 55/57 113-49-89

Peter the Great A/O
CABLE-SATELLITE
TELEVISION St. Pb.
Excellent opportunity to advertise to the residents in Saint Petersburg

Sredneokhtinskiy pr., 52...526-66-31
Fax..............................526-66-24
Telex .... 121637 DISK SU

☎ TELEVISION REPAIR
ТЕЛЕВИЗОРЫ, РЕМОНТ
FERNSEHGERÄTE, REPARATUR
TELEVISION, REPARATION
TV, REPARATION

See also ELECTRICAL, REPAIRS.

Baltik-Sputnik (Sputnik-TV)
Litovskaya ul., 10 245-83-49
Fax 275-74-34
Orbita-Service
Kosmonavtov pr., 25....... 299-81-08
Hrs: 10 - 19
Polyus-Servis
Kuznetsovskaya ul., 44.... 298-29-66
.... 298-24-32
Hrs: 10 - 20
Atele Po Remontu Televizorov
Krasnoputilovskaya ul., 12
.... 183-14-74
Atele Po Remontu Televizorov
Veteranov pr., 96 152-55-91
Atele Po Remontu Televizorov
Nab. Oktyabrskaya, 64 263-65-96
Atele Po Remontu Televizorov
Shkolnaya ul., 7 239-84-41
Atele Po Remontu Televizorov
III Internatsionala ul., 18
.... 156-46-93
Atele Po Remontu Televizorov
Bolsheokhtinskiy pr., 1 222-87-00
Atele Po Remontu Televizorov
Gavanskaya ul., 13 217-21-16
Rekord
Prosveshcheniya pr., 62
.... 598-89-09
Soneks
Professora Popova ul., 7/8
.... 234-58-00
Fax 234-55-04
Torgovyy Center Baltiya
Zverinskaya ul., 38 233-05-33
.... 233-45-17

Tekhnicheskiy tsentr N 3
Gertsena ul., 14............... 315-08-86
.... 315-61-56
Info.................................. 315-61-65
Information of TV Repairs in each region
Remont televizorov

Info Radio repair.................. 164-88-37
Info Kirovskiy...................... 184-34-94
Info Moskovskiy 298-19-89
Info Oktyabrskiy.................. 315-61-65
Info Petrogradskiy............... 233-05-33
Info Smolninskiy.................. 105-16-09

☎ TELEVISION SALES
ТЕЛЕВИЗОРЫ, ПРОДАЖА
FERNSEHGERÄTE, VERKAUF
TELEVISION, VENTE
TV, FÖRSÄLJNING

See also ELECTRICAL SUPPLIES/GOODS

Imported and Russian televisions can be bought at a large variety of shops including domestic ELECTRICAL SUPPLIES GOODS shops as well as some the INTERNATIONAL SHOPS and COMMERCIAL SHOPS. You can even get your own personal satellite TV system installed. Try the following shops:
Elektronika
Gagarina pr., 12 299-38-49
Eridan
Zagorodnyy pr., 11 314-23-18
Hrs: 10-14, 16-19, closed Sun & Mon.
Estonia
P.S., Bolshoy pr., 72 232-25-10
Hrs: 10-14, 16-19, closed Sun., Mon
Signal
Nekrasova ul., 4 272-02-59
Shop of "Radiotekhnika" Riga
Hrs: 10-14, 16-19, closed Sun., Mon.
Rigonda
Moskovskly pr., 171........ 298-08-40
Hrs: 11-14, 16-20, closed Sun., Mon.
Rubikon
Lesnoy pr., 19................ 542-00-65

SKIF, *Satellite TV System*
Satellite TV System Sales & Installation in Northwest Russia
Astra 1 & 2, Nordic, CNN & Other
Vosstaniya ul., 32........... 275-53-45
Fax 275-58-71
Telex..................... 621110 SKIF SU
Hrs: 9-18, $ or rubles, English, French

Zolotoy Klyuchik (Golden Key)
Marshala Govorova ul., 10 184-83-53
Hrs: 10-14, 16 -19, closed Sun, Mon

☎ TELEVISION STATIONS
ТЕЛЕВИЗИОННАЯ СТАНЦИЯ
FERNSEHANSTALTEN
TELEVISION, STATIONS DE
TV, STATIONER

St. Petersburg is served by four TV stations and by several cable TV systems in different areas of the city.

The four TV stations are:
Channel 1: "Ostankino" National channel (concerts, culture, news, films)
Channel 2 "TV Petersburg" (Saint Petersburg's own independent TV with films, interviews, roundtables, local news, concerts and advertising)
Channel 3: "Rossiya" National channel (sports, news, films, features)
Channel 4 "Educational" (foreign language lessons, physics, economics educational films)
Availability of cable TV depends on location.

Petersburg Radio & Television Centre
Chapygina ul., 6 232-02-21
Petersburg TV
Chapygina ul., 6
TV................................. 234-07-16
Petersburg Radio
Rakova ul., 27
Radio 219-96-16

Television Advertising

Petersburg Television Studio
Chapygina ul., 6 232-78-70
.... 232-78-69
EM Advertising West Germany
Chapygina ul., 6 234-22-20
Teletsentr
Chapygina ul., 6 234-78-36
.... 219-96-00
TV-Neva Show-business
Pushkinskaya ul., 10, office 9
.... 112-32-73
.... 112-32-78
.... 112-32-79
Fax 112-36-29
Telex .... 121031 NEVAT SU

☎ TELEX
ТЕЛЕКС
TELEX
TELEX
TELEX

Telex, a form of telegraph, operates independently of phone lines and in some circumstances can be the only way to send information quickly. It is still popular in Russia and Europe where the fax is less common. Most BUSINESS SERVICES CENTERS offer "telex" services.

☎ TEMPORARY HELP
ВРЕМЕННАЯ РАБОТА
ZEITARBEIT
TRAVAIL TEMPORAIRE
VIKARIER, EXTRANIÄLP

There are no well-established temporary employment agencies as in the West. For something similar, try these:

Leningrad College of Radio Electronics
P.S., Kirovskiy pr., 21/14 . 232-66-37
.... 232-47-18
Modern Clerical School
Enquiries........................ 113-69-21
.... 299-68-34
Professional Technical College No. 2
Varshavskaya ul., 7......... 296-16-90
.... 296-29-54

☎ TENNIS
ТЕННИС
TENNIS
TENNIS
TENNIS

BAST Sports Centre

The Place to Relax

Tennis courts, sport halls, exercise room,
Sauna & massage

Raevskogo proezd, 16 552-55-12

Fax 552-39-36

Open 24 hours/day, English & Spanish

Lawn Tennis
  Metallistov pr., 116 540-75-21
  Courts 540-60-92
    Shaping, sauna, swimming pool
    Outdoor courts. May- October

Kirov Stadium
  Krestovskiy Ostrov, Morskoy pr., 1
  Administrator 235-48-77
  Rent courts from 4/15/92 -10/15/92

Tennis Court   **Kort Tennisniy**
  Primorskiy Park Pobedy 235-20-77
  235-16-88

☎ THEATERS/BALLET
    ТЕАТР, БАЛЕТ
    THEATER/BALLETT
    THEATRE/BALLET
    TEATER/BALETT

*For seating plans of Mariinskiy Theater,
Russian Academic Bolshoy Dramatic
Theater, Theater of Opera and Ballet,
Bolshoy Philharmonic Hall, Kappella
Glinka, and Bolshoy Concert Hall
October, see pages 246- 251 of this
book. The names of theaters are
changing rapidly and these are accurate
as of June 15, 1992. There is a Russian
book of seating plans for all theaters,
palaces of culture, and sports arenas,
called* Teatry, kontsertnye zaly, dvortsy
kultury, dvortsy sporta Leningrada(1984).

Academic Comedy Theater
  Nevskiy pr., 56 314-26-10
  Box office 312-45-55
    Metro: Gostinyy Dvor

Benefits Theater
  Nab. reki Moyki, 24 314-07-36
    Metro: Kanal Griboedova

Russian Academic Bolshoy Dramatic
    Theater (n. George Tovstonogov)
    (former Maxim Gorkiy Theater)
  Nab. reki Fontanki, 65. ... 310-04-01
  Box Office 310-92-42
    Metro: Gostinyy Dvor

Bolshoy Puppet Theater
  Nekrasova ul., 10 272-82-15
  Box Office 273-66-72
    Metro: Gostinyy Dvor

To Direct Dial The USA
DIAL 8, wait for Dial Tone
DIAL 101 + Area Code + #

Boris Eyfman's Contemporary Ballet
  P.S., Lizy Chaykinoy ul., 2
  232-02-35
  Director 232-18-62
  Fax 232-18-62
    Metro: Petrogradskaya

Bolshoy Chamber Hall
of the Academic Choir
      Bolshoy Kamernyy Zal
      Akademicheskoy Kapelly
  V.O., 4-ya Liniya, 15
  Administration 213-34-88
  Box office 213-44-90
    Metro: Vasileostrovskaya

Baltiysky Dom *Youth Theater*
  Park Lenina, 4 232-62-44
  Box Office 232-35-39

Bryantsev Theater for Young Audiences
  Pionerskaya pl., 1 164-06-79
  Box Office 112-41-02
    Metro: Pushkinskaya

Buff Theater
  Narodnaya ul., 1 263-65-12
  Box office 263-67-67
    Metro: Lomonosovskaya

Circus
  Main Arena
  Nab. reki Fontanki, 3 210-43-90
    Metro: Gostinyy Dvor

The "Shapito" Circus
  Avtovskaya ul., 1a 183-15-01
  Box office 183-14-98
    Metro: Avtovo

Chamber Music Theater
  Krasnaya ul., 4, office 9
  314-09-55
    Metro: Gorkovskaya

Theater Estrady
  Zhelyabova ul., 27 314-70-60
    Metro: Nevskiy Prospekt & Gostinyy Dvor

Concert Hall in the "St. Petersburg "Hotel
  Nab. Vyborgskaya, 5/2 542-90-56
  Box office 542-80-51
    Metro: Ploshchad Lenina

"Experiment" Drama Theater
  "Theater of Miniatures"
  Kirovskiy pr., 35/75 233-92-76
  Box Office 233-94-28
    Metro: Petrogradskaya

Glinka Kapella (Choral Hall)
  Nab. reki Moyki, 20 314-10-34
  Info 314-11-59
  Box Office 314-10-58
    Metro: Nevskiy Prospekt

Hermitage Theater
  Director 311-90-25
    Metro: Nevskiy Prospekt

Interernyy Theater
  Nevskiy pr., 104 273-14-54
    Metro: Ploshchad Vosstaniya

Komissarzhevskaya Theater *(Drama)*
  Rakova ul., 19 .... 311 08-49
  Box Office 311-31-02
    Metro: Nevskiy prospekt

Central Concert Hall
  Lenina pl., 1 542-09-44
    Metro: Ploshchad Lenina

Yuri Dimitrin

Librettist

Playwright, librettist, musicals, rock operas
Scripts for company presentations
Please call 164-79-51
Fax 164-79-51

Otkrytyy Theater
Vladimirskiy pr., 12 113-21-90
.... 113-22-07
Metro: Vladimirskaya & Dostoevskaya

Lenin Sports-Concert Complex
Yuriya Gagarina pr., 8 298-48-47
Box office 298-41-96
Metro: Park Pobedy

Malyy Dramaticheskiy Theater
Rubinshteyna, 18 113-20-94
Metro: Vladimirskaya & Dostoevskaya

Malyy Zal (Small Hall) Philarmonic
Nevskiy pr., 30 312-45-85
Box office 311-83-33
Metro: Nevskiy prospekt

Malyy Theater Of Opera & Ballet (Musorgskiy)
Iskusstv pl., 1 314-37-58
Metro: Nevskiy prospekt & Gostinyy Dvor

Mariinskiy Theater of Opera & Ballet

(Formerly Kirov Opera & Ballet)
The leading theater of St. Petersburg

Artistic Director - Valeriy GERDIEV

Teatralnaya pl., 1/2
Director 114-44-41
.... 114-43-44
Administrator 114-12-11
Box office 114-43-44
Fax 114-45-40
Telex .... 121460 Kirov SU

Mariinskiy Theater's

CHAMBER CHOIR OF CHURCH MUSIC

Ethereal•Exquisite•Excellent

Listen to Mariinskiy Theater's best voices sing great Russian church & choral music in St. Pb.'s most beautiful Cathedrals.

Music by Tchaikovsky Arkhangelsky, Bortniansky, and Chesnokov

Looking for additional bookings in the United Stated, Europe & Japan for the fall of 1992 & 1993

Artistic Director - Valeriy Borisov

Teatralnaya pl., 1/2 315-69-32
.... 114-72-74
Fax: 114-45-40

Molodezhnyy Theater *Youth Theater*
Nab. reki Fontanki, 114
.... 292-68-70
Metro: Nevskiy prospekt & Gostinyy Dvor

Musical Comedy Theater
Rakova ul., 13 277-87-31
Metro: Nevskiy prospekt & Gostinyy Dvor
Closed for repair

The Music Hall
Park Lenina, 4 233-02-43
Box office 232-92-01
Metro: Gorkovskaya

Musical Theater of Rimsky-Korsakov
Teatralnaya pl., 3 312-25-07
Box office 312-25-19

October Concert Hall
Ligovskiy pr., 6 277-69-60
Metro: Vosstaniya

The People's Theater
Rubinshteyna ul., 13 312-34-84
Metro: Vladimirskaya/Dostoevskaya

Philharmonic Concert Hall of St. Petersburg
Mikhaylovskaya ul., 2
Bolshoy Zal (Grand Hall)
.... 110-40-85
Box Office (Day) 311-73-33
Box Office (Evening) 110-42-57
Metro: Gostinyy Dvor

Comedian's Refuge
Priyut Komedianta
Gogolya ul., 16 312-53-52
Metro: Nevskiy prospekt

Puppet and Marionettes Theater
Nevskiy pr., 52 311-19-00
Metro: Nevskiy prospekt & Gostinyy Dvor

Pushkin Drama Theater
Ostrovskogo pl., 2 311-61-39
Box Office 312-15-45
Metro: Nevskiy prospekt & Gostinyy Dvor

The Chamber Music Theater Company

"St. Petersburg Opera"

Listen to chamber operas in St. Pb.'s most beautiful palaces by best young voices in Russia

Theater at its best.

Artistic Director - Yuri Alexandrov

Please Call 315-67-69
or fax 271-40-22

Sharmanka Kenematicheskaya (Cinematique)
Moskovskiy pr., 151-a 297-26-66
Metro: Elektrosila

Smolny Cathedral Concert and Exhibition Complex
Rastrelli ul., 3 311-35-60
Box office 271-91-82
Metro: Chernyshevskaya

Theater on the Liteynyy
Liteynyy pr., 51 273-63-63
Box office 273-53-35
Metro: Vladimirskaya & Dostoevskaya

Theater of the Musical & Drama Institute
Mokhovaya ul., 35 273-15-92
Closed for repair
Metro: Chernyshevskaya

Theater of Puppets' Tales
Moskovskiy pr., 121 298-00-31
Metro: Moskovskie Vorota

Yusupov Palace
Nab. reki Moyki, 94
Administrator 314-30-66
Ticket Office 314-98-83
Metro: Ploshchad Mira, Sadovaya

Zazerkale Children's Theater
(Through the Looking Glass)
Strelninskaya ul., 11 235-36-18
Metro: Petrogradskaya

☎ **THEATRICAL TICKET OFFICE**
ТЕАТРАЛЬНЫЕ КАССЫ
THEATERKASSE
THEATRE, VENTE DE TICKETS
TEATER, BILJETTKONTOR

You can buy tickets to most ballets, theaters and concerts at the THEATER & CONCERT HALLS, at the many little kiosks called Teatralnaya kassa *(Театральная касса) located at the entrances of metros and on the sidewalk of St. Pt. or at the Central Box Office on Nevskiy Prospect, 42. It will be much cheaper than through "Intourist", but the selection of seats may not be as good. See our SEATING PLANS on page 246-251.*

Central Box Office No. 1
Nevskiy pr., 42 311-31-83

Kassa No. 2
Sredniy pr., 27 213-18-85

Kassa No. 6
P.S., Bolshoy pr., 40 & Kolpinskaya ul.
.... 232-58-63

Kassa No. 9
Bolsheokhtinskiy pr., 10
.... 224-23-92

Kassa No. 11
Metro Vladimirskaya 311-11-89

Kassa No. 12
Nevskiy pr., 39 310-42-40

Kassa No. 13
Metro Gostinyy Dvor 251-99-88

Kassa No. 16
Moskovskiy pr., 41 292-31-74

Kassa No. 22
Dumskaya ul., 2
(Intourist) 314-95-87

Kassa No. 28
Nevskiy pr., 22/24 311-15-39

Kassa No. 30
Karla Marksa pr., 80........ 245-30-16

Kassa No. 35
Moskovskiy pr., 182........ 298-24-95

Kassa No. 39
Metro Leninskiy pr. 254-91-31

Kassa No. 41
Sadovaya ul., 24/26........ 310-46-77

Kassa No. 45
Metro Narvskaya............. 259-77-84

Kassa No. 58
Metro Pushkinskaya 251-90-19

Kassa No. 63
Nab. kan. Griboedova, 2B
.... 219-16-10

Kassa No. 65
Nevskiy pr., 184 271-51-40

Kassa No. 74
Nab. Dvortsovaya, 46 (Hermitage)
.... 311-19-20

Kassa No. 113
Metro Krasnogvardeyskaya
.... 528-15-15

Kassa No. 117
Nevskiy pr., 107 272-65-12

☎ **TICKET BUREAUS**
ПРОДАЖА БИЛЕТОВ
KARTENVORVERKAUF
VENTE DE TICKETS
BILJETTFÖRSÄLJNING

See also AIRLINES and BUSES

Railroad Tickets
Nab. kan. Griboedova, 24
.... 162-33-44

River Boat Tickets
Obukhovskoy Oborony pr., 195
.... 262-55-11

For info on terminals only, not for tickets.

☎ **TIME & TIME ZONES**
ВРЕМЯ И ВРЕМЕННЫЕ ЗОНЫ
ZEIT & ZEITZONEN
HEURE, TEMPS
KORREKT TID (FRÖKEN UR)

For the exact time (in Russian) ..08

St. Petersburg goes on Daylight Saving (Summer) Time on the last Saturday of March and goes off Daylight Saving on last Saturday of October.

St. Petersburg is 3 hours ahead (later) than Greenwich Mean Time and is in the same time zone as Moscow.
Call 315-00-12 (in Russian) for the time difference with a particular city. You can ask there for English operator (if needed).

11 am	St. Petersburg
10 am	Baltics, Kiev, Helsinki ,Tel Aviv
9 am	Warsaw, Paris, Berlin, Rome, Madrid and Prague
8 am	Lisbon, Dublin, London
3 am	New York,
2 am	Chicago,
1 am	Boulder, Colorado & Los Angeles
13 pm	Sverdlovsk, Pakistan
14 pm	Tashkent
15 pm	Novosibirsk
16 pm	China
17 pm	Japan
19 pm	Vladivostok.

☎ TIRES
АВТОПОКРЫШКИ
REIFEN
PNEUS
DÄCK

See also AUTOMOBILE PARTS

Everything for the auto PARTS
Parts, accessories & supplies
for foreign cars, truck, buses
Specializing in Volvo, Mercedes, VW, Opel
Our Shop on Gogolya ul., 19, near Astoria Hotel
Gogolya ul., 19 315-97-58
Fax 292-00-28
Telex .... 121412 LTOS SU
M-F,10 a.m. -6 p.m., Eng, $

Tire Shop
  V.O., 16-ya Liniya, 49
  Manager 213-01-30
      Hrs: 9-20, Sun: 14-16

☎ TOBACCO
ТАБАК
TABAK
TABAC
TOBAK

Western cigarettes can also be bought in most INTERNATIONAL SHOPS *and many* COMMERCIAL SHOPS *and* KIOSKS.

Gavana No. 1
  P.S., Kirovskiy pr., 2 233-52-53
Tabak No. 24
  Sadovaya ul., 42 310-11-05
Tabak No. 35
  V.O., 7-ya Liniya, 36 213-60-82
Tabak No. 38
  Ligovskiy pr., 65 164-48-47
Tabak No. 57
  Nevskiy pr., 64 314-42-58
Tobacco
  Rimskogo-Korsakova pr., 13
  314-84-14
      Hrs: 9- 17,
Tobacco
  Sadovaya ul., 29 315-94-96

☎ TOILETS
ТУАЛЕТЫ
TOILETTEN
TOILETTES
TOALETTER

See RESTROOMS

☎ TOURS - RUSSIA
ЭКСКУРСИИ ПО РОССИИ
REISEN DURCH RUSSLAND
TOURISME ET EXCURSIONS EN RUSSIE
UTFLYKTER - RYSSLAND

See also TRAVEL AGENCIES,
TOURS - SAINT PETERSBURG

Breakwater
  Martynova ul., 94 235-27-22
Elista Tur
  Khalturina ul., 7 275-66-35
  Fax: 275-34-88

Griffon
  ul. Petra Lavrova, 9 275-71-21
  Tours and Excursions in any language

Interaries
  Profsoyuzov bul., 4, rm. 26
  314-92-37
  Fax 311-81-39
INTOURIST,
  See Tourist Company Saint Petersburg
Panorama
  Khalturina ul., 19 312-48-88
  311-89-55
Temp-Service
  Nevskiy pr., 176 271-04-86
  Fax 278-12-10
Inturianta (Russian-Irish JV)
  Korablestroiteley ul., 14 ... 356-41-85
Leningradskoe Aksionernoe Obyedineniye po Turizmu
  Rakova ul., 3 314-08-74
Retur Rekreatsionno-Turisticheskiy Kompleks (Russian-Swedish JV)
  Voynova ul., 28 273-96-83

SPUTNIK
Educational tours & exchanges
Tourist facilities throughout Russia
Chapygina ul., 4, rm. 27 .. 234-02-49

Visa-Turs
  Please call 230-44-21
  They are going to change address in July.
Lenturs
  Primorskiy pr., 4/6 239-57-89
VET Cooperative
  Nab. reki Fontanki, 90, bldg. 1, apt. 17
  314-42-26

ULIXESS TRAVEL AGENCY

Boat trips to monasteries on Lake Lagoda
Excursions to Moscow, Novgorod, Pskov
Tours throughout the Commonwealth
Lesnoy pr., 61, Bldg. 1 245-09-30
.... 555-88-97
Hrs: 10-17, English, German, Finnish

Valentina - Reisen

Explore Siberia and the Silk routes
Cruises and Tours to Siberia & Central Asia
Podezdnoy per., 3a 311-78-23

Varyag Tours

History, art, church & literary tours
Dance, ballet and rock music programs
Book your custom tour at your travel agency
Arranged also in St. Pb. on 24 hours notice.
Kamennoostrovskiy pr., 27
St. Petersburg, 197022, Russia
Tel. & Fax...................... 232-03-60
Telex ....121101 VARAG SU

☎ TOURS SAINT PETERSBURG

ЭКСКУРСИИ ПО ГОРОДУ
С.-ПЕТЕРБУРГУ
EXKURSIONEN IN ST.PETERSBURG
TOUR DE VILLE,
SAINT-PETERSBOURG
TURISTBYRÅ

See also TOURS-RUSSIA and TRAVEL
AGENCIES, BOAT EXCURSIONS,
AIR CHARTER.

*Here are a few firms and individuals
specializing in tours of Saint Petersburg
and the surrounding areas. They often
offer tours to the rest of Russia also.*

Union of Architects

ARHITECTURAL & HISTORICAL
TOURS
OF SAINT PETERSBURG

And the Palaces of Pushkin, Pavlovsk,
Petrodvorets, Lomonosov, & Gatchina

Lead by professional architects

Gertsena ul., 52.....................312-04-00
.....................................311-22-19

The City Code for Saint Petersburg
Dial 812 + Number

ARCHITECTURAL TOURS
OF ST. PETERSBURG

Explore architectural & historical Saint Petersburg
with three experienced professionals who will share
their love and knowledge of St. Pb with you.
Walking tours, canal tours & autotours
Museums, & Music, Parks & Palaces
Tours in English or German
Please call as far in advance as possible.
Please call...............................298-43-59

A. J. EST S.U
Russian Language Tours

St. Petersburg, Moscow, Odessa
Profsoyuzov bul., 4, Entr. 6 .. 110-64-96
Telex .... 121732 CGTT SU

BAST Sports Centre Tours
Individual Tours Across Russia

Drive-yourself or go with our drivers
in our automobiles (Audi's)
Raevskogo proezd, 16 552-55-12
Fax 552-39-36
Open 24 hours/day, English & Spanish

CULTURAL EVENINGS

by the **Professional Movie Actors Guild**
Enjoy an evening with actors, musicians, and
performers from the leading theaters and
studios of Saint Petersburg and their friends
from the world of literature and art

Dinner, art exhibit and music
In English and Russian
Nab. reki Fontanki, 11, rm. 8
Tel. & Fax 312-79-67

City Excursion Bureau
Dispatcher 210-93-50
For foreign tourists.......... 210-91-05
.... 210-92-67
Hrs: 10-13, 14-18, closed Sat, Sun
Leningrad City Excursion Bureau
Nab. Krasnogo Flota, 56
.... 311-24-45
Elista Tur
Khalturina ul., 7 275-66-35
Fax: 275-34-88

Griffon
Petra Lavrova ul., 9 275-71-21
Tours of St. Petersburg in any language.

Helen
Private Car with English Speaking guide
For tours of historic regions
Lermontovskiy pr., 43/1
....113-08-60
Hrs: 9-18. Closed Sat, Sun

Interburo
Sredniy pr., 88 355-46-96
All kinds of services 355-46-95
Hrs: 10-18, closed Sat, Sun

ITUS
Dzerzhinskogo ul., 47 310-93-94
.... 310-87-43
Fax: 310-93-97

Kvint
Nab. Krestovskaya, 3 556-26-53
Hrs: 10-18, closed Sun

LASAN
Guides and cars for private tours of
St. Petersburg and surrounding areas
Rakova ul., 23................. 164-27-05
Hrs: 10-22, $, Eng

Len Art
Nevskiy pr., 40................ 312-48-37
Molen
Ogorodnikova ul., 29 259-92-16
Pamyatniki Kultury
Voynova ul., 35a 273-30-50

PETER THE GREAT
PERSON TO PERSON TOURS
Specialized guides
for your special interests

Let us show you the shops, markets,
factories, museums, the best restaurants, art
galleries, concerts, theater, and night life.

Visit villages, farms & forests.
The parks & palaces of
Pushkin, Pavslosk, & Petrodvorets.

From early morning to late at night.

English, German & other languages..

Reasonable rates.

Dmitrovskiy per., 16............ 311-80-19
Fax.. 526-66-24

Hrs: 8-23 English, German, French

PROFI *Travel Agency*
Guided tours for groups and individuals
throughout St. Petersburg & suburbs
Yakovlevskiy per., 2 298-86-68
English, German, Finnish

Retour
Voynova ul., 16.............. 273-96-96

SAINT PETERSBURG TRANSIT
Personal Introduction
to Saint Petersburg

For Businessmen and Their Wives
Individuals and groups

Let us show you how to enjoy our city
From our museums and restaurants to our
shops, metro & farmer's markets.

Our staff speaks English, German, Swedish,
Finnish & most European & Oriental Languages
Dumskaya ul., 3.................. 314-89-84
Tel. 555-55-54
Hrs: 10-22, Rbl & $

Sputnik (For travelers from 14 to 32)
Chapygina ul., 4 234-02-49
Guides Department 234-96-90

Tour Firm Eksta
Let us introduce St. Petersburg to your
guests & friends.
V.O., 4-ya Liniya, 45 213-00-71

Tourist Company "St. Petersburg"
(Formerly "Intourist")
Isaakievskaya pl., 11 315-51-29
For guides 272-78-87
Daily: 10-17:30

Troika Tours
The Nights of St. Petersburg Tour
Four exciting days and nights
Complete tours include Hermitage, Peter
and Paul Fortress, sightseeing, Pushkin or
Pavlovsk, great restaurants & gala dinner
including the Famous Troika Show.
From $270 depending on hotel.
Zagorodnyy pr., 27 113-53-76
Fax 310-42-79
Telex.................. 121299 TROJK SU

Turist
Nab. reki Moyki, 58......... 311-35-74
.... 311-25-20
Excursions around the city & to the suburbs.

☎ TOY STORES
ИГРУШЕЧНЫЕ МАГАЗИНЫ
SPIELWARENGESCHÄFTE
MAGASINS DE JOUETS
LEKSAKSAFFÄRER

Toys can be bought in DLT, department stores and in special toy stores called Igrushki (игрушки).

DLT (Dom Leningradskoy Torgovli)
DLT Trade House
Zhelyabova ul., 21/23...... 312-26-27
Toys are on the first floor.

Detskiy Mir (Children's World)	
	Детский Мир
Moskovskiy pr., 191........	293-50-75
Prosveshcheniya pr., 46-1	
....	597-33-16
Sedova ul., 69................	560-61-92
Shkolnaya ul., 6	230-87-01
The Complete Store for Children's Clothing, Shoes, and Toys	

Igrushki Store No. 13
Obukhovskoy Oborony pr., 81
.... 265-13-01
Igrushki Store No. 55
Prosveshcheniya ul., 78
.... 557-87-09
Igrushki Store No. 37
Sofiyskaya ul., 29........... 268-64-93
Igrushki Store No. 12
Sadovaya ul., 32 310-06-65
Igrushki Store No. 59
P.S., Bolshoy pr., 38 232-52-43
Igrushki Store No. 91
Suvorovskiy pr., 15......... 271-59-67
Zolotoy Klyuchik No. 23
Marshala Govorova ul., 10
.... 184-83-18

☎ TRADEMARKS
ФАБРИЧНЫЕ МАРКИ, ТОВАРНЫЕ ЗНАКИ
WARENZEICHEN
MARQUES DE FABRIQUES
FÖRETAGSREGISTRERING

☎ TRAIN INFORMATION
ЖЕЛЕЗНОДОРОЖНАЯ ИНФОРМАЦИЯ
ZUGAUSKUNFT
TRAINS, INFORMATIONS
TÅGINFORMATION

See RAILWAY STATIONS

☎ TRAMS (TROLLEYS)
ТРАМВАЙ, ИНФОРМАЦИЯ
STRAßENBAHNAUSKUNFT
TRAM, EXCURSIONS EN
SPÅRVAGN TROLLEY

Trams operate from 5:30 in the morning to 1 am at night.

Trams are what Americans call "Trolleys" and differ from "Trolley Buses" which are buses powered by electricity from overhead wires (like trolleys). Public transport is the basic means of transport for most residents of St. Petersburg and can be the best way to get somewhere, especially when there are no taxis in sight. They are often very crowded at rush hour, but push your way on anyway.

To use the tram, trolleybus or bus, you need to have "transport coupons" called "talony" (ТАЛОНЫ) or a "monthly transport card". Buy "talony" coupons at specialized kiosks selling transport coupons and cards, at Rospechat kiosks, in the bus, trolley bus or tram, and in shops. When you get on, you are supposed to punch them yourself with a simple punch attached to the wall of the trolley. In crowed trams, if you pass your "talony" along, people will help you punch the talony. The fares are changing quickly. "Monthly transport cards" come in different forms and can include suburbs. For more information about the "transport cards", see METRO.

SIGN FOR PUBLIC TRANSPORT		
A	**m**	(tram sign)
BUS STOPS on street	TROLLEYBUS STOPS on street	TRAM STOPS hanging on wire

On our Traveller's Yellow Page's CITY MAP OF ST. PETERSBURG, the TRAM lines are indicated in SOLID RED lines, boxes and numbers, the BUS lines are indicated in SOLID BLUE lines, boxes and numbers, the TROLLEYBUS LINES are indicated in DOTTED RED LINES, boxes and numbers. Buy a metro map and also a transport map of St. Petersburg called Skhema Passazhirskogo Transporta (Схема Пассажирского Транспорта) *at kiosks, Rospechat and book stores. They are in Russian, but the number routes are clear.*

☎ TRANSLATION SERVICES
ПЕРЕВОДЫ, СЛУЖБА
ÜBERSETZER/DOLMETSCHER
TRADUCTION, SERVICE DE
ÖVERSÄTTNINGSBYRÅER

*St. Petersburg is well supplied with
translators and interpreters in all languages,
many of whom are graduates of the
Philological Faculty of the St. Petersburg
State University.*

Astra
P.S., Bolshoy pr., 82, apt. 17
.... 230-88-29
Hrs: 10 -12 , 13-17, closed Sat, Sun

AsLANTIS
A Consortium of Certified Interpreters
For Your Business Negotiations & Trips
Fax & Phone Translation and Transmission
Tel...............................297-26-14
Fax/Tel...........................298-90-07
We can answer your call in English

Aurora Publishers
Nevskiy pr., 7/9
.... 312-42-36
.... 312-38-19
Hrs: 10-13, 14-18, closed Sat, Sun
Belye Nochi
Tarasova ul., 10 224-25-00
All kinds of translation
Hrs: 10 - 21, closed Sun
City Center Translation
Bronnitskaya ul., 15 112-65-15
.... 292-50-96
Oykumena
Please call 238-42-72
*Written translations, interpreters for
business meetings. Hrs: 12 -17*
Innokon
Pushkinskaya ul., 10, apt. 27
.... 164-53-68
*Translation of technical documents from
German to Russian, interpreters for
business meetings in German.*
Inter
Bronnitskaya ul., 15 259-62-52
Interpreter
Please call 560-15-64
*Translation of technical texts
from English & Spanish.*
Interpreter
Please call 232-13-42
Translation of Scandinavian languages
Introkon
Marshala Govorova pr., 52
Please call 252-10-08

Kontakt Student Center at St. Pb.
Electrotechnical University
Prof. Popova ul., 5 234-69-59
Translators for business & travelers
English, German, French, Dutch & Swedish
Lentour
Isaakievskaya pl., 11
Interpreters (except English)
.... 312-24-33
Interpreters (English) 312-12-46
Technical translation 210-09-33
Fax .... 311-63-90·
St. Petersburg joint-stock company
Nikos
Nab. kan. Griboedova, 123, apt. 111
.... 114-53-71
*Translation of technical documentation,
interpreters for business meetings.*
Retur Business Center
Hotel Astoria, Gertsena ul., 39, fl. 2
.... 210-58-66
Translating Russian: Daily: 9 - 21

SAINT PETERSBURG TRANSIT
Translators and Interpreters
English & European & Oriental Languages
Personalized Instruction in Russian
Let our staff introduce you to St. Pb.
Dumskaya ul., 3 314-89-84
Tel. 555-55-54
Hrs: 10-22, Rbl & $

Sezam
Zheleznovodskaya ul., 66, apt. 116
.... 350-45-42
Translation Services
.... 525-88-83
Written translations from English
Translater/Interpreter
Please call...................... 542-76-46
Spanish to Russian; Russian to Spanish;
Medical Expert

Varyag Business Center
at Hotel Oktavian,
Sredniy pr., 88, fl. 4
.... 232-03-60
Fax 356-85-52
Telex................ 121101VARAG SU
Interpreting and translating, Daily: 8 - 20

Znanie
Krasnoy Konnitsy ul., 10, rm. 19
.... 278-50-35
.... 278-50-01
Znanie Society
Liteynyy pr., 42, rm. 2..... 273-20-49

☎ TRAVEL AGENCIES
ТУРИСТИЧЕСКИЕ АГЕНТСТВА
REISEBÜROS
VOYAGES, AGENCES
DE/AGENCES
RESEBYRÅER

The tourist industry and travel agency situation has changed dramatically in the past year. The once powerful Intourist Agency has been split into many independent hotels, travel agencies and travel services and the competition between travel agencies and tour-excursion services is growing. Quality in many hotels is being rapidly upgraded.

Association of Travel Bureaus,

Hotels & Restaurants

Representing the Tourist Industry

in Saint Petersburg

Please call 311-70-75

Aeroprit..............At Pulkovskaya Hotel
  Pobedy pl., 1.................. 299-42-55
  291-28-66
  Fax................................. 108-41-58
American Express
  at Grand Hotel Europe
  Mikhaylovskaya ul., 1/7 ... 315-74-87

EPOL
Travel
Agency

A Full Service Travel Agency
All-Inclusive Tours of Saint Petersburg,
Moscow, Kiev and the Baltics
SPECIALIZING IN CUSTOM TOURS IN RUSSIA

Art, Ballet, Music & Theatrical, Church
Pilgrimages, Architecture, Photography,
Sports, Mountaineering, Hunting & More.

Business Travel Arrangements & Transit

  Liteynyy pr., 6/1 279-50-60
  Fax............................... 279-50-66
  Hrs: 9:30-18:00, English, German, French

Central Travel Bureau of SPCT
  Zhelyabova ul., 27 315-45-55
SPCT Travel Bureau for Tour Sales
  Zhelyabova ul., 27 312-15-36
Byuro Puteshestviy
  Zhelyabova ul., 27 312-21-56
  311-55-51
CIS Travel
  Nevskiy pr., 40, rm. 48.... 311-96-10
  Fax............................... 110-55-10

Contact, Tourism for students
  Prof. Popova ul., 5 234-69-59
Etno
  Lenina ul., 30................. 235-12-65
  Fax................................. 232-08-22
Elista Tur
  Khalturina ul., 7.............. 275-66-35
  Fax:............................... 275-34-88
Helen
  Lermontovskiy pr., 43/1 ... 113-08-60
  251-19-78
  Fax................................. 113-08-59
Intant Tour
  Blokhina ul., 15 230-98-40
  Director.......................... 230-47-06
  Hrs: 10-15, closed Sat, Sun
Interburo
  V.O., Sredniy pr., 88, flr. 3
  366-77--74
Intourist
  (See Tourist Company Saint Petersburg)
Intourservice
  Dzerzhinskogo ul., 69 113-59-83
  Fax................................. 113-35-69
Len Art (Finland)
  Nevskiy pr., 40................ 312-48-37
  Fax................................. 110-66-14
  This address will soon change.
Lentur
  Nab. reki Karpovki, 25 232-68-63
  Fax................................. 232-70-90
  Telex....................121350 VEPS SU
Tourist Service A.O."NIVLOL"
  Muchnoy per., 3, rm. 3.... 310-53-64

---

 from 1989
Co., ltd.

A Name You Can Trust in Travel

Your Full Service Travel Agency
Smolnyy, "Porch" 9, Tel./fax...... 273-08-71
Telex................121350 VEPS SU, Attn. SITI

Sovaminco
  Khalturina ul., 27 314-94-49
  315-84-59
  314-21-66
Sovintour
  Smolnyy, entry 9 271-64-66
  Fax................................. 273-08-71

St. Petersburg Council for Tourism
Head Office: Italyanskaya ul. 3
St. Petersburg 191011 , Russia

Partner in Travel with:
  Balkan-Holidays............. 279-61-44
  Interlen 110-67-68
  Milano 219-16-38
  Lengatur 311-78-62
  Sicily 311-70-75

❋❋ *SPCT* ❋❋

St. Petersburg Council
for Tourism

Leader in travel and tour services
in the St. Petersburg Region

Head Office: Italyanskaya ul., 3
St. Petersburg 191011 , Russia

Tel 314-87-86, 110-67-39
Fax 110-68-24, 311-93-81
Telex .... 121128 TUR SU

12 Hotels

Oktinskaya****	227-44-38
Gavan***	356-85-04
Russ**	273-46-83
Mir**	108-51-66
Fedorovskiy Gorodok[1]	476-36-00
Repinskiy**[2]	231-65-09
Repinskiy Camping[2]	231-68-84
Terioki[3]	231-38-54
Losevskaya**[4]	(279)6-72-29
Nakhimovskaya (camp)[6]	
	(278)6-51-17
Poddubskaya (camp)[6]	(272)7-74-83
Tolmatchevskaya*[7]	(272)7-43-73

[1] Pushkin, [2] Repino, [3] Zelenogorsk,
[4] Losevo, [5] near Priozersk,
[6] near Luga, [7] near Tolmatchevo

Travel & Tour Service Bureaus

Central Travel Bureau of SPCT
Zhelyabova ul., 27....... 315-75-36
SPCT Travel Bureau for Tour Sales
Zhelyabova ul., 27....... 312-15-36
Regional

Volkhov	(263)22-611
Vyborg	(278)206-46
Gatchina	(271)387-40
Kirishy	(268)231-89
Kolpino	484-12-50
Lodeynoe Pole	(264)200-81
Luga	(272)228-02
Petrodvorets	473-12-09
Priozersk	(279)21931
Sestroretsk	231-66-09
Tikhvin	(267)23349
Tosno	(261)21679

Other Travel Services

Intourbureau	356-86-58
Coaches (TOURIST)	225-06-55
Tourist Club	311-14-19
Tourist Sports Union	311-42-75
Auto-Moto Tourist Club	312-08-56
Institute Of Tourism	235-50-66

Sputnik (International Youth Travel)

Chapygina ul., 4	234-02-49
	234-35-00
	234-65-27
	234-93-86
Director	234-35-00
Foreign department	234-99-54
	234-65-37

Tourist Company "St.Petersburg"
(Formerly "Intourist")

Isaakievskaya pl., 11	315-51-29
For guides	272-78-87
Pulkovo-2, Airoport	
Information	291-09-17
Arrival & Pick-ups	122-98-63
Departures	291-68-23
Pulkovo-1, Airport, Information	
Arrivals & Departures	123-85-90
	104-33-29
Railway stations	277-08-00
Sea-Passenger	355-13-30

Daily: 10-17:30

TURBUS

Sapernyy per., 16 273-00-67

ULIXESS TRAVEL AGENCY

Boat trips to monasteries on Lake Lagoda
Excursions to Moscow, Novgorod, Pskov
Tours throughout the Commonwealth

Lesnoy pr. 61, bldg. 1 245-09-30
.... 555-88-97

Hrs: 10-17, English, German, Finnish

Valentina - Reisen

Explore Siberia and the Silk routes
Cruises and Tours to Siberia & Central Asia

Podezdnoy per., 3a 311-78-23

Varyag Travel Agency

Full Service Travel Agency with Correspondents
Throughout Russia and Europe
Kamennoostrovskiy pr., 27
St. Petersburg, 197022, Russia

Tel & Fax 232-03-60
Telex .... 121101 VARAG SU

Hrs: 10-19, $ & Rbl, MC, V, Amex, EC

☎ **TRAVEL BOOKS/GUIDES**
to St. Petersburg
ПУТЕВОДИТЕЛИ ПО
САНКТ-ПЕТЕРБУРГУ
REISEFÜHRER FUR
ST. PETERSBURG
GUIDES DE VOYAGES POUR
ST. PETERSBOURG
RESEGUIDER,
ST. PETERSBURG

*As of June 1992, most English
language guides were still available only
outside of Russia, except for our
Traveller's Yellow Pages of Saint
Petersburg 1992. See below. Here are
some of the best.*

Baedeker's Leningrad, 1991, 295p,
$15.95. *"Best general guide to Saint
Petersburg. Look for new edition soon.
The German edition is already out."
Editors of TYP $12.95*

Bantam's Soviet Union 1991. 1990, 562p. $17.95. *Good coverage in all areas of the former USSR. Look for an update soon.*

Blue Guide to Moscow and Leningrad. *1989, 392p $16.95" Still the classic "must-bring". Best on history, architecture, art, music, culture with great walking tours.*

City Breaks in Moscow & Leningrad. 1990, 80p. $6.95. *Another short guide, but rapidly outdated.*

Essential Moscow and Leningrad. 1991, 128p. $7.95. *A good start for the tourist.*

Fodor's 1992, Russia, the Republics and the Baltics. 1991, $17.00

The Harper Independent Traveler, Soviet Union. 1990, 352p. $10.95. *"Good tours and well written with historical, cultural, and practical information."*

Hippocrene Insider's Guide to Moscow, Leningrad & Kiev. 1990, 175p. $11.95.

Insight City Guides. Saint Petersburg (Leningrad) 297 p. $19.95 . *Excellent guide to Saint Petersburg, with photos and cultural & historical commentary. APA Publications, 1992.*

Leningrad Atlas Turista. 1990, 95p. *Available in kiosks in Russian.   Excellent street maps.*

Leningrad Guide 1990. 1990, 134p *Available in Kiosks in English , very useful with good transportation information on buses, trains, and metro.*

Leningrad Success Guide. *Available in kiosks in English, useful but incomplete with good maps.*

Lonely Planet USSR 1991 810 p. 21.45 *Interesting with lots of good information and maps.*

Moscow-Leningrad Handbook including the Golden Ring. 1991, 205p. $12.95.

The Visitor's Guide to the New Saint Petersburg. 171 pp. $12.95 *Practical insider information from a different point of view. A perfect companion to our Traveller's Yellow Pages.*

The Traveller's Yellow Pages For Saint Petersburg, 1992-1993 with City Map, July 1992, 256p plus large fold-out map, $6.95 plus shipping and handling. The first Yellow Pages for St. Petersburg and the most up-to-date, full of useful

information and 4000 telephone numbers and addresses listed under 432 categories from Accounting Firms and Art Galleries to Yachts and Zoos. Ideal for the tourist,, students, business traveler and resident. Published by InfoServices International, Inc. NY, USA and Telinfo, Saint Petersburg, Russia.

In Russia, copies can be obtained at
    TELINFO, ✉190000, St. Petersburg, Russia, Nab. Reki Moyki, 64,
    ☎ ...... (812) 315-64-12, 315-98-55,
    Fax: ..... (812) 315-73-41, 315-74-20
For the rest of the world:
    InfoServices International, Inc.,
    ✉ 1 Saint Marks Place, Cold Spring Harbor, NY 11724, USA ☎ (516) 549-0064, Fax: (516) 549-2032, Telex: 221213 TTC UR

☎ TRAVELER'S CHECKS
ДОРОЖНЫЙ ЧЕК
REISERCHECK
CHEQUES DE VOYAGE
RESECHECKAR

See BANKS and CURRENCY EXCHANGE

As of June 15, 1992, travelers checks could still be cashed in St. Petersburg only for rubles. Cash them at Vnesh-econombank at Gertsena ul.,29 or at the American Express office in the Grand Hotel Europe. Many other banks refuse them. Small amounts (< $100) can be cashed into dollars when purchasing items at the better hard currency shops.

While credit cards are increasingly accepted in many shops, restaurants and hotels, Travelers checks often are not accepted in place of dollars in some transactions.

There is now a VISA CASH MACHINE at St.-Petersburg Saving Bank.

☎ TRUCKING
ПЕРЕВОЗКИ ГРУЗОВЫЕ
LASTTRANSPORT
CAMION, TRANSPORTS EN
LÅNGTRADAR TRANSPORT

The advertisers in this section are the real professionals in the industry with modern fleets and extensive experience in international transport. For trucking and moving of goods within the city, see also MOVING COMPANIES.

A HISTORICAL DATE
1894-1917   *Reign of Nicholas II Assassinated 1918.*

Lenavtotrans
Nab. kan. Griboedova, 5
.... 314-66-76
Fax................................. 314-66-76
Telex 191186
Trucking inside city & international

Lenvneshtrans
Mezhevoy kan., 5 251-41-97
Fax:............................... 186-28-83
Telex: .... 121511 SVT SU

Neva
Novgorodskaya ul., 19..... 271-88-64
.... 274-96-18

Romar International Inc.
Elagin Ostrov, 10 239-09-01
Fax 239-12-61

☎ TRUCK PARK
АВТОСТОЯНКИ ДЛЯ
ГРУЗОВИКОВ
PARKPLÄTZE LASTKRAFTWAGEN
PARKINGS, CAMION
PARKERINGSPLATSER LASTBIL

High Security   **AUTO PARK**
Cars, Trucks, Buses
Varshavskaya ul., 42........ 296-58-20
Near the Russia Hotel
Daily 24 Hrs English, $ & rbl

Sovtransavto
Vitebskiy pr., 3............... 298-46-50
.... 298-10-50
Fax............................... 298-77-60

☎ TRUCK SALES
ГРУЗОВИКИ, ПРОДАЖА
LASTKRAFTWAGEN, VERKAUF
CAMION VENTE
LASTBIL, FÖRSÄLJNING

SOVAVTO ST PETERSBURG

VOLVO Truck Sales
Volvo Authorized Truck Dealer
Sales, Service, Repairs & Parts
Used Volvo & Maz Trucks
Large Stock of Used Trailers
Distributor of Volvo truck parts for Russia
Full Warranty in Russia and Abroad
Vitebskiy pr., 3 298-46-50
Fax 298-77-60
Telex...................................... 121535 AVTO
Hrs. 8:30-17:30, English, German

SOME HISTORICAL DATES

1898	*Russian Museum, founded in 1895, is opened in the Mikhail Palace*
1914	*St.-Petersburg was renamed as Petrograd*
1917	*1917 Revolution*
1924	*Petrograd was renamed as Leningrad after Lenin's death*

☎ TRUCK SERVICE & REPAIRS
ГРУЗОВИКИ, ОБСЛУЖИВАНИЕ И
РЕМОНТ
LASTKRAFTWAGEN, SERVICE
UND REPARATUR
CAMION, REPARATION
LASTBIL, SERVICE OCH
REPARATION

SOVAVTO ST PETERSBURG

TRUCK SERVICE
TRUCK AND TRAILER
REPAIRS and PARTS
Volvo, DAF & Maz trucks
All Russian & European trailers
Large inventory of tires, brake parts, axles
Warranty work
Factory tested mechanics, modern paint and
test facilities

Vitebskiy pr., 3 298-55-56
Shushary Railroad Station...............293-73-71
Fax..298-77-60
Telex...................................... 121535 AVTO
Mon-Sat, 7-22, $ & rbl., German,
Translators available

☎ TV DOCUMENTARY
ТЕЛЕВИДЕНИЕ, СЪЕМКА
DOKUMENTAR FERNSEHEN
TELEVISION DOCUMENTAIRE
TV, DOKUMENTÄRER

See VIDEO/FILM PRODUCTION

☎ TYPEWRITER REPAIR
ПИШУЩИЕ МАШИНКИ, РЕМОНТ
SCHREIBMASCHINENREPARATUR
MACHINES A ECRIRE,
REPARATION
SKRIVMASKINER, REP.

Suvenir
Baskov per., 4 272-41-67
Hrs: 10 - 18
Usluga
Lermontovskiy pr., 1/44
.... 114-63-57
.... 114-36-64
Hrs: 9-14, 15-19, closed Sun

☎ TYPING SERVICES
МАШИНОПИСНЫЕ РАБОТЫ
SCHREIBDIENSTE
DACTYLOGRAPHIE, SERVICE DE
SKRIVMASKIN, SERVICE

See also BUSINESS SERVICES CENTERS,
SECRETARIAL SERVICES

"REFERENT" Atele mashinopisnykh rabot
Liteynyy pr., 28 272-45-80
Optima
Chaykovskogo ul., 36 273-78-82
Typist
Poeticheskiy bul., 1, bldg. 1, apt. 77
.... 516-37-70
Russian, English
Typist
Please call 588-48-63
Hrs: 16 - 23

☎ UMBRELLAS
ЗОНТИКИ
SCHIRME
PARAPLUIES
PARAPLYER

*Buy umbrellas (zontik or зонтик) at
haberdashery shops called "galantereya"
(галантерея), raincoats at a department
or clothing store.*

☎ UNIVERSITIES
& INSTITUTES
УНИВЕРСИТЕТЫ И ИНСТИТУТЫ
UNIVERSITÄTEN UND INSTITUTE
UNIVERSITES ET INSTITUTS
UNIVERSITET OCH INSTITUT

*Saint Petersburg is a leading
educational and research center in Russia
with major universities, technical
educational institutes, major research
institutions and leading medical research
centers. Here we list major educational
institutions including technical institutes.
The research institutes associated with
the university are listed under
INSTITUTES-RESEARCH.*

*The leading educational institute in St. Pb
is the Saint Petersburg State University,
formerly the Leningrad State University.
Its faculty and facilities are situated on
Vasilevskiy Ostrov as well as throughout
St. Pb. and Petrodvorets (Peterhof).*

Academy of Civil Pilots
Akademiya Grazhdanskoy Aviatsii
Pilotov ul., 38 122-37-81
Dukhovnaya Adademiya i Seminariya
Nab. Obvodnogo kanala, 17
.... 277-33-50
Frunze Naval College
Nab. Leytenanta Shmidta, 17
.... 213-71-47

International Humanities University
Faculties of Law,.Business, Philology,
Journalism and Political Science
Pulkovskaya ul., 11 126-42-89
.... 589-70-83
Marine University   *Morskoy Universitet*
Lotsmanskaya ul., 3 114-07-61
Mining University
Gornyy Universitet im. Plekhanova
V. O., 21-ya Liniya, 2 213-60-78
Pedagogical University
Pedagogicheskiy Universitet
Nab. reki Moyki, 48 312-44-92
Russian-American University
Rossiysko-Amerikanskiy Universitet
Chalturina ul.,6 314-00-01
St.Petersburg Jewish University
St. Peterburgskiy Yevreyskiy Universitet
Please call 298-47-10
St.Petersburg State Technical University
*Sankt-Petersburgskiy Gosudarstvennyy
Technichesky Universitet*
Politekhnicheskaya ul., 29
.... 247-20-95
University for Economics and Finance
Finansovo-Economicheskiy Universitet
Nab. kan. Griboedova, 30/32
.... 310-50-24

ST.PETERSBURG STATE
UNIVERSITY
*Sankt Petersburgskiy
Gosudarstvennyy Universitet*
Nab. Universitetskaya, 7/9
Info............................... 218-20-00
Foreign department secretary
.... 213-11-68
University Scientific Library
Nab. Universitetskaya, 7/9
.... 218-95-46

FACULTIES & DEPARTMENTS
Applied Mathematics & Process Control
Petrodvorets,
Bibliotechnaya pl., 2 428-71-59
Biology & Soil Sciences
Nab. Universitetskaya, 7/9
.... 218-08-52
Chemistry   Petrodvorets,
Universitetskiy pr., 2 428-67-33
Economics
Chaykovskogo ul., 62 273-40-50
Journalism
V.O., 1-ya Liniya, 26 218-59-37
Geography & Geoecology
V.O., 10-ya Liniya, 31/33. 213-06-27
Geology
Nab. Universitetskaya, 7/9
.... 218-94-68
History
V.O., Mendeleevskaya Liniya, 5
.... 218-95-72
Law Faculty
V.O., 22-ya Liniya, 7 213-49-49
Oriental Languages & Studies
Nab. Universitetskaya, 11 218-95-17

(St Petersburg Universities Continued)

Philology (Languages)
Nab. Universitetskaya, 11
.... 218-08-42
.... 218-78-41

Philosophy
V.O., Mendeleevskaya Liniya ,5
.... 218-94-28

Physics
Petrodvorets
Ulyanovskaya ul., 1 428-71-00

Psychology
Nab. Makarova, 6 218-00-01

Russian Languages Studies
Nab. Makarova, 6 218-94-12

Sociology
Rastrelli pl., Smolnyy 1/3, entr. 9
Secretary....................... 274-33-30

University Institutes and Facilities
See INSTITUTES, RESEARCH

Technical Educational Institutes

Aviation Instrumentation Institute
Institut Aviatsionnogo Priborostroeniya
Gertsena ul., 67 210-70-18
.... 312-21-07

Construction Engineering Institute
Inzhenerno-Stroitelnyy Institut
2-ya Krasnoarmeyskaya ul., 4
.... 259-51-91
.... 292-20-26

Electrotechnical Institute
Elektrotekhnicheskiy Institut
Prof. Popova ul., 5 234-25-82
.... 234-89-47

Engineering Economics Institute
Inzhenerno-Ekonomicheskiy Institut
Marata ul., 27 112-06-33
.... 112-02-16

Hydro-Meteorological Institute
Gydrometeorologicheskiy Institut
Malookhtinskiy pr., 98
.... 221-41-63
.... 221-25-96

Railway Engineering Institute
Institut Inzhenerov Zheleznodorozhnogo Transporta
Moskovskiy pr., 9 310-25-21
.... 310 17-24

Pharmaceutical Institute
Khimiko-Farmatsevticheskiy Institut
Prof. Popova ul., 14
.... 234-57-29
.... 110-56-35

Film Engineers Institute
Institut Kinoinzhenerov
Pravdy ul., 13................. 315-72-85
.... 113-27-30

Institute of Culture (Library Science, Cultural Facilities Management)
Kultury Institut
Nab. Dvortsovaya, 2/4..... 314-11-21
.... 312-95-21

Machine Tools Building Institute
Institut Mashinostroeniya
Polyustrovskiy pr., 14...... 540-01-54
.... 540-21-76

Mechanical Institute
Mekhanicheskiy Institut
1-ya Krasnoarmeyskaya ul., 1
.... 292-23-94
.... 292-23-47

Physical Culture Institute im. Lesgafta
Fizicheskoy Kultury Institut imeni Lesgafta
Dekabristov ul., 35.......... 114-40-13
.... 219-51-39

Polygraphical Institute of Moscow.
Leningrad Branch Moskovskiy Poligraficheskiy Institut
Dzhambula ul., 13........... 164-65-56
.... 315-06-37

Agricultural Institute
Selskokhozyaystvennyy Institut
Pushkin: Leningradskoe shosse, 2
.... 470-05-39
.... 470-04-22

Theater, Music and Cinema Institute
Institut Teatra, Musyki i Kinematografii
Mokhovaya ul., 34 273-15-81
.... 273-10-72

Textile and Light Industry Institute
Institut Tekstilnoy i Legkoy Promyshlennosti
Gertsena ul., 18.............. 315-16-83
.... 315-75-25

Refrigeration Industry Institute
Tekhnologicheskiy Institut Kholodilnoy Promyshlennosti
Lomonosova ul., 9 315-36-17
.... 219-89-36

Technological Institute of Pulp & Paper Industry
Tekhnologicheskiy Institut Tsellyulozno-Bumazhnoy Promyshlennosti
Ivana Chernykh ul., 4 186-53-40
.... 186-57-44

Chemistry-Technological Institute
Khimiko-Tekhnologicheskiy Institut
Zagorodnyy pr., 49 259-47-99
.... 259-48-39

Precise Mechanics & Optics Institute
Institut Tochnoy Mekhaniki i Optiki
Sablinskaya ul., 14.......... 233-89-29
.... 238-87-94

Veterinarian Institute
Veterinarnyy Institut
Moskovskiy pr., 112........ 298-36-31
Sea & River Transport Institute
Institut Vodnogo Transporta
Dvinskaya ul., 5/7........... 259-03-25
.... 251-12-21
Painting, Sculpture & Architecture Institute
Institut Zhivopisi, Skulptury i Arkhitektury
Nab. Universitetskaya, 17
.... 213-61-89
.... 213-21-11
Electrotechnical Institute of Communication
Electrotechnicheskiy Institut Svyazy
Nab. reki Moyki 61.,........ 315-89-10
.... 315-32-27
Institute of the Trade
Institut Torgovli
Novorossiyskaya ul., 50
.... 247-78-06
.... 247-80-49
Northern-West Correspondence
Politechnical Institute
*Severo-Zapadnyy Zaochnyy
Politekhnicheskiy Institut*
Khalturina ul., 5.............. 110-65-61
.... 110-62-62

INSTITUTES FOR CONTINUING
EDUCATION & POST GRADUATE STUDY

*There are about 20 technical institutes for
post-graduate studies and continuing
education for managers and specialists in
different branches of an industry for
example, the Institute for Managers of
Building industry. Here are three for
doctors and teachers.*

Institute for Post-graduate
Studies for Physicians
*Institut Usovershenstvovaniya
Vrachey im. S.M.Kirova*
Saltykova-Shchedrina ul., 41
.... 272-63-43
Teachers (City) Post Graduate Studies
*Institut Usovershenstvovaniya
Uchiteley (gorodskoy)*
Lomonosova ul., 11 313-34-30
Teachers (Oblast) Post Graduate Studies
*Institut Usovershenstvovaniya
Uchiteley (oblactnoy)*
Chkalovskiy pr., 25-a....... 235-16-32

☎ VETERINARIAN
ВЕТЕРИНАРЫ
TIERÄRZTE
VETERINAIRES
VETERINÄRER

*There are numerous municipal and private
veterinarians in St. Pb. Here are two.*
Basis
Please call...................... 296-63-62
At your home, Hrs: 12-21
Veterinarian
Please, call..................... 217-36-96

☎ VIDEO/FILM
PRODUCTION
ВИДЕОФИЛЬМЫ,
ПРОИЗВОДСТВО
VIDEOFILMPRODUKTION
FILM VIDEO, PRODUCTION DES
VIDEO, FILM PRODUKTION

Aprel Video
Please call...................... 267-33-45
.... 267-25-72
.... 267-27-73
Globus Film
Tolmacheva ul., 12 314-87-64
Film Consulting
Kirovskiy pr., 10 233-97-47
Fax 233-21-74

Lennauchfilm
Melnichnaya ul., 4........... 265-01-51
Fax 567-70-24

Lenfilm
    Kirovskiy pr., 10 232-83-74
    Fax................................ 232-88-81
Lentelefilm
    Chapygina ul., 6 234-77-75
    Fax................................ 234-39-95
Luch Studio
    Leninskiy pr., 134 254-80-16
Peterburgskiy Predprinimatelskiy Dom
    Info 177-74-59
Rumb
    Zaytseva ul., 41 183-46-39
    Fax................................ 185-08-69
Russkoe video
    Nab. Maloy Nevki, 4........ 311-35-23
Tayny veka
    Sadovaya ul., 53, rm. 59
    310-65-37

TRIONIKS, film-video production
Documentary & Advertising Videos
    Scripts, Takes, Editing, Dubbing
    Povarskoy per., 8............. 112-38-44
    Fax............................... 112-53-59
    Telex .... 121222 SPRES SU

---

7 V I D Studios
Video Productions
Shooting, Editing, Sound Effects
Dubbing in Russian, English & Japanese
Kamennoostrovskiy pr., 42 . 230-80-22

Znanie
    Liteynyy pr., 42, apt. 2...279-52-85n

☎ VIDEO EQUIPMENT AND REPAIR
    ВИДЕО ОБОРУДОВАНИЕ
    VIDEOAUSRÜSTUNG/ZUBEHÖR
    EQUIPMENT VIDEO
    VIDEO, UTRUSTNING

Globus
    Kirovskiy pr., 21, rm. 122
    .... 232-89 83
Photo Repair
    Nevskiy pr., 20............... 315-49-88
    Repair domestic equipment, Hrs: 11-20
Polyus-Servis
    Kuznetsovskaya ul., 44
    298-29-66
    298-24-32
    Repairs of domestic TV & video equipment.
    Hrs: 10 - 20

☎ VIDEO RENTAL / TAPE RENTAL / SALES
    ВИДЕОКАССЕТЫ, ПРОКАТ
    VIDEOKASSETTENVERLEIH
    CASSETTES VIDEO LOCATION
    VIDEO, UTRHYRNING

Remember that there are two video tape standards: the European standards for European TV's and VCR, called "PAL" and the American standard for American TV's & VCR called NTSC.

The Russians use SECAM, which is similar to the European standard PAL. Thus, ordinary American VCRs will not play ordinary Russian or European video-cassettes. And vice versa, American video cassettes can not be used in Russian or European VCRs. They can be converted from one format to another.

Video rental outlets are found all over in St. Petersburg.

Elektronika Gallery & Shop
    Yuriya Gagarina pr., 12
    299-38-49

☎ VISA REGISTRATION (OVIR)
    ОВИР
    VISA-AMT
    VISAS, BUREAU DE
    VISUM, KONTOR

At present, you must still register your passport with OVIR. (Department of Visas and Registration). If you are staying at a hotel, they will automatically do this for you. If you are living with a friend or in a rented apartment, you should also be registered with OVIR, especially if you want to extend your visa.

To extend your visa, you must comply with certain regulations from the very beginning of your stay including registration of your passport. For any extension, you usually need to have an official statement requesting an extension, and if you are staying in a rented apartment or private home, permission to stay a longer time. You then take these papers along with your visa and $20 to OVIR (listed below) and apply for an extension. They are pretty efficient there.

Department of Visa and Registration for Foreigners
    Saltykova-Shchedrina ul., 4
    Secretary....................... 278-24-81
    Info.............................. 278-24-83

☎ VISA SERVICES
ВИЗОВЫЙ СЕРВИС
VISA-DIENST,
VISAANGELEGENHETTEN
VISAS, SERVICES DE
VISUM, SERVICE

*You still need a visa to travel to
Russia. If you are traveling with a travel
agency or a tour, they will take care of
this problem. Now, however, there are
many other ways to get a visa. Your host
in Russia can issue you a personal
invitation, but usually, your invitation will
come from some sort of organization,
institute, or official agency, stating that
they take all responsibility for your needs.
For example, some of the new Bed &
Breakfast Associations also get you the
visa. There are also visa services that will
help you get the "invitation" that is
necessary for a visa if you are not
traveling on a travel agency tour. In
addition, there are visa services that will
help you get a visa quickly from the
Russian Embassy for a price. The Russian
Embassy in Washington now has
accelerated processing for an additional
charge: regular processing is $20, five-
day service is $30, overnight service is
$60. A multiple entry visa for business
purposes can be obtained under special
circumstances and cost $120 for a six-
month visa. In New York you can get a
visa from the Russian Consulate.*

☎ VOLLEYBALL CLUBS
ВОЛЛЕЙБОЛЬНЫЕ КЛУБЫ
VOLLEYBALLVEREINE
VOLLEYBALL CLUB DE
VOLLEYBOLL

Avtomobilist Volleyball Club
   V.O., 2-ya Liniya, 5 218-69-51

☎ WAREHOUSES
СКЛАД
LAGERHAUSER
ENTREPOT
LAGER

See STORAGE

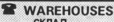 MCT EUROPE

CONTAINER STORAGE IN ST. PB.

MEZHEVOY KANAL, 5 251-86-62
FAX 186-83-44
TELEX .... 121691 MCT SU

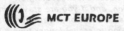
The Country Code for Russia
⇨ **7** ⇦

☎ WATCHES
ЧАСЫ
UHREN
MONTRES
ARMBANDSUR/KLOCKOR

*You can buy watches in specialized
departments of the DEPARTMENT
STORES, in specialized shops called
"Watches", (chasy, Часы) and in many
small commercial shops.*

Bure Salon
   Nevskiy pr., 23 314-66-82
   Director 110-63-11
       Hrs: 10 - 19:30
Chasy (watches) No. 34
   P. S., Bolshoy pr., 30 230-70-78
       Hrs: 10 - 19
Chasy (watches) No. 89
   Sredniy pr., 27 213-18-56
       Hrs: 10 - 19
Chasy (watches)
   P.S., Bolshoy pr., 65 232-04-66
       Hrs: 10 - 19
Chasy (watches)
   Nevskiy pr., 32/34 311-30-95
       Hrs: 10 - 19
Chasy (watches)
   Nevskiy pr., 93 277-13-62
       Hrs: 10 - 19
Chasy (watches)
   Moskovskiy pr., 192........ 298-17-47
       Hrs: 10 - 19
"Raketa" Watch Department
   *at the Gostinyy Dvor, Department Store,
   Sadovaya Liniya*
   Nevskiy pr., 35 110-52-49
Kristall No. 1.
   Nevskiy pr., 32/34 311-30-95
       Hrs: 10 - 19

☎ WATCH BATTERIES
ЧАСЫ, БАТАРЕЙКИ
BATTERIEN, UHREU
PILES POUR MONTRES
UR, BATTERIER

See COMMERCIAL STORES &
WATCH REPAIRS
*Buy watch batteries in specialized
departments of big DEPARTMENT
STORES (Univermag), WATCH SHOPS,
and in some repair shops. An extra watch
battery, however, may save a lot of time,
especially if it is an unusual size.*

☎ WATCH REPAIRS
ЧАСЫ, РЕМОНТ
UHRREPARATUR
HORLOGERIE
KLOCKREPARATIONER

Bure-Salon
   Nevskiy pr., 23 314-66-82

Watch Repair	Remont Chasov
Babushkina ul., 131	262-44-17
Hrs: 11 - 20	
P.S., Bolshoy, pr., 65	232-04-66
12-ya Krasnoarmeyskaya ul., 11	
....	251-42-15
Liteynyy pr., 45	273-64-05
Hrs: 10 - 19	
Ligovskiy pr., 173...........	166-56-33
Hrs: 11 - 20	
Nevskiy pr., 63...............	315-57-86
Nevskiy pr., 136.............	277-05-86
Vladimirskiy pr., 3...........	113-21-22
Hrs: 11 - 20	
Vladimirskiy pr., 5...........	113-13-81

All types of watch batteries
Hrs: 11 - 20

☎ WATER
ВОДА
WASSER
EAU
VATTEN

Don't drink the water. Many Russians don't drink tap water in Saint Petersburg and you should probably not drink the water either. Avoid cold tap water and ice, and items rinsed in cold tap water, both in winter and especially in summer, even though the water is frequently tested.

Water Treatment:
1. Boil for 10 minutes, or
2. Iodine treatment (Tablets of Potable Aqua, Globulin or 2 drops of iodine per liter of water, 1/2 hour)

Possible health problems. Water is almost always a problem for world travelers and Saint Petersburg is no exception. In addition to the usual problems, St. Petersburg was thought by some to have a problem with "Giardia Lamblia," a parasite found throughout the world (especially in the clear mountain streams with the mountain sheep grazing nearby). The symptoms may appear after weeks or months and include stomach cramps, nausea, bloated stomach, watery, foul-smelling diarrhea and frequent gas. The current state of this problem is unresolved. One medication thought ot be effective is Metronidazole, but it is only to be used only under care of doctor. See MEDICAL CARE AND CONSULTANTS.

Getting fluids. Getting enough fluids can be a problem. Drink lots of weak tea, soft drinks and beer. Mineral water can be salty. Juices are usually OK. The best strategy is to boil all your water and to put extra hot water from morning coffee and afternoon tea in pitchers and bottles. You can use a little one cup water heater (bring with you). Some inhabitants use water filters such as charcoal filters (bring with you). In an emergency, use water purification tablets (bring with you) and brush your teeth and fill your water bottles with the hottest tap water available.

Water Supply Interruption.
The hot water to apartments & offices is often supplied by central power stations. In summer, they turn off the hot water for "planned repairs" for two weeks or more. Take a sponge bath & boil some water.

☎ WEATHER
ПОГОДА
WETTER
TEMPS, MÉTÉO
VÄDER

See CLIMATE

For four day weather forecast in Russian, dial 001.
For monthly weather forecast for the entire country, dial 062.

Weather Bureau
Prof. Popova ul., 78
.... 234-13-92

☎ WEIGHTS & MEASURES
МЕРЫ ВЕСА
MAßE UND GEWICHTE
POIDS ET MESURES
VIKTER & MÅTT

See are TABLES OF WEIGHTS & MEASURES *on page 242-244.*

☎ WHAT TO BRING
ЧТО ВЗЯТЬ С СОБОЙ
REISECHECKLISTE
CE QU'IL FAUT AMENER
VAD TAR JAG
MED/RESECHECKLISTA

See CLIMATE *for a discussion of clothes.*

The supply of most goods is rapidly increasing in St. Petersburg. Some things, however, are still in short supply or time-consuming to find. So, to save time and money, and to be sure to have essential things, consider bringing the following items (listed in order of priority) not only to Russia, but on most trips. Three *** are essential, two ** are very useful and difficult to find, and one * are convenient.

*** All prescription medicines and prescriptions (in generic form)

*** *Medicine for Giardia Lamblia (Metronidazole, but consult doctor while using), and an antibiotic for bacterial dysentery.*
*** *Small packages of Kleenex and pre-moistened witch hazel packets.*
*** *Extra pair of glasses / contact lenses hearing aids, and their prescriptions.*
*** *Special batteries for cameras, hearing aid and watches.*
*** *Contraceptives/condoms, feminine hygiene products. (These items are increasingly available in PHARMACIES and INTERNATIONAL SHOPS.).*
*** *Photocopies of passport, visa, other documents, air ticket (two places)*
*** *Business cards (many)*
** *Standard first aid items: antibiotic cream, cortisone cream, fungal cream, powder, band aids, moleskin for blisters, pseudoephedrine, antihistamine, aspirin, Dramamine, thermometer, small needle, tweezers, Pepto-Bismol, Immodium, alcohol wipes, Q-tips. & "single use hypodermic needles" of an injection.*
** *Swiss army knife*
** *Small flashlight*
** *Toilet paper (roll)*
** *Small transformer and plug converters to round plugs(if needed)*
** *Small multi-voltage hair dryer*
** *Decaffeinated coffee & tea.*
** *1/2 liter plastic water bottle*
** *Small water heater, 2% iodine water tablets (Potable Aqua, Globulin)*
** *Flat water stopper & bar of soap*
** *Special batteries (AA & D are usually available in hard currency shops).*
** *Sunscreen, lip salve, sunglasses*
** *Mosquito repellent*
** *Foldable nylon string bags (for shopping)*
* *All special film in x-ray proof bag (Regular film is now widely available)*
* *Dried fruit, meat, soups, dried milk for coffee*
* *Thermos insulated mug & spoon & knife*
* *Walkman radio/ tape with tapes and batteries, blank cassette tapes, small short wave radio*
* *Umbrella & Binoculars & Alarm Clock*
* *Travel guides*
* *Dictionary, phrase book, guidebook & Address-phone book, extra pens and pencils, pen refills, lead, erasers, Scotch tape, plastic folders, paper clips and rubber bands.*
* *Laundry soap, 15 ft of light nylon line & clothes pins, lightweight plastic clothes and pants hangers, shoe polish, small plastic bags, needle and thread, etc.*

☎ WOMEN'S CLOTHING
ОДЕЖДА ДЛЯ ЖЕНЩИН
DAMENBEKLEIDUNG
VETEMENT POUR FEMMES
DAMKLÄDER,

See CLOTHING, WOMEN'S

☎ YACHT CLUBS
ЯХТ-КЛУБ
JACHTKLUBS
YACHT-CLUBS
SEGELKLUBBAR

Malakhit
Please call...................... 311-45-64
Neva Yacht Club
Nab. Martynova, 94 235-27-22
Yacht Club of Marine University
Nab. Martynova, 106....... 235-61-02
Yacht Club
Nab. Martynova, 92 235-43-50

☎ ZOO
ЗООПАРК
ZOO VERMIETEN
ZOO
ZOO

The Zoo
Park Lenina, 1
Info............................... 232-28-39
Metro: Gorkovskaya

SOME HISTORICAL DATES

1941-1944	*Blockade of the Leningrad*
1953	*Stalin died*
1985 - 1991	*PERESTROYKA*
1991	*Leningad renamed Saint-Petersburg*

To Contact The Editor of
The Traveller's Yellow Pages
TELINFO
✉190000, St. Petersburg, Russia:
Nab. Reki Moyki, 64
Tel................315-64-12, 315-98-55
Fax 315-74-20, 312-73-41

For the rest of the world
InfoServices International, Inc.
✉ 1 Saint Marks Place
Cold Spring Harbor, NY 11724, USA
Tel...................USA (516) 549-0064
Fax .... (516) 549-2032
Telex..................... 221213 TTC UR
Telinfo is a wholly-owned subsidiary of InfoServices International, Inc. NY, USA

The Suburbs of Saint Petersburg

LOMONOSOV • PAVLOVSK • PETRODVORETS • PUSHKIN

We include telephone numbers and addresses of basic services, banks, hotels, museums and restaurants in four suburbs of St. Petersburg. Most of this information was collected personally by our staff. Our readers are invited to add to this list.

LOMONOSOV
ЛОМОНОСОВ

Lomonosov is 40 km west of St. Petersburg. The commuter train to Lomonosov leaves from the Baltic Station. Get off at Oranienbaum-1 Station, an hour from the city. From May to September hydrofoils go to Lomonosov from Morskaya Pristan on Vasilevskiy Island (V.O.) near Tuchkov Bridge every 30 minutes.

BANKS

Bank
Yunogo Lenintsa pr., 63 .. 473-16-04
Hrs 9-13

CAFES

Chudesnitsa
Krasnogo Partizana ul., 16
.... 422-39-29
Hrs 11 - 20

CHURCHES

Archangel Michel Cathedral
Sobor Arkhangela Mikhaila
Yunogo Lenintsa pr., 63 .. 422-39-62

CITY COUNCIL LOMONOSOV

Gorodskoy Sovet Narodnykh Deputatov
Pobedy ul., 6-a 422-46-08
Hrs 10 - 18

DENTISTS

Dentist
Stomatologicheskaya Poliklinnika
Sverdlova pr., 2 423-03-49
Hrs 8 - 21

DRY CLEANING

Dom Byta
Yunogo Lenintsa pr., 32 .. 422-38-63
.... 422-37-97
Hrs 10 - 19; lunch break 14 - 15

HOSPITAL

Hospital   Bolnitsa
Leninskaya ul., 13 423-07-69

JEWELLERY

Akvamarin
Yunogo Lenintsa pr., 53... 422-31-19
Hrs 10 -19

LAUNDRY

Dom Byta
Yunogo Lenintsa pr., 32... 422-38-63
.... 422-37-97
Hrs 10 - 19; lunch break 14 - 15

LEGAL ADVICE

Legal Advice
Yuridicheckaya Konsultatsiya
Yunogo Lenintsa pr., 43/6 422-47-56
*Mon, Tue, Thur 9 - 19; Wed,
Fri 9 - 18; Sat 9 - 13*

MARKETS

Market   Rynok
Rubakina ul., 4 422-44-49
Hrs 9-20

MILITIA (POLICE)

Traffic Police   GAI
Kronshtadtskaya ul., 5..... 423-02-32
Hrs 9 - 18

MINISTRIES, RUSSIAN

Internal Affairs Department   UVD
Kronshtadtskaya ul., 5
Duty 423-07-02

MOVIES

Zarya
Filatovykh ul., 14 422-74-27

MUSEUMS

Katalnaya Gorka
Yunogo Lenintsa pr., 48... 422-37-53
Hrs 11- 17, Cls Tue
Chinese Palace   Kitayskiy Dvorets
Yunogo Lenintsa pr., 48... 422-88-06
.... 422-37-53
Chinese Kitchen   Kitayskaya Kukhnya
Yunogo Lenintsa pr., 48... 422-88-06
Palace of Peter III   Dvorets Petra III
Yunogo Lenintsa pr., 48... 422-37-53

NOTARY PUBLIC

Notary Public   Notarialnaya Kontora
   Yunogo Lenintsa pr., 43/6
   423-08-89
        Tue, Thur 10 - 19; Sat 9 - 13;
        lunch break 13 - 14

PARKING LOTS

Platnaya Autostoyanka (24 Hrs)
   Yunogo Lenintsa pr., 67 ....No Phone
Platnaya Autostoyanka
   Oranienbaumskiy pr......... 422-47-50

PHARMACIES

Pharmacy   Apteka
   Pobedy ul., 2 422-77-60
        Hrs 8- 21
Pharmacy   Apteka
   Yunogo Lenintsa pr., 55/8
   422-60-13
        Hrs 9 - 21

POST

Post office
   Krasnykh Partizan ul., 27
   422-97-87
        Hrs 9-19

RENTALS (furniture, bicycles, TV)

Petrodvortsovyy District
   Yunogo Lenintsa pr., 34
   ....422-89-31#

TRUCKING

Transagenstvo
   Yunogo Lenintsa pr., 63
   423-07-14
        Hrs 8-17

VISA REGISTRATION OFFICE

OVIR
   Kronshtadtskaya ul., 5..... 423-00-28

PAVLOVSK
ПАВЛОВСК

Pavlovsk is about 30 km south of St. Petersburg and is known for its Palace of Paul I and large beautiful park in the French style. The electric commuter train from Vitebsk Station leaves every 20-30 minutes and takes about 30 minutes.

BANKS

Bank No 502
   Krasnykh Zor ul., 16/13 ... 470-61-03
        Hrs 10-20

BATHS

Banya
   Lunacharskogo ul., 12 470-60-53
        Hrs 8-20 Closed Mon, Tues, Wed

BAKERIES

Bulochnaya
   Krasnykh Zor ul., 2.......... 470-60-14
        Hrs 10-19

BOOKS

Books   Knigi
   Krasnykh Zor ul., 25........ 470-23-92
        Hrs 10-19

CAFES

Zolushka
   Marata ul., 21 470-24-20
        Hrs 11-20

CHURCHES

Voenno-Polevaya
   Oborony ul., 1 .... No Phone#

CITY GOVERNMENT

Gorodskoy Sovet Narodnykh Detutatov
   R. Lyuksemburg ul., 11/16470-20-27

HAIR CUTTING

Parikmakherskaya
   Krasnykh Zor ul., 11 470-60-64

LAUNDRY

Laundry   Prachechnaya
   Krasnykh Zor ul., 2.......... 465-13-27

MEDICAL CARE

Poliklinika No. 67
   Marata ul., 1 470-21-71
        Hrs 8-20

MINISTRIES

Internal Affairs Department   UVD
   Marata ul., 17 470-20-26

MOVIES

Rodina
   Krasnykh Zor ul., 7.......... 470-61-94

MUSEUMS

Pavlovskiy Dvorets
   Revolyutsii ul., 20 470-21-56
   470-21-55
        Closed: Fri., first Mon.
        Hours: 9.00-17.30

PARKS

Pavlovsk Park
   Revolyutsii ul., 20 470-21-55
   Tour bureau 470-21-56

PHARMACIES

Pharmacy   Uptake No. 100
   Krasnykh Zor ul., 14........ 470-60-73
        Hrs 8-21

PHOTOGRAPHY

Photos *Hrs 11-19* **Fotografiya**
Vasenko ul., 28.............. 476-94-78

POST

Post-Office
Libknekhta ul., 8/14 470-20-66

RENTALS

Rentals of TV, furniture, etc.
Atele prokata
Detskoselskaya ul., 6 470-61-06
Hrs 10-19

RESTAURANTS

Leto
Krasnykh Zor ul., 35........ 470-62-16

SHOE REPAIR

Shoe Repair **Remont Obuvi**
Vasenko ul., 28.............. 470-24-14
Hrs 10-19

SHOPS

Children's Shop **Detskiy Mir**
Kommunarov ul., 12/15 ... 470-25-71
Hrs 9:30-22

TAILORS

Making/mending of clothing **Atele**
Detskoselskaya ul., 17 470-62-13
Hrs 10-18

PETRODVORETS
(PETERHOF, PETERGOF)
ПЕТРОДВОРЕЦ
(ПЕТЕРГОФ)

Petrodvorets, also called "Peterhof" in English or "Petergof" in Russian, is about 30 km west of St. Petersburg on the Gulf of Finland. It is known for beautiful palaces, parks and especially for fountains. The electric commuter train leaves from Baltic Station to Novyy Petergof Station every 30 minutes and takes about 40 minutes. From Novyy Petergof Station, take bus No. 350, 351, 352, 356. It is about 10 minutes to the Park. From May to September you may go to Petrodvorets by hydrofoil from Hermitage (Dvortsovaya Naberezhnaya). It leaves every 20 minutes and takes about half an hour.

BAKERIES

Bulochnaya, No. 9
St. Peterburgskaya ul., 41 427-97-30
Hrs 7:30-19

BANKS

Bank
Mezhdunarodnaya ul., 10
.... 427-54-88
Hrs 10-20
Commerce Bank
St. Peterburgskaya ul., 12
.... 427-53-64
Hrs 9:30-12:30

BATHS

Lenina bul., 10 427-35-88
Hrs 8-21, Cls Mon, Tue

BOOKSTORES

Books **Knigi**
Avrova ul., 10 427-76-74
Hrs 10-19

CAFES

Chayka
Kominterna ul., 4 427-96-01
Hrs 11-18

CHURCHES

St.Peter & Paul Cathedral
Sobor Svyatogo Petra i Pavla
St. Peterburgskaya ul., 32
.... 427-92-68

CITY GOVERNMENT

Gorodskoi Sovet Narodnykh Deputatov
Kolpinskaya ul., 7 427-79-15

DENTISTS

Dentist **Stomatologicheskaya Poliklinika**
Proletarskaya ul., 1 427-70-88
Hrs 8-20

GAS STATION

AZS 99
Frunze ul., 2.................. 427-91-12
AZS 17
St. Peterburgskaya ul., 67
.... 427-92-19

HOSPITAL

Hospital **Bolnitsa No. 37**
St. Peterburgskaya ul., 20
.... 427-92-49

HOTEL

CHAYKA
Shakhmatova ul., 16 428-68-42
Hotel of Watch making factory
Gostinitsa Chasovogo Zavoda
Chicherinskaya ul., 11 428-70-02

LAUNDRY

Laundry **Prachechnaya**
Lenina bul., 10 427-35-88
Hrs 8-17

MARKETS

The Market   **Rynok**
Torgovaya ul., 8 427-90-57
Hrs 8-18

MILITIA (POLICE)

GAI Traffic Police   **GAI**
Frontovaya ul., 8a........... 420-12-47

MINISTRIES, RUSSIAN

Internal Affairs Department   **UVD**
Morskogo Desanta ul., 1.. 427-74-02

MOVIES

Aurora
St. Peterburgskaya ul., 17
.... 427-54-54

MUSEUMS

Museum "Bolshoy Petergofskiy Dvorets"
Kominterna ul., 2 427-95-27
Hrs 11-18, Cls Mon
Museum "Dvorets "Cottage"
Kominterna ul., 2 427-99-53
Hrs 11-18, Cls Mon
Museum "Marli"
Kominterna ul., 2 427-77-29
Hrs 11-18, Cls Tue
Museum "Ekaterininskiy korpus"
Kominterna ul., 2 427-91-29
Hrs 11-18, Cls Tue
Museum of Benua family
Kominterna ul., 2 427-50-39
Hrs 11-18, Cls Mon

NOTARY PUBLIC

Notary Public   Notarialnaya Kontora
St. Peterburgskaya ul., 28 427-98-40

PARKS

Parks and Fontains of Petrodvorets
Kominterna, 2 427-95-27

PARKING LOTS

Avtostoyanka N 5
Konoplyashnikovoy ul., 5
.... 427-78-42

PHARMACIES

Pharmacy No. 3   Apteka No. 3
Kalininskaya ul., 6........... 427-05-78
Decorated in old Russian style
Hrs 8-20

POST

Post office
St. Peterburgskaya ul., 15
.... 427-53-91
Hrs 8-21

RESTAURANTS

Parkovyy (closed for repair)
Avrova ul., 14 427-90-96
Petrodvorets
Nizhniy park, ... 427-93-90

SHOE, REPAIR

Shoe Repair   Remont Obuvi
Razvedchikov bul. 427-14-41
Hrs 10-20

TAILORS

Making & mending of clothes   Atele
St. Peterburgskaya ul., 29
.... 427-92-49

TELEX

Post office
St. Peterburgskaya ul, 15
.... 427-53-91
Hrs 8-21

TRUCKING

Lentransagenstvo
St. Peterburgskaya ul, 8/9
.... 427-74-27
Hrs 9-18

TV/RADIO REPAIR

Repair of radio equipment
Ozerkovaya ul., 45 427-23-00
Hrs 10-19

VISA REGISTRATION OFFICE

Morskogo Desanta ul., 1
.... 427-77-12

WATCHES

Raketa
St. Peterburgskaya ul., 60
.... 420-29-66
Fax 420-28-04

PUSHKIN
(TSARSKOE SELO)
ПУШКИН
(ЦАРСКОЕ СЕЛО)

Pushkin is 24 km south from the city and known for its Catherine Palace in the Baroque style, parks and also for the Lyceum where Pushkin, Russia's favorite poet, studied in 1811-1819.

The electric commuter trains leave every 20 minutes from Vitebsk Station and the trip takes about half an hour. Get off the train at Detskoe Selo (Детское Село) Station.

BANKS

Bank
Oktyabrskiy Bulvar, 16.... 470-02-06
.... 470-00-28
.... 470-02-01
Hrs 10 -13

CAFES

Ermitazh
Kominterna ul., 21 476-62-55
Hrs 12 - 23; lunch break 17 - 18

CHURCHES

Church
A. Vasenko ul., 15........... 465-81-97
Sophia Cathedral   Sofiyskiy Sobor
Sofiyskaya ul., 1............. 465-47-47

CITY GOVERNMENT

City Government   Gorodskoy Sovet
Oktyabrskiy bul., 24........ 466-24-18
.... 466-24-19
.... 466-24-07
.... 466-62-81

CLOTHING REPAIR

Clothing Repair
Marksa ul., 58................ 470-74-01
Hrs 10 - 19; lunch break 15 - 16

CONCERT HALLS

Church
A. Vasenko ul., 15.......... 465-81-97

DENTISTS

Dentists
Pushchina ul., 33............ 470-10-17
.... 470-10-10

DRY CLEANING

Dry Cleaning   Khimchistka
Leningradskoe shosse, 13/1
.... 465-99-88
Hrs 10 - 19; lunch break 14 - 15

DEPARTMENT STORES

Gostinyy Dvor
Moskovskaya ul., 25 466-26-05
Hrs 11 - 20

EMERGENCY MEDICAL CARE

Emegency Medical Care
    Skoraya Meditsinskaya Pomoshch
Moskovskaya ul., 15 470-74-31

GAS STATIONS

Gas Station No. 1
Zheleznodorozhnaya ul.,... 470-16-77
Gas Station No. 2
Vasenko ul., 1................ 476-57-31

GIFT SHOPS

1-go Maya ul., 30/42....... 470-76-70
Hrs 11 - 19

HOSPITAL

Hospital   Bolnitsa
Proletkulta ul.,5/7 470-34-19

HOTELS

Fyodorovskiy Gorodok
Admiralteyskiy pr., 14 465-03-97
.... 476-36-00
Pushkinskaya
Shishkova ul., 32/15 465-94-07
.... 465-88-37

LEGAL ADVICE

Legal Advice
    Yuridicheskaya Konsultatsiya
Pushkinskaya ul., 22 466-48-82
.... 466-54-92
Hrs 9:30 - 19

MARKETS

Market   Rynok
Truda ul.,...................... 476-87-56
Hrs 8 - 18

MILITIA (POLICE)

Militsiya
Pushkinskaya ul., 34 476-78-24
.... 470-34-18
Info.............................. 470-02-02
Traffic Police   GAI
Pos. Tarlevo, Novaya ul., 1
.... 466-48-76

MOVIES

Ruslan
Marksa ul., 42 470-03-73

MUSEUMS

Museum "Modern Art Gallery"
Marksa pr., 40/27 466-55-81
Hrs 11 - 17; lunch break 14 - 15
Op Sat, Sun
Museum "Pushkin Lyceum"
Komsomolskaya ul., 2 465-86-63
Hrs 10- 17, Cls Tue
Region Museum
Truda ul., 28 466-55-10
Hrs 10 - 17, Cls Thu, Fri
Museum "Pushkin House"
Pushkinskaya ul., 2 476-69-90
Hrs 11 - 18, Cls Tue
Palace of Catherine I
Yekaterininskiy Dvorets - Muzey
Komsomolskaya, 7 470-34-29
.... 465-53-08
Hrs 10 - 17, Cls Tue

NOTARY PUBLIC

Notary Public   Notarialnaya Kontora
Pushkinskaya ul., 20 466-54-94

OPTICIAN

Optika
Leningradskoe shosse, 13/1
.... 466-20-59

POST OFFICE

Post Office   Pochta
Revolyutsii ul., 31 466-47-94
.... 466-48-09
.... 466-44-17

PHARMACIES

Pharmacy   Apteka
Revolyutsii ul., 51 476-86-72

PHOTOGRAPHERS

Photographers
1-go Maya ul., 30/42 470-76-41
Hrs 11 - 20; lunch break 13 -14

RADIO REPAIR

Radioequipment Repair
Shkolnyy pr., 23 470-70-32
.... 466-64-13
.... 466-64-07

RENTALS (furniture, bicycles, TV)

Pushkinskiy District
Leningradskaya ul., 45
.... 470-11-33

RESTAURANTS

Shampur
1-go Maya ul., 39 470-74-23
Hrs 11 - 22;
Vityaz
Moskovskaya ul., 20 466-43-17
.... 466-43-18
Hrs 12 - 23; lunch break 18 - 19

SHOES, REPAIR

Shoes Repair   Remont Obuvi
Kominterna ul., 60-a 470-10-33

SHOPS

Gloriya
1-go Maya ul., 39 470-33-76

TELEGRAPH

Telegraph
Revolyutsii ul., 52 466-44-18
.... 470-49-01

THEATRE TICKETS BOX-OFFICE

Theatre Tickets Box-Office
Teatralnaya Kassa
1-go Maya ul., 29 470-98-25
Hrs 16 - 19; Sun 13 - 16:, Cls Sat

TICKETS AIR

Aeorflot Tickets   Kassa Aeroflota
Leningradskaya ul., 1 470-13-06
.... 466-48-65

Major Cities near Saint Petersburg

NOVGOROD • PSKOV • VOLOGDA • VYBORG

Information on these important nearby cities is difficult to find in Russian as well as in English so we sent our staff there to collect information and addresses of the most important services, shops, banks, museums, etc. Our readers are invited to add to this list.

NOVGOROD
НОВГОРОД

The dialing code is 816

Novgorod is located on Moscow-St. Petersburg Highway about 190 km south of St. Petersburg. Novgorod, more than 1000 years old, is famous for its Kremlin, and churches of 9-13th centuries. Daily train leaves from St. Petersburg from the Moscow Station at 5:55 p.m. and from Vitebsk Station at 7 p.m. and take 4 1/2 hours. The auto trip takes about 2 1/2 hours.

AIRPORT

Airport
Yurevskoe shosse 7-42-42

AUTO REPAIRS

Sovinterservices
Oktyabrskaya ul., 15 2-14-90
Hrs 8-17

BUSES

Autostation
Vokzalnaya pl., 7 7-53-47
Hrs 6-23

BAKERIES

Bulochnaya
Lva Tolstogo ul., 11 7-64-00
Hrs 9-19

BANKS

NOVOBANK
Slavnaya ul., 50 3-61-67
Hrs 9-17

BOOKSTORES

Prometey
Leningradskaya ul., 13 7-82-96
Hrs 10-19

CAFES

Lakomka
Leningradskaya ul., 11 3-61-08
Hrs 9-19

Posad
Bolshevikov ul., 14 9-48-49
Russkaya kukhnya
Komsomolskaya ul., 14 7-60-15

CITY GOVERNMENT

City Council   Gorodskoy Ispolkom
Pobedy pl., "Dom Sovetov"
.... 7-25-40
Region Council   Oblastnoy-Ispolkom
Pobedy pl., "Dom Sovetov"
.... 7-81-88

CUSTOMS

Customs
Yurevskoe shosse, Airport
.... 7-81-16

DENTISTS

Stomatologicheskaya poliklinika No. 1
Lenina pr., 34/13 3-57-58
.... 3-32-11

DRY CLEANING

Khimchistka
Grigorovskoe shosse, 19a 7-13-39
Khimchistka
Gagarina ul., 25a 3-48-13

EMERGENCY MEDICAL CARE

Emergent Medical Care
Skoraya Meditsinskaya Pomoshch
Oborony ul., 24 03
Hrs 7-18

GAS STATION

AZS No. 2
Leningradskaya ul., 92 2-54-60
AZS No. 3
Moskovskoe shosse 3-37-81

HAIR/CUTTING

Lada
Lenina pr., 20 3-14-91
Hrs 8-20

Salon krasoty
Leningradskaya ul., 13 7-32-22
Hrs 8-20

HOSPITAL

Central hospital   **Bolnitsa**
Shtykova ul., 18 7-72-31
Info 7-20-70
Hospital   **Bolnitsa**
Kolmovo ul., 6 2-57-53
Info 2-53-47

HOTEL

Intourist
Dmitrievskaya ul., 16 7-50-89
Rossia
Nab. Alexandra Nevskogo, 19/1
.... 3-41-85
Sadko
Gagarina pr., 16 7-53-66
.... 7-70-93
Volkhov
Nekrasova ul., 24 9-48-49

LAUNDRY

Laundry   **Prachechnaya**
Gagarina, 25a 3-48-13

LAW FIRMS

Legal Advise
Yuridicheskaya konsultatsiya
Suvorovskaya ul., 4 3-07-76
Hrs 0-18

MARKETS

Market   **Rynok**
Zhelyabova ul., 15 7-73-55

MEDICAL CARE

Poliklinika (private)
Mira pr., 13 2-27-93
Maternity hospital No. 1
Rodilnyy Dom No. 1
Komarova ul., 9/11 7-20-36
Maternity hospital No. 2
Rodilnyy Dom No. 2
Derzhavina ul., 1 3-44-13
Emergency room   **Travmedpunkt**
Dekabristov ul., 12 7-27-44

MILITIA (POLICE)

GAI Traffic Police
Suvorovskaya ul., 2 3-41-49

MINISTRIES, RUSSIAN

KGB
Leningradskaya ul., 2/10 7-26-96
Internal Affairs Department   **UVD**
Leningradskaya ul., 2/10 7-45-38

MOVIES

Novgorod
Lomonosova ul., 9 2-04-30

Oktyabr
Lenina pr., 26 3-34-55
Rodina
Leningradskaya ul., 12 7-30-12

MUSEUMS

Museum "Novgorod Kremlin"
Kreml, 11 7-36-08

NOTARY PUBLIC

Notary Public
Notarialnaya kontora No. 1
Leningradskaya ul., 4 7-80-22

PARKS

Kremlin park
Kreml, ... 7-71-56
Park
Lenina pr, ... 3-07-70

PARKING LOTS

Autostation (Pay)
Zhelyabova ul., 15 7-64-30

PHARMACIES

Apteka
Leningradskaya ul., 14 7-30-04
Hrs 8-22
Apteka
Lenina pr., 37 3-59-06
Hrs 8-20

PHOTOGRAPHERS

Photography
Chernyakhovskogo ul., 74
.... 7-52-12
Hrs 9-19

POST

Post office
Gertsena ul., 1 7-24-11
.... 7-53-72

RESTAURANTS

Detinets
Kreml 7-30-15
Hrs 12-24, $ & RUBLES
Intourist
at Hotel
Dmitrovskaya ul., 16 9-42-88
.... 9-42-91
Hrs 12-24
Kafe Posad
Bolshevikov ul., 14 .... 9-48-49#

RESTROOMS

Toilets (pay)
Kremlin
Railway Station
Market

SHOPS

Rus
Leningradskaya ul., 25......... 7-45-13
Shop
Lenina pr., 52.................... 3-29-71
Hrs 9-19

SOUVENIRS/GIFTS

Souvenirs/Gifts
Leningradskaya ul., 6 7-73-45
Hrs 10-19
Souvenirs/Gifts
Lenina pr., 5 9-92-37
Hrs 10-19

TAXIS

Taxi (to order)
Studencheskaya ul., 31 9-30-38

THEATRE

Drama Theater
Dmitrievskogo ul., 16 7-37-16

TICKETS

Aeroflot Tickets   **Kassa Aeroflota**
Vokzalnaya pl., 7 7-40-02
Rail Tickets
          Zheleznodorozhnaya Kassa
Vokzalnaya pl., 7 7-40-35
Bus tickets   **Avtobusnaya Kassa**
Vokzalnaya pl., 7 7-61-86
Info 7-53-47

TRANSLATORS

Intourist
Dmitrievskaya ul., 16........... 7-42-35
Hrs 9-18

TRAVEL AGENCIES

Intourist
Dmitrievskaya ul., 16........... 7-42-35
.... 7-50-89
Fax 7-41-57
Telex 121076
Hrs 9-18, $, Rubles & credit cards
Travel agency
Nab. Al. Nevskogo, 19/1...... 3-23-11
.... 3-53-32
Hrs 9-18

TV/RADIO REPAIR

Ekran
Grigorovskoe sh., 38, kor. 4 . 2-40-10

VISA OFFICE

OVIR
Leningradskaya ul., 2/9........ 9-04-25

PSKOV
ПСКОВ

The dialing code is 81122.

Pskov is located 265 km south of St. Petersburg on Pskov Lake. Founded in 903 and known as Novgorod's little brother, Pskov is also famous for its Kremlin and churches. The daily train leaves from St. Petersburg's Warsaw Station every 2 hours and it takes about 7 hours to get there. From Airport Pulkovo-1 there are daily flights on 9:15 p.m. and also on Monday, Wednesday, Friday at 8 pm.

AIRPORT

Airport
Germana ul., 34.................. 2-22-15

AUTOSERVICE / REPAIRS

Autovaz
Rizhskiy pr., 74 3-27-14

BAKERIES

Bulochnaya
Oktyabrskiy pr., 22 3-38-91
Hrs 9-20

BANKS

Akobank
Gogolya ul., 2 2-47-74
Hrs 10 - 17
Bank
Oktyabrskiy pr., 8 2-36-82
Hrs 10-17

BOOKSTORE

Books   **Knigi**
Rizhskiy pr., 41 6-43-81
Hrs 10-19

BUSES

Bus Station   **Avtovokzal**
Vokzalnaya pl., 21 2-40-01
Hrs 5-24

CAFES

Kuorio
Kiseleva ul., 8 6-25-41
Hrs 12-24, Cls Tue

CITY GOVERNMENT

City Council
Gorodskoy Sovet Narodnykh Deputatov
Nekrasova ul., 22................ 2-33-45

City Executive Committee
Ispolkom Gorodskogo Soveta
Narodnykh Deputatov
Nekrasova ul., 22 2-26-67
Oblast Executive Committee
Ispolkom Oblastnogo Soveta
Narodnykh Deputatov
Nekrasova ul., 23 2-30-69
Hrs 10-18

CHURCHES

Russian Ortodox Church adminitration
Eparkhiya
Leona Pozemskogo ul., 83a.. 2-40-07
Holy Trinity Cathedral
Svyatotroitskiy Sobor
Kreml, 1 2-39-20

CUSTOMS

Customs   *Tamozhnya*
Yana Fabritsiusa ul.,............ 3-02-87

DENTISTS

Dentist
Stomotologicheskaya poliklinika
Oktyabrskiy pr., 29 3-89-90
.... 3-89-96

DEPARTMENT STORES

Central Department Store   *Univermag*
Sovetskaya ul., 13 2-37-09
Hrs 10-20

DRY CLEANING

Snezhinka
Nekrasova ul., 42 2-19-30
Hrs 9-17

EMERGENCY MEDICAL CARE

Emergency Medical Care
Skoraya meditsinskaya pomosh
Komunalnaya ul., 21 3-43-07

GAS STATION

AZS No. 1
Gdovskoe shosse................ 3-45-91
AZS No. 3
Rizhskiy pr., ... 6-09-41
AZS No. 32
N. Vasileva ul.,................... 3-59-61
AZS No. 44
Leningradskoe shosse,......... 2-48-16

HAIRCUTTING

Lyudmila
Oktyabrskiy pr., 14 3-87-36
Hrs 9-20
Ruslan
Oktyabrskiy pr., 22 2-07-20
Hrs 9-20

INTERNATIONAL SHOP

In Hotel "Rizhskiy"
Rizhskiy pr., 25 6-22-23

HOSPITAL

City Hospital   *Gorodskaya Bolnitsa*
Komunalnaya ul., 23............ 9-92-14
Regional Hospital   *Oblastnaya Bolnitsa*
Malyakova ul., 2 2-47-03

HOTEL

Oktyabrskaya
Oktyabrskiy pr., 36 3-99-12
Rizhskaya
Rizhskiy pr., 25 6-22-23
Turist
Krasnoznamenskaya ul., 4.... 2-51-51

LAUNDRY

Laundry   *Prachechnaya*
Sovetskaya ul., 42 "B" 2-37-73
Hrs 11-19

LEGAL ADVICE

Legal Advice
Yuridicheskaya Konsultatsia
Komissarovskiy per., 2......... 3-93-55
Legal Advice
Yuridicheskaya Konsultatsia
Leona Pozemskogo ul., 45
.... 2-09-93

MARKETS

Market   *Rynok*
Vorovskogo ul., 6 2-30-08
Hrs 7-18

MEDICAL CARE

Poliklinika No. 1
N. Ostrovskogo ul., 19 2-53-57
Emergency room   *Travmedpunkt*
Komunalnaya ul., 21............ 9-92-54
Maternity hospital   *Rodilnyy Dom*
Kuzbasskoy divizii ul., 22 6-76-64

MILITIA (POLICE)

GAI Traffic Police
Truda ul., 75 3-67-12

MINISTRIES (RUSSIAN)

The Committee of Foreign Affairs
Nekrasova ul., 23................ 2-23-56
Hrs 9-18
KGB
Oktyabrskiy pr., 48 2-16-49
Dept. for Internal Affairs   *MVD*
Komissarovskiy per., 2......... 2-49-85

MOVIES

Oktyabr
Lenina pl., 1 2-20-74
Smena
Oktyabrskiy pr., 17a 3-97-34

MUSEUMS

State Historical-Architecture Museum
Nekrasova ul., 7 2-33-10
Hrs 10-18, Cls Mon

NOTARY PUBLIC

Notary Public   Notarialnaya Kontora
Petrovskaya ul., 24 6-15-94
Notary Public   Notarialnaya Kontora
Sovetskaya ul., 85 3-87-37

PARKS

Puskin City Park
Oktyabrskiy pr., 34 3-91-42

PARKING LOTS

Parking Lot
Marksa ul., 3 2-33-86
Parking Lot
Rizhskiy pr., 25 6-76-12

PHARMACIES

Pharmacy   Apteka
Rizhskiy pr., 31 6-45-71
Hrs 8-20
Pharmacy   Apteka
Oktyabrskiy pr., 16 2-24-43

PHOTOCOPYING

Copying of documents
Profsoyuznaya ul., 2 3-47-36
Hrs 10-20

Canon Technical Centre at Pskov

CANON PHOTOCOPIERS
Authorized Sales and Service
Pskov

Inzhenernaya ul., 4
.... (81122) 24628
St. Pb. Fax 166-36-24
St. Pb. Tel .... (812) 269-05-04

PORT

River Terminal   Rechnoy port
Krasnoarmeyskaya ul., 2/7
.... 6-54-11

POST

Post office
Sovetskaya ul., 7 2-18-42

RESTAURANTS

Riga
Rizhskiy pr., 25 6-76-34
Hrs 12-24
Tourist
Krasnoznamenskaya ul.,4 3-35-21
Hrs 12-24

SHOPS

Orbita
Rizhskiy pr., 41 6-44-52
Hrs 10-19
Trade Center   Torgovyy Tsentr
Yana Fabritsiusa ul., 5 2-87-17
Hrs 10-20

SOUVENIRS/GIFTS

Souvenirs/Gifts
Oktyabrskiy pr., 32 3-38-13
Hrs 10-18

STADIUMS

Mashinostroitel Stadium
N. Ostrovskogo ul 3-56-72

TAXI

Taxi (to order)
Kozinskogo ul., 6 9-40-31

THEATER

Pushkin Drama Theater
Pushkina ul., 13 2-23-98

TICKETS

Tickets for Aeroflot   Kassa Aeroflota
Rizhskiy pr., 29/21 2-62-62
Hrs 9-20
Tickets for buses   Autobusnaya Kassa
Vokzalnaya ul., 21 2-40-01
Tickets for trains
Zheleznodorozhaya Kassa
Vokzalnaya pl., ... 2-37-37
Booking for tickets 9-50-32

RAILWAY STATION

Railway Station
Zheleznodorozhnyy Vokzal
Vokzalnaya pl., ... 2-37-37

TELEGRAPH

Telegraph
Oktyabrskiy pr., 31a 2-19-72
Hrs 8-22

TRANSLATIONS

Intourist
Rizhskiy pr., 25 6-22-54
.... 6-75-13
Hrs 9-18

TRAVEL AGENCIES

Intourist
Rizhskiy pr. 25 6-22-54
Hrs 9-18

Pskov Travel Agency
Kreml, 6 2-51-58
Hrs 9-18

TV / RADIO REPAIR

Orbita
Rizhskiy pr., 41 6-25-71
Hrs 9-17

VISA REGISTRATION OFFICE

OVIR
Oktyabrskiy pr., 48 9-51-39
Hrs 9-17

VOLOGDA
ВОЛОГДА

The dialing code is 81722.

Vologda is located in 850 km north-east of St. Petersburg. Founded in 1147, Vologda is famous for Vologda lace. Trains leave from St. Petersburg from Moscow Station daily at 7:35 p.m. It takes about 13 hours to get to Vologda. Also there are daily planes from Airport Pulkovo-1 at 5:30 p.m.

AIRPORT

Airport
pos. Dorozhniy 2-06-86
Info 2-14-62

AUTOSERVICE / REPAIRS

Autostation
Voroshilova ul., 16 2-45-18
Everest
Sovetskiy pr., 66 5-09-22

BAKERIES

Bulochnaya
Lenina pr., 4 2-06-90
Hrs 8-20.

BANKS

Vologdabank
Kremlevskaya pl., 12 2-30-53
Hrs 8-17.

BOOKSTORES

Books   **Dom Knigi**
Mira ul., 38 2-30-18
Hrs 10-18.

Books   **Politicheskaya kniga**
Mira ul., 14 2-42-38
Hrs 10-19.

BUSES

Bus Station   **Avtovokzal**
Babushkina ul., 10 2-04-52
.... 2-94-90
Hrs 5.30-24.

BUSINESS CARDS

Pushkina ul., 25, office 421 . 2-61-33
Hrs 9-17.

CAFES

Mercuriy
Pobedy pr., 8 2-36-93
Hrs 12-23.

CEMETERIES

Administration
Sovetskiy pr., 53 2-05-04
Cemetery
Poshekhonskoe shosse 2-10-16

CHURCHES

Russian Orthodox Church Administration
Eparkhiya
Voroshilova pr., 93 2-32-77
.... 2-12-20

CITY GOVERNMENT

Executive Committee of Oblast Council
Ispolkom Oblastnogo Soveta
Narodnykh Deputatov
Lenina ul., 15 2-23-80
Executive Committee of City Council
Ispolkom Gorodskogo Soveta
Narodnykh Deputatov
Kamennyy most, 4 2-00-42
Hrs 10-20
Commerce Administration
Upravlenie Torgovli
Lenina ul., 15 2-06-05
Planning Committee
Planovaya Komissiya
Lenina ul., 15 2-03-03

CUSTOMS

Customs   **Tamozhnya**
Komsomolskaya ul., 36 4-12-12

DENTISTS

Dentist   Stomotologicheskaya poliklinika
Batyushkova ul.,9 2-10-86
Hrs 9-19.

DEPARTMENT STORES

Department Store   **Univermag**
Klara Tsetkin ul., 4 2-24-43
Info 2-32-80
Hrs 10-20.

DRY CLEANING

Dom Byta
Klary Tsetkin ul.,3 2-51-59
Hrs 9-20.

EMERGENCY MEDICAL CARE

Emergency Medical Care
        Skoraya Meditsinskaya pomoshch
Chekhova pr., 17 2-12-82
Info 2-61-94

FOOD STORES

Tsentralniy
Gertsena ul., 14 2-97-71
Hrs 10-19.

GAS STATIONS

AZS No. 6
Chernyshevskogo ul., 149.... 2-27-03
AZS No. 35
Uritskogo ul., 132a 2-96-46
AZS No. 37
Mudrova ul., 40 5-69-22
Neftebaza
Turundaevskaya ul., 6 2-63-51

HAIRCUTTING

Parikmakherskaya
Sovetskiy pr., 6 2-34-81
Hrs 10-20
Fantaziya (Fantasy)
Chernyshevskogo ul., 103.... 9-09-91
Hrs 10-20

HOSPITALS

City Hospital No. 1
        Gorodskaya Bolnitsa No. 1
Sovetskiy pr., 98 2-01-23
Info 2-05-25
Emergency room................. 6-57-06
Regional Hospital   Oblastnaya Bolnitsa
Lechebnik, 17 2-13-80
Info 3-02-50
Ophthalmological Hospital
        Glaznaya bolnitsa
Poshekhonskoe shosse, 25 .. 2-07-95
.... 3-11-10

HOTELS

Vologda
Mira ul., 92 2-30-79
Oktyabr
Karla Marksa ul., 7 2-05-69

HUNTING

Soyuz
Chernyshevskogo ul., 114.... 4-24-20
.... 2-76-09
Fax .... (817-22) 4-24-20
Hrs 9-18.

LEGAL ADVICE

Legal Advice
        Yuridicheskaya konsultatsiya
M. I. Ulyanovoy ul., 14 2-55-72
.... 2-05-94
Hrs 10-19

MARKETS

Market   Rynok
Batyushkova ul., 3a............. 2-16-95
Hrs 7-18.

MEDICAL CARE

Maternity Hospital   Rodilnyy Dom
Pirogova ul., 24 2-27-70
Maternity Hospital   Rodilnyy Dom
Chernyshevskogo ul., 68...... 2-11-40

MILITIA (POLICE)

GAI Traffic Police
Sammera ul., 6................... 6-39-39

MINISTRIES, RUSSIAN

Internal Affairs Department   UVD
Mira ul., 36 9-44-94
KGB
Menzhinskogo ul., 58 2-10-00
.... 9-90-46

MOVIES

Rodina
Chernyshevskogo ul., 23...... 2-07-74
Salut
Lenina ul., 14 2-25-81
.... 2-04-91
Sputnik
Molodezhnaya ul., 5 2-29-86
.... 2-28-86

MUSEUMS

Art Gallery (Museum)
        Kartinnaya galereya
Kremlevskaya pl., 3 .... 2 14-33
Hrs 10-18.
Regional Museum
        Kraevedcheskiy museum
Orlova ul., 15 2-25-11
Hrs 10-18
House of Peter I   Domik Petra-I
Sovetskiy pr., 47 2-27-59
Hrs 10-18

NOTARY PUBLIC

Notary Public Notarialnaya kontora No. 1
Uritskogo ul., 44................. 2-21-22
Hrs 8-17.
Notary Public Notarialnaya kontora No. 2
Gogolya ul., 89................... 6-50-27
Hrs 8-17

PARKS

Park
Pobedy pr., ... 2-16-97
Park
Nekrasova ul., 48 6-30-85

PHARMACIES

Pharmacy   **Apteka**
Mashinostroitelnaya ul., 5 2-71-19
Hrs 8-20.
Pharmacy   **Apteka**
Mayakovskogo ul., 35 2-20-19
Hrs 8-20.

PHOTOCOPYING

Ampersand
Pobedy ul., 3 kv.18, ... 5-96-46
Everest
Sovetskiy pr., 66 5-09-22
.... 5-13-59

PHOTOGRAPHERS

Photo
Mira ul., 7 2-20-43
Hrs 10-18.
Photo
Lenina ul., 4 2-45-03
Hrs 10-18

RAILWAY STATION

Railway Station
            Zheleznodorozhnyy Vokzal
Mozhayskogo ul.,33 B 2-06-73

RESTAURANTS

Mishkolts
Voroshilova ul., 37 2-51-38
.... 2-92-34
Hrs 12-23
Sever
Pobedy ul., 6 2-26-00
.... 2-16-92
Hrs 12-24
Vologda
Mira ul., 92 9-67-94
.... 9-67-17
Hrs 12-24.

REPAIR OF CLOTHING

Repair of Clothing   **Dom Byta**
Klary Tsetkin ul., 3 2-51-59
Hrs 9-20.

REST ROOM (TOILETS)

Mozhayskogo ul., 33 B

SHOPS

Shop for children   **Detskiy Mir**
Mira ul., 11 2-26-22
.... 2-21-85
Hrs 10-19

SOUVENIRS/GIFTS

Souvenirs/Gifts
Lenina ul., 13 2-45-25
Hrs 10-18
Vologda Souvenirs
            Vologodskie Suveniry
Chekhova ul., 12 5-14-81
Hrs 10-19

TAILORS

Dom Byta
Klary Tsetkin ul., 3 2-51-59
Hrs 9-20.

TAXIS

Taxi
Mira ul., 5 2-45-60
Taxi
Torgovaya pl., 11 2-11-32

TELEGRAPH

Telegraph
Lermontova ul., 27 2-48-76
.... 2-05-68
Hrs 8-22

TELEPHONE

Telephone Station
Gertsena ul., 41 2-04-25

TICKETS

Tickets for Aeroflot
            Kassa Aeroflota
Gertsena ul., 45 2-33-02
Hrs 10-19
Railway tickets
            Zheleznodorozhnaya Kassa
Gertsena ul., 45 6-45-55
.... 6-45-49
.... 2-46-77
Info 2-27-04
Hrs 9-19
Bus tickets   **Avtobusnaya Kassa**
Gorkogo ul., 86 6-53-88
Hrs 9-19
Tickets for river transport
Gertsena ul., 45 6-71-00

THEATRE

State Drama Theater
Sovetskiy pr., 1 2-60-69
.... 2-61-06

TRANSLATIONS

Batyushkova ul., 11 office 508
.... 5-21-70
Hrs 10-18

TRAVEL AGENCIES

Intourist
Klary Tsetkin ul., 26 2-60-63
Hrs 9-18
Sharm
Kalinina ul., 17 2-15-01
Hrs 8-17

TV/RADIO REPAIR

Gorkogo ul., 113 2-73-29
.... 2-70-11

VISA REGISTRATION OFFICE

OVIR
Mira ul., 30 2-60-21

VYBORG
ВЫБОРГ

The dialing code is 278.

Vyborg is the border town on the St. Petersburg-Helsinki highway, 160 km north-west of St. Petersburg. Vyborg is one of the oldest cities in Europe. Fast trains to Helsinki leave daily on 6:20 a.m. and on 3:55 p.m. from Finland Station and take 1 1/2 hours. Electric commuter trains leave from Finland Station every hour or two. The trip takes about 2 1/2 hours by train or by car. On the highway to Helsinki, there are two border crossings to Torfyanovka (to Vaalimaa) and at Brusnichnoe (to Nuijamaa). There are scheduled sailing to/from Finnish ports.

BANKS

Vneshekonombank
Leningradskiy pr., 14 25-523

BARS

BERRY BAR
Zheleznodorozhnaya ul., 7 25-942
Hrs 9-24

BUSES

Bus Station   **Avtovokzal**
Zheleznodorozhnaya ul., 7 25-942

CAFES

Brigantina
Yuzhnyy Val., 16 25-317
Hrs 12-23
Pantserlaks
Luzhskaya ul., 1 26-301
Hrs 11-21

CAMPING

Repino StpbTC Camping
Primorskoe Shosse, 419... 231-68-39
.... 238-35-50

CITY GOVERNMENT

City Council of Vyborg
Sovetskaya ul., 12 24-723
Hrs 9-18
Committee of Foreign Trade Affairs
.... 78-320
Economic Chamber
Sovetskaya ul., 12 21-300
.... 24-792

CUSTOMS

Customs   **Tamozhnya**
Zheleznodorozhnaya ul., 9/15
.... 26-697
Vysotsk 52-578
Brusnichnoe 70-504
Poselok Luzhayka......... 96-1-21 263
Port 28-859
Torfyanovka...................... 28-470

DRY CLEANING

Dry Cleaning   **Khimchistka**
Lenina ul., 11 20-452
Hrs 10-20

DEPARTMENT STORES

Department Store   **Univermag**
Lenina ul., 11 20-452
Hrs 9-20

EMEGENCY MEDICAL CARE

Emergent Medical Care
Skoraya Pomoshch
Mayakovskogo ul., 2 24-012

GAS STATION

AZS No. 1
Vokzalnaya pl., 1 23-553
AZS No. 3
Leningradskoe shosse........... 96-759

INSURANCE

Ingosstrakh
Leningradskiy pr., 31 25-704

HARD CURRENCY SHOP

Beriozka
Leningradskiy pr., 19 21-455
Hrs 10-19
Beriozka
Zheleznodorozhnaya ul., 15 ... 21-798
Hrs 10-19
Helen
Kutuzova bul., 7, bldg E........ 24-932
Hrs 10-19

Helen
   Vokzal................................ 28-429

Ross
   Dimitrova ul., 1..................... 20-955
   Hrs 9-24

HOSPITAL

Regional Hospital   Rayonnaya Bolnitsa
   Oktyabrskaya ul., 2.............. 25-641

HOTEL

Druzhba ★ ★ ★
   Zheleznodorozhnaya ul., 5..... 21-654
Ship "Korolenko" (hotel on the ship)
   near hotel "Druzhba"............ 94-478

JEWELLERY

Almaz
   Krepostnaya ul., 43.............. 20-373
   Hrs 10-19

LAW FIRMS

Law Firm   Advokatskaya kontora
   Vodnaya Zastava ul., 6a 28-941
   Hrs 9-18
Legal Advice
             Yuridicheskaya Konsultatsiya
   Krepostnaya ul., 41.............. 23-170

MAPS

   *There are several good maps/guides
   available for Vyborg at* INTERNATIONAL
   SHOPS.

MARKETS

Market   Rynok
   Severnyy Val, 1 25-313
   Hrs 8-18

MEDICAL CARE

Gorodskaya Poliklinika
   Onezhskaya ul., 8 25-309
   Hrs 8-22
Maternity Hospital   Rodilnyy Dom
   Leningradskoe shosse, 24/26 23-992

MILITIA / POLICE

GAI Traffic Police   GAI
   Leningradskiy pr., 13............ 25-590
   Hrs 9-18

MINISTRIES, RUSSIAN

Internal Affairs Department   UVD
   Leningradskiy pr., 13............ 24-726
   Hrs 9-18
KGB
   Krepostnaya ul., 28.............. 22-838
   Hrs 9-18

MOVIES

Rodina
   Mira ul., 7.......................... 20-204
Vyborg
   Krepostnaya ul., 25.............. 21-370

MUSEUMS

Regional Museum
                  Kraevedcheskiy Musey
   Vyborgskaya krepost............ 21-515
   Hrs 10-18

NOTARY PUBLIC

Notary Public   Notarialnaya kontora
   Mira ul., 10......................... 22-515
   Hrs 9-18

PHARMACIES

Pharmacy No. 7   Apteka No. 7
   Vokzalnaya ul., 4 96-807
Pharmacy No. 18   Apteka No. 18
   Lenina pr., 22...................... 20-448
   Hrs 9-19
Pharmacy No. 87   Apteka No. 87
   Sadovaya ul., 11.................. 25-578
   Hrs 9-18

PORTS

Sea Terminal   Morskoy vokzal
   Severnyy Val, 1 93-220

POST

Post
   Sportivnaya ul., 4 25-124

TELEGRAPH

Telegraph
   Moskovskoe shosse., 26....... 25-049

RAILWAY STATION

   Vokzal................................ 96-406

RESTAURANTS

Sever
   Lenina pr., 11...................... 21-837
   Hrs 12-24

SHOPS

SPORTS EQUIPMENT

Spartak
   Moskovskiy pr., 11 25-957
   Hrs 10-19

SOUVENIRS/GIFTS

Souvenirs *(Hrs 10-19)*
  Severnaya ul., 12.................. 21-921

TRAVEL AGENCIES

Intourist *(Hrs 9-18)*
  Zheleznodorozhnaya ul., 5..... 24-760
Sputnik
  Leningradskiy pr., 31............ 25-047
Travel agency
  Storozhevoy Bashni ul., 11.... 20-646

Sovtransavto

SOVAVTO ST PETERSBURG

VYBORG TRUCK PARK

**FUEL, SERVICE and REPAIRS
WAREHOUSE and SECURE PARKING**

On the Helsinki - St. Petersburg Road at Vyborg

Tel ....(278) 2-14-63

VISA REGISTRATION OFFICE

Visa Registration *(Hrs 9-18)*   **OVIR**
  Leningradskiy pr., 51............ 25-861

✦ ✦ ✦ ✦ ✦

CALENDAR OF EVENTS IN ST. PETERSBURG

When	Where	What	Phones
AUGUST			
August	Smolnyy cathedral	Concerts of the Smolnyy cathedral chorus (sacred, ancient Russian music)	311-35-60
August	Smolnyy cathedral	Exhibition "They are bringing me a horse". (Painting, utensils, applied arts)	311-35-60
August	Jewish association	Jewish arts seminar	275-14-65 275-14-59
August	Russian museum	National arts and its collectors	314-34-48
August	Russian museum	The past of the Russia in medals, coins and badges.	314-34-48
August	Benua museum	Toneta's principles (bentwood furniture: wood and metal tubes)	427-50-39
August	Russian museum	Khuindji painting exhibition	314-34-48
August	Benua museum	Sigizmunda Mey exhibition.	427-50-39
August	St.-Petersburg City Historical museum. (Petropavlovskaya Fortress)	"Petersburg menu". (Commandant's House)	238-45-11
August	Hermitage	"Playing cards". History of the life in Russia. (Alexandrovskiy Hall of the Hermitage)	219-86-25
August	Pushkin museum	International Great Parade of Military & Historical Societies	311-38-01
August	Ethnography museum	"Special Larder". Unique jewelers of Russian Empire	219-11-74
August	Ethnography museum	Sacred music concerts of Chamber chorus at the Marble Palace	219-11-74
SEPTEMBER			
September	Smolnyy cathedral	Concerts of the Smolnyy cathedral chorus (sacred, ancient Russian music)	311-35-60
September	Smolnyy cathedral	Exhibition "They are bringing me a horse". (Painting, utensils, applied arts)	311-35-60
September	Russian museum	Khuindji painting exhibition	314-34-48
September	Benua museum	Sigizmunda Mey exhibition.	427-50-39
September	St.-Petersburg City Historical museum. (Petropavlovskaya Fortress)	"Petersburg menu". (Commandant's House)	238-45-11

September	Hermitage	"Playing cards". History of the life in Russia. (Alexandrovskiy Hall of the Hermitage)	219-86-25
September	Ethnography museum	"Special Larder". Unique jewelers of Russian Empire	219-11-74
September	Ethnography museum	Sacred music concerts of Chamber chorus at the Marble Palace	219-11-74
September	Veterinary Institute and GIDUV	International seminar "Problems of the modeling of pathological processes of human beings and animals and using of biologically active preparations"	278-11-60
September	Mendeleev Institute	European Scientific Conference "150 years of State System of the Ensuring Unified Measurement"	259-10-11
September 31 -October 6	LenExpo	International Fair "Russian Farmer"	355-19-96 298-98-97
September	LenExpo	National Exhibition of China	355-19-96 298-98-97
September, 22-26	LenExpo	International Exhibition "PAP-FOR 92" (Forest complex & Pulp & Paper industry).	355-19-96 298-98-97
September, 15-20	House of Peace Friendship with Peoples of Foreign Countries.	Exhibition Lenexpo-Germany	210-49-00
September, 28-30	House of Peace Friendship with Peoples of Foreign Countries.	International Congress "Through Quality to Business"	210-49-00
September	Automotoclub	International Cinder Track Racing.	210-49-00
September	Automotoclub	Cinder Track Racing. (Championship of Russia)	274-22-56
September	Automotoclub	International Supermotocross	274-22-56

OCTOBER

October	Russian museum	Exhibition of works of Shubin (Russian artist)	314-34-48
October	Smolnyy cathedral	Exhibition "They are bringing me a horse". (Painting, utensils, applied arts)	311-35-60
October	Benua museum	Sigizmunda Mey exhibition.	427-50-39
October	Ethnography museum	"Special Larder". Unique jewelers of Russian Empire	219-11-74
October	Ethnography museum	Sacred music concerts of Chamber chorus at the Marble Palace	219-11-74

October, 1-5	House of Peace Friendship with Peoples of Foreign Countries.	International Congress "Through Quality to Business"	210-49-00
October, 2-5	All-Russian Electromechanical Institute of Communication	II International Conference on Fiber Optics	
October, 24-25	Leningrad Association of Ballroom Dances (At the "Jubilee" Sports Palace)	"BALTIC-CUP-92" International Contest of Ballroom Dances	314-89-95
October	LenExpo	Construction Materials-92	355-19-96
October	LenExpo	Exhibition "Security and guarding"	355-19-96
October	LenExpo	Exhibition "New Technologies in Metalworking Industry"	355-19-96
October	LenExpo	"Hospital-92"	355-19-96

NOVEMBER

November	Russian Museum	Exhibition of Falk's works	314-34-48
November	Fedor Dostoevskiy Museum	International Conference "Dostoevskiy and World Culture"	164-69-50
November	Ethnography museum	Sacred music concerts of Chamber chorus at the Marble Palace	219-11-74
November	LenExpo	International Fair "The Children's World"	298-98-97
November	LenExpo	Informational and Computer Systems	298-98-97

DECEMBER

December	Russian Museum	Exhibition "Soviet Art of 1930-1950"	314-34-48
December 26-January 8		Second International Music Festival "Christmas Meetings at the Northern Palmira"	110-55-09
December	LenExpo	IV Exhibition of Scientific, Technical and Production Firms"	355-19-96
December	LenExpo	Artistic Works	355-19-96

NEW NAMES IN SAINT PETERSBURG

Names are being changed quickly in Saint Petersburg. The name of Leningrad was formally changed to SANKT-PETERBURG (САНКТ-ПЕТЕРБУРГ) after a vote by the citizens in June 1991. Even before that vote, street names were being changed. "Soviet" name plates were being removed from the street sign, and statues of Lenin and other Soviet heroes were disappearing. After the vote, the process accelerated and now more than 50 street names have been changed back to their original pre-1917 names. Some of these have been listed below.

In this first edition of the Traveller's Yellow Pages for Saint Petersburg, we have used the "old Soviet names" and not the "new pre-1917" names because most people still use the old Soviet names, most signs have the old Soviet names, and most guide books and stationery use the old Soviet names. The "name" situation is changing rapidly, so be alert to the problem. Our list of street name changes should help.

Many other names were changed, also. For example, the "Opera and Ballet Theater named after Kirov" has been changed to "Mariinskiy Theater." Often, pre-1917 institutions took back their pre-1917 names. In general, in our Traveller's Yellow Pages, we have used the newest names available for theaters, universities, enterprises, and so forth. Many names with "Leningrad" have been changed to "Saint Petersburg". For example, the "Leningrad State University" is now the "St. Petersburg State University" and the hotel "Leningrad" is now the hotel "Saint Petersburg". Some venerable institutions, like have been broken up into several small parts, For example Intourist lost most of its hotels when they became independent organizations, its transport branch is now the independent "Intourist Transport", and its travel agency functions now survived in the much smaller "Travel Agency of Saint Petersburg". In sum, life and names are changing quickly in Saint Petersburg. Very confusing, but very exciting as the new system emerges from the old.

STREET NAMES - OLD and NEW
НАЗВАНИЯ УЛИЦ - СТАРЫЕ и НОВЫЕ
STRASSEN NAME - ALTE und NEUE
NOMS DES RUES - ANCIENS et NOUVEAUX
GATUNAMN - GAMLA och NYA

Old name (''Soviet'' name) of the street	New name of the street	Старое название улицы	Восстановленное название улицы
Anny Ulyanovoy ul.	Polozova ul.	ул. Анны Ульяновой	ул. Полозова
Bratstva ul.	Malyy Sampsonievskiy pr.	ул. Братства	пр. Малый Сампсониевский
Brodskogo ul.	Mikhaylovskaya ul.	ул. Бродского	ул.Михайловская
Voinova ul.	Shpalernaya ul.	ул. Воинова	ул. Шпалерная
Voytika ul.	Vitebskaya ul.	ул. Войтика	ул. Витебская
Gaza pr.	Staro-Petergofskiy pr.	пр. Газа	пр. Старо-Петергофский
Dzerzhinskogo ul.	Gorokhovaya ul.	ул.Дзержинского	ул. Гороховая
Zhelyabova ul.	Bolshaya Konyushennaya ul	ул. Желябова	ул. Большая Конюшенная
Kalyaeva ul.	Zakharevskaya ul.	ул. Каляева	ул. Захарьевская
Karla Marksa pr.	Bolshoy Sampsonievskiy pr.	пр. Карла Маркса	пр. Большой Сампсониевский
Kirovskiy pr.	Kamennoostrovskiy pr.	Кировский пр.	Каменноостровский пр.
Kommunarov pl.	Nikolskaya pl.	пл. Коммунаров	Никольская пл.

Old name ("Soviet" name) of the street	New Russian name of the street	Старое название улицы	Восстановлен-ное название улицы
Krasnoy Konnitsy ul.	Kavalergardskaya ul.	ул. Красной Конницы	Кавалергардская ул.
Krushteyna kan.	Admiralteyskiy kan.	кан.Круштейна	Адмиралтейский кан.
Mayorova pr.	Voznesenskiy pr.	пр. Майорова	Вознесенский пр.
Maksima Gorkogo pr.	Kronverkskiy pr.	пр. Максима Горького	Кронверкский пр.
Marii Ulyanovoy ul.	Grafskiy per.	ул. Марии Ульяновой	Графский пер.
Mira pl.	Sennaya pl.	пл. Мира	Сенная пл.
Smirnova pr.	Lanskoe shosse	пр. Смирнова	Ланское шоссе
Ogorodnikova pr.	Rizhskiy pr.	пр. Огородникова	Рижский пр.
Olega Koshevogo ul.	Vvedenskaya ul.	ул. Олега Кошевого	Введенская ул.
Petra Lavrova ul.	Furshtatskaya ul.	ул. Петра Лаврова	Фурштатская ул.
Podbelskogo per.	Pochtamtskiy per.	пер. Подбельского	Почтамтский пер.
Profsoyuzov bul.	Konnogvardeyskiy bul.	бульвар Профсоюзов	Конногвардейский бульвар
Rakova ul.	Italyanskaya ul.	ул. Ракова	Итальянская ул.
Skorokhodova ul.	Bolshaya Monetnaya ul.	ул. Скороходова	Большая Монетная ул.
Sofi Perovskoy ul.	Malaya Konyushennaya ul	ул.Софьи Перовской	Малая Конюшенная ул.
Tolmachyova ul.	Karavannaya ul.	ул. Толмачева	Караванная ул.
Fotievoy ul.	Eletskaya ul.	ул.Фотиевой	Елецкая ул.
Fofanovoy ul.	Enotaevskaya ul.	ул.Фофановой	Енотаевская ул.
Khalturina ul.	Millionnaya ul.	ул. Халтурина	Миллионная ул.
Shchorsa pr.	Malyy pr. P.S.	пр. Щорса	Малый пр. П.С.
Kirovskiy most	Troitskiy most	Кировский мост	Троицкий мост
Komsomolskiy most	Kharlamov most	Комсомольский мост	Харламов мост
Pestelya most	Panteleymonovskiy most	мост Пестеля	Пантелеймоновский мост
Pionerskiy most	Silin most	Пионерский мост	Силин мост
Svobody most	Sampsonievskiy most	мост Свободы	Сампсониевский мост
Skver na Ostrovskogo pl.	Ekaterininskiy skver	сквер на пл.Островского	Екатерининский сквер
Detskiy park Oktyabrskogo rayona	Yusupovskiy sad	Детский парк Октябрьского района	Юсуповский сад
Sad im. F.E.Dzerzhinskogo	Lopukhinskiy sad	Сад им.Ф.Э. Дзержинского	Лопухинский сад
Park Chelyuskintsev	Udelnyy park	парк Челюскинцев	Удельный парк
Vosstaniya pl.	Znamenskaya pl.	пл.Восстания	Знаменская пл.
Griboedova kan.	Ekaterininskiy kan.	кан. Грибоедова	Екатерининский кан.
Dekabristov pl.	Senatskaya pl.	пл. Декабристов	Сенатская пл.
Ostrovskogo pl.	Aleksandriyskaya pl.	пл. Островского	пл. Алек-сандринская
Pestelya ul.	Panteleymonskaya ul.	ул. Пестеля	Пантелеймонская ул.
Revolyutsii pl.	Troitskaya pl.	пл. Революции	Троицкая пл.
Stachek pl.	Narvskaya pl.	пл. Стачек	Нарвская пл.
Truda ul. & pl.	Blagoveshchen-skaya ul. & pl.	ул. и пл. Труда	Благовещенская ул. и пл.

THE METRIC SYSTEM OF MEASUREMENT

Linear Measures

1 kilometer (km)	=	1000	meters
1 hectometer (hm)	=	100	meters
1 decameters (dm)	=	10	meters
1 meter (m)	=	1000	millimeters
1 meter (m)	=	100	centimeters
1 decimeter (dm)	=	10	centimeters
1 centimeter (cm)	=	10	millimeters
1 millimeter (mm)	=	0.1	centimeter
1 millimeter (mm)	=	0.001	centimeter

Square Measures

1 square kilometer (km^2)	=	100 hectares
1 hectare (ha)	=	10,000 m^2
1 square meter (m^2)	=	10,000 cm^2
1 square meter (m^2)	=	10^{6}mm^2
1 square centimeter (cm^2)	=	100 mm^2
1 square millimeters (mm^2)	=	0.01 cm^2

Cubic Measures

1 cubic meter (m^3)	=	1000 (dm^3)
	=	1,000,000 cm^3
1 cubic centimeter (cm^3)	=	1000 (mm^3)
1 cubic millimeter (mm^3)	=	0.001 (cm^3)

Liquid Measures

1 kiloliter (kl)	=	1000	liters
1 hectoliter (hl)	=	100	liters
1 dekaliters (dl)	=	10	liters
1 liter (l)	=	10	deciliters
1 liter (l)	=	100	centiliters
1 liter (l)	=	1000	milliliters
1 liter (l)	=	1000	cm^3
1 deciliter (dl)	=	10	centiliters
1 centiliter (cl)	=	10	milliliters
1 milliliter (ml)	=	0.001	liter
1 milliliter (ml)	=	1	cm^3

Weight Measures

1 metric ton (t)	=	1000	kg.
1 kilogram (kg)	=	1000	grams.
1 gram (g)	=	1000	mg.
1 milligram (mg)	=	0.001	gram.

US & British Cooking Measures

Volume Measures

1 teaspoon	=	5	milliliters
1 tablespoon	=	16.5	milliliters
1 cup	=	264	milliliters
1 pint	=	528	milliliters

BRITISH-AMERICAN UNITS OF MEASUREMENT AND METRIC EQUIVALENTS

Linear Measures

English		Metric	
1 inch (in.)	=	25.4	millimeters
	=	2.54	centimeters
1 foot (ft)	=	12	inches
	=	30.48	centimeters
	=	0.3048	meters
1 yard (yd)	=	3 feet = 36 inches	
	=	0.9144	meters
1 mile (ml)	=	5280	feet
	=	1760	yards
	=	8	furlongs
	=	1.6093	kilometers
1 naut. mile	=	6080	feet
	=	1.832	kilometers
1 inch	=	12	lines
	=	2.54	centimeters
1 line	=	6	point
	=	2.1	millimeters
1 point	=	1/72	inch
	=	0.3528	millimeter
0.03937 inches	=	1 millimeter	
0.3937 inches	=	1 centimeter	
39.37 inches	=	1 meter	
3.2808 feet	=	1 meter	
1.0936 yards	=	1 meter	
3280.8 feet	=	1 kilometer	
1093.6 yards	=	1 kilometer	
0.62137 miles	=	1 kilometer	

Square Measures

English		Metric	
1 square inch	=	645.16	mm^2
	=	6.4516	cm^2
1 square foot	=	929.03	cm^2
	=	9.2903	dm^2
	=	0.092903	m^2
1 square yard	=	0.83613	m^2
1 acre	=	43,560	ft^2
	=	0.4047	hectare
1 square mile	=	2.5900	km^2
0.001550 square inches	=	1 mm^2	
0.15500 square inches	=	1 cm^2	
0.10764 square feet	=	1 dm^2	
10.764 square feet	=	1 m^2	
1.1960 square yards	=	1 m^2	
2.47 acres	=	1 hectare	
0.38608 square miles	=	1 km^2	

Cubic Measures

English		Metric	
1 cubic inch	=	16.387	cm^3
1 cubic foot	=	1728	$inches^3$
1 cubic foot	=	0.028317	m^3
1 cubic yard	=	27	ft^3
1 cubic yard	=	0.76455	m^3
1 cubic mile	=	4.16818	km^3
0.061023 cubic inches	=	1	cm^3
35.315 cubic feet	=	1	m^3
1.3079 cubic yards	=	1	m^3
0.23990 cubic miles	=	1	km^3

Liquid Measures

British/US		Metric	
1 US fluid ounce	=	29.57	milliliters
1 Br. fluid ounce	=	28.4	milliliters
1 US pint	= 16		fluid ounces
	=	0.4732	liter
1 British pint	=	20 fluid ounces	
	=	0.570	liter
1 quart	=	2	pints
1 US quart	=	0.94635	liter
1 British quart	=	1.140	liter
1 gallon	=	4	quarts
1 US gallon	=	3.7854	liters
1 British gallon	=	4.546	liters
1 US barrel	=	119.24	liters
1 British barrel	=	160.42	liters
1 Barrel of oil	=	158.98	liters
0.033814 US ounce	=	1	milliliter
33.814 US ounce	=	1	liter
1.0567 US quarts	=	1	liter
0.26417 US gallons	=	1	liter

Weight Measures

Troy (precious metals)

1 carat	=	200	mg
1 grain	=	0.064799	g
1 ounce	=	31.103	g
1 pound (lb)	=	0.37324	kg

Avoirdupois (common)

1 ounce (oz)	=	28.350 g
1 pound	=	0.45359 kg
1 centner (British)	=	50.6 kg
1 centner (US)	=	45.3 kg
1 centner (Russian)	=	100 kg
1 ton (short)	=	907.18 kg
1 ton (long)	=	1016 kg

Avoirdupois Equivalents

15.432 grains	=	1 gram
0.035274 oz avoir	=	1 gram
3.5274 oz avoir	=	100 grams
2.2046 pounds	=	1 kilogram
0.98421 ton (long)	=	1 ton metric
1.1023 ton (short))	=	1 ton (metric)

Dry Measures

English		Metric	
1 quart	=	1.1012	liters
1 peck (pk)	=	8.8098	liters
1 bushel (bu)	=	35.239	liters
0.90808 quarts	=	1 liter	
1.11375 pecks	=	1 liter	
0.028378 bushel	=	1 liter	

Temperatures

Fahrenheit		Celsius
212	—	100°
176	—	80°
140	—	60°
122	—	50°
104	—	40°
102	—	38.9°
100	—	37.8°
98.6	—	36.6°
90	—	32.2°
86	—	30°
80	—	26.6°
70	—	21.1°
68	—	20°
60	—	15.5°
50	—	10°
40	—	4.4°
30	—	-1.1°
32	—	0°
20	—	-6.7
14	—	-10°
10	—	-12.2
0	—	-17.8°
4	—	-20°
-10	—	-23.3°
-31	—	-35°
-459.67	—	-273.15°

Celsius = (Fahrenheit - 32) / 1.80
Fahrenheit = (Celsius × 1.8) + 32

Old Russian Measures

1 versta (верста) =
    = 500 sazhen (сажень)
    = 1066.78 meters
1 sazhen = 3 arshin (аршин)
          = 2.13356 meters
1 arshin = 16 vershok (вершок)
          = 0.71 metres
1 vershok = 0.0444 meters
1 pood (пуд) = 16.38 kg
1 kilogram = 0.06105 pood
1 desyatina (десятина)
    = 2400 $sazhen^2$ (кв. сажень)
    = 109.254 arcres

APPROXIMATE CLOTHING AND SHOE SIZES

MEN'S CLOTHES

Suits & Coats

American		36	38	40	42	44	46	48
		S	← M →		L	← XL →		
European		46	48	50	52	54	56	58
Russian		46	48	50	52	54	56	

Shirts

American	14	14½	15	15½	16	16½	17	18
	← S →		← M →		← L →		← XL →	
English	34	36	38	40	42	44	46	48
European	36	37	38	39	41	42	43	45
Russian	36	37	38	39	41	42	43	45-46

Shoes (All size comparisons are approximate.)

American	6½	7	7½	8½	9½	10	10½	11½
English & Ger.	6	6½	7	8	9	10	10½	11
European French			39	41	43	44½	45½	
European Italian	38	39	40	42	44	45	46	47
Russian	37	38	39	41	43	44	45	46

Socks

American	9½	10	10½	11	11½	12
English	9½	10	10½	11	11½	12
Russian	39	40	41	42	43	44

WOMEN'S CLOTHES

Dress & Coats

American	6	8	10	12	14	16
	S	← M →		← L →		XL
English	8	10	12	14	16	18
European		40	42	44	46	48
Russian	44	46	48	50	52	54

Shoe (All shoe sizes are approximate and should be checked.)

American	4½	5½	6½	7	7½	8	8½	9	9½
English	3	4	4½	5	5½	6	6½	7	7½
German	3	4						7	
Italian		36	36	37		38	39	40	41
French	35½	36½	37	38	38½	39	40	41	41½
Russian	33½	35	35	36	36½	37	38	39	40

CHILDREN'S CLOTHES

American	4	6	8	10	12	14
English (in.)	43	48	55	58	60	62
European (cm.)	125	135	150	155	160	165

Editor's note: This information is only approximate and there were considerable
differences in the data for shoe sizes. Readers are invited to contribute
more precise information to this table.

SEATING PLAN OF
Mariinskiy Theater of Opera and Ballet
(Formerly Kirov Theater, 1625 Seats)

Teatralnaya pl., 1   Tickets: 114-43-44
Bus: 22, 27, 43, 50, 100   Administration: 314-43-44
Tram: 1, 5, 15, 21, 33, 42   Map: F-6

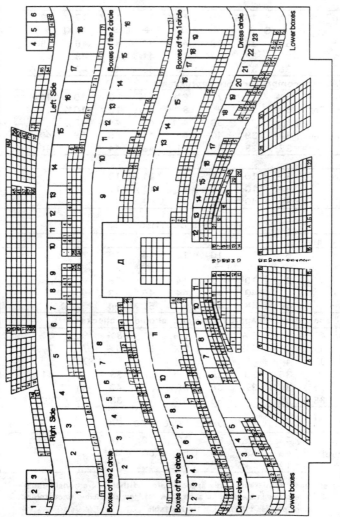

Mariinskiy Theater of Opera and Ballet

SEATING PLAN OF
Malyy Theater of Opera and Ballet
Academic Malyy Theater of Opera and Ballet n.a. Musorgsky
(1239 Seats)

Iskusstv pl., 1
Bus: 14, 22, 25, 27, 44, 45,
Tram: 2, 3, 5, 12, 13, 14, 34
Trolley: 1, 5, 7, 10, 14, 22
Metro: Nevskiy prospekt, Gostinyy Dvor

Tickets: 212-20-40
Administration: 214-37-58
Map: J-8

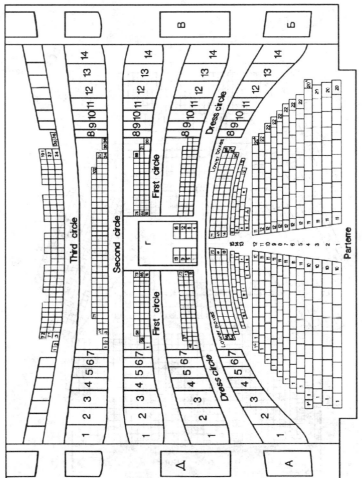

Malyy Theater of Opera and Ballet

SEATING PLAN OF

Russian Academic Bolshoy Dramatic Theater by Tovstonogov

(Formerly Gogkiy Theater, 1402 Seats)

Teatralnaya pl., 1

Tram: 2, 5, 13, 15, 14, 28

Trolley: 1, 3, 5, 7, 8, 9, 10, 15, 17, 14, 22

Metro: Nevskiy prospekt, Gostinyy Dvor

Tickets: 310-92-42

Information: 310-04-01

Map: J-7

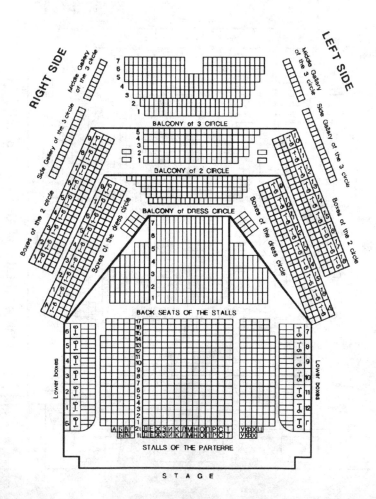

SEATING PLAN OF

Bolshoy Philharmonic Hall

Philharmonic n. a. Shostakovich

Bolshoy Hall

(1318 Seats)

Mikhaylovskaya (formerly Brodskogo) ul., 2   Tickets: 110-42-90

Bus: 14, 22, 25, 44, 45,   110-42-57

Tram: 2, 3, 5, 13, 14, 34   Administration: 311-73-33

Trolley: 1, 5, 7, 10, 14, 22   Map: J-8

Metro: Nevskiy prospekt, Gostinyy Dvor

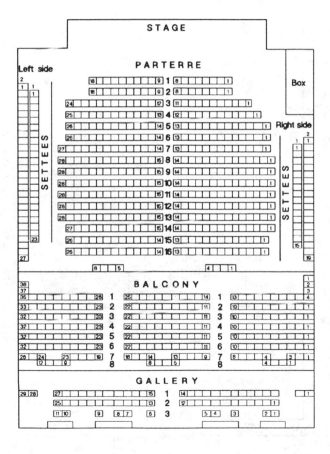

SEATING PLAN OF
Glinka Cappella (Choral Hall)
Academic Cappella n.a. Glinka

Nab. reki Moyki, 20   Tickets: 314-10-58
Bus: 14, 22, 44, 45   Administration:314-10-34
Trolley: 1, 5, 7, 10, 14, 22   Information: 314-11-59
Metro: Nevskiy prospekt, Gostinyy Dvor   Map: H-8

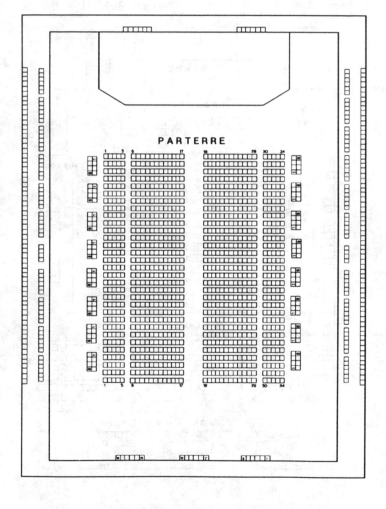

SEATING PLAN OF
Oktyabrskiy Concert Hall
Bolshoy Concert Hall "Oktyabrskiy"
(3738 Seats)

Ligovskiy pr., 6

Bus: 22,

Tram: 10, 13, 16, 17, 19, 28, 32, 44, 49

Trolley: 1, 5, 7, 10, 14, 22

Metro: Ploshchad Vosstaniya, Mayakovskaya

Information: 277-69-60

Administration: 277-74-00

Map: L-8

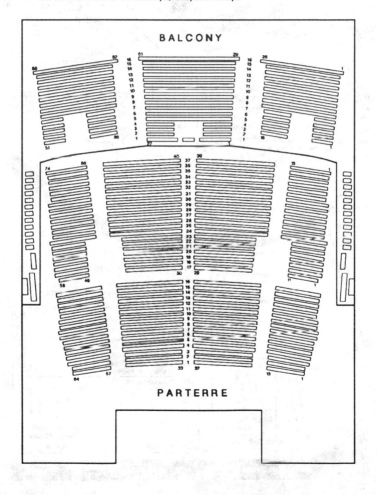

NEVSKIY PROSPEKT

From Neva to Kanal Griboedova

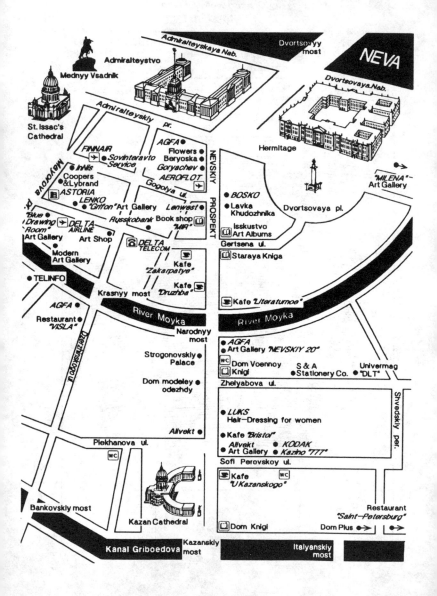

NEVSKIY PROSPEKT
From Kanal Griboedova to Liteynyy prospekt

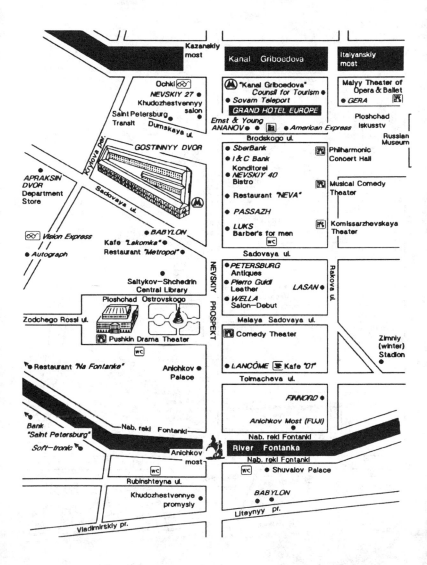

NEVSKIY PROSPEKT

From Liteynyy prospekt to Ploshchad Vosstaniya

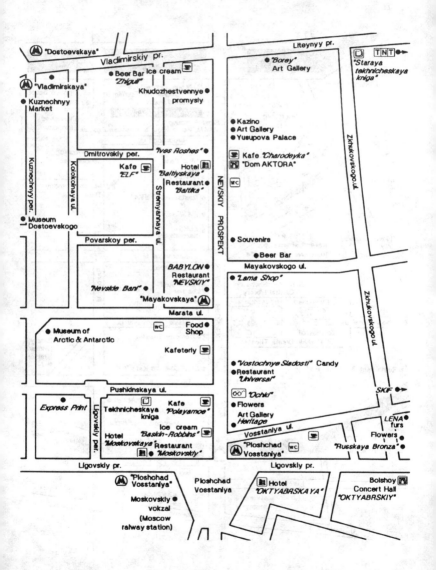